Through Anthroposophy
to the
Universal Church

The author in 1968, at age sixty-seven

BERNHARD MARTIN

Through Anthroposophy *to the* Universal Church

⊕

A Spiritual Memoir

with letters from
Valentin Tomberg

Angelico Press

First published in English
by Angelico Press 2023
© Angelico Press 2023
Translation by Stephen Churchyard
and James Wetmore © Angelico Press 2023
Introduction © Angelico Press 2023
All rights reserved

For information, address:
Angelico Press
169 Monitor St.
Brooklyn, NY 11222
www.angelicopress.com

The publisher gratefully acknowledges the
author's daughter Christiane Martin for her generosity,
Michael Frensch (recently deceased) and Harrie Salman
for their contributions to the Introduction, and
Richard Bloedon for his editorial review

Authorized for printing by the Church
Speyer, June 10, 1950
Episcopal Ordinaire
Dr. Haussner, Vicar General

978-1-62138-939-2 (pbk)
978-1-62138-940-8 (cloth)

Cover design: Michael Schrauzer

To My Children

Veronica, b. January 15, 1940
Christiane, b. January 21, 1943
Gottfried, b. July 30, 1946

CONTENTS

Introduction

WHO WAS BERNHARD MARTIN? HIS AUTOBIOGRAPHY
Von der Anthroposophie zu der Kirche: Ein geistiger Lebensbericht,
published here for the first time in English, offers deep insights into
this man, who spent his life crossing borders.

Bernhard Martin was born on June 3, 1900 in Frankfurt, Germany, into a family of Reformed Protestants. He died on August 9,
1985. His father did not have any connection to a church, although
he carried a copy of *The Imitation of Christ* by Thomas à Kempis
wherever he went. He was a supreme court counselor, who died
when young Bernhard was thirteen years old. His mother was only
loosely associated with any real church life. He was sent to the "Sunday school" of the church until the age of his confirmation, but after
that the need to participate in church life gradually disappeared. At
his elementary and secondary schools "the ungodliness of the age
was like a constitutive force." The same went for his time in higher
education, where he devoted himself to music and law in particular:
"I was hungry in a deeper sense, and needier than most students: a
misfortune, yes, but also (since my path in life subsequently led me
to clarity and a nourishing worldview), a stroke of good fortune." A
fateful over-specialization had proliferated in almost all courses of
study. Meaningful connectedness was lacking even in *Germanistik*
(the study of German life and letters), medicine, theology, and
other fields of instruction.

After two years of study, Martin's soul was so fragmented that he
sought out a sanitarium. There, his encounter with Freud's work
seemed to offer "what was missing": "Psychoanalytic 'care' leads to

* With grateful acknowledgment to Michael Frensch and Harrie Salmon for the
guiding threads of this introduction. ED

i

the level of the sub-individual, there where in the end one person is equal to another, where it is not humanity that is decisive, but the domination of fundamental drives." The sub-individual can only be ruled by a "higher element," which, however, had not yet developed in Martin. "Unbelief, helplessness, and doubt were alive and at work in me.... I could not imagine how I might ever discover a flow of strength in my life that would give it meaning."

In 1924, Bernhard made a new beginning by moving to Hamburg, where he apprenticed in an export business. While there, the behavior of his boss occasioned in him great distress of conscience and he spontaneously went to a Catholic priest for confession. This was his first experience of the Catholic church. And it would be another twenty years before his next experience of Catholicism. In 1925, he left Hamburg and wrote a manuscript called *Manfred: The Story of a Dying Man*, "a kind of interior autobiography," as he put it. That same year, Bernhard returned to university, commencing a course in German studies and philosophy in Munich. Although he was now able to follow his studies without damaging his health, "inside" he was living "in a dark prison, an inner dungeon."

Through a friend, Martin then encountered the work of the founder of Anthroposophy, Rudolf Steiner, who, as he put it, saved his life: "A still-hidden organ for the truth was being addressed as it had never been addressed before." A "detoxification process" began, leading in due course to the freeing-up of spiritual powers within him. Martin felt himself gradually to be more and more "fittingly" acquainted with "what God expects from us human beings—admittedly, not in the sphere of the church, but in a sphere that is free, and outside tradition."

To the question "what is Anthroposophy?" Martin answers with Steiner's words: "Anthroposophy is a path of knowledge that leads what is spiritual in the human being into what is spiritual in the cosmos.... It is a science of experience, yet one not related to what is earthly and given to the senses only, but also and essentially to the supersensory, metaphysical, and spiritual foundations of that earthly, sensory world." For although, as Martin writes, the encounter with Anthroposophy develops in the human being an organ for the perception of the invisible, "the sense for truth and the strength for truth emerge differently in different people." Moreover, the idea of reincarnation and karma helped Martin find the path to humility. He could now understand his own relationship to the world and to nature in a way that led gradually, not only to his recovery, but also to an inner transformation. The unity and the depth of the anthroposophical worldview gripped him. Martin is quick to emphasize, however, that "the essential part comes about through a 'higher I'— essentially, through the being of Christ."

In the end, Martin's religious need led him to the Christian Community, a "community for religious renewal" that had been set up with the help of Rudolf Steiner. For a few years, he was able to engage intensively with this. Indeed, he was crucially indebted to it, above all to its liturgy. The Christian Community became so important to him that he began training for its priesthood, but after a few semesters he had to give this up, as he lacked the health and strength required to carry out this vocation.

In the period of transition that followed, Bernhard worked at several jobs, among them as a librarian in Leipzig and as an editor in Berlin. In early 1937 he began his life-long profession as an editor at the Bärenreiter Publishing House in Kassel (a Protestant firm with a supra-denominational orientation). In 1938, he married Ingeborg Pfister. In due course, four children were born to them.

At Bärenreiter, Martin soon became one of the editors of the journal *Neue Schau, Monatsschrift für das deutsche Haus* [New view, a monthly for the German household], a responsibility he kept until his retirement in 1965. He published dozens of his own articles in the journal, and a number of short works on spiritual topics. He wrote poems and aphorisms as well. He also published in the journal *Du Selbst* [Yourself] and the Catholic journal *Geist und Leben* [Spirit and life], a journal for asceticism and mysticism.

Between 1942 and 1944 Martin had, as he writes, "now and then caught sight of the writings of a man who seemed to have come to grips with the anthroposophical spirit in a deeper and more individual way than I had ever before seen, even in the work of those figures worthiest of respect." In the beginning, he had only heard this man's name, but then was able to spend several weeks in a home where most of his works were available. The style of these writings gave him the impression of being the presence of the words of an "initiate." This man was Valentin Tomberg (1900-1973), with whom Martin would have seven long conversations between June 11, 1944 and April 18, 1948 in Bad Godesberg and Kassel. These conversations marked the beginning of an enduring friendship, in the course of which Tomberg introduced Martin to the spirituality of the Catholic church. Looking back on this first meeting with Tomberg (of which a fragmentary record of what was said still exists),[1] Martin writes:

> Now I found myself faced with a person who awakened in me the impression that greatness did not only lie behind us, but also lived among us. The Catholic reader can perhaps picture the effect of this on my soul by imagining what it would be like if a Doctor of the Church of the stature of St Thomas Aquinas were to appear among us today. I cannot sufficiently emphasize how deeply happy the experience made me, how greatly I had thirsted for such "originality." […] I was so bold as to ask for permission to visit him, and although he was living in seclusion, he invited me for a conversation. The first encounter (which was not to remain the only one) was solely concerned with anthroposophical and personal questions. We talked about "spiritual direction." But this phrase points to much more than an exclusively religious affair, as it might seem to anyone who lives only in the world of prayer, or who only knows the *phrase* "spiritual direction," rather than the thing itself. I hardly dared step into the room where the conversation was to take place. And I know even now that at its end I was filled with the thought: "Master, we have toiled all night, and taken nothing: nevertheless, at thy word I will let down the net." I let it down, and it was not in vain that I did so!
>
> Not long afterwards I learned, to my great astonishment and regret, that this man with whom I was now, blessedly for me, acquainted, was close to the Catholic church. I simply could not situate this. The Catholic church was in my view spiritually obsolete, a power opposed to "progressive thinking," in which people

---

1. In this autobiography, Martin chose not to mention Valentin Tomberg by name, but instead describes him on this occasion simply as given in the quote above. Martin's notes of these conversations, as well as twenty-one sometimes very instructive letters, were presented to me by his youngest daughter, Christiane Martin, when I visited her on March 17–18, 2004 in Bergen, North Holland.

lived on in a "purely emotional" piety, dependence, and unfreedom. Although I was perfectly ignorant of the Catholic church, I bore deep within myself, even in early 1944, all the prejudice and revulsion towards everything "Catholic" instilled in me by the Protestant thought of the turn of the century, and that had only been strengthened by my membership in the anthroposophical movement. [...] Could this spirit then, who seemed to me unconditionally strong in his knowledge and worthy of trust, really be close to the Catholic church? For he seemed to me to be strong in knowledge and worthy of trust precisely *because* he embodied the spirit of Anthroposophy in his thinking, and in a way I had never before encountered. [...] But the fact was that this revered man stood close to the Catholic church, and this threw a new burning and disturbing question into my life. [...]

I asked for a second interview. This too was granted to me, and we spent almost a full day in conversation about the question of Anthroposophy and the church. During this exchange, my impression of the spiritual eminence of my host was confirmed. Moreover, the firm wall of my prejudices against the Catholic church was for the first time pierced, and pierced deeply. What I had previously examined only through the spectacles of deep-set prejudices (or had not examined at all) was now illuminated for me in its true nature and—so far as this was possible in a single conversation—clarified. True, no questions were answered; rather, more were raised. . . . The spirit with whom I had been led further along had his reasons for having left his anthroposophical activities behind him, and it must have been at around this time that he entered into the Catholic church. Whether his reasons might ever become mine was at that time entirely unclear, and I would then have held it to be impossible. In our first interview he had rightly thought it appropriate (since I was of course very distant from the Catholic church) to speak to me only in such a way as my power of comprehension and my concerns permitted. He did, on his level, what I would always do on mine, according the expression, "what matters is not conversions, but Christ."

The present book appeared in the summer of 1950. Since his first visit to Tomberg in 1944 (as the war raged around them), Tomberg and Martin had become good friends; and the friendship soon spread to their families, who often visited each other. At the end of the war, Martin, a deeply religious man, as we have seen, came to some essential insights into Catholic Christianity that opened up new paths for him and prompted him in 1946 to convert to Catholicism.[2] Later the same year, Martin sent Tomberg the manuscript of the present book, as he was interested to know Tomberg's opinion of it. Since the book recounts experiences, some of which also mirror Tomberg's own process of development "through Anthroposophy to the church," and since this topic had been the subject of intensive conversations between the two friends, one can assume that much of this found its way into Martin's book. Tomberg could only agree with the reasons for Martin's conversion:

> Even after having read only the first part of your book, I can say with a completely clear conscience and most genuine conviction that what I have read is a work of *moral genius*, and can do good only to the spiritually-aristocratic reader, the sole kind of reader, indeed, who can be thought of for this book, with its true tolerance (that is, an understanding unsullied by fear or hatred) of the "heresies" of the modern age, its confidence that Catholic Christianity is a "powerful competitor" able to fully engage with *all* the intellectual trends of the present, and its intimate insight into just *how* (in what manner and fashion) it can *be* that "all roads lead to Rome"—i.e., with its true tact.
>
> What I most prize in the work is the unconquerable weapon of modesty and honesty, which really can say *everything*, conserve *everything*, and critically evaluate *everything*: a method I described above as partaking of *moral genius*. As far as style and form are concerned, I can say little more than that, here too, they are as masterfully handled as they usually are by you.
>
> In your most recent letter you write of your "favorite topic": failure, falling short as man, citizen, person, Christian, spiritual pupil, etc. I don't have the least occasion to contest the subjective and objective details of this failure; I would only say something very simple regarding it. If my dear friend Bernhard were *not* a failure, but a contented, self-assertive, robustly successful "great guy"—I would hardly be able to be so fond of him. And if I myself, who am

---

2. Unlike Tomberg, however, Martin remained a member of the Anthroposophical Society for the rest of his life.

faulty, feel this way, then "how much more does our Father in heaven, who is perfect." That is the more decisive aspect of the question, considered within the realm of *love*.

If I now consider it in the light of *truth* also, the following can be said: what is needed is not to shake off the cross, but to become one with it in such a way that even one's weaknesses and faults become creative strengths and *new* virtues. Is it not well worth enduring a series of failures, if in the end these failures flow together into modesty? Or (as you put it), is it not well worth being "incapable of anything oneself," so as to learn to pray that God's power should work miracles? Or, to be "inarticulate," so as to master a language in such a way that it becomes a pattern for all languages? Or, "not to be sociable," so as to stand close to those people and beings who represent the conscience of the world? The cross of our weaknesses and our failings is the *field of action* upon which the miraculous operations of grace unfold. Farewell. I shall write again soon. Valentin.[3]

Two weeks later, Tomberg returned the second part of Martin's manuscript. Now it became clear that the book not only earned his approval but, in addition, that in his view it filled a significant gap that was of great importance also for Tomberg's life-decisions. He expressed his gratitude to Bernhard Martin by thanking him

> for the confidence and, in particular, too, for the joy I found in this work. I have nothing essential to add to the "preliminary critique" I sent you earlier. Except, perhaps, that with this work a gap is filled that I had perhaps once thought it my duty to fill—and now it has been done in a way that I could have striven for, but could never have attained. I therefore thank you for the work on purely personal grounds as well.

The correspondence between Martin and Tomberg continued to deepen. Several particularly important letters related to the central theme of this book will be found in the Appendix, along with reviews from the side of both Catholicism and Anthroposophy, and an important early article on Christ in Anthroposophy. The friendship continued between the Martins and the Tombergs until the latters' deaths in 1973.

---

3. Valentin Tomberg to Bernhard Martin, letter of July 3, 1949, RKT-Archiv.

Publications

The Mystical Element in the Poetry of Christian Morgenstern, 1931.

Monograph on the German painter Karl Thylmann.

Three monographs on Goethe.

"Der Christus-Impuls in Rudolf Steiners Buch *Wie erlangt man Erkenntnisse der Höheren Welten*," n.d., typescript, included in the Appendix in translation as "Christ in Rudolf Steiner's Book *Knowledge of the Higher Worlds and Its Attainment.*"

Und setzet ihr nicht das Leben ein—Drei Kriegsbetrachtungen, Bärenreiter Verlag, Kassel, 1941 (20 pp).

Die zwölf Monate, Bärenreiter Verlag, Kassel, n.d. (72 p).

Von der Anthroposophie zu der Kirche: Ein geistiger Lebensbericht, 1950.

Denken und Tun, Stuttgart, 1955, aphorisms (111 pp).

Geschlechtsnot und ihre Heilung, Stuttgart, 1956 (205 pp).

Über die Anthroposophie zum katholischen Glauben (printed brochure, summary of his autobiography, 23 pp).

Ein Spruchbuch von der Ehe (aphorisms on marriage).

Ein Spruchbuch von das Vaterunser (aphorisms on the Lord's Prayer).

Foreword

THE PRESENT WORK DOES NOT ARISE FROM ANY NEED on its author's part to discuss the course of his life *per se*, but from an intention to contribute something, so far as he is able, to the development of the Good in the world, and to the service of the Church. It is not a biography in the usual sense of the word. It portrays but few external events and experiences. Very little is said of the characteristics of other people, and almost nothing else of the sort that can make other biographies quite gripping. It keeps as strictly as possible to the task of setting out the development of the author's *worldview*. This is what is meant by calling it a "spiritual memoir." Such a spiritual memoir is neither an external nor a psychological document. It does not so much describe feelings, inclinations and disinclinations, longings, personal maturity or immaturity, and so on, as it does ideas—which of course do always have an effect on feelings and actions, as they ought to and must. The model for the study (if it is not too immodest to put it thus) is not Goethe's autobiographical *Truth and Fiction*, but St Augustine's *Confessions*. This is why the author makes public here many things about his life that, from a worldly and personal point of view, it might have been better not to speak of, and that would have been easy to pass over in this account. Indeed, had he been thinking of his own interests, it would have been imperative to keep silent about them! Do we not often, however, owe more to someone's personal confession than we do to a merely generalizing exposition of truth? Is it not sometimes helpful to know of the wrong directions another person has taken, and of the stages along his way? Things sometimes happen in life which one can only decide to talk about for this very reason. Yet every person can learn such things along his own life's way, for each of us has encountered plenty of warning signs and signposts, whether hidden or revealed.

For his part, the author was for many years an anthroposophist and a member of the religious denomination called the Christian Community. Both Anthroposophy and the Christian Community have in one way or another come to the notice of Catholic and Protestant Christians, and many people are looking to form a judgment about them, but without quite having been able to. Perhaps the experiences set down in this book will help some of these people to do so. In their essence, both movements, Anthroposophy and the Christian Community, can only be disclaimed by the Church. But even so (or indeed, precisely on this account), for many people it would be a good thing to know what these movements are like in more detail, and to understand this disclaimer for themselves. For, in our day, the judgment and the injunctions of the Church obviously only have effect insofar as people allow them to. For better or worse, the individual person's understanding of things can in many respects no longer be left out of account. Recent history demonstrates this so indubitably that it would be superfluous to serve up examples here. The present study may, however, prove more instructive than studies treating Anthroposophy and the Christian Community solely in the light of doctrine. The author thus begins with a description of the movements mentioned as they initially (and for a long time afterwards) affected him personally, and only arrives at judgment in the course of this exposition. Perhaps in this way some people will be spared one or another of the side alleys down which my life took me. Anyone who understands the Church, who loves it and who lives in it, needs no religious or spiritual renewal springing from any other source.

Like the Catholic and Protestant churches, Anthroposophy and the Christian Community are many-sided, many-layered institutions that can never be exhaustively represented in a limited context. How many portraits can be painted of a single person! In how many different ways can even a single oak tree be depicted! Why, then, should we imagine that spiritual powers can be an easy matter to represent using only readily applicable formulas? Owing to the current trend whereby quotations are torn out of context, repeated over and over again, and unreflectingly taken at face value, the author would like to say right at the outset that his judgment can be taken only as a whole, and not in its individual parts. Anyone who cites individual passages taken out of context is acting arbitrarily and fabricating a distorted image. Correlatively, thorough study and serious engagement with Anthroposophy *can* bring benefits. Any superficial toying with the intellectual legacy of Anthroposophy can only engender confusion. The truth of these propositions will become clear in the course of this study to anyone who reads it with attention.

Since every person is an indispensable part of the whole of humanity, every person contributes for good or ill to humanity's development, even a person who has never become conscious of so doing. He contributes, however, not only through his personal faith and the way he personally leads his life, but also through wrestling with the truth, through what is inside his consciousness, through his attachment to supra-personal spiritual objects. Everything depends upon the personal testing of the individual in life. More-over, all ideas and professions of faith, no matter how correct they might be, are meaningless in an individual's life if they do not corre-spond to deeds. In the last analysis, however, deeds are nourished by ideas. If, then, there were no ideas prompting and representing the coming-into-being of what is truly good, in the long run good deeds themselves would be impossible. Humanity is only of service when it lives in the consciousness of truth; its drives are reliable only inso-far as they are effectually interspersed with ideas. To this extent, every spiritual path that is travelled seriously, even that of the most ordinary people, has significance for the whole. It is not irrelevant whether a person strives for the good only as an isolated individual, or whether he lives in some way in the Christian faith, whether he only (as it is usually put) "believes" in a "universally Christian" church, or whether he belongs to the Catholic church—that is, whether he finds and takes the path to the Catholic church, to the church that has to propound, and has propounded, the plenitude of truth. The author does not say this because it is part of the church's doctrine and because he has accepted it as such, but because he has *discovered* it for himself and has *confirmed* its truth for himself.

3

As far as is possible within its allotted space and with the means available, the present study wishes to bear witness to the truth of the Church. Its aim will have been achieved if any seeker after that truth has been spared one spiritual false trail or another, or if by its means even only a few people acquire a more truthful picture of the Catholic Church than they possessed before—if, that is, some are strengthened in their faith in the church or even brought only a little further along the path towards the church, which does in truth represent the "universal" church of Christ on earth, as is expressed by its title, "Catholic" Church. Perhaps it may also help one or two Catholic Christians to arrive at a clearer grasp of what the "one holy and apostolic church" (*una sancta catholica et apostolica ecclesia*) actually *is* in the divine and human reality of our Church.

Kassel-Wilhelmshöhe, May 18, 1950,
on the fourth anniversary of my conversion
DR. BERNHARD MARTIN

1

Childhood and School

CONVERSION IN THE SPIRITUALLY TURBULENT PERIOD of the Counter-Reformation (Angelus Silesius) was one thing. It was another to have been converted in the emotionally rich age of Romanticism (Friedrich Schlegel). And it was still another to have been converted in the materialistic nineteenth century (Cardinal Newman), an age in which the powers of ungodliness expressed themselves concertedly as never before in history, and in which those who were "of good will" (*bonae voluntatis*) had also, accordingly, to stand together. Hence, it is fitting to specify that the year of my own birth was 1900, and that the events of my life have gone by in lock-step with those of our era itself, that of the twentieth century.

To avoid misunderstanding, I should say something by way of introduction, something already well enough understood by everyone, but that it is of particular importance to bear in mind here. Children and adolescents, at least until they are twenty-one years of age, are in general shaped by their environment. They are not yet in a position to arrive at valid judgments of their own. Thus, what I have to relate about my Protestant childhood in no way touches on the problem of Christian professions of faith or Church membership, but is merely a personal account. Certainly, many Catholic Christians could say about their own early lives things similar to what I say in what follows about my own early years in the Protestant church. Even if in the course of my early development I (unfortunately) fell away from the Protestant church, and will need to speak about that truthfully here, this does not constitute a criticism of that church, nor does it imply that such a thing could never have happened in the Catholic Church. The question of church affiliation only arose for me *later* in my life. And better or worse personal experiences as a child could neither have furthered this nor prevented it. In my opinion, personal experiences (always so "subjective") should never be used as "proofs" either for or against any particular "camp."

My childhood took place in an age when the Second German Empire was coming to its end. My early youth ran its course through the years of the First World War. Then followed the first German Republic, and then Adolf Hitler's so-called Third Reich. After this came the conquest and occupation of our homeland by its opponents and its partition into two strictly separated portions, with the clash of East and West at its heart. Naturally, it is impossible to foresee with any clarity what will happen in the future; but even so, it is clear enough that the struggle between good and evil (which is not intended as a reference to any particular political power blocs) is becoming ever more apparent, and that forces hostile to Christianity are becoming ever more powerful both in the East and in the West (as well as in the Center), and that whatever it is humanly possible to do to counteract this trend must be done by those who wish to serve the Good. Why should God stand by us if each of us does not do all that is humanly possible in this regard?

I grew up in a Christian household. My father had been guided to a high degree of faith, renunciation, and humility by an unusually severe lot in life. He lived (although admittedly without having any connection to a church) strongly and vitally through Thomas à Kempis's book *The Imitation of Christ*, and everything that goes along with it. He had a copy of the *Imitatio* with him as early as his honeymoon, and kept it always by his side. My mother was also a Christian. She too had been through unusual sorrows and privations, and in them and through them had in the course of time come to partake in things that those who have not been tested, who are "happier," evidently find so difficult to achieve, or never do achieve. She too was only loosely associated with any real church life, and even that with reservations.

My parents were Reformed Protestants. The distinction between Reformed and Lutheran Christianity was not especially important to them. They wanted to be *Christians*. They regarded theological and dogmatic distinctions, facts, and problems as less important than the guidance of Christ himself, something that, in truth, it is indeed possible for human beings to attain and to fulfill in any situation in life. In our domicile there lived, in addition to my parents themselves, a simple, devout lady named Hedwig. Though a "domestic servant," she was in every way part of the family. In her humility, selflessness, and sheer faith she was a pure and almost perfect example to us—or at least should have been so to me. Unfortunately, however, I cannot say that I appreciated her true worth in my childhood and youth. Only in later years—after the obscurity and weakness, the religious "self-sufficiency," and the darkness of my unusually long period of development had at last given way— did I learn to prize the significance of simplicity. Our day began and ended in prayer or devotion. It was a habitual and natural custom, too, for us to say grace—which was said by an adult, not a child. We were mindful in praying not only of our own salvation but also that of others. One prayer we often used contained the following fine verses:

> Let all my kin
> in Thy hand rest, O God.
> Let all the people, great and small,
> Commended be to Thee.

For us, Christmas was not just a family celebration, and Easter merely a party featuring brightly-colored Easter eggs. We celebrated the birth of Jesus Christ and his Resurrection from the dead.

The great and decisive events and truths of the world were also commemorated. For many years, I went early and often to the Protestant service for children—not out of my own need, but because this was "how things were done" and it was unimaginable to do otherwise. But I went for another reason too. The children received, every time we visited, an issue of a periodical to be obtained only if they were present there in person. We were promised that at the end of the year everyone who possessed all the issues for that year would have them bound up into a book. The prospect of possessing this book drove me (I was already something of a completist) never to miss the children's service. This service, which (symptomatically enough) was called "Sunday school," I attended until my confirmation lessons began, that is, until I turned thirteen. So, religious nurture was never absent in those early years of my life.

Critical thoughts and feelings, however, of the sort the young are wont to have, surfaced for me early on with respect to the children's service. Of course, I would not have been able to frame these thoughts and feelings in words at that time. Today I might express them roughly as follows—although it may be (who can be certain about this sort of thing?) that something of adult judgment, only in seed-form then, may unavoidably be mingled with them: "Grown-ups don't take this children's service as seriously as they should. They have it because they think it is good for us children, but somewhere in themselves (and in an important part, too) they don't believe in what we are being taught."

Perhaps this thought of mine was unfair to those involved, who (looking back now), I suspect were as honest and serious about it as they were able to be. But this era (recall that we were living in the Germany of the Empire) did not on the whole permit the depth and immediacy of the religious life that is widespread today, that as a matter of principle is always called for and is always possible.

It was impossible, however, for the ordinary person to be conscious of the "spirit of the age." Indeed, the question is to what extent the leaders understood that spirit or worked against it in any way. Only in missionary work was there any notion that a person might have to suffer and die for the sake of his Christian faith. But that was a distant exception. It had nothing to do with what happened here at home. Did we not live in a Christian country in which everything was well-ordered, and upon which God poured out his blessings? Individual people certainly did their best. Perhaps they were also deeper and more authentic than they seemed to my precocious, childishly critical mind. But there was undeniably something desolate here, without any one person being to blame for it. I don't think it ever occurred to anyone that they might need to bear witness to their faith with their own blood.

It was characteristic of the children's service I am speaking of that it was purely pedagogic. There was no celebration of the liturgy, nothing that really called upon the powers of the heart, nothing that prompted real worship. Essentially, the service was just a lesson into which songs and prayers had been inserted. The "Christianity" of that time went along readily and easily with a great deal that (if it

Childhood and School

had been sound) it should in fact have opposed. Moreover, from my very youngest days I noticed again and again that in many ways Protestant Christians did not "go to church" (in the basic sense of that expression), but went to hear a particular pastor "at church," and then critiqued his sermon. Recently, many serious Protestant Christians have tried to overcome this problem. But how can this succeed if the sermon is still taken to be the main point of a "service," and if (since it is always the performance of a particular person) it can hardly fail to be noticed by attentive auditors whether the sermon was "good" or "not good"?

During my first three years at school I learned the main parts of the Lutheran catechism, Bible stories, prayers, and a few songs. At school, too, the day began with a prayer. One of the prayers most often recited began with the words, "Lead me, O Lord, and guide my path with your Word!" But it should be explained (here as before) that I did not really "believe" in the teacher's praying. If I can put this in words drawn from my present stage of life, praying in school seemed to be more about "setting the right tone," of good behavior, of being well-brought-up—whereas the teacher leading the prayer did not give the impression of actually wanting to be led by anybody! In retrospect, the teacher clearly appears to me rather as a person girded with ambition and a strong sense of self. I do not say this by way of criticism of this capable and well-intentioned teacher (and doubtless there were similar teachers who were Catholics). But what I have mentioned does seem to me one of the distinguishing features of the time, a feature that could often enough be "observed" but seldom "seen through." Together with other features like it, this was one of the reasons why Christianity did not properly take root in me. We can only speak with conviction to children of our "path" through Christ, and of the way we lead our lives to this end, if in truth we want to be led by Him ourselves—and if personal, civic, and patriotic matters do not, on their own, account powerfully sway our resolve.

If I am not completely deceived, even well-intentioned and devout people of the time lived in a state of inner conflict not often remarked upon: their Christian religious life was not related to the whole; in essence, it lived on its legacy, on custom, and was too

9

much relegated to a personal realm. By this I mean not so much the effects of that life, but rather what people thought privately. In "society" at that time, speaking of God or of matters of faith invited scorn. Any who did so (for example, the great Bodelschwingh)[1] were conspicuously out of line, and were either accepted on account of their bold originality or inwardly rejected. The events that lit up one's life, that "made it worth living," were *not* those occasioned through Christ but those that happened, or could have happened, in church. On the whole, politics, culture, and diversions of every sort occupied a place in the life of the soul that, if Christian life were healthy, would belong to the encounter with Christ and the Christian life. If I may put it like this, people's eyes lit up if they had a nice summer trip ahead of them, or if they were going to see a production of *Maria Stuart*, or to a banquet, etc. Never in my childhood did I see anyone's eyes light up at the thought that the Sunday service was going to begin in half an hour's time—and I do not think I am the only one who never saw this! It was a hallmark of the age: Christianity was not the main priority.

These observations are not meant to be taken in a spirit hostile to life. Psychologically speaking, it is quite natural that a happy event (whether expected or not) will generally produce a stronger feeling of joy than a regularly expected action like going to church. It is, rather, of differing "tenors of life" that I am speaking: one such tenor can validate the external and cultural, another the world of truth and essence. At the time I am describing, the Christian element was on the whole not what determined the core; it was no more than an "extra" in life. And generally speaking, all this remained the same in subsequent decades. The difference between then and now is that with the passage of years we have come to see that we are no longer living as a Christian nation in a Christian country, but in a nation and a country surrounded by something very different indeed from Christianity, where there just "happens to be" something called

---

1. Friedrich von Bodelschwingh, "the Younger" (1877–1946), German pastor, theologian, and public health advocate, who resisted National Socialism. His father of the same name, "the Elder" (1831–1910), founded the Bethel charitable foundations, still operating today. ED

Christianity and the church. At that earlier time of which I am reporting, this now obvious fact was still hidden, although it was already in the works. Water cooled down far enough suddenly freezes; confusions gradually prepared suddenly become visible (I speak of the outbreak of the First World War in 1914). But who among us see now, or saw then, the preparatory processes at work before the course of events suddenly made them visible?

My Christian surroundings did not succeed in convincing me in a way appropriate to my understanding, as a child, of the irrepressible, inexorable strength at the heart of Christianity: its readiness for sacrifice. Admittedly, the fact that these surroundings did not have such convincing power certainly had something to do also with my own nature. I can easily imagine having had different pastors, different teachers, a different Sunday school—yet the result would have been the same. For truly, the ungodliness of the age was like a constitutive force. To be caught in that ungodliness was then the rule, to be free of it the exception. In my case also, this spirit of the age proved stronger than the admirable teachings with which I was supplied; moreover, I always had good relations with the individuals concerned, and had no grounds for reproaching any of them, either then or now. On one occasion, for example, there was an exhibition of missionary work. I still recall the many astonishing exhibits that held my attention: a reconstructed tribal hut, weapons, drums, pictures of churches. Here and there were collection boxes into which we were encouraged to drop coins in support of the mission. On the top of these boxes was a figurine of a kneeling black child who nodded each time a coin was dropped into the box. How superior we must have seemed to ourselves, as German Christian children! How unimaginable for us was the thought that somewhere in Africa there might be just such a box on top of which a blond German child nodded when a coin was tossed in! How thoroughly this whole feeling of being a "Christian" was saturated with an invisibly racist, nationalistic, cultural arrogance! No church flag flew over this exhibition of missionary work (there was no such flag at that time for the Protestant church), but hovering above it was the black, red, and white German flag, as also (in the background) German plans for colonization, a powerful German fleet, and everything that went with His Majesty the German Emperor—in sum, the notion that the world stood in need of being "made whole" by "Germanity." German colonization, at least (when compared with other colonial practices), was decently carried out. Christianity was not appealed to for political ends. Germany was only part of a general European imperialism, and did nothing out of the ordinary. But it may well be asked today whether and to what extent it was violating its own presiding idea. Only someone who thinks there never was any particular spiritual or even religious work for Germany to do will disapprove of the foregoing words.

Examples like the one I have just mentioned could easily be multiplied. It could be "shown" that the Christianity of that period, at least Protestant Christianity (but probably Catholic Christianity also), had on the one hand fallen too much under the spell of the cultural and political, while on the other hand remained too shadowy and taken for granted to awaken real enthusiasm. I believe the situation was similar in all countries and could have been observed at work in similar ways everywhere. Beneath the deceivingly well-ordered surface of life, however, everything that was to unfold over the following decades was already in preparation. And did we, as a collectivity, ever wake up to this reality at the time? Did we, as a collectivity, realize along that way just what that "time" really signified? Every person to any degree able to "see through" the state of the age, and to allocate to merely worldly things the place in this life that they truly deserved, must be grateful they proved able to still do so.

In secondary school (*Gymnasium*), which I entered at the age of nine and attended till my eighteenth year, things carried on just as before with respect to the Christian life. Here, too, morning prayer was customary. Every week commenced with an hour of devotion, for which the whole school assembled in the hall. Here too (perhaps with one exception), I was unable to find any teacher for whom there were not a great many more important things in life than the subjects of prayer and devotion. Religion was for them just one subject among many others. We studied the Bible, church history, and Protestant apologetics, as well as songs, psalms, and so on. All this, however, was just one field of instruction alongside others. The Christian and religious element was in no way set above anything else, nor were other subjects ever related even in the least way to what was taught in our religious studies. On closer inspection, it could not be seen how Latin, Greek, or history, studied from a purely political standpoint, could have anything to do with the Christian faith or with Christian truth. Did life have any higher meaning whatsoever? Ought we hopeful young seedlings not simply be put in a position to take our place in a respectable middle-class profession of some kind, to be successful in life, and to secure a good reputation and sufficient wealth? One great occasion in school life was the celebration of victory over the French at the battle of Sedan in 1870. Another was the Emperor's birthday. Later still, celebrations of German victories in the world war became occasions on which (we did not really understand why) we were given a whole day off from school. For what sort of life, then, was school really preparing us?

This question brings another in its train: For what is school a preparation *today*? Have the conditions of the age improved at all in this respect? Here is not the place to go into this question in detail. I mention it only because I do not wish to be in any way unfair. Indeed, the people of the era of my childhood can be credited with not having been swept up in these catastrophes in the same way we were swept up in our own later age. Their religious naivety was much more excusable, if one can put it like this, than ours. Today, too, Christian and religious life is confined to a limited domain. It has been shown that one is not a Christian simply because one cultivates certain external routines and customs, but by virtue of deciding for Christ, by virtue of believing, hoping, and loving— together with a readiness to follow the *ultimate* consequences of that decision. The kingdom to which we Christians belong is not of this world. But we *are* meant to bring its spirit *into* this world— something never more needful than now.

The spirit of my secondary school figures in my memory as a grey, devouring, disabling monster. Why, after all, should one number the stripes of the tulip or count the molars of the preserved animal specimens presented to us, if nothing of the thought that nature is a divine revelation, a divine gift, and the site of God's action in the world for human beings, was ever granted access to our natural history lessons? Why should we care about the best wines the contemptible Romans drank during the years of the Empire's decline, or about the peacock feathers with which they made themselves vomit in order to dine another time on an empty stomach? What did it matter (as I once had to explain in an essay) that Schiller brought the character of Wallenstein "humanly closer to us"? Why did we have to learn astronomy, which worked in terms of light-years, which saw the earth as a cosmic "speck of dust" with no trace to be found of the meaning of life or of human dignity, which was devoid of any idea of God, and turned all qualities into quantities?

Even what we learned of theology was better suited to destroy reverence and faith than to awaken them. For our instructors, here was no burning ideal, no binding example. As seventh-year pupils, we once read the Mark's gospel in full. The classes in which this study took place, however, ought really to have been called lessons in philology, not lessons in religion. Christ, the radiant, benevolent, loving, central spirit of the whole, did not come alive even in "religion lessons," let alone in others! There were certainly political, cultural, and poetic "ideals"—for instance, a romantic enthusiasm for "antiquity," doctrines of the just state, a German claim to the world, belief in a consistent law-like development within nature, and so forth—but these were all matters of disconnected details. What we learned only prepared us for our later earthly vocations, for a certain "cultural" life, not for a life that could be revealed as meaningful, God-given, and obligated to God. If you aspired to become a navigator, you had to study mathematics; if you wanted to become a salesman, you had to learn geography and English; if you aspired to become a pastor, you had to learn Greek and Hebrew—it was "all the same," whichever field you might aspire to.

This fragmentation of life stood right before our eyes, but who among us really noticed, who among us struggled against, or tried to change, the fact that this so-called "spiritual and intellectual life" was in reality only too well-suited as a preparation (not directly, but indirectly) for war and violence? True life was not nourished in this way—not mine, not that of the other pupils. Nor was it so at my school only, but at any school of that time, as far as I knew. How do matters stand now in this regard? I can only say that happy is he who sees things as they are, who finds the springs of life, who *decides*! Before moving on, however, let me first present a few more instructive hallmarks of the religious life of that period.

I was eleven years old when my grandfather died and I witnessed his burial, which was a most solemn one, at least in the external sense of top hats and slow-moving processions. But how very remote this burial was from the spirit of the deceased himself, who would have been more grateful for a single real intercessory prayer than for the moving eulogy or for chorales or trombone music, however finely performed! But in the Protestant Christianity of that age there was no such thing as intercession for the dead. Graveside solemnities were on one hand a consolation for those left behind, and on the other a "final tribute." I can only regard it as a sign of unwittingly sound judgment on my part that these solemnities did not in any way have a hold on me. To anticipate for a moment my later life, I can say that all the Protestant burial services I ever attended had the same basic features. The deceased person was honored with a final tribute and those left behind were consoled. In the Protestant world even today, any sense of the connection between the living and the dead seems dormant. Every living, believing Protestant Christian is grateful when another living person thinks of him by way of intercession; but that the dead could benefit from such service, and in fact stand in need of it, has tragically disappeared from the Protestant consciousness, at least as far as I could ever tell.

To resume, upon our return home we children began a happy game, and I remember how I suddenly grew ashamed of our happiness. This was not because I felt grief about losing my grandfather, but because it entered my mind that it was not "permitted" to feel happy on such a day. Who told me this? It could only be that there was a split between my own being and the being I had (admittedly with good intentions) been taught to be. How differently would such a day of mourning have passed if it had been ordered around an actual intercession for the dead! Something similar happened one Good Friday. On a pleasure outing, we children were scolded for our cheerful play: we were told we ought to behave in accordance with the gravity of the day. After all, Good Friday is, apart from Christmas and Easter, the "highest" Protestant feast day in the church year. One is supposed to meditate upon the sacrificial death of Jesus Christ with the utmost attentiveness. As I was only a child, this admonition had naturally not entered into my most inward being. Rather, it had struck me in a certain way as no more than a religious convention. I had no real understanding of the meaning of Christianity. Now, the mystery of Christ's sacrificial death is truly an unfathomable mystery. But even so, there are different levels on which it can be grasped, and different doors that open upon it—not excepting doors through which even a child with some intimation of what is at stake might pass. Unless very highly gifted, a child is of course unable to grasp the whole mystery, but adults can impart some vignettes of it, some things that catch the child's attention and are humanly persuasive. This is just what the child's soul draws life from. It is just such elements as these that can become the "door."

In saying these things, I am not certain whether or not I am being fair to the grown-ups who were around me, or whether only my own slowness was to blame. But I had the impression that, for the grown-ups, even the duty to be grave in demeanor was more a matter of taking the right tone, and of custom, than an expression of present experience and realization. Even today I still have the impression that the whole age was like that. Indeed, people as a whole were almost all like that then. This became why, by degrees, I grew estranged from Christianity. In the long run there were no spiritual or conventional threads attaching me to it any longer. I needed nourishment for my being, along with inspiring human examples, but did not find them. The world in which people considered it sufficient to allocate perhaps two hours a week to religion (two hours with no effective relationship to the rest of one's life) seemed desolate to me, and still seems so. Sadly, the misfortune I am pointing to has by no means diminished in recent years. Let those whose task it is to introduce children to what is good in life see to it that a resolve to overcome this two-hours-a-week piety emanates from themselves as adult models of moral behavior! In a couple of decades' time, how many of those now growing up will level these the same criticisms regarding their younger years against *their* own "grown-ups"?—Although, please understand, my intent is not to criticize but to offer insight into how the world was at the turn of the twentieth century.

In my first years at secondary school I had a friend, the son of a pastor, whose parents had a charming little weekend house ten miles or so from the city. Once in a while I would be invited there on a Sunday. There was no question of going to church there. Nature had, so to speak, taken God's place. Everyone thought this just fine. Even the profession of Protestant pastor was in many ways "one profession among others," just as religious studies was "one lesson among others." Naturally, the pastor was obliged to serve at the church in the city at ten o'clock, but could then head out to the country, leaving his pastorate behind, so to say. The springs of the power of Christianity, a power that could give meaning to life as whole, were lacking not only here, but everywhere. Since I am saying something to the disadvantage of this pastor, I would add that the pure and hearty joy this individual took in nature was nonetheless a fruitful and quite unforgettable impulse in my life.

As regards my confirmation, unfortunately I cannot think of the lessons leading up to it without shuddering. The priest who taught them, a gentleman of many titles, was without question far too much at home in political and military life to be able to awaken actual repentance or to open the way into the mystery of Christ. He once told us that every week he had to write an edifying essay for the soldiers, that the essay had to contain precisely two thousand syllables, and that that was no easy matter. I thought: why are you telling us this? We could not yet share in this difficulty, so were we supposed to admire his achievement? I mention this only as a sign of those times. Many other signs of this sort could be given.

Then came my confirmation. It was for me an agonizing solemnity because I did not feel what I was supposed to feel. My inward soul was empty—or, rather, stuffed with good intentions. I had no receptivity. Neither, in any case, was there a living stream for me to receive. I saw myself as being at fault. To myself, I seemed especially worthless—not, unfortunately, in the sense of that true repentance which can be brought about by forgiveness, but in the sense of being split in two with a disabling embarrassment that became even greater for having to be concealed on the outside. At that time I once (and only once) knelt in church. My genuflection had, however, not been prepared for by anything in my life up to that point. I had never seen grown-ups kneel. And so this act of kneeling remained for the time being a one-time experience in my life, a gesture that, because it could not be inwardly realized, induced no feelings of devotion in the many spectators behind us, but only embarrassment. Whether I received the body and blood of the Lord, I cannot say. All I know is that, although I did not possess a true faith, the host and the chalice were presented to me nonetheless.

The examples I have given are neither coincidental nor merely personal. Here, in connection with the following passage, is a proof of this. The wife of an optician, whom I had befriended, half of whose patients were Protestants and half Catholics, said to me in 1946 or 1947 (not in 1916 or 1917, the time of which I am presently speaking) that when one asked Protestant children to kneel, they did not know how to, whereas Catholic children could immediately kneel at the examination bench. Furthermore, she said that a figure of the cross found on a table of illustrations for young children was mostly described by Protestant children as an airplane, whereas Catholic children always described it as a sign of the cross. The optician's wife, who was not a churchgoer, reported these observations without the least sign of reproach, without a tone of righteousness, without any wish to do either side down. Perhaps I may add here that, in many a Protestant church service, I heard the words of the apostle to the Gentiles spoken, to the effect that "at the name of Jesus every knee should bow" (Philippians 2:10), and often wondered how it could have come about that such an unequivocal admonition should not be obeyed. However that may be, in my childhood and youth I unfortunately acquired the view that kneeling was no longer up-to-date, as twentieth-century people had gotten beyond all that.

As was customary, I received many gifts on the occasion of my confirmation. I can sort them into two groups. To the first group belongs a picture of Kaiser Wilhelm II in military grey, a large picture of Hindenburg with a marshal's baton, and a picture of a German torpedo-boat rushing into combat, all three in very tasteful frames. In the other group belong such "edifying" books as *Youth is Sacred*, Brother W. Forster's *How To Live*, and so on. My notion regarding these books was that their purpose was to edify. And yet, as it seemed to me, neither those who had given them to me, nor indeed the entire generation of grown-ups, were entirely serious on this point of intended edification. The books seemed to have more to do with instruction or advice about adolescence than anything else. Notwithstanding all this, I did try for many years to be in earnest about such edification, although this was more of an intellectual effort than anything that could satisfy my heart. In reality, Christianity as it then presented itself, and as indeed it all too commonly presents itself today, was an "ideological superstructure" of life, not something that awoke joy, bestowed meaning, or supplied inner strength.

After I had been received into the congregation (this being part of the meaning of Protestant confirmation), the need to partake in its life gradually withered away. I was heading towards total secularization. Naturally, I did not at that time consider this a deficiency—and as far as I knew, neither did any of my comrades. My closest friend during these years was a Jew with whom I shared a love of poetry. Religion was not at the center of our personal or public lives. It was a "private matter," or not even that. In public life even today, religion is anything but the center of things; and as far as can be seen, this is likely to remain the case. Nonetheless, it can much more readily be at the center of people's personal lives today than was the case forty years ago. And for an increasing number of people it does indeed stand at the center.

In my life, by contrast, it was music that became more and more important at that time. I lived *in* it and *with* it. I owe a great deal to Beethoven. He stirred and satisfied my young soul as no religious book or church service had been able to do. And not only Beethoven. I went frequently to symphony concerts and operas, and devoted many hours to learning to play the piano. Beyond this, and in part owing to the fact that school left me yawningly empty, I immersed myself more and more in poetry. From Goethe's *Iphigenia* and Schiller's *Bride of Messina* I came to grasp above all the splendor of the German language. With joy, I breathed in the verses of *Iphigenia*, as well as the powerful rhythm of the choruses in the *Bride*. Meanwhile, the New Testament and Christian truth stood in the background. But everyone thought that was just fine. I would have to say that, at that time, I was hardly aware of having met anyone at all to whom the Christian faith meant as much to them as music and poetry did to me. And yet, strangely enough, a certain powerful Protestant self-consciousness remained present to us, even if I cannot specifically identify any individuals responsible for it.

As I recall, we did have *one* Catholic in our class, and somehow I "knew" that one could never quite trust Catholics, that one had always to reckon with a certain lack of forthrightness on their part, that in general they practiced a duplicitous morality. In fact, however, I was completely ignorant of Catholic church life. In our part of the city, there was no Catholic church. I had never entered one. Nevertheless, a strong aversion to everything Catholic hung around us then. Our religious instruction (unreligious and intellectualistic as it was in other respects) was devoted entirely to celebrating Protestant Christianity. If ever Catholicism did get a passing mention, it was the Catholicism of the fifteenth and sixteenth centuries. Not only that, but it was sure to considered in isolation from the facts of previous Christian ecclesiastical history. Martin Luther was celebrated as a monumental figure who had led us to freedom and the true Christianity; indeed, he was celebrated as the founder of Church history itself! Before him, of course, there had been *only* Catholicism. But so far as I can recall, no mention was made of that! The nature of the Holy Mass, the meaning of the vows of poverty, chastity, and obedience, the veneration of the Mother of God, sacramentalism—all these aspects of Catholicism, and others besides, could hardly be broached in a truthful manner in a Protestant religious studies at that time. Martin Luther's burning of the papal letter of excommunication, his text *On the Babylonian Captivity of the Church*, his marriage to the nun Katharina von Bora, and other things besides, were set before us as *victories* for God! We learned more about Gustavus Adolphus than about the life of St Francis, the teachings of St Thomas Aquinas, and the work of St Ignatius Loyola all put together.

Martin Luther's shadow darkened much that it would have been far more important to shed light upon than teaching us inexperienced students "adolescent" Bible criticism and Protestant "self-consciousness." In this respect, it seems that times are changing, and that they will continue to do so. At that time, however, Protestant "self-consciousness" was anything but humble and grateful; it was presumptuous, saturated with politics, and to a great extent not Christian at all. How otherwise could it have persisted in people to whom actual Protestant Christianity did not mean very much? Even in later years, I often noticed such a denominational self-consciousness in Protestant Christians, who were not nearly serious enough about their church to be justified in setting it apart from the positive practice of the Catholic church. At that time, all the people in my field of vision were *proud* of the fact that Protestant Christianity (the "national church"!) was preoccupied with the emperor and the fatherland, whereas the "Ultramontanists"[2] were regarded practically as traitors. For Protestants, the "world" was on the whole a very great deal more important than "God."

Naturally, such a way of putting things is far too simple to adequately describe so complex a context. Nor am I saying that I think it would have been proper to prepare us only for "God," and not for the "world." But it was a godless world that we were being prepared for! It was the world in which the Great War would shortly break out, in which all the frightening premonitory signs of that war (and all that was soon to follow therefrom) were accepted as "going without saying." Who ever asked, at that time or later, about the connection between the catastrophic war years and human sin, between what was then called "spiritual life" and the actual course of events? Taken as a whole, God's presence was conceived for the most part as for the purpose of blessing German weapons and helping the good German cause onwards to victory. Walther Flex's poems, which

---

2. Ultramontanism ("beyond the mountains") is a clerical political conception within the Catholic church that places strong emphasis on the prerogatives of the church, as contrasted with Gallicanism, the belief that civil authority over the church is comparable with that of the pope—a situation not dissimilar to that of the "national" Protestant church in Germany still today.

21

with a certain shimmering quality bring together national feeling and Christianity, were typical of that time. To allude to the title of one of his books (*The Wanderer between the Two Worlds: An Experience of War*), we were at best wanderers *between* two worlds, not *in* them.

After I had drifted away from Christian and church life, I joined the *Wandervögel*[3] and went on many "hikes" over the course of the years. For the most part, these treks took up a single Sunday, on which, of course, we did not go to church—but others lasted longer. The idea that Sunday was "the Lord's day" had disappeared from my outlook. We enjoyed the peal of the bells with a certain Romantic sense for their beauty, and (not to put too fine a point on it) regarded the village churchgoers as pleasant window-dressing. For our part, we tried to find satisfaction only in nature itself, in folk traditions, in cooking our own meals, in primitive ways of life, in midsummer festivals, in hiking with our comrades. The *Wandervögel*, understandable as a reaction against the excesses of civilization, and to this extent commendable, should also have been seen in an intellectual-historical context and in the context of religious history.

I must here confess that I myself never felt wholly at home in the *Wandervögel* because one of its distinguishing features was a certain break with the tradition of spiritual life. This could not suit me, and yet for a long time I felt more at home in the *Wandervögel* than in Christianity and at church service. For me, it was really no longer necessary for any bells to peal. Was this not also characteristic of that age as a whole? And taken as a whole, are things really any different today? We have now found out with blinding clarity that in the end, merely taking delight in nature and in what is primitive furnish no sort of protection against moral chaos. Is humanity today in such a state that church bells might peal with any justification? Who

3. The *Wandervögel* ("wandering birds") was a popular German youth movement between the turn of the century and the early 1930s, a movement that conceived of itself as protesting against industrialization by means of hiking. ED

still takes his hat off at the sound of them to say a prayer? Who might even seriously think of doing so? Any who think responsibly about this example of the disappearance of piety will agree with the view that we should hold on to whatever signs and symbols we still can—for once they have disappeared, it will be difficult, or impossible, to reintegrate them into our lives. But while they yet exist, it is always possible to breathe new life into them. Even today, and despite everything, streams of blessing continue to pour out from the pealing bells, blessings that can hardly be prized too highly...

However much fulfillment I drew from music, poetry, and nature, at the end of the day I was indescribably impoverished, disconnected from the source of life, in no position to discover anything essential, satisfying, or gratifying. More closely considered, all my participation in cultural life was but a surface phenomenon. It could not be otherwise, for man does not live by bread alone, and neither does he live by the "bread of culture" alone.

The sphere of mystery was unknown to me and closed to me. I cannot say for a certainty whether or not the mystery dwelt in a place completely inaccessible to me, but in my childhood and youth I had only come to know a Christianity devoid of mystery, a Christianity served up in pedagogical fashion. And let me add that this remark is not (as a friend once opined) a consequence of my having only gotten to know Reformed, rather than Lutheran, Christianity—which latter has a richer liturgy. Lutheran Christianity was not unknown to me. But people can mean very different things by the word "mystery," and anyone who does not know the mysteries of the Catholic church from his own experience (that is, who knows only the distinction between "Reformed" and "Lutheran" Christianity), will understandably judge these things in a quite a different way than will the Catholic Christian. There can be no argument about this. Nor should an argument be *started* about it!

Looking back, I might say that I was always thirsting for what is universally human, for what is beyond nationality, for the reality of divine governance—which, although it may indeed conflict with what is "earthly," also gives us the strength to live on and with this earth in the right way. But there was nothing and nobody who could assuage this thirst. It was a thirst in the depths of my soul, hidden from sight. Even I knew nothing of it, and so cannot imagine how any good spirit at that time could have made me aware of it, let alone have assuaged it. Everything I have been saying about the state of the age at that time must in the end be understood as self-criticism and confession.

Seen from this perspective, there were two "take-aways" from my final years at school that proved to be of great significance for me (including for the path that would later lead me into the Catholic church). The first of these was the work of Richard Wagner. I know very well how embattled Wagner is today, how he can be described as a "man of his time," as decadent, superficial, estranged from the spirit of Christianity. And in all honesty, for many years now I haven't felt the least need to see or listen to any of Wagner's operas. But this is not the place to discuss Wagner's relationship to Schopenhauer, say, or to the philosophy of his time. All that need be said here is that at the time in my life of which I am now speaking, he rescued me. My relationship to him went beyond a merely musical one. What I felt in him, or through him, and what I have to thank him for, goes far beyond musical stimuli and gratifications. I can best indicate what I mean with the word "mythical." The day I saw *Siegfried* for the first time (when I "saw" it, that is, rather than merely hearing it) was one of the most important in my life. This work became for me the image of supreme reality, of supreme efficacity. I did not think to question whether it was Christian, non-Christian, or pre-Christian. Rather, I took from it only what was good and what made for the good. I too wished to become a dragon-slayer. I exulted when, in the second act, the monster was felled and the hero understood what the wood-bird was saying. I breathed in the spirit of victorious conquest. I intuited something, at least, of the triumph of the archangel Michael over the Adversary, and I thought myself happy in the company of mythical heroes. This may have been foolish, but to my soul it was a reality—indeed, a reality that lay in the direction of the Christian mystery, however distant from the life of Christian liturgy *Siegfried* might be, both on the surface and in its content. None of my teachers at school, none of my comrades in the *Wandervögel*, no poem of Goethe's, then moved me nearly so much as the figure of Siegfried, and much of what stood around him. *Logos spermatikos!*…[4]

Something similar held true of Wagner's *Parsifal*. Here again, over and above the musical element, it was the mystery-act or mystery-image that cast a spell on me. Just as I had had no feeling for Brunnhilde in *Siegfried*, so here too I had none for the beautiful flower-maidens or the wicked Kundry. But the mystery of the "Grail" did not pass me by without leaving a trace! At least that is how it seems to me now, against the background of the rest of my life. It may perhaps be that *Parsifal* has an alienating or even repulsive effect on anyone already at home in the liturgy of the Church; but at the time, I had no experience whatever of the liturgy of the Church. And so the twice-performed scene of the Lord's Supper, so unlike the church liturgy I had till then known, awoke and nourished my slumbering feeling for liturgy. Admittedly, I could not then suspect that (nor to what extent) Wagner's *Parsifal* only exhibits in a distant, fragmentary copy what is present as a reality in the Church. Nor did even Richard Wagner open up to me anything that could nourish the very core of my being. But since all that was on offer otherwise was the prospect of improving one's vocabulary, solving mathematical problems, noting down historical facts, or memorizing Bible sayings, this sound-poet of genius could indeed bring good things to my life.

That was the first thing that truly affected me in my final years at school. Now we come to the second thing. In Autumn 1917, ten of us twelfth-graders were sent to bunk with a farmer and help in the potato harvest. We had by then read the opening sections of Goethe's *Poetry and Truth*, and there came to life before my eyes the scene in which little Wolfgang assembles a kind of altar on his father's music desk in such a way as to concentrate the rays of the rising sun through a magnifying glass and set alight a cone of incense. What happened for me was this. One day, with a comrade who soon became a friend, I built by the bank of a river a small stone altar and decked it out with fruits and flowers. As the full

4. The generative principle of the universe that creates and takes back all things.

moon was rising over the nearby wood, I set fire to some twigs on this "altar" while my friend played songs on his violin. Now, from an objective point of view, this was no great event. But for me it became a symbol nonetheless, and no bad one at that. Regarded superficially, this was merely an imitation of Goethe, stemming from the instinct for play. But the scene that night filled me with an intimation of liturgical, cultic reality. It was for me not a sign of some drift towards nature-worship, nor was there any danger of such a thing (albeit this danger did come closer to us later). I never had anything to do with nationalistic or anti-Christian ideas and cults, either outwardly or inwardly. But even so, a promise was made that night—even if I could not then have said to whom the promise was made! Today I can say it: it was the promise of Christian liturgical worship, a promise that, admittedly, could never be kept by Protestant Christianity. Unexpectedly, something very serious and significant had emerged out of a mere game, which had itself been prompted by a work of literature. Already that night I was aware of what I am speaking of here; it was not something I noticed only later. On occasion—something announces itself like this, from out of the unconscious, something that only later acquires life and a specific shape in the full light of consciousness.

Here I must ask my Protestant friends to excuse my remarks about Christian liturgical worship. I well understand that they may believe Christian worship and efficacious liturgy exist in the Protestant church just as much as in the Catholic church. Moreover, I know from many experiences of my own that Christ himself can work the effects of his grace in any time and at any place. But what I mean here by "Christian liturgical worship" is something my Protestant friends can know only from the outside. I do not hold it against anyone if they value Catholic liturgy less than it deserves. But I must also bear witness that Catholic liturgy is more sublime than any outsider can imagine.

The night-scene I have described was unfortunately an isolated incident, unremarked upon and without immediate sequel in my life. It eased my heart more than it impelled my thinking. That thinking of mine (if one can speak of the "thinking" of an average seventeen- or eighteen-year-old) was still closely bound up with the spirit of the age and of my schooling, despite all my dissatisfaction with these—that is, the seed had sprouted, although not in the sense intended by my teachers. The world of the Bible, of hymns, and of churchgoing had become unreal and shadowy to me. We had not really been brought up in a Christian way, but in a humanist and idealist way, with an added modicum of natural science. All the good impulses and ideas of any kind acquired in school presupposed a tenacious, healthy feeling of life—a will towards, and the strength for, the struggle for survival. People who possessed the latter certainly could manage to pass through this educational mill, or another like it, without visible damage and hardly noticing the absence from their lives of any imparted meaning.

The fragmenting of my spiritual life that took place in school was to continue in my life as a whole. It was my destiny to find myself in situations where, from out of the greatest forlornness, I would have to search for the meaning of life and its divine source of strength in the void, in hard and apparently hopeless efforts lasting for years. From time to time, I was likened to the "pure fool" Parsifal. One thing about the comparison was true: I was about to embark upon those wanderings that Parsifal had to undergo between acts two and three of Wagner's opera. School, and all its training, had left me empty. Despite Goethe and Schiller, Beethoven and Wagner, Parsifal and night-time sacrifices, despite the *Wandervögel* and the Christian parental home, I was on my own—without any noticeable relationship to the world of God, without the power or the desire to pray, without even an intimation of the "mountains from which help comes to us." Moreover, in place of all these things I lacked, I was full of a certain arrogance, full of the joys of culture, full of "Protestant" self-consciousness, and full of many an ideology.

Notwithstanding all I have described, ten months before the end of my time at high school I was given my diploma and sent off with high hopes and great expectations. Along with others in my peer group, I had been called up for military service! We, the youngest and least capable, were supposed to help win a world war that had already been lost. I did not speak to anybody at the time who saw through the madness of this pointless arrangement—or derangement! Moreover, even if my experiences of the world as it had come to meet me till then were quite simple and personal, they still seem to me characteristic of that whole period of time, and in many ways of our own even more horrifying age. One could quite well be a "Christian" without applying Christian truth to the situation in which the world found itself. Indeed, except in relation to one's immediate personal affairs, one could perhaps *only* be a Christian precisely because one did *not* so apply it.

Many people, understandably, hold the view that what is decisive for a child's religious development is not only church and school, but above all the parental home. One might see in my narrative an implicit condemnation of that parental home, but such a view would be quite out of place. My father died when I was thirteen years old, and so had no influence on my spiritual development at all. My mother was, as I have said, a Christian, but she was not active in the church, nor did she take any active part in the solution of the problems of the age. How could it be her business to answer questions like "how is German Idealism related to Christianity? What is the significance of modern natural science? What does the close connection between church and state mean?" But still, such questions did not become any the less important, or come any closer to being answered, just because one lived in a "Christian parental home"—that is, a typical middle-class home of the turn of the century, which cannot in itself occasion reproach. Without any further qualification, it seems to me in any case far too rationalistic to make parents responsible for the religious development of their children. After all, everyone can only do his best, and success or failure does not lie at human discretion, but is always a matter of God's grace.

In the oath of loyalty I had to take to the flag at the commencement of my military service, I was given yet another striking indication of the spiritual situation around me. What was an oath? What was God, the Omnipotent One "in whose presence" the oath was to be taken? Moreover, I was by far not the only one without a living relationship to God. None of the other eighteen-year-olds who had to swear loyalty to "their" emperor had such a relationship to him. None of us saw in this oath-taking more than a superficial act drawn from tradition, which at bottom meant nothing and did not commit us to anything. A rifle lock was a great deal more real to us than the "love of God." Going on leave was much more important to us than going to church. Cigarettes and butter were infinitely more significant to us than Bible sayings and sermons, not only for us two hundred poor recruits, but for almost everyone.

If matters had been otherwise in this respect, the world war would either not have broken out, or it would have gone differently. There often flitted shadow-like through my heart the saying from John's epistle that was engraved in marble on my father's gravestone, which I had taken also as my confirmation motto: "And the world and its desire are passing away, but those who do the will of God live forever." (1 John 2:17) But what was "the will of God"? What was "forever"? What was I myself, that I should "abide" forever? When my military service ended five months later, I went to university—to study law.

2

University and Psychoanalysis

THERE IS OFTEN A HIDDEN YET NOT WHOLLY UNFATH-
omable relationship between the spiritual or religious life as it is led
at any one time and the external facts and events of history. We
might indicate that relationship by saying that all deeds proceed
from ideas. For example, the Crusades were the destined consequence of corresponding ideas; the struggles of the Reformation
would have been unthinkable without the spiritual movement at
their core; or again, the workers' movement of the nineteenth and
twentieth centuries would not have come into being, or would have
gone differently, had it not developed out of particular ideas of the
time. And such connections between ideas and deeds are not just at
work in specific, readily identifiable outer events, but are present
also between the outer tendency of an entire age and the ideational
or spiritual life led within it. The world wars of our century, and
everything horrifying that happened in their wake, would not have
broken out, would not have taken so inhuman and diabolical a
form, had humanity as a whole held to different ideas, had it
believed in something other, in something Other that deserved the
appellation "Christian." But this was not the case. Taken as a whole,
all the catastrophes of the two World Wars, both great and small,
were an unmistakable sign and inevitable consequence of the godlessness into which modern humanity had fallen. Here is not the
place to investigate this subject in detail, for it would take considerable time and trouble to make this point to any who have not
already come to see it for themselves. And yet some effort in this
direction need not be futile; indeed, it may well be instructive to
turn our attention to the nature of our cultural institutions with the

intention of finding possible ways to change them—since, *summa summarum*, the same is true today as was true decades ago.

Institutions of higher education as they were at the turn of the twentieth century (and for the most part still are) provided no spirit of peace, nor did they open up that source of strength by whose means alone all destruction can be counteracted. "Normal" people could indeed pass through these institutions to the degree they did not object to the "life" they were preparing them for, and were willing to settle for no more than to find a place in just this "life." For most people it went without saying that one would spend ten, eleven, or twelve years in the classroom, become a soldier and fight (whether with enthusiasm or not) for Germany's "just cause," and if need be fall in that cause or be maimed for it. True, alongside such people were others who knew they had an inner vocation and were later able to take their part in bringing about the good, even though (or perhaps precisely because) they found the general spiritual life of the time unhealthy, and suffered from it. But such people were a decided minority. I myself belonged to neither of these types, but to a third. The drive towards the good (and strength to work for it) was not so innate to me that in due course it would inevitably have taken effect, no matter the circumstances. When I was growing up, I was lacking not only in a sufficient store of cultural and academic background, but also in any awakening to or nourishment of my innate being. I could not truly *inhabit* a world where spiritual life in general was wholly secularized and fragmented. I could only *exist* there, and do so in horror. Because I was by nature all too receptive and susceptible, all the ills of the public spiritual life around me (including the deeper causes at work behind them) exerted a powerful effect on me.

Even when I left school, I was a completely secularized and fragmented person. For me it was not at all self-evident how one should live; my own power of thinking was not yet developed, and my own special case was, in a way, a symptom of how matters stood with the public world of culture. It is for this reason alone that I dare to speak of my own life's course—for, generally speaking, what is merely personal ought to remain a private matter. Looking back, I can only regard it as healthy, in a deeper sense, that I was not infected with the "spirit" of my school or with the "spirit" of the age as they pressed in upon me. And it seems to me as though, in a more public and vulnerable way than for most people, I underwent a portion of the destiny of the age in my own personal destiny.

The present work is not meant to depict my personal experiences, but rather the path along which my worldview developed. I must therefore make clear what I mean by "worldview." The word should *not* be taken as designating whatever one happens to think at a particular time, for such passing ways of looking at the world do not at all accord with the deeper reality of one's life. Someone may think himself an "idealist" even though in truth he is very attached to material things. Someone else may think himself a "materialist" even though it might be more true to describe him an "idealist." Subjective mental contents are not always an adequate expression of objective states of affairs. There is a "Christianity" that is only "at home" in mental finesse, and its proponents cannot otherwise be distinguished from non-Christian people. Then again, there is a life lived in accordance with the Christian mystery that is nevertheless unaccompanied by any mental confession of the truth of Christianity.

A considerable gulf can open between the organism of the will, the world of deeds, and the organism of thought, not only in terms of moral perfection or imperfection (this goes without saying, and is almost our universal lot), but even in respect of life, of the will itself. In reality, quite other thoughts often determine our life than we may believe to be the case. Only too often, the spiritual element can become nothing more than an "ideological superstructure." Artistic, moral, philosophical, or religious ideas are not always the truly decisive ones, even when they may seem so. When I use the expression "worldview" here, however, it is, precisely, decisive ideas that we are thinking of. Viewed outwardly, I left school as a thoroughgoing "idealist," whereas in reality I was, if not a full-on materialist, at least a person lacking the spiritual strength or ability to set my own goals. Where and what, then, are "ideas"? It was my task to seek them out. I had to struggle for them. But first, I had to struggle for a "worldview" to guide my search.

The spirit of university life dovetailed with that of my secondary schooling. It was the same spirit, only here more splendid and powerful. That element from which the university takes its name, "universality" (*universitas*), was no longer present. On the whole, the universities had long since become mills of mere professional training. I cannot set this out in detail at this point. For now, the following remarks and examples will have to suffice. Lectures and research projects were taking place in every subject that the human spirit has ever explored. But there was no common bond joining them. The individual areas of research and expertise strove towards different goals. The bond between them had long since been rent asunder. Previously, that bond had been secured and preserved by means of the seven liberal arts, above all theology. The break-up of the old *universitas* was a process stretching over centuries of secularization, decline, and increasing human self-glorification. In my time, this process seemed to have reached a culmination. And the worst thing was that in general this eventuality entirely escaped notice—or, at a minimum, was not taken with the gravity it warranted. For most people, the pressing need to find practical means of survival was so powerful that they did not think any the worse of the university for having shrunk down to the primary function of preparing them for one or another "profession" in life. Indeed, most came to expect no more than this. At university one can train to be a priest, a doctor, a lawyer, a paleontologist, and so on, but what is the meaning shared among all these, what is their inner connection?

When I say that the individual fields of research and expertise did not possess a shared meaning, that is not quite correct. In reality they did indeed, and still do, share the same source and goal. If pursued according to "realist" principles (in the Scholastic sense), they could still in our day be developed from and held together by the same fundamental concepts. But how few in any of the individual fields of research can think as far as God-given, God-rooted reality! The *centripetal* force that initially defined and united the respective fields of research has been overtaken by the *centrifugal* force that fragments them. The eternal center has been progressively forgotten. Everything has been pushed more and more towards the periphery, towards the world of appearances, towards "concrete-ness"—a tragic positivism indeed! If a natural scientist happens to be "devout," if his research or method leaves "space" for the idea of God, this space must not be filled with yet more science, but instead with something from the domain of the soul or spirit. There was not earlier, nor is there now, any "natural science" able to proceed from the spirit of God that deduces matter from spirit or that is faithfully certain of the origin and goal of "nature." Yet only just such a natural science could be healthy and in accord with reality. What is earthly and material has become overwhelmingly decisive for modern humanity. Hence the fragmentation of the former unity; hence the disconnectedness of the multiple fields of study that now stand alongside one another; hence their dangerous specialization—indeed, even their war (whether open or concealed) of all against all, which yet again (as we were saying above) is the consequence of ideas, or rather, of *not* having ideas.

In light of these facts, the life of universities in the modern age in general appears superficial in the literal sense of the word. (This of course is not meant to be a blanket characterization of individual researchers in their particular fields.) For the sense-perceptible material world *is* in truth only the surface of total reality. An approach essentially oriented towards the material and sense-perceptible is always superficial: it does not return to the objective foundation, to the divine ground. Moreover, it is a God-given truth that *in principio erat verbum* (in the beginning was the Word). In this sense, academic life—when seen as a whole—lacked and still lacks the *principle*. Only in theological lectures was the principle ever mentioned; and like everything else in the intellectual life of the university, these lectures concerning religion and Christianity lacked any real spiritual or intellectual connection with the other subjects. What did the teaching and purposes of an art historian, a legal scholar, or a medical student have to do with the content of theological lectures—with the principle of all things, with the original nature of the world? Was there a living, meaningful connection to be seen between chemistry and jurisprudence, between astronomy and theology, between German studies and medicine, between musicology and technology?

I am well aware that in our day we are for the most part unaccustomed to a thinking that gets to the bottom of things—and so, to most people, questions of this sort may seem exaggerated, self-serving, even self-aggrandizing. But they are nonetheless justified. It is even dangerous that almost everyone settles for a specialist education, taking it as a given that the various fields of enquiry simply line up alongside one another with no purposeful connection between them. Five hundred years ago, this lack of purposeful connection was not taken to be axiomatic, nor will it any longer be axiomatic in another five hundred years. The catastrophes of modern life stem from the fact that properly human spiritual life was first split off from God, then turned towards itself, and finally fragmented in the way described. Over time, these catastrophes were prepared in the invisible realm, in the field of thinking, so that now—in the visible, cultural, economic, and political realms—something is appearing that could never have done so, had it not been summoned up by means of ideas. "Summoned up by means of ideas"? Admittedly, this expression stands in need of explanation, for surely it goes without saying that no one actually imagined in detail the catastrophes that then actually took place. But the fact nonetheless remains that through the "how" and the "what" of ideas, both the divine powers and nature were so far ejected from the human domain, and their workings so greatly hindered, that previously unknown powers could now enter and take effect.

To put it concisely, he who does not hold to the world of the angels will in the long run fall victim to the devil, whether knowingly or not. The higher world and the lower world meet in humankind. Humankind is the field upon which the higher and the lower worlds contend. Just as the human organism is healthy only when its members work together, so too the social community is healthy only when its members (not only classes, nations, and so on, but also its cultural-spiritual fields) are in accord with each other. And just as the human organism can live in a healthy way only if it receives the necessary nutrition and the necessary supply of air, so spiritual life can live in a healthy way only if it receives the necessary strengthening and fulfillment from God, or from the divine spirits. Only when once again we possess "universities" wherein the individual disciplines work "with the same basic concepts" and are thus unified at their core rather than merely through their particular outer aims—only then will social life be healed at its core.

Of course, I would not have been able to express ideas of this sort at the outset of my studies. But I did bear them within myself as a feeling, a disappointment, a pain, a need, and a hope—even as, already in my school days, I had borne all their fragmentation and disconnection. As someone who lacked any real education of the core of my being, the damage done by the public "world of culture" was fraught with deeper consequences for me than for a "healthy" person.

I went to university to study law, but still I had no clear idea of what I would do with my life. I chose jurisprudence mostly for want of any better idea. It was said in those days (another sign of the times!) that those who did not know what they wanted to do should study law, because many things could come of that. And this is true, provided that one has a tough will and the strength to fit in with the world as currently ordered. In my case, however (unfortunately, or rather, in truth, fortunately), nothing would "come of it." I went to the lectures in the expectation, even the need, that they might awaken and nourish my weak and slumbering self. But no such awakening call or nourishment came my way. Here I can only offer some essential outlines of what I mean.

Jurisprudence is meant to serve the right, or law, as it was laid down originally by God and thereafter handed down and upheld by responsible human individuals. But in the lectures I attended, there was not even the least intimation that law might have anything to do with God, or that the study of law might have anything to do with actual, objective rights. To attain any comprehension whatsoever of what law really is, I would have had to search out for myself in old books a picture of what might summon up real joy in legal work. But jurisprudence as I got to know it was just one subject among others, merely a professional training. It was not the "blindfolded goddess" it was meant to be. It was no goddess at all! The spirit of "positivism" had taken it over. Jurisprudence had lost its eternal source. My take on this state of affairs (certainly with some exaggeration and generalizing from personal experience), was that jurisprudence had arrived at the "apotheosis of formalism," and so I turned my back on it. At that time I was as yet unable to see what splendor, what moral life, what *divine life* had once inhabited jurisprudence, and could do so once again. Moreover, I was unable to see how working at spiritually reanimating jurisprudence might, in fact, be well worth the trouble.[1]

The following semester, I was a "natural scientist," and alongside physics and chemistry tried to master differential calculus. The physics teacher began his seminar with the words, "when Galileo met resistance to his discovery that the earth moved around the sun, he said 'yet it does move'; and so I say to you, gentlemen, 'yet England is to blame for the war!'" This was received with thundering applause and then the physics lecture began. Some years later this teacher took his own life. Taken together, these facts may serve as an emblem of the spirit of the university and its contradictions.

However helpless I might have been in respect of my academic life, a sense was at work beneath this outward helplessness and incapacity, a sense that sought what was right and fruitful in the spiritual life. To this end, I resolved to join some sort of student association. For me, there was no question of joining the cadets or a student fraternity, or a club for my major field of study, or even the "free German movement." There was in Marburg, however, from the time before the war, an association with a unique character and aim, given the rampant secularization of the time. It was called the "Academic Association," and I became a member. Its basic idea was that nothing should bind us together other than the fact that we were academics. Accordingly, an "academic evening" was held every week in which one of the members gave a talk about his field of

1. As pointed out in the Introduction, while this book was being written, Bernhard Martin was in touch with Valentin Tomberg who had recently published two books (one being a doctoral dissertation) on precisely this subject of reanimating, or regenerating, jurisprudence: *The Art of the Good: On the Regeneration of Fallen Justice* and *Jus Humanitatis: The Right of Humankind as Foundation of International Law*. Moreover, two years after the present book was published (1950), Tomberg completed a final, work in this field: *International Law and World Peace*.

study, ending in a general discussion. All fields, not excepting all political perspectives (something quite incredible at the time), were represented, and the subsequent discussions were conducted at a high intellectual level. Anyone who conformed himself to this requirement was thereby acknowledging the true "spirit of the "university," the spirit of unconditional knowledge, or "presupposition-less science," as we understood it—and, since the "universality" mentioned earlier had simply been lost, each speaker had to commence his presentation within the bounds of his own field of study. In this connection, the Academic Association respected the freedom of its members in a manner hardly to be found anywhere else at the time. Members were neither committed to "demanding satisfaction" under a code of honor, nor united in rejecting such a code. Rather, each member personally recorded his own position with respect to any such "demand for satisfaction" in a sealed envelope. Then, should a conflict arise, he was only obliged to conduct himself in the manner he had himself laid down, and only then was that made known to the other party.

Admittedly, the Academic Association did not answer the question I had had to face more than any other—i.e., how to strengthen one's being and give meaning to life (including meaning within a fragmented academic life). Nor were lectures on art history and philosophy of any use to me in this regard, even though I enjoyed attending both, particularly those in the history of philosophy, which acquainted me with so many great ideas. But even with some rudiments of understanding how Spinoza, Leibniz, Kant, or Schopenhauer thought about the world and humankind, the best I came away with was an intellectual overview that in the end did not really clarify the question of my *own* relationship to the world. One of the Association's members received a doctorate under the direction of Paul Natorp for an outstanding study in the field of Kantian philosophy, but he clearly did not live for the spirit of this philosophy. It was the other way around: it was with the aid of the spirit he *did* live for that he engaged with Kantian philosophy in the first place. I realized that one must have sufficient inner certainty of one's own in order to take any pleasure in an intellectual overview, and in particular to participate in the spirit of the presiding intellectual overview that had come to define all areas of the humanities at that time. I, however, did not possess such certainty in my being. To the contrary, I was hungry in a deeper sense, and needier than most students: a misfortune, yes, but also (since my path in life subsequently led me to clarity and a nourishing worldview), a stroke of good fortune also.

At the time I am speaking of, Oswald Spengler's pessimistic idea of the "decline of the West" hung persuasively and seductively in the air, and was widely discussed. Unpracticed and unfortified as I was, solving the basic question the book posed lay beyond my ken; yet I also somehow felt it was expressing a truth. As yet, I knew nothing of St Augustine's idea that "although the world is collapsing, Christianity is not collapsing, because Christ does not collapse." For me, all things metaphysical had become mere verbiage. I had fallen victim to the world of appearances. I was incapable of thinking things through from first principles. In place of this, Nietzschean ideas seductively (even if never wholly convincingly) enthused me, although I never assimilated them very well. That there was more "knowledge" in my body than in my best wisdom, or that God was dead and now the superman should live—these, thankfully, were ideas I never fully grasped in the sense intended by this author. But it was only consistent with my take on the world during this period of my life that I should get mixed up with Nietzsche. At that time he had not yet been taken up as a component of the history of philosophy, but was still a "living" philosopher, so to speak, whom one might rather approach directly. Whosoever loses the awareness of God must, however, in one way or another, arrive at atheism, and consequently an overvaluation of what is earthly and human. This conundrum was not, however, altogether my case.

Yes, I had indeed slipped away from the divine, but in a certain way I had also slipped away from everything human. I was unable to take any idea deriving from a human being seriously enough to put its stamp upon my life. Discontented with jurisprudence, as I was at the time, it could well have happened that I might sign up as a *studiosus theologiae*. I sought out Rudolf Otto, author of the book

The Idea of the Holy, and was able to speak with him about the matter. He thought it quite possible that one might become a theologian even if one were incapable of praying—which was the case for me at that time. His advice was well meant. In the course of theological study, perhaps one really can arrive at the faith one needs in order to be a pastor, but no Catholic theologian could have given such advice as Rudolf Otto gave to me—nor, I hope, would any Protestant theologian do so today. Such at state of affairs was symptomatic of that age, and more particularly of Protestant life in that age, and I could no longer take root in such an age. I don't mean this as a criticism. The ways of men differ immensely, and although as a Catholic one can and may believe in the uniqueness of the Catholic church, one ought not in any way to depreciate the personal paths taken by other Christians. In both Catholicism and Protestantism there is as much horrifying half-heartedness as there is supreme purity and giftedness.

So there I was, seated at the feet of a scholar of the New Testament, who, all the while looking gladly through the window into the distance, recommended to me St John's gospel. But here also no fruitful connection was made between the "matter" discussed and the core of my being. Even such a course as this was just "one subject among others," rather than anything inspiring that might direct me to the spirit of my origins. Meanwhile, doubt settled deep within me. Even theology did not rescue me for the living.

Then, during a vacation, I resolved to begin again with medicine. But it did not take very long for me to recognize that I, so helpless in the world of the senses, would never be able to master the many details of medical specialties. In a certain way I had now traversed the "four faculties," and with Faust could say:

> I've studied now Philosophy
> And Jurisprudence, Medicine—
> And even, alas! Theology—
> From end to end, with labor keen;
> And here, poor fool! With all my lore
> I stand, no wiser than before…

Unfortunately, these words are not merely a nice quotation but express with cruel precision just how things stood with me after four semesters. I really was "no wiser than before" (in fact, I was just as stupid and incapable!); and I really was a "poor fool" in having no idea what I should do. And so I had to interrupt my studies without being able to decide on some other profession. The idea that I "ought to study," I now realized, came to me from the history of my family and corresponded as well to certain prejudices in which I was still caught up. Yet at the same time I knew it was also an expression of the being within me that demanded to be developed. I could not serve as a carpenter or a gardener, just as I would never have been able to become an engineer or competent businessman. No matter the measure of money and stipends available for such pursuits, such considerations could not attract me or satisfy my need to find out how things stood with the matter of awakening and forming my own being. This latter could only happen through intellectual work, however, and for this, higher education was necessary—despite its manifest deficiencies and limitations. But first I had to leave the life of higher education and hide away for a while.

It was then that I resigned from the Academic Association, no longer feeling worthy of membership. The presiding officer who read out my letter of resignation remarked: "A member with no falsehood in him!" He may have been right as far as my underlying nature was concerned; and yet it was the right thing for me to leave. At that time, the Academic Association was the best a student association (one that wanted to be more than a mere club) could be, and many years later I noticed that the famous and venerable Martin Rade immediately attributed to it a particular value when I mentioned to him that I had once belonged to it. But he also said the Association had opened up the question of the university in a way that was merely formal rather than substantive, that proceeded from first principles (i.e., from method to the "matter at hand") to the source and ground of all real and possible individual specialties. And so there I was, no longer part of the Association. In truth I had already inwardly released myself from this community of friends.

I found it necessary now to make my way to a sanitarium. I chose one quite beautifully situated in the Alps, from which one could look far into the distance of the Upper Bavarian plain and over to the distant mountains of the Allgäu range. Here I was set to manual labor: first as gardener, then for a long while as a servant on the estate belonging to the sanitarium. I did not lack bodily strength. I put my whole self into it, whether in summer hay-harvests or in winter wood-chopping. On one occasion I climbed up the Zugspitze and back down before cycling fifty kilometers and then appearing for work at the appointed time next morning, something that could ordinarily only be done by experienced outdoorsmen.[2]

During this period I came to prize the work of Stefan George. Despite the poet's strong preference for pagan antiquity, I count this as having been among the good things in my life. At the time, I loved C.F. Meyer's novella *The Saint*, and couldn't read it often enough. I explored with wonder the Upanishads, of which I had a large scholarly edition. I did not, however, work through them in any systematic way. I also explored the works of Lao Tzu and Zhuang Zhou. Zhuang Zhou's anecdote of the two ladies has remained unforgettable to me. "A landlord had two wives, an ugly one and a beautiful one. He honored the ugly one, and despised the beautiful one. Zhuang Zhou asked a servant at the inn why this was. The servant answered that the beautiful one knew how beautiful she was, and we do not see her beauty; the ugly one knew how ugly she was, and we do not see her ugliness."

In these years, too, music was very important to me. We played Mozart over and over again. And then there were Bach and Bruckner too, composers to whom I dedicated myself. Thus I did not live without some personal gain amid the "two cultures of music," as August Hahn called them. Religion, Christianity, prayer, sacrament, church: all these were at that time empty words to me.

In compensation, however, I loved the earth and the sky all the more—the spring meadows, the cloud-play upon the mountains, the pure crag-lines in the distance. As in the words of Goethe's *Iphigenia*, "where the sun unlocked the heavens before me," I often thought of Upper Bavaria, of the beautiful foothills of the Alps,

---

2. The Zugspitze, at 2962 meters, is the highest peak in the Wetterstein mountains and in Germany.

where I loaded hay wagons, chopped wood, plaited straw hats, traveled by mule, and on the mountainsides gazed into the far distance. All this, however, concerns only the outward framework of life. The real treatment at the sanitarium had to do with psychotherapy, of which for various reasons it is difficult to give an account here.

The two academic years I had behind me by this time had given me many essential things from a variety of fields of knowledge, but it had done so in a piecemeal form, as could not have been otherwise at that time in a university—nor could it be otherwise today. It had neither awoken nor fortified in me any living connection with the spirit of God. On the contrary, it had only strengthened the feeling of weakness and abandonment I had suffered from already at the end of my school days. And so I found myself in a sad situation that cannot be described solely as a personal illness but also as a "sign of the times." Taken as a whole, "the times" was in a very real sense as sick as I was as a poor student. But this illness usually hid behind an overgrown, inauthentic busyness, and was thus for the most part neither seen nor suspected. This explains why it will require some effort for me to describe my predicament at the time. Nonetheless, I must overcome this difficulty. After all, only by first exposing an illness can one describe the healing that followed.

So, then, I must confess that in the sanitarium where I lived for well over two years, I was deeply and selflessly loved by the wife of the leading doctor. She took me into her heart, fretted about me as a mother does over her child, and strove mightily to ensure that the slumbering consciousness of her pupil would open itself to the world and to the spirit of God. Such caring love sets up an emotional bond that can oblige one to keep silence about anything that might work to the disadvantage of the other person. But still, however much love and personal gratitude might prompt me to remain silent about psychotherapy, this spiritual memoir, such as I envision it, demands that I speak of it.

The therapeutic work at the sanitarium followed the principles of Sigmund Freud's psychoanalysis. Freud had discovered the significance of the "unconscious" in human beings, and of their slumbering (and also deviant or repressed) drives. He went on to define a whole school of psychology that only later was taken in a more intellectualistic direction by others. One factor holding sway in the "unconscious" is the sexual drive. This drive doesn't always govern the unconscious in an organic way that furthers life, however, for the drive concerned belongs not only to our physical life but to our psychological life as well. Moreover, it can happen that if someone's "instinctual life" is not sufficiently worked through by their consciousness, it can have a damaging effect in that person's unconscious as a result of particular repressive "complexes." If then such complexes (which can go back to an overwhelming event or "trauma" suffered at some time in the past) emerge from the unconscious into consciousness, under certain circumstances harmony can once again be restored in the patient's life as a whole, and the spirit can once again develop in an undisturbed fashion. In drastically abbreviated form, this is the essence of Freudian psychoanalysis. The means by which what is going on (or going wrong) in the unconscious is brought to light is, among other things, the analysis of dreams. Dreams, which emerge from the unconscious and most often bear tidings of something far from waking consciousness, can be illuminated by means of all sorts of "associations."

Now, since those treating me were of the opinion that I was affected by such complexes, these had to be sought out, "abreacted," and thus rendered harmless. In this way, the spirit that had supposedly been repressed on account of some trauma could be led towards its true vocation. To this end, whatever dreams I had were analyzed, and where possible illuminated by means of associations. But as it turned out, no complex could be found, so none could be dispelled. We searched for one with great patience, but in vain. Unfortunately, this search was not limited to personal discussions. I also acquainted myself with psychoanalytical writings. I can only speak of this with great pain because to do so I must call to mind quite precise matters pertaining to the people who in other ways did me so much good. I say this, because in the end I came to regard these writings, together with the "therapy" they extolled, as dangerous and destructive. Through this experience, my imagination was poisoned in an enduring way with ideas that were evil, *very* evil. My thinking, which, despite my secondary school years and four semesters at university, was still in a certain sense a blank slate, was now overwritten with things best left unspoken. This spiritual "nutriment" certainly found a receptive audience generally, but in my case it was handed to me on a platter—which was all the more painfully distasteful for having been served to me by people (who thus bear responsibility for it) whom I still love, and whom I will always love. Anyone who doubts the justification for the Church's "Index" (its directive not to read certain books) may, admittedly in a grotesque way, gain some insight into its importance by looking into some psychoanalytical texts, particularly psychoanalytical "case histories" of the sort I then devoured. Those who take the trouble to do this may perhaps then come to understand that it may be far preferable to leave some things unread than to seek to "make up one's mind" about them, and that it can be good to protect others from the influence of what is evil. Would it not have been good in just this way if Hitler's *Mein Kampf* and Rosenberg's *Myth of the Twentieth Century* had remained unread, if there had been a tribunal to prevent the intellectual dissemination of their poisonous false doctrines?

Perhaps if someone were to begin such psychoanalytical treatment against the background of a relatively stable life situation, or with prior familiarity of one kind or another with what psychoanalysis entails, they might be able (in some degree, at least) to survive the search for "associations" and "complexes" without great damage. But in my case, I had nothing so firm to fall back on—those elements of the world of Christian and humanist-idealist culture that had so far gotten through to me had not yet reached as far as my innermost being. True, they had not remained solely an outward cultural veneer, but neither had they produced in me a settling and illuminating effect. But now, with these psychoanalytic procedures, my core *was* being reached—if not the core of my spirit, then certainly the core of my soul. There was even, on the part of my consciousness (which had previously remained mostly free from lower things) a certain inclination towards the dark world that these procedures had summoned up. It was most unfortunate that all this was handed to me just when, belatedly, I was in a state of receptivity in which I involuntarily took everything much more to heart than can have been intended by my well-meaning therapists.

There is indeed a system in psychoanalysis, and it is more comprehensive than that of individual fields such as anatomy or botany. Human consciousness and dream-life do indeed participate in the whole universe, or at least they can do so. This is not the place, however, to offer an exhaustive exposition of Freudian science. I can only describe its effect on me personally, which was like that of the famous dragon's teeth in the myth of the Golden Fleece. I now believed the goal of everything in life, culture, and religion was "love-fulfillment." I seriously believed (and I cannot have thought up this absurdity on my own) that it was not only pleasurable sport to seduce girls, but that it was my duty to do so—and even that it was expected of me. Yet I shrank back from this "duty," believing I could never be as "masculine" as it seemed my "therapy" expected of me. This state can best be described as one of a bewildered loss of all healthy feeling. Naturally, such psychoanalytic doctrine—the whole of it—could only have emerged from outside the Christian faith and the Christian church. Moreover, the damage it does is in large measure connected to the fact that it takes partial truths for the whole. It is a science lacking any connection whatsoever with God.

Now, the sanitarium was only about three hundred yards from the fine local village church, but the spirit of that church never found its way into the therapy practiced at the sanitarium. In that therapy there was not a word said about the Mother of God, about angels, saints, or a higher reality; nothing about Christian faith, the Christian church, or the mystery of the divine. Everything that, by means of devotion and inspiration, prayer and grace, can alone make the soul truly healthy, was excluded. The sole topic for discussion was myself and my "unconscious." None of the things I have just mentioned were in my unconscious. The simple truth is that psychoanalysis, a purely this-worldly procedure, lacks any true ideal. As the youngest child of purely natural-scientific research, it can at best leave the divine world unmentioned, so that human beings can busy themselves with earthly matters alone, rather than undertaking to lead them towards true healing. Psychoanalysis has nothing whatsoever to do with that health which in truth is alone worth talking about. For, what is it to "be healthy"?

There is no perfect health (or rather, no health worth striving for) that is not to be found in the fundamental attitude *Domine, non sum dignus, ut intres sub tectum meum, sed tantum dic verbo, et sanabitur anima mea*: "Lord, I am not worthy to have you come under my roof, but only speak the word, and my soul shall be healed." (Luke 7:6–7) I do not mean that these very words must be used. I know there are countless different paths to salvation and to the Savior. But I believe I know today that without the Savior there is no salvation. Indeed, "There is salvation in no one else, for there is no other name under heaven given among mortals by which we must be saved." (Acts 4:12) The "health" sought in Freudian psychoanalysis as I became acquainted with it, however, was a health that did no justice to this truth. It was, instead, a purely earthly "health" with the help of which one could just as well become a criminal or war pilot as become in some sense a Christian. It is a great danger that in our day the "obvious" universal view is that to be healthy means to be unimpeded in one's earthly power to act—whereas such a "health" as this ought instead to be diagnosed a horrifying, shattering, sickness! But all this is just another sign of the spirit of our age. Taken as a whole, present-day humanity has fallen further from divine governance than ever our ancestors did. It "masters" vast provinces of ideas, fields of research, and universally-recognized categories of "reality"—into which, however, not the least awareness *of* the divine, not the least connection *with* the divine, have ever found their way.

Naturally, there is some justification in calling someone capable of action "healthy," but this concept of health would *itself* only be healthy in the full sense if brought into a living connection with that concept of health about which I have just said what most needs to be said. Physical ailments like pneumonia, a broken leg, or a septic ear can be successfully treated without thinking about God, the meaning of life, or sin. But a sickness of the soul cannot be treated with true success if such concepts as faith, prayer, the meaning of destiny, redemption, divine judgment, and eternal life are either unknown or left out of consideration. This truth is incontrovertible, regardless of how many people may believe otherwise. It goes without saying, of course, that anyone unfamiliar with the level of life being spoken of here—a "depth" that is not psychological, but pneumatological—will hold a contrary opinion. I once heard a chief physician at the sanitarium laugh out loud as he remarked that Charlotte von Stein had been a silly goose not to go to bed with Goethe—rather than furthering his mental culture![3] This sort of attitude is not without consequences for the one who expresses it, or for anyone who falls under its influence.

It is painful for me to write these things because (as I already felt at the time, and later learned to be the case) the leading figures of the sanitarium were by no means wholly estranged from Christianity. The chief physician I just mentioned was at the time passionately translating John's gospel! He regularly held Christian celebrations in his home in which I would gladly have taken part—but they were not open to "patients." How much good these people might have done, had they let those entrusted to their care participate also in their Christian life and quest! How differently might fifty minutes of psychotherapy have gone had it begun with a prayer. But, indeed, the truth is that nothing of the Christian spirit finds its way into "therapy."

So, "pure fool" that I was,[4] not yet capable of thinking for myself, I was brought into contact with dominating ideas that the therapists would certainly never have wanted to summon up in me, and whose subsequent germination and growth it should have been their task to notice and prevent. Living directly in conflict with everything sacred and Christian, I regarded psychoanalysis as the correct "worldview," which in my view at that time was always and everywhere valid, and ought therefore to be universally disseminated. With deepest conviction I said to a friend of mine, who at that time was a candidate in theology and had pointed me to the truth of Christianity, that the entirety of his Christian doctrine was not at all "presuppositionless" but in fact derived from tradition,

3. Charlotte von Stein (1742–1827) was a playwright and lady-in-waiting at the Weimar court, where she was a close friend of Schiller and Goethe, and exercised a strong influence in particular on Goethe's life and thought.
4. Allusion to the hero of Wagner's *Parsifal*, who is so described in that opera.

and for that reason could only be upheld from a position of unfreedom. At the time, naturally, I believed myself to be free. But in fact I was totally helpless in life. I was a nobody who had allowed myself to be inflated with unpleasant fantasies and "objectives." What sort of "freedom" was that? It was a freedom of protest, where "freedom" mostly meant, not freedom to *do* anything, but freedom *from* something. Moreover, in recent decades have we not become all too familiar with a supposedly free rebellion at every level against genuine values? In this light, my own rebellion, although lived out in completely hidden fashion, can also serve as a general symptom of how far and how hard was the path from this infernal rebellion to simple, truthful faith!

Sigmund Freud and his disciples never thought out the possible ultimate consequences of their doctrine, just as they had never fully fathomed its origin. They were children of their time, a time of objective godlessness, in which natural science, anthropology, psychology, and so on had almost nothing to do with what theology teaches, or with what the prayerful petition of all Christian liturgy has in mind. Once upon a time the whole world, the whole field of human consciousness, was God's territory. But this territory has been conquered bit by bit by an enemy power. One of the "brigades" of that enemy power, certainly only one of many (but a very dangerous one) in its extensive army is called "psychoanalysis." Only a "total" Christian perspective on the world, together with the practical consequences of that perspective, can save us. Those who were treating me were well-intentioned, but they failed to see that it was one thing ethically (even with a selfless attitude) to focus fixedly on the "unconscious," and quite another to deal with such a situation as I was then in—void of any worldview, and both spiritually hungry and psychologically malleable.

Every person, whether highly cultivated or of a simpler nature, is an idea of God, and is consequently called to his own consciousness and his own responsibility. This is why care for the life of consciousness is so important. It is through such care that the individuality is nurtured and revealed. By contrast, psychoanalytic "care" leads down to the sub-individual, where everyone is alike, where there is no humanity, but only the drives. In this domain, the necessary order can only be brought by something able to establish rulership over it—whether we call that something our being, our ego, our spirit, or anything else. Because this higher element called to establish rulership had not yet developed in me, the dose of psychoanalysis I received could only damage me. The general or collective elements in me were summoned up without my individuality having been correspondingly prepared, or rather, without having been given the chance to be so prepared. This was to have consequences for my life, consequences that need not be spoken of here in detail. What I can say is that however undeveloped my consciousness was, what happened was a "leap from the pinnacle of the temple." I blame no one but myself for this, even though from a psychological point of view one might regard the whole business as a spiritual temptation.

It is dangerous thing that, whereas psychoanalysis has a concept of "feelings of inferiority," it has no concept of "guilt." Feelings of inferiority disturb us, but they do not burden us. Where possible, we talk ourselves or busy ourselves out of them, but nothing ethically valid is needed to overcome them. The penitence that impels forgiveness is something quite different. At a later stage in life it became my task to turn my feelings of inferiority into an awareness of guilt. Feelings of inferiority come from the devil and draw us away from God. Awareness of guilt comes from God and leads us back towards Him. Moreover, a consciousness that goes deeply into things knows itself to be responsible for things of which, from an externally human point of view, it needn't really to have accused itself. One must learn to say about *everything* bad, and without *any* reservation: *mea culpa, mea culpa, mea maxima culpa* ("through my fault, through my fault, through my great fault")! Equally, one is permitted also to observe objectively the playing out of destiny on the world's stage. What follows below is my attempt to do just that.

The present godlessness, worldliness, and lack of spirituality of humankind's collective spiritual life, within which psychoanalysis (and many other things typical of the time) represents only an extreme point, was (with a few exceptions) monstrous. The "world"

in which (or as a result of which) I had fallen ill could offer no "sanitarium" in which that illness might have been healed. The inner task of my life, which was to seek a source of strength and meaning for an empty, wavering, vulnerable inner life, had only now become fully clear to me. The story of my youth, including my early studies and the time spent in the sanitarium, had led me to the most extreme form of the experience: "You are afraid in the world." What lay yet before me was to find the truth that would redeem me and make me whole: "I have said this to you, so that in me you may have peace. In the world, you face persecution. But take courage; I have conquered the world!" (John 16:33)

The spirit of Freudian psychoanalysis is poison. It is poison in every case, not in mine only. It is poison even when by its means a "cure" may be achieved. But, for the sake of truth, let me add that in saying this I am referring to outright, unalloyed Freudian psychoanalysis and to the effect this had in my particular case. For even at that time (and increasingly thereafter) psychoanalysis has moved forward in a more positive direction—to the point that, as I write today, there are not only many psychotherapists who properly situate sexuality right from the outset, but also many whom one must acknowledge as being fully Christian. Indeed, from time to time a friend of mine who works as a psychotherapist has patients referred to him from the confessional by one of the most well-known Catholic priests in Germany. The priest would certainly not have taken this step had he feared that those patients would meet with an un-Christian influence there. It is enough to mention this here, however, rather than to embark on detailed descriptions of the various psychotherapeutic schools, doctrines, and methods in detail.

3

Businessman and Student

IN 1924, I WAS GIVEN THE OPPORTUNITY TO MOVE TO Hamburg and apprentice in an export business, and I took it. In doing so, I had no more specific a goal in view than finding some sort of entry into "life." Hamburg, at that time the largest German city after Berlin, filled with the air of the open sea, was rebuilding its export business, which had been languishing in the wake of the First World War. After the period of hyperinflation, with its million- and billion-mark notes, the *rentenmark* had at last been introduced, and its purchasing power was enabling the resumption of international trade.[1] The business I was engaged with was a department of a large firm that, owing to the improved economic situation, was rapidly developing. It's main business was exports to East Asia, and I was soon busy preparing faithful and reliable invoices in dollars and pounds (offering for sale pencils, raw materials, pianos, pins, and so on), and both writing and deciphering encoded telegrams. My boss, a big businessman of the unscrupulous kind, who sported three gold watch chains over a correspondingly expansive belly, and was willing to tread over not only one dead body but a whole heap of them to achieve his purpose, was very happy with me. The "solidity" I seemed to have brought with me was, it seemed, just what he needed. What I mean is that I was a predictably "calculable" quantity in his planning. In his mind, he probably envisioned me ensconced in China or Japan as a company secretary, earning thousands for him. But he had miscalculated. As a predictable man of the "real" world, he understandably imagined that the aspirations of his

1. The *Rentenmark* was a new currency introduced in Germany in October 1923 in an attempt to control inflation.

"solid" apprentice could be aimed at nothing other than worldly success and its attendant pleasures. What he lacked, however, was the imagination to grasp that there is also an inner, spiritual, divine world, and that it is possible for someone to be split between the outside and the inside, between the world and the spirit, between one's outward role in life and one's inner concerns.

When a year later I left the firm and turned my back on the admittedly imposing edifice of Chile House (as the business was called), he cut me off completely, most likely because he was lamenting the generous wages he had paid me almost from the beginning on account of my performance. For this type of person there are only two questions in life: "How can I make as much money as possible?" and "How can I most enjoy my life in spending it?" Everything else for him is only a means to personal ends. Both of these questions were inwardly unknown to me. Roughly put, *my* questions were: "How can I find the right shape for my life to take?"; "How will I find the strength to live in this horrible world?"; and "What do I need to do in order to fulfill, at least to some extent, the meaning of my life?" And, not to forget, these questions were at work in a soul that possessed no sort of self-confidence, very little trust in other people, and no trust at all in God!

Business, as I got to know it in Hamburg, seemed to me an intolerably sterile and stultifying vocation. It filled my soft, impressionable heart with crippling horror. I was able to do what was required of me professionally, but in soul I was in no way connected to all this, even by the thin thread of an instinct for play that might have found it satisfying to prove successful at something so foreign to my nature. In my year in Hamburg, then, I lived a double life. The solid apprentice businessman was my exterior, behind which lived despair, discontent, insecurity, and a longing for fulfillment. On the other hand, there were visits to the theater and to concerts, good books were read, and a certain social circle cultivated. I had friendly connections at some houses in Flottbeck, where I could be received not as an apprentice, but as a person.

I led a double life in a second sense too, however. Actions resulting from the spirit of my psychoanalytic "worldview" stood in melancholy contradiction, not to that fine young-businessman exterior, but to my own self-respect and my own conception of myself. This double life fit quite well with my surroundings at the time. Here is a relatively innocent example. Our boss once walked benevolently through the rows of desks and asked an apprentice, the son of a Hamburg business magnate rolling in money, "Hey, how are your girlfriends?" The apprentice answered, "I only have one girlfriend, Herr O." To which the boss replied, "Sure, we only have one *official* girlfriend, but that's not the whole story" (and it should be noted that we knew he spoke from experience). This annoyed me (even then I was bad at tolerating any "double life"), and I retorted, "You must not think, Herr O., that everyone does as perhaps you once used to!" A horrified silence followed, but the boss went his way without issuing a reprimand. I had spoken honestly enough, yet sometimes I seemed to myself like Dorian Gray,[2] whose inner face, a face destined to be revealed one day, was so terrifyingly at odds with his outer appearance,.

Fortunately, after an occasion on my part of just such behavior as referred to on the part of my boss, I fell into great distress of conscience, and, impelled by despair, betook myself to a Catholic confessional, said what was on my mind, and denounced myself. The priest listened to me with great calm and a palpable kindness. He was accustomed to hearing of such sins. He could not absolve me sacramentally, since the Catholic sacrament of absolution is open only to Catholic Christians (which obviously doesn't mean that no non-Catholic penitent can obtain forgiveness), but he spoke in such a way that I left the confessional comforted, strengthened, and with good intentions. *That was my first experience of the Catholic Church.* It ought to have made me pay attention. Regrettably, however, it was lost to view for years, with no further consequences. There was no other confessional like the one I had visited in the whole of Hamburg. Why did I forget it? Why didn't it become a magnet and stimulus to me to begin a new and better life right then and there?

---

2. The main character in Oscar Wilde's novella *The Picture of Dorian Gray* (1890), who sold his soul in order to remain always as youthful as he had been when a portrait had been painted of him: the picture would fade, but not Dorian Gray himself.

Because my will was weak and the psychoanalytic poison still had me in its coils. It took many more years for me to root it out of my soul and spirit. Later, some time after I had left Hamburg, I set myself the deliberate goal of ridding myself of it—but that was a goal not to be achieved overnight. Angels do not so easily overcome demons, who cling close to anyone already in their clutches…

When the year in Hamburg was at an end, I returned for the summer to the charming little village in Upper Bavaria. I was no longer a patient, however, as it was now clear even to the therapists that I harbored no "complexes" to be pulled out like a tooth. I do not frankly know whether they ever realized that they had inflicted something upon me psychologically in a manner equivalent to treating a physical illness for years with unsuitable and toxic medications. Now, however, it was I who was on the spot, having myself been entrusted with treating a female "patient" psychoanalytically! I did this with all the integrity I could muster, and my charge, a tragically unhappy and inwardly insecure person, at least fell no further under evil's spell.

During this summer an event of great import for my life took place: I wrote my first book. Once before, when I was about twenty-one years old, I had penned a series of hymnic compositions in the style of Nietzsche's *Zarathustra*. After this first foray, any capacity to express myself (apart from musical improvisation) had fallen asleep. It was a novel, a kind of interior autobiography. The title was *Manfred: The Story of a Dying Man*. This "Manfred" (a contraction of Martin and Friedrich, and the name by which I was called in my childhood and youth) was of course me. For no external, immediately compelling reason, Manfred was traveling toward death in a state of agonized suffering. To his good fortune, however, he had a child. The child was called Bernhard, and the final chapter envisioned Berhard's ascent, as if in anticipation of the fate I imagined for myself, and that was then still completely hidden from me. *Manfred* was not written in naturalistic style, but in a style all its own: endless repetitions with a certain magical power drilled pessimistic thoughts into the soul, which however had the effect of drawing me out of myself. Over and over again, tirelessly, to the point of exhaustion, strikingly pictorial short sentences framed a mostly purely interior content. It may be that a remote model for the form this book took was provided on the one hand by Nietzsche's *Zarathustra*, and on the other by the discourses of the Buddha with their recurrent phrasing. The content, however, was entirely my own.

With a friend's help, this unhappy book came close to publication, but thankfully it never got that far, and in the course of time all the copies I had made were destroyed. The lesson of this time was that just as there is a nurturing from above and a nurturing from below, so is there also a spiritual influence from above and another from below. There was certainly no good spirit behind *Manfred*; but as I later noticed, it did have precursors, contemporaries, and kindred spirits enough in "modern art." Stylistically, *Manfred* belongs to the epoch of expressionism; morally, it belongs to the realm of literary deconstruction that was gaining the field in the twenties. In any case, what could I—spiritually a void and morally a minus sign—have to say?

When the summer of *Manfred* had passed by, I left the sanitarium. I resumed my studies, now in Munich. My state was much altered from that of my earlier studies. First of all, the objective effects of all that had previously stood in the way of a healthy relationship with the spirit of the university were present, to which were now added the experiences of incapacity I had passed through, and which were themselves not without consequences. Whereas at the outset of my first period of study I had been expecting help and nourishment from outside, I resumed university life now with the awareness that nothing was to be expected from that direction. Thus, it was a question of commencing a period of "study" from which, at least to begin with, no essential nourishment, indeed no essential goal of any kind, was expected. The main point of taking the step was to enable me to live in a large city and in an intellectual atmosphere. What was to come of this new beginning would only emerge in the course of time. But it did indeed emerge, for intensive effort and divine grace would eventually join forces to reveal meaning, and to bring me strength.

Every university has its unique quality. Things are different in Hamburg from what they are in Marburg, different in Bonn from what they are in Munich. As regards the essential spirit of the university, however, there is no great difference: they all reflect and exhibit the spirit of the age I sketched earlier and that can be characterized with the keywords secularization and fragmentation. I say (and will have further occasion to say) that these two keywords are not in the slightest meant to be pejorative as regards individual academic teachers or individual scholarly achievements. Only those have a right to criticize who have earned that right through the requisite accomplishments. In invoking these words I mean only to cast light upon my need to become a person of faith, and as well as to illustrate my opinion of the true task of the university: to form one's being and draw out one's spirit. It is in this sense, then, that I met with the same secularization and fragmentation I had encountered years before. I would like to offer here a small but telling example of what I mean by this, one that can stand for dozens of others, but that experience has shown to be quite difficult for a modern person to understand, and therefore to truly take seriously.

The spirit of "presuppositionless" science prevalent in the university was perfectly suited to critiquing sentences like the following: "Goethe bestowed immortality on Ulrike von Levetzow."[3] The critique runs something like the following. What does this sentence really mean? Is not every person a unique individual who bears their meaning, their task, their fulfillment (or lack thereof) in themselves? Cannot even someone upon whom a famous man "bestows immortality" fall victim to eternal perdition? Does no

3. Theodore Ulrike Sophie von Levetzow (1804–1899) was a friend and the "last love" of Johann Wolfgang von Goethe. The seventeen-year-old girl first met Goethe in 1821. The poet, then 72, was so carried away with her wit and beauty that he thought for a time of marrying her, and urged Grand Duke Karl August to ask for her hand in his name. Rejected, Goethe left for Thuringia and addressed to her the poems that he afterward called *Trilogie der Leidenschaft*, which include the famous *Marienbad Elegy*. Ulrike later confessed that she was not prepared to marry, and angrily denied a liaison with Goethe. She remained unmarried all her life and died at the age of 95 in Bohemia. ED

divine judgment adjudicate righteously and irrevocably on the form of our lives after death? Is not immortality bestowed upon us by God, the Creator and Lord of all life, irrespective of whether we happen to have been friends with this or that important person? In sum, then, what can it mean to say that Goethe bestowed immortality on Ulrike von Levetzow?

Well, it just means that if Goethe had not loved her and not written poems about her, we would not be talking about Ulrike von Levetzow any more, over a century later, which is indeed the case, and we know quite well that the sentence quoted will be understood in just this sense by almost everyone who reads it. And yet, it is dangerous to appropriate the word "immortality" (which ought by rights to describe a metaphysical, objective, divine fact) to refer to something entirely different. One cannot with impunity misplace and conflate concepts and the meanings of words. In a hidden but not insignificant part of their being, those who speak of "immortality" in this way lose the sense for what immortality actually is, even if they do not notice this loss. The idea, so balefully exhumed later by National Socialism from the ancient past (and to which it swore fealty), that fame among one's successors was something worth striving for (all without thinking it through to its conclusion, and put to anti-Christian purposes) was grounded in the spirit of the university, though not there alone. There is no question that in the age of Scholasticism a sentence so unholy as the one we are here considering could not have been uttered, and that at that time even among the nominalists a word meant nothing other than what a speaker or writer was thinking. Undeniably, one could indeed at that time deny immortality, but one could *not* speak of immortality when what one really meant was to be remembered by posterity.

What I am saying here illuminates the spiritual situation I again encountered at university. It provides yet another example of the fact that "individual fields were not working with the same basic concepts"—the field in this case being literary history and logic or metaphysics. How little it takes (and in how many places) to point out the same ruination of the spiritual life so evident in this little example! It is a grave circumstance indeed, and one not without serious implications for the external course of historical events, that for most of our contemporaries what is meant by something said or written can so readily be dispensed with, and that their organ for detecting truth is so atrophied that such examples as we are discussing pains them not in the least. Truly, when the devil is called the father of lies, this is not meant figuratively, but literally. Any deviation from the truth, even so "innocent" a one as this, is not without its consequences. Naturally, at the outset of my second period of study I would not have been able to express all this in the way I have done here, but I certainly did feel the harmfulness of what I have mentioned. I sensed, at least, that the symptoms I am at pains to describe were but small signs of something more, standing behind them. To have drawn any essential nourishment from university life as it was then, I would have had to be a Catholic theologian—something for which, in my case, the necessary prerequisites were absent.

Here is another example. It was part of the spirit of "scholarship" then prevalent that works of art handed down from the past were discussed and critiqued solely from an "art-historical" perspective, without regard to the essence of the worldview that may have gone into their making. Buildings, sculptures, etc., bequeathed to us by the spirit of Christianity (or for that matter, by the spirit of Buddhism, Confucianism, Egyptian culture, or that of Greece) were received solely as works of artifice, on the grounds that this was the best way to do them justice. While the original "substance" in them was pointedly ignored, our own correlative contemporaries' "insubtantiality" passed entirely unnoticed. What sort of a world was this, where one learned about the development of architecture from the Romanesque to the Gothic to the Baroque, where one could correctly recognize and classify the style and period of any work of art, where one could blithely inventory the merely formal, exterior, "expression" of these works of art in complete dissociation from their essential nature—as though the pious, faithful, gifted artists who brought them to realization had done so simply with a view to giving us an entertaining occasion later, and at several removes, to critique and confabulate about them? If one is completely disconnected from the attitude and aims of the artist, if one feels no obligation towards his concerns in life, can one really understand his work? However "significant" and "expressive" an altar painting may be in the mind of a modern, is not its essence irremediably closed to anyone for whom the altar does not mean what it meant to the artist who originally created it? What does it really matter to know, for example, that this wood-carving of the altar dates from the second half of the fifteenth century and is likely to have been made in the Rhineland? How feeble, how superficial must soul-life have become in order that such an approach can be considered satisfying! Our age is capable of exhibiting the face of the Crucified with the caption "Head of a man," or of depicting the right leg of Paionios' sculpture of Nike (the Greek goddess of victory!) as a separate limb, in order to "better display" how "perfectly" the "female body" was portrayed in classical antiquity! What is evident in this, and in everything that goes along with it, is a lack of reverence, a "cerebral greed" that is full of consequences for the world of external deeds and that has lost nothing of its effect by having long since become officially approved and so widespread that it is hardly possible any longer to see matters otherwise. The core of one's being cannot be nourished by this sort of thing. Ought not the university to nourish one's being, even the being of those who are no longer really looking for any such nourishment? I set down such thoughts here reluctantly, but my doing so is not a question of mounting a critique, or of any personal pretensions, but to offer a sign of life and some insight into our present spiritual crisis of struggling for a worldview in the most fundamental sense of the word. Truly it is a question of overcoming a sickness that shows itself in only too many forms and that ought to be wrestled to the ground everywhere it appears.

In my new setting, I was surrounded mostly by young people to whom it was natural to lead a double life. They demanded nothing more from the university than a professional training, while the real joys of life they sought out in student communities, on dance floors, and, especially in Munich, from nature. Munich is near the mountains, and many would head for the Alps for the weekend whenever they could. In a deeper sense, one could even say that

Munich is not only near the mountains, but that the mountains have a real effect on the city, even if not to the same extent they do in Innsbruck. In the mountains, all differences of rank would fall away, as they probably still do today. *Lederhosen* and a "Stein" of beer are the symbols of a general, all-inclusive humanity. There is nothing like it in any other German city, and the good side of this quality also had its effect on academic life. In this sense it was good to be in Munich (even if I had no dealings with the Stein of beer).

At first I attended only a few lectures. My plan of work in German Studies was to come into focus only later. As things stood, it sufficed that I had again set foot on academic ground, which I both loved and feared. True, for all the many stimuli and accomplishments it offered, the university was on the whole a barren place, though not so barren as the large Chile House of my year in business had been. At the end of the day, in the university things did not come down to money but to the life of the spirit or mind, even if this spirit was one of fragmentation. And in the field of intellectual history, it was really only a spirit of the past—for here, historicism ruled. In German studies, as elsewhere, there were two professors: one was called Brecht; the other, von Kraus. A joke circulated among the students: *Geh zu Brecht, bis dir Kraust, und geh zu Kraus, bis du Brechst!* ("Go to Brecht till you're crimped up tight; go to Kraus till you burst!"). I never saw anyone take seriously the terrible reality expressed in this joke, which is why I even trouble to mention it. Most people evaded the basic problem and took life as it came. They were only undertaking a *Brotstudium*, studying in order to make a living.

Among my close acquaintances I experienced two "cases" that seemed symptomatic then, and still do. Independently of each other, and at different times, two friends—both of whom had originally been set on studying in the philosophy department—transferred to the medical faculty (one of them after one semester, the other after two) in order to be free from the sort of questions that were much more "in your face" in the philosophy faculty, and that had to be dealt with by anyone who did his work thoroughly. Both became very capable medical specialists; but by taking this route, they evaded tasks and decisions that, as far as I had seen, had originally been more important for them than the new course embarked

62

upon. One of the two, who later became an "enthusiastic" National Socialist, once said to me with pride and satisfaction: "We National Socialists have it good. We do not need to think. We need only do what we are told!" He was entirely unaware that a view of life appropriate to a recruit in the barracks was gaining the upper hand over his spirit, and that he was gradually losing any connection with the realm of the mind. There were then, and there still are today, all too many people who exemplify the type of "academic" who numbers among his ideals "not needing to think." Indeed, a whole history of politics in recent decades could well be written from the standpoint of its connection with the history of the life of the mind, and of academia as a whole. As for me, I still needed time before my own independent spirit could begin to stir. I not only had to wrestle with what I was thinking about, but had also to acquire the *strength* to wrestle with it. In this wrestling, I had to do not only with morality and immorality (*moralibus et immoralibus*), but also with my very being—that of which these terms could be predicated.

Existence, life, and the meaning of life were unclear and questionable to me—not because I needed to acquire by means of *ideas* a so-called justification for existence, but in the fundamental structure of my life itself. Anyone who has the force and will to live within himself (i.e., anyone who does not seriously consider suicide), ought to seek sources of *strength*, not ideas, about life. A great many clever books on the subject of what is "best" in life have been and will be written and read—but all the while, for those busied with these books (whether writers or readers), the course of reality flows on quite independently of them. Only seldom do the prerequisites for life and the premises of books connect. What we need is a spiritual life that has an immediate connection with reality. A spiritual life lacking such a connection is not really worthy of the name.

Before long, an illuminating idea came to me. It was something, really, that went without saying, something that ought to be decisive for everyone who means to seek truth rather than settle for opinions. And it is applicable to all areas of life! I had noticed that, in our age, mere philosophizing provides no liberating point of connection with the source of spiritual life, the source of truly human life. Apart from whatever those who engage in it might otherwise gain, philosophizing is in no way enriched just because this or that nimble thinker contrives to "explain" some fundamental concepts and their consequences so "convincingly" that a throng of admirers gather round him, adopt his doctrine with firm conviction, and undertake to spread it further. Had I not been so agonizingly impaired by the manner of my life, who knows but that I might eventually have been capable, in some small measure, of founding such a "school." But even had this happened, what real gain could there have been in it? How vast is the number of enthralling but invincibly subjective ideas abounding all around us! Yes, there can be a certain fascination in becoming acquainted with different intellectual perspectives (every person, after all, is a "world" unto himself), but ought I simply to follow some leading thinker merely as a matter of "personal taste" embedded in my particular make-up, or without further ado to adopt the "reasons" suggesting to me that I should do so? I did not so much care to know how the world might seem to this or that gifted or particularly graced individual. I wanted to know how the world truly *is*. There are already far too many interpretations and explanations on offer, whether served up by Barth or Husserl, by Eucken or Natorp, by Johannes Müller or Haeckel. I confess that at the time of which I am speaking I would not have been able to express this thought so clearly. I do so today because it accords with my reality at the time. I did not need a second-hand worldview, but an immediate one; not a subjective worldview, but an objective one. I needed ideas that not only confirmed what was present, but that summoned up something not present, something that could lift my inner nothingness, my anxiety, my world-weariness off its hinges. Did ideas of this sort exist?

I had nothing at all in common with the church. Protestant Christianity had never really been home to me. Not one of the people I had met there had been in a position to recognize the distress of my life, far less to alleviate it. It is no criticism of the noble and faithful people with whom I was brought together—but is essentially a *self-criticism*—to say that in Protestant Christianity as a whole, on a supra-personal level, a certain desolation prevailed. It seemed to me that an ancient, once powerful heritage of faith, now somewhat in decline, was being handed on there. At one point, I sat for several weeks reading Karl Barth's commentary on the Epistle to the Romans, a work that had a great influence in the Protestant church in the nineteen-twenties. But I became neither more astute nor more devout as a result. This work, like many others of the same sort, was too intellectualizing for me—or else, perhaps, it required precisely the strength of heart that I lacked, something that still needed to be awoken. Even then I was at least aware enough to know that, while Karl Barth interpreted the Epistle to the Romans in this way, someone else might interpret it differently. How is it possible for one person to interpret this way, and another that way? What is at the bottom of it? How does it come about that in the Protestant church one "theological school" can supersede another? What is at the bottom of theology as a whole? What is at the bottom of the sciences, or of human life as such? My questions were directed towards the discoverable answer of an *In principio erat* (or rather, *est*) *verbum*: "In the beginning was (or rather, is) the Word. I heard and read the most varied thoughts, but they did not fit with each other. They did not reach the core of my heart—which unfortunately (to be honest) was at that time dedicated to "presuppositionless" science. I did not know then that there is *no such thing* as being wholly without presuppositions, because there are many presuppositions above us and beyond us without which the very act of thinking itself would not be possible. I did not know then that those who take themselves to be free from presuppositions are not free from them, but merely ignorant of them.

I had no connection at all with the Catholic church. The confessional event in Hamburg I described earlier had remained an isolated incident. The wondrous organism of the Catholic church was unknown to me. At most, all I saw were the spots on her garment, not her being. Or rather, not even the spots: I saw nothing at all! From my youth onwards I had borne within me the feeling that the Catholic church was a nefarious institution preoccupied with power, out-of-date, hostile to the German fatherland, and at bottom even un-Christian. This was the after-effect of the culture wars of the Bismarck period, when Protestant Christianity stood in a

dangerously unquestioned alliance with the state. Recent events
have clearly shown how inappropriate any such alliance must be.
Today, the culture wars over Catholicism in the Bismarck period are
seen quite differently (even on the Protestant side) than was the case
fifty or sixty years ago. At the turn of the century, however, the alliance of Protestant Christianity with the fatherland had not yet been
broken. At that time people felt themselves to be standing with the
"head of state" against the "Ultramontanists,"⁴ whereas in our day
people mostly feel as though they are standing with the trans-
national Catholic church against every form of state omnipotence.
That is the fruit of the most recent events. In the previous period,
however, this could not yet be the case, and it was amid the effects
of that epoch that I passed my childhood and youth.

The aversion to Catholicism in Protestant life at the turn of the
century was nourished not only by pedagogical ideas warding off
Catholicism, but also by a certain "style" in the whole sense of life
then. As I have mentioned before, there prevailed at that time what
one could call a "denominational sense of self" that essentially
rested on *protest*. It was as if we had a share in freedom because we
saw Martin Luther as the figure who embodied the ideal of freedom
itself. This sense of self can be so strong that those who carry it fall
into complete unbelief, pure this-worldliness, and utter godlessness, much more readily than they can even begin to consider the
truth and meaning of the Catholic church. For example, I had an
uncle who was quite detached from Protestant church life, but who
shared the prevailing "patriotic" attitude in his rejection of Catholicism. I have often met people of this sort. Moreover, I myself was
unfortunately in a similar situation. After all, I could live for years
in a village in Upper Bavaria without once going to church; I could
go past a monastery church in complete blindness, without taking it
in from any point of view other than that of "art"; I could study in
Munich without even setting eyes on Catholicism. The only church
I went to from time to time was Russian Orthodox, and I did so, not
in a spirit of religious search, but in one of romantic detachment.
And at least once I bent the knee on the feast of the Transfiguration

4. See page 21, note 2.

at the Andechs Abbey, together with those believers from whom I was then a world away. How, in a real or apparent search for the truth, can one's eyes be held hostage in this way? Truly, there is such a thing as "not seeing with seeing eyes, nor hearing with hearing ears." Since I was incapable of *looking* for anything in the Catholic church, I was incapable of *finding* anything there. To the vanishing extent that I had ever considered the matter, it was simply "in my blood" that the Catholic church had to be rejected. Where, then, should I seek?

Unbelief, helplessness, and doubt were alive and at work in me, and at a dangerous and decisive level of the soul, a level upon which depends one's ability—or inability—to live. I could not imagine how I might ever discover a flow of strength in my life that would give it meaning. I did not experience any such strength. And as for my thinking, although it was predisposed to freedom, it was still under the spell of my lot in life. At that time I held suspect all ideas, even those that did not come from the church—but especially those that did!—of being delusions, of coloring and clouding the truth. I lacked the strength to believe in anything, let alone to believe in Christ. I was full of misgivings toward anything alien to me. Empty as I was in my deepest inner being, I became a doubter of everything, a mere man of intellect, a helpless, "guilty–not guilty" nihilist. In these "best years of my life" I resembled a dead leaf that had fallen from the tree, not a young and growing plant.

Today, as a Catholic Christian, I can say that I was thirsty, at least in the bottom of my soul, for the "water of life." I lacked any experience of or belief in the omnipresence and help of Christ. I was a "prodigal son" who ought to have set out and returned to his father. At that time, however, words like these lacked any appeal for me. They were incomprehensible to me. I needed my being to be perceptibly and efficaciously connected to that of the world, to the spiritual element in the world, to God. But against this stood my undeveloped, unbelieving, spoiled nature. And despite all my efforts, my thinking was superficial, my feelings self-seeking, my will embryonic and weak.

I was banging my head not so much against a brick wall as against sheet metal. Oceans of fire danced before my eyes, ever and again. Within me seethed world-weariness and anxiety. Not only this, but also an almost active nihilism—not, indeed, as a consequence of anything that had happened to depress me, but as a reaction on my part merely to my existing in this world. Anyone who had spoken to me at that time of "gratitude towards God" or of some kind of obligation towards him, would have received the following answer, delivered with full intention: "God did not have to create me. And if I could make one request of him, it would be that he at once permanently annihilate me and free me from this existence."

I was unable, however, to speak about this situation. With the exception of my novel *Manfred* in 1925, my awakening spirit was unable to express itself in any way. Although outwardly unimpeded, I lived inwardly in a dark prison, separated from the world by thick walls that neither I nor anyone else could break down. Although I was not wholly without gifts, I was unable to say anything, unable to find the words for anything, unable to give anything shape. There are inner prisons as well as outward ones. I was twenty-eight years old when at last the first lines of verse emerged that, whether good or bad, at least broke through the prison walls and to that extent had a liberating effect. I had experienced and suffered from hesitancy for years, to an almost intolerable degree: "the pain that can be *spoken* of is small!" Understandably, my first verses were of an expressionistic kind, and depicted my situation in partly uncanny, yet true, images. For example:

> There you go with deep-riven skull,
> whence bursts an iceberg-sea.

Happy is he who is unfamiliar with such a situation, and who can regard such words merely as "literary expressions" of an age now gone by! These words, unfortunately, expressed all too precisely not only what I felt, but also how matters really stood around me. I now know this exactly, or can at least remember it. But happily, I am now far distant from my own bewilderment. In the course of that year, something evil fell away more and more, and something good arose in its stead. Fifteen years later, a woman who had not seen me for about that long asked, "How is your head these days? In those days it was always so full of fire and bafflement...," and I had trouble remembering how things had been with me. And yet, for the purposes of this memoir, I have had to remember—and memory says that words like those I have quoted were not exaggerations. No, when seen from the inside, they were very sober statements of the truth.

From time to time the first signs of something good were emerging. Not only to someone in pain, and not just to someone especially troubled, the following words of riper experience may apply:

> Build altars of your tears.
> Mindful of Lot's wife's sudden turn to stone,
> Plunge into your sea of longing,
> And in your torment's rainbow find God!

Typical of that time is the following poem, which (one might hope) may be completely unintelligible to most people, but actually expresses very precisely how I was at that time.

> Today we no more weep, but clench
> What once were tears to stone,
> And mutely lay up vaults mortared with our pain,
> Into whose darkened chambers, dispirited, we stare.
>
> We soon ourselves are stone, chiseled by machines
> Into lurid blocks of conflict, that soon,
> 'Midst thunder, pave a massive highway
> High above the rails our guts lay down.
>
> Then comes the garish glare. Piercing lights
> Dance like a dark-flickering cataract.
> Sharp, naked points in a sea of flame
> Rain down around us—grenade after grenade!
>
> Then comes the vortex, O shapeless horror.
> Something spectral—banners—pour out from a *maw*.
> You are *sucked out*! From your dead mouth
> *Nothing*—no least tatter—pours out!

Today I would describe this poem simply as an expression of complete separation from God. I was, however, "sucked out" in this way, not only in my worst moments, but frequently—essentially all the time. And for a long while I was a battlefield not only for the clash between good and evil, but also between spirit and spiritless-

69

ness, between being and not-being, between giving myself over to being and withdrawing from being. And in each case, the second term was dangerously preponderant.

I mention all this only because it shows what sort of help was to be sought for such a state of sickness, of sin, of the sickness of sin. "The light shines in the darkness," and it shone down even into this darkness. The course of destiny, and the good, which increasingly came into my life, only become clear when there is no doubt about the degree of darkness. There *are* situations in which the "spectral banners from a maw" being sucked out—and the active power of "Nothing"—can in an uncanny way be living, immediate experiences.

Human beings are usually protected by the healthy natural connection between body and soul from experiences of the kind I was having. In every situation, God himself is at work within the body in which we live and move and have our being. Godlessness is always only a psychological and spiritual condition, not a corporeal one. If there is a healthy connection between body and soul, something good and divine always "pours out" from the body into the soul, something that is, however, admittedly often misunderstood and misused. The situation is different if the connection between soul and body is not a normal one, but a loose one, and when the soul is still undeveloped, weak, and susceptible. Then it is more strongly exposed to the real influence of something lower and evil, to the "spectral," to the "maw"—to the "Nothing."

The power of these elements can then be overwhelming, and anyone who wishes to be healed in such a situation must call on and breathe in a higher power of matching strength. What led me out of this situation was my encounter with Anthroposophy: not suddenly, but gradually; not completely, but to a great degree; not without hard and exacting work on my own part, but at bottom as a gift of divine grace. And in the situation in which I then found myself, even today I do not know what spiritual voice would have been able to penetrate into the depths of my soul's dungeon, if not the voice of the founder of Anthroposophy, Rudolf Steiner.

4

Anthroposophy

ALMOST AT THE BEGINNING OF MY SECOND PERIOD at university, a friend gave me a lecture by Rudolf Steiner to read. It was the first lecture from the series "From Jesus to Christ," and dealt with the distinction between Jesuitism and Rosicrucianism, and their different spiritual methods. It made an impression on me. The lecture's style contrasted with such writings as set out a worldview with which I was already familiar. I sensed, obscurely, that here a different, more penetrating, spirit than I was accustomed to was addressing me, a spirit who was not just adding a hundred-and-first opinion to the hundred possible opinions on a subject, but was instead speaking from his own power of vision. Moreover, hearkening to what he had to say was rewarded in a different way than was usual. Behind all my anxiety and doubt, a still-hidden organ for the truth was being addressed as it had never been addressed before. This was true, if not of the very first work of Steiner's I read, then at least of the first group of his works that I read.

The same friend introduced me to the "Christian Community," which called itself a "movement for religious renewal." It was also a matter, for me, of renewing my life—this I knew and recognized, despite all my weaknesses, confusion, and doubt. The Christian Community, which was then about four years old, held regular Sunday services under the title of the Act of the Consecration of Man. There was a priest and a liturgical rite consisting of four parts: a "proclamation," a "sacrifice," a "transformation," and "communion." All was strange and new to me. At the time I had not the slightest acquaintance with the Holy Mass. The priest (for such he clearly was, although he was addressed as a "pastor") wore a long white gown, the "alba," and a colored overgarment that changed according

71

to the season, which was called a "chasuble." I took exception to the words "Act of the Consecration of Man."[1] It seemed to me too long, too highbrow, not Christian enough; and for a long while I felt somewhat ashamed of it, even after I had become accustomed to feel myself to belong to the Christian Community, as happened later.

This feeling of belonging developed very slowly. I was obscurely attracted by the "liturgy," as the Act of the Consecration of Man was called (many members just called it the "Act") but it was, like a mountain range, very hard to climb. I knew nothing of Catholic liturgy; my sense for liturgy was completely undeveloped, and the usual Protestant Sunday services, or at least the ones I was familiar with, were very unlike this one. For the most part, the words used in it only distantly recalled Christian tradition. Almost everything was new. At least, that is how it seemed to me, and I did not then know about the inner relation of the Act of the Consecration of Man to the sacrifice of the Holy Mass. I did not know that the Act of the Consecration of Man, which is of course only an indicative rather than an exhaustive designation, represented a contemporary reworking of the communion liturgy. This observation is not intended dogmatically. From a dogmatic point of view there can self-evidently be no "contemporary reworkings" of the Church's liturgy. The rite as a whole was, at least, substantial. It was not to be grasped merely by the intellect, and made demands upon one's sense of self, as well as being rousing and nourishing.

At the beginning of the "sacrifice" (I can only speak of a few details here) it was not God, but the "foundation of the world"[2] that was addressed. The "foundation of the world" was to receive the sacrifice. This was an equivalent to the passage where in the communion rite we pray *suscipe, sancte Peter, omnipotens aeterne deus, hanc immaculatam hostias* (accept, holy Father, almighty, eternal God, this spotless sacrifice). I did not like the expression "foundation of the world." Philosophical thought told me that the "foundation of the world," if it was not to be mere words, was supposed to invoke a

---

1. *Menschenweihenhandlung.*
2. *Weltengrund.*

being; and as it seemed to me, the word "God" must say the same thing more meaningfully. Why, then, did a new description have to be introduced for the same "thing"? It is not a matter of words, after all, but of the thing itself, of this or that being. And to whom can we sacrifice, other than God, the almighty, the creator of heaven and earth? I asked my friend why the expression "foundation of the world" was used, rather than "God." He smiled, explained that my ideas were in some way antiquated, and said, without any deeper explanation, that it came to the same thing. My question had admittedly originated merely in my intellect, and my friend was right to regard an exchange of merely intellectual opinions as unproductive. But my question was nevertheless justified. I posed it again later, when nobody could accuse me of asking a merely intellectual question; and later still, I found out the answer myself. The Act of the Consecration of Man was intended for people who had lost any living relationship with tradition, and who were now to be brought back to the path of Christian thinking, feeling, and willing in such way as not to be put off by ancient features that might repel them. Now, I was, and all too decidedly, just this sort of person myself; and so, for a long while I was myself of the opinion that everything had to be "new," that only what was "new" was substantial.

It was impossible for me quickly to assent to all this, since I was burdened with doubts and resistances. Spiritually speaking, I was as timid and cautious as a fawn who is ready to bound away at any moment. But through all my cautious doubt, through the prison bars of my intellect, I had a dim intimation that something rousing and fortifying had here contacted the depths of my being. I did not brood too much over the Act of the Consecration of Man, but attended it often, even if irregularly.

The friend who had introduced me to the Christian Community was of the opinion that this form of Christian liturgy would be the right one "for a couple of hundred years." This qualification seemed to me correct, yet unfortunate. It may indeed be significant that more or less my first thought in the Christian Community was that "foundation of the world" and "God" described the same being. What, then, was the point of the new word? Later, I more and more thought: should we judge questions concerning our worldview or the Church from the standpoint of our own soul or our own personal needs? Doesn't the truth have to be sought for in a spirit of the greatest possible selflessness? The rite of Holy Communion and the Catholic church will still be alive when, after "a couple of hundred years," the language of a "movement for religious renewal"—new for now, and addressed to a small group of people—would have ceased to exist. Principled, transpersonal, selfless thinking leads to the Church; I owe my conversion to the fact that I was capable of principled thinking, and needed it. Anyone who seeks personal experiences and stimuli (I heard this word used in the Christian Community so often that I was completely fed up with it), and who starts out from or remains stuck with what he personally needs rather than starting out from the idea of *a* whole or *the* whole, will hardly or never be able to fit in with principled thinking, and yet will always stand in need of it.

These are the sorts of thoughts I had to wrestle with over many years. It should be said right away that the spirit of Anthroposophy saved me from collapse, and that I came closer to the spirit of Anthroposophy through the form it took in the Christian Community. I was, however, slow to understand either Anthroposophy or the Christian Community, and it took a long time before I was able to let either have a strong effect on the core of my being. If I were to set out in these pages the first few steps of the almost infinite staircase I climbed, it would make a very dull portrayal. So it will be better to give an overview of some key features of Anthroposophy and of the Christian Community—and to describe Anthroposophy first, even though it was the Christian Community that was important to me initially.

What is Anthroposophy?

A sufficient and completely satisfactory answer to this question cannot be given in a few sentences or a few pages, even by a person who lives entirely in and through its spirit, and who has completely mastered its language. Rudolf Steiner, its founder (1861–1925), often pointed out that our earthly language is really only adequate to earthly things, i.e., that it proves unreliable in regard to the spiritual, the "spirit world," or "higher worlds." Anthroposophy, however, not only refers to the spiritual, but is itself something spiritual, so one can only ever speak of it through imperfect intimations. Can one ever exhaust in words the beauty of an apple tree in blossom, the nature of a person, the splendor of a starry sky in winter? Can the nature of the Catholic church, or of the mystery of Christianity, be set out in a few sentences or a few pages? In spiritual matters, however, many people would like to be enlightened in short order, without reflecting that this cannot be done adequately, and that if they try, they will remain stuck at the same level as an encyclopedia.

Only one who loves, believes, and champions a worldview can speak wholly in its spirit. Karl Adam rightly remarks in his *The Nature of Catholicism* that only a believing Catholic is in a position to portray truthfully the nature of the Church. Friedrich Heiler, who was once a Catholic Christian, did indeed often sing the praises of the Catholic church in his later life, but was by then only able to portray from outside what he had previously known from within. In any worldview deserving of the name, not only thinking, but also the will, prevails. No worldview can be wholly understood by means of the intellect alone, and none can be seen as it appears to itself from the standpoint of another. The anthroposophist is not in a position to see the nature of the Church as the Church may and must see and understand itself. But nor can Anthroposophy be seen from the Church's standpoint as it must appear to itself and to its proponents.

I myself was for many years in a position to discuss Anthroposophy in a way satisfactory to those who at the time were my friends in this worldview, without ever making them think that I had not grasped the nature of Anthroposophy. At that time, at least, I was speaking from *within* Anthroposophy, as far as my situation allowed it, rather than *about* Anthroposophy. Now, however, I face the task of speaking about it, and it will therefore be impossible to content my former friends in the way I would once have been able to. In the sphere of disputes between worldviews there is, understandably, no such thing as complete objectivity apart from what presents itself to the ordering intellect alone; and the situation is the same when it comes to a worldview and a religion. In reality, even if the intellect is concerned with many worldviews, it can strictly speaking only describe or intimate them from outside. Is a living picture of what is knowingly combated ever available to the one combating it? From everything I experienced in my Protestant childhood, and above all after everything I experienced in the anthroposophical movement too, it seems impossible, or at least very seldom possible, to me. And yet, there must be spiritual combat. And yet, the Church must reject the anthroposophical worldview taken as a whole. And yet, some sort of picture of Anthroposophy, at least of a preliminary kind, must be drawn from the standpoint of the Church.

Here, however, where the full trajectory of a destiny is to be shown, where it would be untruthful and ungrateful were the author to deny what Anthroposophy has done for him, and where the author's conversion in itself harbors a certain critique, it seems best to me not even to attempt to paint an "exhaustive" picture of Anthroposophy, but to say just enough about it for the whole of Anthroposophy to become imaginable, and for the path taken by the development of my own worldview to become clear. And it seems to me, too, that the great respect I bear within myself for Anthroposophy as a creation of Rudolf Steiner will be best shown in this way. What, then, is Anthroposophy?

Rudolf Steiner himself once answered this question with the following short sentence. "Anthroposophy is a path of knowledge that leads what is spiritual in the human being into what is spiritual in the cosmos." On this accounting, Anthroposophy is in the first place not a doctrine, or a learnable sum-total of statements about the world and human beings, or a theoretical system from which one could then draw practical consequences, as one can from Kant's or from Schopenhauer's philosophy. Anthroposophy is not philosophy, not something that results from reflection or from speculation. It is a science of experience, but one not related to what is earthly and given to the senses only, but also and essentially to the supersensory, metaphysical, and spiritual foundations of that earthly, sensory world. It is related to these foundations in a way that (if he can understand how to breathe in Anthroposophy and how to make it real) it enables a person who is at first tied down to that sensory world to make contact with supersensory, divine beings and sources of strength. I will try to explain this in a way that makes no prior assumptions.

It is obvious to every person that stones, flowers, animals, people, the sun, the moon, and the stars exist. Where do they come from? By what means do they come to exist? What is their content and meaning? To these and similar questions, Anthroposophy gives an answer that is neither the answer self-evident to people of faith as a matter of principle—"from God"—nor an answer that is intellectually learnable (or at least it will not of be any use to anyone to learn it thus), but an answer that leads one to observe, experience, and attain insight for oneself. Rudolf Steiner chiefly addressed people's capacity to think. He did not want the thoughts he conveyed to be accepted without question, but to be examined, tested, experienced. He claimed to speak about the supersensory background and efficacious essence of our life and being on earth from personal experience alone. And I had the impression—an impression that increased until it became complete certainty—that this claim was justified, and that that was just why Rudolf Steiner deserved to be trusted.

This gives only a first intimation of what Anthroposophy "is." It is relatively easy to say something reasonably adequate about personal situations and developments in a few words. There we are dealing with a limited area, an individual human case. But Anthroposophy, or, as Rudolf Steiner called it, "the science of the spirit," relates to absolutely everything that is present in spirit and in spirits, and in how they reveal themselves within our cosmos. As I said before, it is not adding a hundred-and-first opinion about the world and life to the hundred that already exist. It really is a "science of experience." It can, or ought to, or could actually "lead what is spiritual in the human being to what is spiritual in the cosmos." What is written and said about this "what is spiritual in the cosmos" by Rudolf Steiner ought, however, to become an incentive to the reader to give *himself* up to the "path of knowledge." The meaning of Anthroposophy consists—I can only bear witness to this, not prove it—in releasing spiritual forces in the human being, and making him more fitting for what God expects from us human beings—admittedly, not in the sphere of the Church, but in a sphere that is free, and outside tradition.

This was just what attracted me in Anthroposophy and bound me to it, a connection that became something ever more nourishing for me. Philosophical contentions, ideas, and assertions have little effect today on what concerns the basis of our destiny. In earlier centuries matters were otherwise. Even as late as 1800, the life of thought was more stimulating and efficacious than it is almost ever found to be at the present day. Today, all philosophizing appears to be something added to life, not something that "holds the world together." This is just what cannot be understood by means of intellectual activity (see the character of "Wagner" in *Faust*). All the intellect can know is something that is earthly, that has therefore come to be— something already closed off and consecrated to death. The world, however, is alive. And we human beings are also alive, and wish to, and ought to, be alive. How? Why? Self-evidently, in principle, with God's help and for God's sake. I have never, so far as I am aware, doubted this, despite all my rebelliousness. But this answer was far too general to be effective. For even the Catholic church—every time the preface to the canon of the Mass is recited—speaks of the governance of the *hierarchies*. There is not only "God." There are also divine (and anti-divine) spirits.

Just as an ordinary person is able to become aware in the countenances of his fellow men of their souls and their spirits, rather than merely of physiological facts, so Rudolf Steiner was able, as far as I could see or detect, to become aware or to "read" in everything that is given to the senses (from the stone to the starry firmament) its soul, its spirit. Whoever wishes to regard living human beings merely as sense-perceptible beings will never grasp anything about their nature, but will be faced only with facts about the sensible world, which, as such, belong in a series with other such facts. Even by consistent materialists, the human being is understood (or are they being inconsistent here?) by means of a spiritual organ that is able to "see" in what is externally visible an element that is invisible from the outside. The contemplation of what is given through the senses alone can never lead to the idea of a sentience that reasons.

Thus, the natural-scientific picture of the world widely disseminated today is, in the literal sense of the word, meaningless. No one knows why the "myriads of stars" are really there. Nor can it be discovered whence the original mass and force (or whatever you may wish to call it) from which the world as we know it is supposed to have developed, really came, and who gave it its inherent laws, and so on. Everything perceptible, indeed everything even rationally conceivable (every thinking person can put this in his own way) must have a cause. And just as, in our earthly life, no work of art comes into being, no letter is written, no garden is planted, no shoe is mended, without a specific consciousness and a specific will standing behind them, so must this also be the case with the world as a whole. The laughter and tears, the work and endeavor of the human being show forth the existence of an invisible being living inside the human body. Only this "is" a person. Only when living on earth is this person also corporeal and sensible, that is, an appearance of the spiritual in the material. So it is with everything that exists.

Behind everything visible, however "merely material" it may seem to be, a spiritual element is determining, bearing, and revealing itself—that is, *a* being, and not only one being, but many. We call them the hierarchies, the choirs of angels, "above" whom at an unimaginable height and distance the Most Holy Trinity is "enthroned," the Trinity that nevertheless runs through all being. This may in large part sound self-evident to believing Catholics. After all, in every Holy Mass resounds the *sanctus, sanctus, sanctus Dominus, Deus Sabaoth! Pleni sunt coeli et terra gloria tua. Hosanna in excelsis!* (Holy, holy, holy, Lord God of hosts! Heaven and earth are full of Thy glory. Hosanna in the highest!). For most of our contemporaries, however, it is anything but self-evident, just as it was anything but self-evident at that time to me. I had, as I have mentioned, lost my connection to the Christian tradition. Everything that came to me in the language of the past was suspicious to me in the innermost depths of my being. I thought roughly as follows.

What does it matter to me what generations immemorial, or a few particular people endowed with grace, once experienced? If all this was only once upon a time, but no longer applies, I cannot, and do not wish to, have anything to do with it. I had never heard anyone speak of the divine, the supersensible, the spiritual in any other language than that of tradition, and it seemed to me (which indeed signifies a sad ignorance on my part) that what was being spoken of in the Christian church was, apart from a few exceptions, not something that could be experienced here and now, but something past and gone, which I could not think could reasonably lay any obligations on us today. Why should it do so? Why should we today believe what was once not only believed but also revealed to and experienced by the first proponents of the faith? The twelve apostles, for example, did not "believe" that Christ was resurrected; they experienced it, and testified to their experience. For many years, St Thomas, often called "doubting" Thomas, seemed to me the great justifying champion of the will to experience. Justifying, because Christ himself came to him and spoke to him. "Reach hither thy finger, and behold my hands; and reach hither thy hand, and thrust it into my side. . . ." At that time, therefore, in the inner Christian circle, it was not faith alone that ruled. There *was* no tradition, no acceptance on the basis of the assertions of others. Thus did I too demand and thirst for living experience.

The situation I am here admitting to, and now regard as sad rather than as praiseworthy, was conditioned by my personal destiny. I neither knew anything of the nature and meaning of the Church (which, to put it briefly, carries the experiences of the past alive into the present and the future supra-personally—and on God's instructions), nor of the meaning of examining through "not seeing," nor of the fact that people receiving grace have indeed in all ages of Christian history "experienced." Today I know that no person is entitled to such an experience as was given to St Thomas, and that we would do well to stick to the words that were spoken to just this Thomas: "Blessed are they that have not seen, and yet have believed." For it is relatively easy to live in the "seeing," whereas to persevere "believing" in "My God, my God, why hast thou abandoned me?" is hard. And just this, too, was what Christ lived out for us in advance; and to perform just this, too, is what belongs to his successors. Each person receives the destined "experiences," however, at the allotted hour.

With these thoughts, however, I neither can nor wish to represent my "thirst for experience" as something entirely unjustified. "Experience" does not only mean having experience of the highest facts about the world. It means stepping altogether beyond what is given and accessible only through the senses; and this can only be healthy. In particular, it contains an effective way of overcoming materialism. Not much is gained when materialism is "overcome" or "refuted" in a merely theoretical way. Insofar as he is truly alive, man actually lives upon higher forces and beings; the more consciously he does so, the better. Even where this happens, there is always plenty of room for faith, in the basic meaning of the word.

Although the belief that one can and must be convinced of the truth about the world from one's own experiences was certainly immodest and pretentious, in reality my task was to overcome my doubt, the paralysis of my soul. In respect of this task, it was of decisive importance for my development that I recognized in Rudolf Steiner a contemporary "person of knowledge," whose insights, however, were not offered as merely personal revelations that everyone now had to believe, but as signs and incentives of knowledge as such—in which every seeker could in time come to share. Put philosophically, the systematic element of Anthroposophy was, *according to the intentions of Anthroposophy's founder*, legitimized, disclosed, and made fruitful by means of its method. Everything Rudolf Steiner passed on in "concrete" statements, in objective expositions from the realm of the supersensory worlds, is at bottom meant as a contribution to the self-knowledge of each individual person. Rudolf Steiner wanted once again to unlock access to the divine and spiritual world for modern human beings, who as a whole have mislaid the organ for the divine and the spiritual, and for the most part have mislaid the organ for living faith as well. Thus, I belonged to just the group of people to whom his thought was addressed.

The necessary strength for this, however (as will be gathered from what has already been recounted), could only be acquired over the course of time. I was excessively cautious, accepted absolutely nothing upon authority, and scrutinized everything as far as I possibly could. So matters stood (at least on the level of intellectual thought), with regard to the whole of my conscious spiritual life. But in my heart, things were rather different. I read many of Rudolf Steiner's writings, attended lectures about his work, and took part in Acts of the Consecration of Man with much benefit, which, in the individual moment, could not always be traced back to my own conscious labors of thinking. The truth offered by Rudolf Steiner was able to become effective within me to the extent that it abated my doubt, hesitation, and defensiveness, and (in the first instance) made possible for me my own free affirmation. It was decisively redemptive for me that in Rudolf Steiner I had to do with a spirit not merely adroit or merely faithful or well-meaning in putting something that came from the past into new words, but to whom the "spirit world" had been laid bare, who referred to it as something self-evident, and who showed how the individual could himself arrive at corresponding experiences, at least in principle. The basic primer in anthroposophical method, which was written in the earliest years of our century and was intended to introduce the individual to meditative exercises, and thus to his own insight, has the pertinent title *Know of Higher Worlds: How Is It Attained?*[3]

Two points may perhaps be interposed here. First, there is a proliferation of anthroposophical texts, and it cannot be my aim here even to name the essential works or to give an outline of the ideas contained in them. The essence of Anthroposophy lies not so much in the What as in the How. One does not become a better anthroposophist by knowing as much as possible of the written corpus of Anthroposophy, but by living out the necessary How of it in one's own life. If this is true for members of the movement, it is also true for outsiders: the essence of the matter is grasped, not by having the "systematic" element unfurled as completely as possible before them, but by acquiring an intimation or intuition of the anthroposophical method. In the context, then, I refrain from giving a reading list, or anything of that kind.

---

3. Hereafter, *Knowledge of Higher Worlds*.

Second, many distorting rumors about and caricatures of both Anthroposophy and its founder have been disseminated. Given what human nature is, that is understandable. Even the enemies of Jesus Christ asserted that he was possessed by the devil. The present study will as a matter of principle have nothing to do with rumor or caricature. I am writing according to the best of my knowledge and conscience, not without experience of the matter—and I write, today, as a Catholic Christian. I know how and why Anthroposophy is to be rejected, and I shall say so later. I believe that to deploy caricatures and personal disparagement is both untrue and unproductive. Here, too, it is the case that only "the truth will set us free," and that only ideas capable of standing up to the truth can really bring about good.

Only in later years did I first engage in detail with the exercises in the book *Knowledge of Higher Worlds*.[4] At the beginning of my time as an anthroposophist I was, on health grounds, and also on the advice of an experienced leading anthroposophist, not yet in a position to do so. But I was also not so immodest as to be disposed to recognize as true only that which was fully disclosed to me through my own experience. On one hand, it sufficed the doubter to sense Rudolf Steiner's spirit, his knowledge, his spirit-knowledge to such an extent that what he presented seemed worthy of trust. On the other hand, however, the truths—the "parts" of the anthroposophical worldview—mutually reinforced each other. Rudolf Steiner himself used the image of a system of planets to capture this, a system in which the individual planets do not follow the earth's law of gravity in their trajectories, yet where they still, together, constitute an organic whole. In the same way, Anthroposophy itself represents a whole whose individual "parts" are illumined not only individually, but also by their relations to the other parts. One must not, for example, defer belief in the power of the angels until one has oneself personally and unmistakably felt the beating of their wings and witnessed it with one's own eyes. One may take it as certain, on the basis of many illuminating ideas about the matter, that the angels are alive and have effects. Moreover, there are in this area what we might call

---

4. Mention an appendix with the relevant article, if this is accomplished.

insights of differing ranks and grades; and anyone who attends to this closely can without a great deal of effort begin to have experience of the governance of the angels. True, he must pay attention, and he must concentrate on the "higher worlds," for angels appear in the earthly world either not at all, or only very seldom. This is just what Anthroposophy calls for and called for: it directs the spirit towards the invisible world without subtracting anything from the visible world. Anthroposophy itself forms the organ by means of which the invisible can be perceived. If, then, I was myself not in a position to test the immense "results of supersensory research," it was important to me that these results did derive from an experience, and that one could hope in principle to also experience them for oneself.

At its core, truth can never be proved. Otherwise, all people on earth would be Christians, there would not be different groups and camps in religion and in worldviews, and the content of the Creed would be the uncontested belief of all people. Truth is known by means of a particular "organ," but the sense for truth and the strength for truth emerge differently in different people. How often and on how many occasions does one person heedlessly fail to be struck by something in which another rejoices, and by which he is deeply stirred! This is the case even in the purely earthly realm, in all matters of culture and the spirit, but is really and truly so in the case of the divine element that pulses through the world and bears it up. It gradually became clear to me that truth must at bottom and in its very nature be unequivocal. And so I was increasingly convinced by Rudolf Steiner's statement that anyone who penetrated into the heights or the depths would leave behind him the strata at which differing opinions were possible, and would find truth itself. Thus Rudolf Steiner's statements (which, incidentally, for the most part agree with those of the truth as communicated by the Church, or which can be brought into concord with it) became more and more worthy of trust to me, and accordingly more and more helpful in building up a positive worldview, in overcoming doubt, lack of clarity, inner weakness, and psychoanalytic poisoning. Many details in this regard, however, served up for me a lifetime's work.

Anthroposophy

Rudolf Steiner developed Anthroposophy out of modern natural science by drawing on certain theosophical teachings coming from the East; the spirit of natural science, which was wholly alien to me, thus gave its stamp to the whole. There were certain details of anthroposophical "doctrine" I could never accept. But that was no great pity, since I was able to accept the most important things, and only a few people have ever in the fullest sense of the word been deeply stirred by all of Anthroposophy. A more comprehensive spirit was at work here, which led so far beyond everything averagely human that one could be glad to have grasped even a little of it. With this, I have come to an important point, which is: why did Anthroposophy become a decisive help to me in my life?

I offered earlier a certain critique of the spiritual work of schooling and the academic life. I suffered greatly from the fact that that life was fragmented into individual faculties, and that the individual areas of research were not working "with the same basic concepts." In Anthroposophy, I found this defect overcome. This simple sentence contains something *unutterably meaningful*: just as my soul had been fragmented and secularized by the fragmentation and secularization of the life of the spirit as a whole (not in its particulars), so the unified anthroposophical world-picture, which can provide an objective overcoming of this evil as a whole, gradually restored my soul to healthy unity.

Rudolf Steiner portrayed the whole development of our visible world, from the "first beginning" to the situation it is in today (in which humankind has become completely deracinated), as a single process of becoming in which the divided beings, in their origin and by their vocation, belong together and are connected to each other. The world-picture that emerged in this way, temporally and spatially, takes from today's science and scholarship both the "theological" and the "natural-scientific" element, both the humanities and jurisprudence, both economics and politics. Behind the person in me who was busy with lectures and books in German studies, music, or education, there was, so to speak, the germ of a second person, who now had an idea of the common source and connection of all these fields in the sense I have indicated, and who (very imperfectly, of course) began to participate in their realization. There was, therefore, a place, a source, from which healing was to be brought, however off-putting (in part) the forms through which its water flowed remained for me. For a sphere of my being, in which I could neither bear the darkness nor make headway by means of my strength alone, it was illuminating and fortifying to me that the elements of the anthroposophical worldview concerning theology and natural science (to repeat only this example) could be traced back to the same root. Thus Christ, described among other things as "Sun-spirit" (an expression, however, which cannot but be misunderstood by almost everyone who is not an anthroposophist), was, here, a figure who had to do not only with the "salvation" of human "souls" (as I had always previously understood) but also with the previous, present, and future development of the entire world. And Anthroposophy does not only teach this as a matter of principle, but also vividly demonstrates it. The figure of Christ stands at the center of anthroposophical "doctrine," just as Christ stood, in a purely external way, at the place of honor in the first "Goetheanum"—the headquarters of anthroposophical spiritual life in Dornach, near Basel, Switzerland, a headquarters that was burnt down in 1923. Christ *is* the heart of our universe. In a worldview grounded upon truth, therefore, He must stand at its center.

Now, Rudolf Steiner also often used the expression "Christ-impulse." The Christ-impulse governs the world from within, and so on. To an outsider, this can seem inappropriate, even impious. That is the case with a good deal of what Anthroposophy deals with. Anyone who only becomes acquainted with small splinters of the great tree of "Anthroposophy," anyone who hears talk of the "etheric body," of "lotus flowers," of the "Old Moon" stage of evolution, or of the "sacrifice of the Thrones," and who hears this without being prepared in advance and is thus not in a position to grasp the meaning of the words or the connection of what is meant with other things, can, understandably, only shake his head in response. Anthroposophy (and in this one respect it is comparable to the Catholic church) is spiritually all-embracing; and something spiritually all-embracing cannot be made intelligible in three or four sentences, although it can easily be distorted in them. The truth of the Church, too, can easily seem absurd to one who is distant from Christianity, if only a few fragments of it come to his awareness. The idea that all beings and domains belong together, however, had a healthy effect on me, despite many off-putting particulars. This effect was not produced overnight, but in a principled way that grew ever stronger. It was the same with a second idea, too, as follows.

I was soon lent the "cycles" of lectures Rudolf Steiner had given on the gospels, on the celestial hierarchies, and on the "mystery of Golgotha" (which were at that time not publicly available). I had completely grown out of the usual ways of speaking about the Bible, which were (how shall I put this?) indebted to tradition, or were offered as edifying. The world of the New Testament had almost disappeared from view for me. Now I was at once enthralled in my innermost being by the way Rudolf Steiner spoke about the gospels, about their content and their intellectual and historical context. This was not only "new" in terms of its style, but it also contained things that had never been said before. I devoured these books, and then read them over and over again. Many secrets were out, many connections demonstrated and expounded; moreover, many ways in which these connections could be applied were developed, and these spoke deeply to me. Here, where it is mostly a question of a personal narrative, it would not be relevant to give details. What matters, however, is that through Rudolf Steiner I was reconnected to the world of the gospels—at first only by means of "knowledge," but later in my heart, too—although it took a long time before I could read the New Testament "correctly" for myself. I gained trust in the world and the spirit of the gospels again, at first in a preliminary way, then more firmly. I came to see (or to think I saw) what inspiration essentially is, and could at least begin to regard Holy Scripture as revelation once again. What a blessing, after so many wrong turnings and doubts!

Anthroposophy also teaches the law of "reincarnation and karma." According to this doctrine, a human being is not alive on earth only once, but over and over again. Individual lives on earth, however, are connected with each other, both in a spiritually organic and in a morally organic way. Everything that is done, omitted, achieved, brought about, neglected, or spoiled in the course of one life determines the form and task of the life or lives that follow it. I was always able to engage with this idea only hypothetically. (Incidentally, the same was true for other people I knew.) I myself did not arrive at any insight deserving the name in this area, but it struck me that the history of humankind was also itself a unity, to the extent that the same beings had gone through the same process of development, rather in the way set out in Lessing's *Education of the Human Race*. According to this, man today, in looking back on earlier cultures, was not merely seeing with astonishment (and also, at bottom, with detachment) something that had been created and brought to maturity by completely different people. Rather, he was looking back on them with a kind of unconscious recollection. The Egyptians, the Greeks, medieval people, and moderns, were in reality much more closely related than could be understood without the help of the idea of reincarnation. The meaning of "evolution," however, is "progress in consciousness." All beings, including man, move towards ever higher levels of consciousness. What that means is not an ever more distinctive power of intellect and vision, as a distant observer might suppose today, but rather a ripening of the whole being. Those beings who are at the highest, or at least at a very high "level of consciousness," have to be thought of as having done away with all personal limitations, as having become pure and selfless, open to the workings of divine spirits, and untroubled by the spirits of the abyss. Their greatest happiness lies in self-sacrifice.

The idea of "reincarnation and karma"—that is, of the human and organic connectedness of different lives on earth—was not only illuminating to me, but also helpful. I was still brooding over a sense of my lot in life, which was not an entirely easy one. Wild, imperious revolt and defiance of God often overcame me. For a long time I was very far from obedience and belief. No preacher of the Church, even if he had spoken with tongues of fire, would, then, have been able to awaken these qualities within me, for my sense for them was simply undeveloped or paralyzed. The idea of reincarnation and of karma worked within me to allow me to accept my fate as something justly allotted to me. I could no longer see myself, as I had previously done, as the object of an enigmatic and arbitrary divine will that seemed to me cruel (the idea that God's will is never arbitrary, but always just, was for a long time entirely beyond my field of vision). Instead I had to posit myself, even if only theoretically, as the cause of my own woes. At that time the idea that we human beings must always accept our lot from God's hand was entirely alien to me. If I thought of "God" at all, it was with the hint of a supposedly just demand. The idea of reincarnation and karma helped me to find the path of humility. And this proved to be curative. It was only much later that I became aware that that idea, considered with *complete* accuracy, is only a displacement of the problem. Does not our being and life originally come from an inexplicable cause? Can anyone quite seriously explain the enormous differences between people in a concrete and intelligible way through "reincarnation and karma"? Is not the almighty "Father" at bottom, and in each individual case, in truth the creator not only of our existence and our life, but also of the tests He sets for us? The central problem of fate is not solved by ideas of reincarnation, but by means of the experience, or the faith, that God is good, fatherly, compassionate; that He is love, whether this idea satisfies our consciousness primarily through emotions, or as a belief, or through intellectual certainty. For the idea of karma rests on an idea of justice that corresponds only to pre-Christian humankind, but that through the voluntary life, suffering, and death of Jesus Christ has been transfigured into another and higher idea. Christ suffered innocently, and even if human beings never suffer innocently, their sufferings can be better "explained" with respect to some kind of existing *cause* for a *purpose* that is certainly present.

I could, therefore, expound the fruitfulness for me of the anthroposophical worldview from a number of different points of view. Here, though, I only want to select one. Rudolf Steiner represented human beings as four-part, or seven-part, beings whose center and actual spirit was called the "I." Man, like everything outwardly visible, possesses a "physical body." And, like everything that is alive and grows and thrives in the world, he possesses an "astral body" (if the reader to whom this term is alien will for the moment let the expression pass) or a "soul body" or "psychic body," like everything that feels and desires—everything that can suffer and experience passion. Alone among earthly beings, man possesses the "I," the bearer and shaper of ideas.

These brief hints cannot possibly make clear the enormous fruitfulness that lies in this picture of man, still less counteract the misunderstandings it can call forth in those unfamiliar with it. This picture of man enables those who can wield it to have uncommonly vivid relations to stones, plants, and animals. It shows in a very concrete and concretely applicable way how we human beings stand both within creation and above it, how we are the "crown" of creation. The plurality of "parts of being"—at first unintelligible and thus very suspect to one unfamiliar with them—does not fragment the idea of the unified human being, any more than the ideas of lungs, heart, blood, and muscles fragment the idea of the bodily organism. Irrespective of whether they are viewed sympathetically or unsympathetically, the words used to name the "parts of being" refer to realities. This picture of the human being, together with the human being's relation to its external and spiritual environment, is not a product of intellect or of "nominalistic" thinking; it is, rather, experienced and drawn up in a purely "realist" spirit. Each word corresponds to an idea, to a concept; and each idea and concept corresponds to an objective reality. In the course of time, my whole relationship to the world and to nature was essentially reshaped with the help of these concepts and what they freed up in me—reshaped, not in the sense that I acquired more experience, but in the sense that I worked through my experience spiritually. In terms of this language, the meaning of life can be specified thus: the "I" is to transform the "psychic" body and the "etheric" or "life" body; indeed, it is to transform the "physical body" to some degree also, to spiritualize it and make it into the most completely unified expression possible of the spirit of love. The human being has an important part to play in this transformation; his part is to provide the preparatory work, so to speak, the *conditio sine qua non* (the necessary condition). The essential part, however, comes about through a "higher I"—essentially, through the being of Christ. In principle, this appeals to what in the Church we call the ideal of holiness; but the Church appeals to it using quite other words, and does not aim at the same kind of intellectual training as Anthroposophy advises for its adherents.

As well as I was able, I worked my way into this and many related things over the course of the years, alongside my studies. It was a sort of *secret sanatorium*, and it saved my life—just as the spirit, the spirit of God, God Himself, is the true healer and savior for all our failings. I came closer to Him in this way that lay so far from the life of the Church. I probably would not have found my way to Him without it. But doubts broke out over and over again. More and more new "reasons" against faith arose, and as soon as one of these had been "refuted," another most often sprang up in its stead. I had only too much personal experience of the fact that truth cannot be grasped by the intellect, but can certainly be destroyed by it. In each situation, the human being comprehends only what he wants to comprehend, even if he has no knowledge of what his deeper will really is. Many ideas that apparently occur spontaneously to the truth-seeking spirit arise in fact from a doubting, self-seeking, habit-bound fundament of the soul. Anthroposophy had a curative effect on this fundament of my soul, but to the extent my soul had still not been healed, it came up with "objections," renounced devotion, and stood in the way to prevent the coming-into-being of the good. Finally, after years, I became an "anthroposophist," i.e., a person who adhered without reservations or objections to Rudolf Steiner's "science of spirit," to its method of research, and to the obligation to serve that science seriously.

For a long time, however, I could not become a member of the "Anthroposophical Society." For many years I shrank back from the spiritual obligations connected with becoming one. Even if entering the Anthroposophical Society cost nothing but an affirmation of the nature of "spiritual research," I took even this with complete seriousness. At university, as at high school, you can trundle along without any commitment of your own, without any personal spiritual obligation. But here it was a matter of an undertaking contrary to "academic learning." Here, personal courage was required. This I could summon up only after a long period of reflection.

What was more, for a long while I did not feel quite at home among the anthroposophists. I did indeed get to know many spiritually independent people, but on the whole I seemed to myself to have fallen among people with whom it was usual *jurare in verba magistri* (to swear by the words of the teacher). What Rudolf Steiner had "said" was, in many cases, not really the beginning, but rather the end of one's own train of thought—and that, with people who never seemed to me to have solved the kinds of problems with which my lot had presented me. A high school teacher once said to me (evidently thinking himself to be voicing something important) that his wish was to live long enough to read everything Rudolf Steiner had said; and he did not seem to be alone in this wish. Joining the Anthroposophical Society thus also required the strength to rise above personal inclinations and disinclinations, to accept belonging without self-seeking, and to be, if not capable of achievements and sacrifices, then at least ready for them. At that time I was still a seeker, almost wholly without any help, and one who sought support and examples in my immediate human circle. Every seeker wishes to see what he seeks embodied in other people. I was often horrified to see how Anthroposophy was "received" and (so it seemed to me) often merely consumed.

At the start of my time as an anthroposophist I was once present as a guest at an anthroposophical Christmas celebration. We read a Christmas lecture Rudolf Steiner had once given. It was much too hard for me. It seemed to me, though, that it was much too hard for the others, too. Yet they themselves did not seem to notice this, or, if they did, they hid it from each other very successfully. I felt that there was a tense atmosphere in the room, and the tension was released only when the lights were lit on the Christmas tree, and apples and honey cakes passed among us. Before that, no sort of joy or gratitude for the birth of Christ was to be detected—not even, of course, in me.

I had experiences like this not only at the start of my time as an anthroposophist, but over and over again in the course of the years, and I think I may say that most adherents of Anthroposophy (apart from those who were leaders by nature) were taxed by such experiences too. Something like an equivalent was going on here, in the field of worldviews, of what happens when people try to learn all about higher mathematics without having grasped the basics. Because one's heart and being are being nourished in some way, it is often overlooked that one cannot really speak of *knowledge* here in the particular sense that Rudolf Steiner intended. Living in and through lectures, presentations, and "impulses" foisted itself in where the intention was supposed to be to experience things for oneself. That is understandable, but it is also dangerous; and strictly speaking, it is a misuse of Anthroposophy, which is supposed to be received by every adherent in the sense given it by its creator. The exercises in *Knowledge of the Higher Worlds* are practiced, so far as I am aware, by relatively few people, and the method of the "philosophy of freedom" as presented by Rudolf Steiner is also correctly practiced only by a few. It is not meaningful to argue about facts and questions of this kind. Nothing can be proved in this connection, either. It is just that I have repeatedly had the experience, right up until very recently, that the concept of insight can be received—and realized or not realized—in starkly contrasting ways.

It was only much later that I really understood that other people usually do not have my particular limitations, but do have their own. The others, too, had probably arrived here from some darkness of their own: their inner selves were not as rich, their spirit not as creative, as I had at first accepted in good faith. Even in Anthroposophy there was and is, so far as I could see, only a small stratum of active and especially gifted people who stood out, and stand out, from the general run of anthroposophists. Nothing could reasonably be expected of the rest, any more than from me, for I too had achieved nothing discernible in the field of Anthroposophy. Certainly it would have been better if they had practiced the *jurare in verba magistri* a little less.

Only in 1930 did I become a member of the Anthroposophical Society, yet still without any real inclination to do so. It took a certain effort of will, too, on objective grounds. My doubts were so far overcome that only the Yes really made itself heard any more. I had understood that feelings were subjective, and should therefore not be allowed to decide matters. For me, belonging to the Anthroposophical Society meant something distantly comparable to belonging to a religious order. I still had no overview of the Society, and no real power to achieve anything, but I took my membership seriously, and wished to be serious about it in the whole conduct of my life, as far as that was possible. What I thought and how I felt about it—and also how the seeds of my finding my way to the Church were already sown in 1930—is shown by the following verses, which were written at around the time of my joining the Anthroposophical Society:

> How gladly, friends, I would be one with you,
> gazing on the great man,
> of whom I too can testify
> that he freed me from the world of illusion.
>
> Yet I have never on earth
> found a great spiritual good so misapprehended:
> *He* wanted to give you courage,
> and *you* have but learned readily and happily what he said.
>
> The truth of the worlds dwells not in a concept
> that human beings can grasp. If you could only
> walk the *path*, here and now!
> You lack the deep refinement of deep humility.
>
> You are still thinking as in the time of your fathers:
> "look how far we have come,
> bringing light to this deep shaft!"
> *That*, friends, is not how one takes hold of eternity.
>
> And it was the intention of the man
> you so deeply venerate to proclaim eternity.
> Take care he does not weigh you down;
> and live—the beginning of deep eternity!

True, a certain intellectual independence manifests itself in these verses, but they are also insolently critical and pretentiously arrogant. At that time, I could not justly claim that I had in any way been freed from the world of illusion. Nor was I in any way more reverent than those who are reproached in these stanzas. I still saw the splinter in my brothers' eyes, without being aware of the plank in my own. I certainly had no inner right to hand out admonitions to others. I was still too much a person of the intellect to grasp the reality of life and to judge others kindly. Years later, I learned this (and from an anthroposophist, Friedrich Rittelmeyer): "only when you speak about another person in such a way that his angel could hear and approve of it, are you really telling the truth." And in my train of thought I tried, later on, to enact this manifestly divine *admonition to purity.* At the time of which we are speaking, though, despite all the tests I had been through, despite all divine tutelage, I still lacked humility. And can one ever say that one has enough of that?

O God, calm my thoughts!
Illuminate my needy heart!

5

The Christian Community

THE ANTHROPOSOPHICAL MOVEMENT WAS FOUNDED by Rudolf Steiner shortly after the turn of the nineteenth and twentieth centuries. Up to that point, Steiner (who was then about forty years old) had published philosophical, literary, and natural-scientific writings, but had not yet publicly announced anything about his insights into the spiritual world. Now he joined the already-existing Theosophical Society, which allowed him to work within it without tying him down to any particular doctrine, whereas many of those who wrote and spoke within that Society upheld a doctrine of spirit already prescribed in advance by the movement's leadership. Rudolf Steiner took on the office of General Secretary for Germany only on being assured that he would be allowed without any restriction to teach spiritual insights he *himself* had arrived at. Nor did he ever give utterance to any other kind of knowledge. Thus, although the Anthroposophical Society only emerged from the Theosophical Society in 1910, it remains true that the anthroposophical movement came into being at the turn of the century.

In the Theosophical Society it was later asserted and put about that Christ too was governed by the law of reincarnation, and that he was on the point of reincarnating himself on earth again in the form of a young Hindu man. Such an idea can only emerge when there is a total lack of clarity about the nature of the God-man. Here, though, Christ was taken as a "great initiate" rather than as the Son of God and the Redeemer of the world. In contrast to this, Rudolf Steiner always upheld the uniqueness and significance of Christ's incarnation, and testified to the divinity of Christ's being. His doctrine therefore proved itself more and more clearly to be incompatible with Theosophy. In the end, a very nasty campaign against him was conducted by foul means, and so Steiner left the Theosophical Society and founded the Anthroposophical Society. In contrast to the Theosophical Society, the Anthroposophical Society upheld in full the doctrine of Christ's redemption of the world. Admittedly it does so in forms whose Christian character can only be detected by outsiders if they pay close attention, forms that also harbor the danger that they may not be taken by the members in the same sense as that in which they were intended by the founder of the movement, Rudolf Steiner.

The Christian Community, of which I am now to speak, was not founded by Rudolf Steiner in his lifetime, but came about through the fact that a number of mostly younger theologians asked Steiner for help in working for Christian renewal in a way that would be adapted to the times. As far as I know, Steiner at first pressed them as to whether such a work of renewal would not be possible within the existing churches, and only after they had given this question a decided negative did he provide help in founding the Christian Community (1921–1922), help that was essentially twofold. First, Steiner gave a series of lectures to the initial group of priests. This put the first collaborators in the movement in a position to begin their work with confidence, with new means, and in a new spirit. Then he also supplied them with a "new liturgy," with the texts of the sacraments that were then to be used in the Christian Community movement, principally with that of the Act of the Consecration of Man. As far as I am aware, this text came about, not through an external or literal revision of the text of the Holy Mass, but rather by means of inspiration. (The word "inspiration" can mean many different things; and by using it, I do not mean to set the origins of the Act of the Consecration of Man and those of the writings of the New Testament on the same level.) The text we now have can indeed be compared with the text of Holy Mass, and can be seen as a modernization of it.

The Christian Community soon spread through many German cities and through neighboring countries (and more recently to the USA, too). Over the course of the years, it has acquired a membership of many thousands of people and has exercised a stimulating influence on the Protestant world far beyond its own membership.

Its priesthood is thought to consist of about 160 people, both men and women.[1] In the movement it is emphasized that woman's "I" has now been sufficiently awakened for her to be equally entitled to deal with what service at the altar requires. I have never regarded this idea either as entirely felicitous, or as sufficiently deeply thought through. From one point of view, it is self-evident that woman's "I" is "equally entitled" with man's. From another, the emphasis upon female rights, although it is very much in the spirit of our time, and has completely triumphed in the secular sphere, seemed to me to belong to a merely temporal women's movement. Anyone who, like the leadership of the Christian Community, believes in reincarnation, ought (so I increasingly thought) in consistency to judge that a feminine and a masculine incarnation present distinct tasks. The fact that in the Church it is only men who serve at the altar (in Protestant Christianity there are exceptions) does not express any masculine eagerness to be in charge, but rather a divine ordering—and there are no "rights" in the *imitatio Christi*. Gertrud von Le Fort demonstrates this admirably in her book *The Eternal Woman*. It is not the "eternal" woman (for whom this is self-evident), but the "temporal" woman, who emphasizes that she has "equal entitlements" and wants to demonstrate this in an external way.

In any case, however, what is the Christian Community? And why does it call itself a "movement for religious renewal"? It is difficult to answer this question, for the same reason that it is difficult to answer the question "What is Anthroposophy?" With the Christian Community, too, it is a matter of a spiritual undertaking that cannot adequately be described in a few words, not even through the best efforts of its adherents. Moreover, the Christian Community results from a fundamental critique of the existing Christianity of the churches, and finds itself in a certain opposition to that existing Christianity. Otherwise it would never have needed to be founded, and would be able to dissolve itself. And just as no spokesperson for the Christian Community can ever speak about the Catholic church in a way that a Catholic Christian would be able to accept without

---

1. It is estimated that the Christian Community now serves about 100,000 individuals. It has proven difficult to determine the current number of priests.

any reservations, so no Catholic Christian can speak in such a way that members of the Christian Community will feel themselves to have been properly understood. It will therefore be impossible, in what follows, completely to satisfy my former friends.

For many years I was in a position to champion the concerns and the spirit of the Christian Community in the way its priestly colleagues wished. I gave lectures in the Community—not of course immediately after my convictions led me to join it, but later on— and often wrote for its periodical. Even when it was banned by the Gestapo, I spoke at the graveside of those members who had died. No one can seriously assert (as might now happen in retrospect) that I had "still" not grasped its essence. I did grasp it, and I have also never forgotten how I thought about it in those years. Even today, I would direct towards the Christian Community anyone whose way to the Church is evidently closed, and to whom the Community could supply something humanly essential. For as a priest of the Church once said to me before my conversion: "It is not about conversions, it is about Christ." The "baptism of desire" can take place anywhere. People inevitably travel along different paths, and it is more important to direct them to a place where their yearning for the good will be nurtured, than to burden them with doctrines to which their ears are closed. The doctrine of salvation and the demands of the Catholic church hold only where there is receptivity to them, not where "invincible ignorance" stands in the way of their being grasped.

By its nature, the Christian Community is a "church," an association of people who wish to serve Christ, and it does so in the following way. At its summit stands the *Erzoberlenker* who, with the assistance of several *Oberlenker*,[2] leads the whole movement. The *Erzoberlenker* presides over larger matters concerning the life of the community, while the *Oberlenker* subordinate to them deal with lesser matters. Individual congregations are represented, led, and cared for by individual priests. The Christian Community thus as a

---

2. The German terms for these functions are often retained in English contexts. *Oberlenker* has the sense of guide or coordinator, and *Erzoberlenker* that of chief or central guide or coordinator (in the sense, as it were, of "horizontal hierarchy"). ED

whole has a hierarchical form, and its structure is similar to that of the Catholic church, on which it is in this respect modeled. The Christian Community, however, came into being without any connection to the tradition of the Christian church. It was founded, with the help of Rudolf Steiner, directly from its own efforts and "out of the spirit." The greatest emphasis was laid on this fact about its coming-into-being, and this was seen as a direct justification of the whole organization.

It is easy to say how the Community's coming-into-being and the life that has sprung up in it is to be judged in the light of dogmatics. Here, though, it is first a matter of saying what effect it had on me and on those who participated in it. I had no connection to the tradition, and no knowledge whatever of the Catholic church. The Christian Community struck me and most of its members as something wholly unlike and incomparable with anything else. I, at least, could only compare it with the organization and church life of the Protestant domain; and when compared with that, it seemed splendid, valid, and straightforwardly convincing. That the Christian Community was outwardly small, and the Protestant church outwardly large, in no way affected my judgment. Even today, Protestant Christianity seems to me, tragically, to lack any sense for hierarchical order. The idea of the "universal priesthood" could in the long run only be inimical to hierarchical structure; and understandably, people became less and less able to see that the idea of the universal priesthood and the various tasks of particular priests were not mutually exclusive, but instead productively complemented each other. There have recently [1950] been promising changes in the Protestant church in this respect too. In the Christian Community, the necessary sense for "hierarchy" was present in advance.

The Christian Community also corresponds to the Catholic church in its sacramental life. It administers the same sacraments as the Catholic church. It possesses baptism, confirmation, confession, an act of the consecration of man, marriage, extreme unction, and the ordination of priests. Admittedly, confirmation is, from one point of view, more closely related to first communion, and, from another, to Protestant confirmation. But it is nevertheless, like Catholic confirmation, administered in an orderly fashion by the "guide" or "coordinator," whose function corresponds to that of a bishop.

I never experienced extreme unction or the last rites in person, and only once did I have any experience of confession, and not a good one (the priest seemed to me to be as much at a loss as I was myself). I was once able to witness the solemn ordination of a priest (a joyful experience for all the participants!), and often to witness baptisms, weddings (including my own), and confirmations. I participated countless times in the Act of the Consecration of Man, which stands at the center of the life of the Christian Community in the same way that Holy Communion does at the center of the life of the Church. Only of that is there a need to give a short overview.

Instead of the prayer of repentance with which every Holy Communion begins, the Act of the Consecration of Man opens with difficult formulas for meditation, which change according to seasons and festivals, and do not recall anything in the language of the Church. Only the Protestant service in its various forms offered me any starting point for a comparison. The Protestant service, apart from the Communion service, is almost devoid of mystery, and consists almost entirely of preaching. Liturgically speaking, it is a dwindling of the full Christian service to its first part only, the "proclamation" that comes before the Mass. The Act of the Consecration of Man, on the other hand, has in my judgment an incomparably deeper objective effect than any form of service of preaching. I say "objective," and mean that literally. Subjectively, effects may differ. Not everyone present at something objectively essential takes from it subjectively what it offers; divine grace reaches us in the most various shapes, and it works in a completely incalculable way.

The "credal prayer" of the Christian Community (corresponding to the Creed) runs as follows:

> An almighty divine being, spiritual-physical, is the ground of existence of the heavens and of the earth who goes before his creatures like a Father.

> Christ, through whom human beings attain the re-enlivening of the dying earth existence, is to this divine being as the Son born in eternity.

In Jesus the Christ entered as man into the earthly world. The birth of Jesus upon earth is a working of the holy Spirit who, to heal spiritually the sickness of sin within the bodily nature of mankind, prepared the son of Mary to be the vehicle of the Christ.

The Christ Jesus suffered under Pontius Pilate the death on the cross and was lowered into the grave of the earth.

In death he became the helper of the souls of the dead who had lost their divine nature; then he overcame death after three days.

Since that time he is the Lord of the heavenly forces upon earth and lives as the fulfiller of the fatherly deeds of the ground of the world.

He will in time unite for the advancement of the world with those whom, through their bearing, he can wrest from the death of matter.

Through him can the healing Spirit work.

Communities whose members feel the Christ within themselves may feel united in a church to which all belong who are aware of the health-bringing power of the Christ.

They may hope for the overcoming of the sickness of sin, for the continuance of man's being, and for the preservation of their life destined for eternity.

Propositions such as these can have quite different effects on different people. One person may, perhaps, only notice what agrees with dogma and what does not agree with it. Another, perhaps, without paying attention to the detail, hears only a certain predominantly Christian sound, or dislikes the strangeness of the language. For still another person the sentences have a broadening, liberating, cheering, and even inspiring effect. In my case they were encountered by a soul that was searching, that had no ear for traditional Christian language, but that wanted truth and nourishment for the core of its being. It was only much later that I compared these propositions with the Apostolic and Niceno-Constanitopolitan Creeds (the latter being the Credo recited during the Mass). At the time in question, and for a long time afterwards, I breathed in their atmosphere, so as to become a participant in truth. From an early stage, the ecumenical breadth and the catholicity they too possess was important and dear to me. The proposition about the Church, when rightly understood, is in accordance with what the Church says about itself. It is not only people with a particular cultural background or with a particular spirit who belong to the Church, but all "who feel the salvific power of the Christ" (it could be said that only those who have received baptism, or the baptism of desire, feel it). The concept of the Church in the Christian Community is, however, "spiritualistic" like that of the reformers, not "realistic" in the Catholic church's sense.

In the Christian Community, as in Anthroposophy, to which it is closely related and committed, and by which it is essentially guided, great emphasis is laid on "consciousness." The Act of the Consecration of Man, and everything else done in the Christian Community, are to be followed with the greatest possible alertness and attention. It was said of the traditional forms of service and of the people who practised them that—*summa summarum*—they lacked a completely "contemporary" consciousness. I can sketch the idea here roughly in the following way.

According to the anthroposophical theory of development, man and humankind have gone through various "stages of consciousness." This is how it was in the past, and this is also how it will be in the future. In the Egyptian cultural epoch, for example, it was the development of the "sentient soul" that was appropriate to the age, i.e., people then lived essentially in "feeling" and were connected to the divine element governing them essentially by means of "feeling." In the succeeding epoch, that of Greek and Latin culture, humanity already enjoyed a more awakened life. It was the age of the "rational soul." Since the fourteenth century AD, humanity finds itself in the epoch of the "consciousness soul." Now there was on the one hand a stronger consciousness of the physical environment, but also, on the other, a stronger sense of the human being as an independent spirit. It is precisely the task of modernity, and in particular of our present age, to develop "consciousness" in this sense. (Here it should be noted that it is impossible for outsiders to take expressions of the anthroposophical worldview entirely in the sense in which they are intended; many texts about or against Anthroposophy therefore score cheap points against citations which, even when they are literally accurate, have a misleading effect. All quotations in the present study are meant positively, even if they unavoidably carry a risk of being misunderstood.) Now, not all people have got as far as achieving a completely contemporary "consciousness." We are, so it is said, surrounded by people who represent the spirit of past epochs within our present day, as, for example, fish and birds were still present even once the "age" of the mammals had really begun. It is our task to do what we can to contribute to the coming-into-being of the good, by developing a "consciousness" appropriate to our age.

This task can be taken very seriously and in a way that is of real use. It can also, however, lead to not entirely happy demarcations over against those of our fellow human beings who lack or supposedly lack a "fully contemporary consciousness," and against their ways of life. Over the course of the years, people who are distant from the anthroposophical movement have often spoken to me about what they called an "anthroposophical arrogance." This arrogance by no means necessarily follows from the spirit of either Anthroposophy or the Christian Community, but appears in people who consider themselves superior to those who do not share their "consciousness," and to those who live among religious forms that these people think can be regarded as rather obsolete. A widespread consciousness of being an elite has resulted from this, a consciousness that does not merely prompt those who have it to service, but also seems to increase their value in their own eyes. Anthroposophy brings many things into consciousness that require a good deal of tact and reflection if they are to be handled correctly. It is hardly astonishing that not all its adherents possess these qualities.

As I write this, I become painfully aware that at that time we always felt it to be in order to see other forms of religious practices and of church life critically, from the consciousness of our own superiority; but that any criticism of our own, whoever offered it, was regarded as a sign of misunderstanding and not taken seriously. We lived by the presumption, requiring no further reflection, that we had been given what was best, most progressive, most productive, and most significant for the future, and that all the means necessary to overcome any sort of defect in the spiritual and religious life, wherever such defects might be found, were in our hands. Nothing "against" the Christian Community could be allowed to stand without correction, even in the most insignificant article. From the Community's side, however, things were too often said about others and their beliefs which must have been hurtful. That has remained so right up to the present day. In *Die Christengemeinschaft*[3] there are many propositions about church life, both Catholic and Protestant, that can only be received as disrespectful attacks. Probably, however, those who were involved did not know this. When I was a member, at any rate, not only I myself but everyone with whom I spoke about this sort of question had no sense of this. We thought we were "painting a portrait," but we were doing so from a place from which we could not see the value of what we were depicting, and from which only a caricature could become visible.

The anthroposophical doctrine of the development of consciousness, when applied to church history, produces something like the following. The Catholic church as a whole is a sign and an expression of a particular stage of consciousness that has already been superseded. Much of what it contains is to be referred to the stage of the "Egyptian" cultural epoch, much else to the epoch of the "rational soul," a medieval spirituality that is no longer "up to date." It keeps its believers in a state of unfreedom and is no longer in accordance with modern man. It is actually obsolete, and in our present time represents something essentially past, although it has retained a liturgical and spiritual life still worthy of respect.

In contrast to Catholicism, in the view of the Christian Community, Protestantism represents a considerable and decided progress in consciousness. It is the sign of a step into spiritual freedom, a step that, admittedly, was made by sacrificing the former spiritual sense for mystery. When compared with Catholicism, Protestantism represents both progress and impoverishment. I often heard the Catholic church described as "Petrine" and the Protestant church as "Pauline." The Christian Community, by contrast, was supposed to

---

3. A periodical of the Christian Community.

represent a third "stage" of Christianity, corresponding to our own age and to the future. It was called "Johannine."

It was held that in this "Johannine" Christianity a higher unity of Catholic and Protestant Christianity had been brought about, a unity appropriate to our age. The liturgical power of Catholicism, well-adapted to mystery, was to be united with Protestant freedom, awakening, or autonomy. In this sense the Christian Community called and calls itself "trans-denominational."

It will be obvious to many people that here, by "Catholic" and "Protestant," what are understood are types of people, types of thinking, and forms of religious life, but that the words lack metaphysical content. Catholic and Protestant are, however, in the first place separated not by representing different religious types, but by the fact that truth appears to each in a different way. The idea of human development—which does not come from the Bible, but from natural science—opens doors to many insights, but also shuts other doors on much that is essential.

Anyone who thinks from the point of view of the history of consciousness, in the way that has been set out above, will find difficulty in feeling part of Christianity as a whole without any reservations. Not so long ago, an essay appeared in *Die Christengemeinschaft* in which some things were described as corresponding to "the age of Catholicism," others to "the age of Protestantism," in contrast to which what the Christian Community held to be true was appropriate "today." There are still, however, Catholic and Protestant Christians alive. And when compared with them, there are relatively few members of the Christian Community. How can the latter accept the former into their hearts, and deeply respect them, if they live by the idea that what other Christians are doing is just not up to date anymore? One of the dangers of the Christian Community lies in its overvaluation of the contents of consciousness and the objective forms of life of religious service. It is more important that we human beings regard ourselves as in need of renewal than that we assert this or that about "the" Church or about Christendom "itself," and think that we and only we have hold of the means of renewal. In the Christian Community I only ever heard or read the expression "Christendom" in this objective sense, disregarding individual people, whereas in life everything turns on whether the individual says "I must renew my life" (or let my life be renewed). One of the priests once said to me that it would be better if we were completely surrounded by modern materialism and if the churches coming from the past had no longer been there to mislead so many people into a Christendom no longer fit for the future (to speak of "Christendom" as *one thing*, in this way!). Another priest thought similarly: the Christian Community could not take part in the Una Sancta movement without damaging itself, since the Community was there precisely to renew everything that needed to be renewed in all the churches. This idea *can* be seriously meant, but it carries the risk of a vain arrogance, and, in the end, of spiritual and religious isolation.

Self-evidently, there is progress in consciousness, and different stages of consciousness among people on earth, and within the Catholic church too. Romano Guardini, Gertrud von Le Fort, or a cultured Jesuit father are on a higher "level of consciousness" than an old dear who can hardly read and just prays the rosary. What would become of the Church, however, if the "most advanced" members left it and wanted to join a special new community of their own? That would lead to a fragmentation of the Christian church. One of the great and wonderful things about the organism of the Church is that its "most advanced" spirits, both priests and lay people, remain at work within it. From the standpoint of the Church, any extra-ecclesiastical association, even one consisting of people who have a particularly pure will to cultivate something good, can only count as sectarianism; and the history of Christianity has often witnessed phenomena of this kind. The Church can never approve of the "Christian Community," however "up to date" it might be. It can only acknowledge the good that may be done by it, in and through individual people.

As far as my experience goes, there are gathered in the Christian Community only people who have fallen away from tradition, who are incapable of receiving any stimulus from the idea or the reality of the Church, and whom the "new" element in the Christian Community helps along the path of life. Many of them know almost nothing about the Church, its teaching, or its history; many who, like me, were not reached in their childhood or youth by the

Church's good news or the reality of its presence, are now paying attention; many turn away from the Church in their later years and find in the Christian Community the revival for which they had longed. The reality of the fates of individuals offers no matter for dogma; later, however, when I got to know Catholic theology, I was often struck beyond measure by how many ideas I found there that I had for many years myself thought were new ideas, ideas that nobody had ever had before Anthroposophy and the Christian Community came into being.

On the occasion of one Christian Community summer conference in Munich at the end of the 1920s, Cardinal Faulhaber warned against the Christian Community from the pulpit of Munich's Frauenkirche. This was certainly, as one of the priests of the Christian Community in Munich said, a sign that the Church was taking some sort of notice of the Community, and it was for this reason gratifying to the Community's priests. Cardinal Faulhaber had to represent the Church against the still young Christian Community; he not only could describe it, but was bound to describe it, as a danger, even if it was perhaps still quite a local one. What did this have to do with me, though—since we are still concerned here with the story of an individual's development? Such a thing does not become intelligible by judging one's earlier situation from the standpoint at which one has arrived later. Moreover, I know that many people came to the Christian path through the Christian Community, and I myself have the Community to thank for my having found my way to Christianity and to the Church. I may and must, therefore, speak of the Christian Community as approvingly as I possibly can. Who can tear out of his own heart a love that was so genuine and good and innocent and full of blessings?

A great number of the ideas I acquired by hearing or reading them in the Christian Community fell into me like good seedcorn, but often, alas, upon stony ground. The ground lay so barren there that it could only very gradually be turned into a productively tilled field. The ideas I received, however, are not only to be compared to seeds, but also to rain and sunshine that make the land fertile. The full weight of these words will be felt only by one who does not form an idea of them on a quick read-through, but immerses himself in the images they summon up: they are *images of truth*, and as such have variously deep effects, depending on the way they are received.

Stronger than any idea was the *effect* of the liturgy. The Act of the Consecration of Man had an enlivening, awakening, nourishing effect on me, not, alas, rapidly, but rather very slowly, laboriously, and often in such a slight way as to be imperceptible. It was not just a matter of a consciousness already prepared to receive new impressions, and to be changed, but rather of my very being, which was sadly imprisoned within itself and burdened with a resistance to anything from outside, even to help. Nothing could make its way into the core of my heart, into the genuine depths of my being: not nature, not culture, not the ideas with which my studies supplied me, nor the human relationships I had. Ideas such as the passages mentioned from the Act of the Consecration of Man, however, and above all the effect of the Act as a whole, sent warmth and life into the dark foundations. It was *not* my own doing that over the years (rather than weeks or months) doubt and unbelief diminished, receptivity to truth grew greater, and a will towards the good was built up within me. It was, rather, a sign of divine grace, and not only in a general form—for the fact that I was permitted to participate in the life of the Christian Community, and especially in its "liturgy," was also a grace.

The liturgy was supposed to be followed with the greatest conscious attention possible. All the words were spoken slowly and loudly. The "liturgy" was intended—not solely, but among other things—as a shared meditation. True, as time went on, I did also have a feeling that God or the "spirit world" (the "foundation of the worlds") was being shouted at a little too much. The words of the beginning of the Holy Eucharist, for example (in the Christian Community, "receive, with the bread, My Body"; "receive, with the wine, My Blood"), which in the Canon of the Mass are spoken quietly, had to reach the furthest corners of the hall. The Old Testament says of the prophet Elijah's meeting with God that God was not in the storm, nor in the earthquake, but in the still small voice of calm. Can one imagine the words *hoc est corpus meum* being shouted at the top of the priest's voice through the whole of the church? No—we hear it loudly enough with our inner ears, and we bend the knee before the mystery in silence. Yet since I was unfamiliar with anything comparable, it seemed to me natural that everything should be spoken this loudly and this evenly. My sense for liturgy had yet to develop.

In light of the fact that we were supposed to celebrate the liturgy as consciously as possible, it would have been appropriate for members to have the sacred texts before their eyes; for the less one must attend to externals, and the less one must exercise one's intellect, the more a meditative devotion is possible. All the liturgical texts were, however, with only a few exceptions, available only to the priesthood. Probably this was to protect the texts from theological criticism. What, though, would the Christian Community say about the Church, if the texts of Holy Mass were reserved to priests alone? From everything I experienced in the Christian Community, I imagine that this would be regarded as an unmistakable sign of priestly domination, of making people's minds up for them, of the unfreedom of believers. The same thing is thus valued differently according to whether it concerns oneself or others. It is difficult to be just, and not to fall victim to existing customs and claims when making one's judgment. I myself, in any case, learnt the Act of the Consecration of Man by heart(!) and was then able to follow everything without any effort, as well as, later, to compare the wording with that of Holy Mass.

The gestures of the Act of the Consecration of Man are sparing when compared with those of the Roman or even the Greek Orthodox liturgy. There is no real kneeling, and the members of the congregation sit fixedly on their seats during the whole solemnity, with the exception of the reading of the gospel, for which all stand in every Christian service. I have often, alas, seen people continuing to sit with their legs crossed even during the consecration; kneeling was taken as a sign of a past "stage of consciousness." In later years I once spoke with one of the priests about the contradiction between sacred events and human gestures. He said it was a matter of experiencing the event in a way that was "as little hindered as possible by bodies." I asked whether he could have sat through Christ's actual, historical crucifixion with his legs crossed, so as better to "experience" the event. But we could not agree about this.

Freedom was very strongly emphasized in the Christian Community, and I was entirely content with this. It was good to attend the Act of the Consecration of Man, but no one insisted upon it. It was good to take communion, but it was not a sin of omission not to do so. Confession was recommended over and over again, but anyone who never went to it was not doing anything wrong. Nor was there any sort of bond of faith for the members; all one needed to do was to "affirm" the liturgy. People who lived in the faith of the Church were held to be unfree; the idea of any sort of church discipline or even order was scorned and was unknown. Goethe was often quoted. I once heard him described, along with Mozart, as a "church father" of the Christian Community, although his remark that "only law can give us freedom" was never mentioned. Tellingly, more than one member at various times said to me, in almost identical words, "I don't want to go to church because I ought to, but because I want to!" That was for many years just my case. For a long time I saw in this "I want to" a sign of freedom. It is very difficult to distinguish freedom from self-will in the conduct of one's own life. If anyone had come to me with "you ought to" or even with "we have to" in those years, I would have dismissed him pronto. The "freedom" practised in the Christian Community can put many people who are unable to recognize or to practise obedience on the path to the good.

Great emphasis was (and still is) placed on the novelty of what was thought and of linguistic expression. In one of the prayers of the "liturgy," for example, it was prayed that "the warming of hearts" should lead to the "illumination of spirits in the being of man." Piety and wisdom, which mean exactly the same thing as this, were and are inconceivable here. I once heard a sermon in which the four parts of the Act of the Consecration of Man were compared with the four phases of a four-stroke car engine, and another in which the colors in the sky before the dawn (blue, green, red) were assigned to faith, hope, and charity. A female priest once said to me that really we should not say "I am the bread of life" but, instead, "the I-am is the bread of life." In a public speech we were given permission not to think of God as being so strict, but rather as "a bit more like Mozart." "Grace," Greek *charis*, was frequently connected with the three graces, and the translations of the New Testament used were often barely even distantly reminiscent of any usual or literal translation.

These are particularly clear and extreme examples. There was much more of the same sort, however. Anyone who in any way lives within the tradition can hardly even imagine how productive a preaching that does not proceed from any doctrinal heritage, but instead from human experience alone, can be. For a long time I could be persuaded, if at all, only by ideas and words that not only corresponded to modern consciousness, but had also been produced by it. Even the new translations can do more good than those who have been brought to the truth by the old ones may think. Here is an example of this principle that shows both the value and the limitations of the worship of the "new." It was usual in the Christian Community, instead of "in the beginning was the Word," to say "in the very beginning was the Word." I once said to a priest, "Beginning and very beginning really mean exactly the same thing. True, perhaps 'in the very beginning' makes some people who don't have happy memories of 'in the beginning' pay attention. After a couple of centuries have gone by, though, 'in the very beginning' will seem just as obsolete as 'in the beginning' does to many people now. Then perhaps some clever person will hit upon the idea that in order to excite people anew, one could and should say 'in principle.' That wouldn't have been worn out yet. And then it wouldn't be too long until someone else notices that 'in principle' is just the same as *in principio*, and *in principio* is the same as the 'in the beginning,' which is so despised today. So it would be good not to overestimate the importance of the words in which we clothe things, but instead to go straight to the things those words signify." We could not, however, agree. I myself took years to see that to anyone who really wants to honor God and to pay Him his due for the creation of the world through the Logos, it is unimportant which word is spoken in an earthly language. "In the very beginning," "in the beginning," "in principle": each of these expressions points to a completely unfathomable sphere that we can never adequately describe in human words. In favor of the reading "in the beginning," it is enough to say that it is simple and venerable, that everyone can understand it, and that a united Christianity needs words that are recognized by everyone. For Christianity as a whole will come apart if little movements get to work everywhere with new expressions that are only recognized by small circles of people.

Friedrich Rittelmeyer, the first "Chief Guide" of the Christian Community, even called Rudolf Steiner (in the title of one of his books) the man who would "lead us to a new Christianity."[4] I thought from early on that there could indeed be new forms or even new initiatives in Christianity, but no "new Christianity." But I agreed with Friedrich Rittelmeyer and all those who thought as he did that the old forms and initiatives had become unproductive, and that everything therefore depended on the new ones, which I too wished to serve. The exclusivity this idea contains and fosters can induce great enthusiasm. Like all my friends with the same view of the world, I thought the whole ecclesiastical Christianity that surrounded us was condemned to die sooner or later, and would fall into such poverty that the only way out would be the anthroposophical movement and the Christian Community. We took our own type of Christianity as an absolute and excused ourselves from looking too closely at any Christian life beside our own.

Unfortunately, I must say that I never witnessed any joy in the Christian Community about anything valuable that came from outside the Community itself. Whatever might happen, it either illustrated a defect in "confessional" Christianity, or was seen as a prefiguring of what the Christian Community itself was trying to do. Often, alas, I had the impression that the priests kept their members together by telling them over and over again what was special to the Christian Community and could be found nowhere else. It is just those people who do not do any of the work of acquiring knowledge themselves, and who are not themselves especially free (free, that is, *to* do things, rather than merely free *from* doing things), who like to hear about the power of knowledge and about freedom. These are painful observations, but the ideas corresponding to them came to me at an early stage. Many outsiders wonder

4. The book is Friedrich Rittelmeyer, *Rudolf Steiner als Führer zu neuem Christentum* [Rudolf Steiner as guide to a new Christianity] (Stuttgart: Verlag der Christengemeinschaft, 1933).

how it can be possible that a small group of people should possess such unshakable self-confidence, such exclusivity, such unlimited pretensions? The following occurrence, which was reliably reported to me, may offer a key to that question.

Rudolf Steiner had given a public lecture at which two Catholic priests had appeared. They could not object to the content of anything he had said; but afterwards they went up to Steiner and told him that they were in agreement with him, but that it put them off that he used such unfamiliar words to express everything, adding that, for their part, they spoke for everyone. Rudolf Steiner objected that although they certainly wanted to speak for everyone, in reality they spoke for a quite particular group of people. The priests insisted that they spoke "for everyone." Then Rudolf Steiner asked, quite specifically, "You wish to speak for everyone, but do all the people of the city actually come to you?" This question the priests had of course to answer in the negative, upon which Rudolf Steiner explained to them, "well, you see, I spoke today for those who do not come to you." Anyone who wants to do justice to the anthroposophical movement—Rudolf Steiner always spoke as an anthroposophist, never for the Christian Community—as well as to the Christian Community must think through the truth in this anecdote properly. There are many people to whom the word "God" says nothing any more, and who tragically confirm in this Nietzsche's notorious formula, "God is dead," yet who are nevertheless not incapable of finding their way back to God's being and to the divine world by means of entirely new words free from such associations. This is how everything "new" in the Christian Community is to be explained, and this is how it can be saving and inspiring—as well as how it can be so difficult for one who essentially belongs to it to think his way out of it!

The Christian Community and the Anthroposophical Society also rescued me, because in them I was able to get to know many significant people who were held up as examples. Friedrich Rittelmeyer, for example, who later proved to be a fatherly friend to me, was a person whom I did not feel I could ever praise enough. I had a friend in Munich who was one of the priests, whom I looked up to with feelings of real and unqualified benevolence. I was also able to meet Michael Bauer, who was the person who, after Rudolf Steiner's death, most fully and purely embodied the spirit of Anthroposophy. I could also describe many people who brought unconditional good into my life, and who credibly made Anthroposophy seem the movement that could help an otherwise fragmented and secularized world out of its predicament. All this must not be forgotten or undervalued, even though my path later led me out of the anthroposophical movement and the Christian Community and into the Church. Catholicism should never lead to the underestimation of human and spiritual values, however and wherever they manifest themselves, but to the affirmation of everything that is positive in the world. And how many significant personalities and Christians there are outside the Catholic church! I think, for example, of Blumhardt, Bodelschwingh, Mathilde Wrede, of the friends of Father Sonnenschein and Brother Paul, and many others.[5] Least of all would I wish to depreciate Rudolf Steiner, who is often misunderstood and reviled, and whom I alas never saw in person, but whom I have heard enough about from eye witnesses to have a strong image of him in my mind. And the following is and remains true.

I owe my increasingly strong recovery in soul and spirit not only to Anthroposophy and to Rudolf Steiner, but also to the Christian Community and to its theology and liturgy, despite the reservations that this short account has had to contain. The Act of the Consecration of Man, in particular, was a curative wellspring for my life. Here my soul, which was at first almost entirely incapable of prayer, of looking upwards, of self-recollection, gradually learned dedication, concentration, and veneration. For such a long time I had not known with what aim I should be studying, but gradually the will formed in me to contribute to the work of the Christian Community myself. I believed that I had enough experience of being tested

5. Blumhardt, probably Christoph Friedrich Blumhardt (1842–1919), Lutheran theologian; Bodelschwingh, probably Friedrich von Bodelschwingh (1831–1910), founder of the welfare institution Bethel; Mathilde Wrede, a Finnish Christian known for her prison work; "the friends of Father Sonnenschein" refers to those who assisted Carl Sonnenschein (1876–1929) a German Catholic priest, theologian and social reformer, and would include the legal scholar Hubertus Prinz zu Löwenstein and the poet Else Lasker-Schüler. The identity of Brother Paul is uncertain. ED

and of suffering to be able to stand by others in those situations, and I did not know that the exercise of the priestly office required more health and strength than I possessed, and that priesthood is a divine, rather than a human office. After my studies were concluded, I wished to enter the vocational seminar of the Christian Community and later to become a priest. Dr Rittelmeyer accepted these ideas amicably, and wished me the strength necessary for the completion of my studies. That this strength was needed was obvious to him too. All those of us who belonged to the circles I have mentioned were in complete agreement about the fragmentation and secularization of modern culture. The decision to become a priest threw a helpful light on many difficulties that faced me in the continuation of my studies. It also shed the necessary light on my relationship with the Christian Community and with everything I had received from it, which I have unfortunately had to portray here with reservations.

At heart, I was admittedly much more an anthroposophist than a member of the Christian Community. I was more adapted towards "thinking" and "knowledge" than I was emotionally predisposed, say, towards priestly leadership, and only people of the latter kind are considered for the priesthood. I had also not become a member of the Christian Community. As far as I can remember, I considered such membership, in contrast to membership in the Anthroposophical Society, to be beneath my dignity. In those years the Christian Community was often thought of as a second-rate organization, and there was no doubt among well-informed circles that the "way of knowledge" was the highest path.

These two movements, Anthroposophy and the Christian Community, should not be confused with each other or equated with each other, even though they may be spoken of together. The Christian Community emerged *from* Anthroposophy, but as an organization it was wholly *independent*. Rudolf Steiner himself emphasized that the Christian Community was not conceived as an anthroposophical enterprise, and he once expressed the difference as follows. "The anthroposophical movement is dedicated to the need for knowledge and brings knowledge; the Christian Community is dedicated to the need for resurrection, and brings Christ" (as reported by Friedrich Rittelmeyer in his book *Rudolf Steiner Enters My Life*). Thus, although nothing in heaven or on earth is greater than Christ, I nevertheless saw, understood, and made my own the fact that, and the reasons why, many anthroposophists did not wish to be members of the Christian Community. In my early years as an anthroposophist I myself witnessed what, even then, I understood to be an ugly attack on the Christian Community from the side of the anthroposophical movement, a serious attack, full of self-righteousness and arrogance.

At that time, I thought that if the "way of knowledge" was the "highest" path, then a mature human being could not be permitted to emphasize his or her own superiority in any way. Or, rather, he simply does not do so! And anyone who does lacks, just for this reason, that very maturity which it is the whole point of the anthroposophical movement to produce. Yet my reservations towards the Christian Community were not entirely unjustified. Even if my own illness prevented me from developing my own being freely, I was not the type of person to be a "member of the congregation." The Christian Community did not, alas, awaken in me any straightforwardly selfless will to serve. But is that any wonder, since Rudolf Steiner, for example, had clearly said that the advanced human being could be "his own confessor," and since all of those who were actively at work in the Christian Community were also anthroposophists, and none of them ever bore witness to the blessing of confession from personal experience? Instead, it was only members of the Christian Community who were to be brought to use this "sacrament." I did not become a member of the Christian Community until 1935, and for a completely external reason: the Anthroposophical Society had been banned by the Gestapo, and it seemed advisable at that time to get confirmation of my membership in the Christian Community, backdated by some considerable time.

When, today, as a Catholic Christian, I look back on that period, and on the way in which I then ranked things, I shudder. How can people of good will evaluate and delimit their "stages of consciousness" in such a way that even purely external consequences can follow from these "stages"? Today I think I have understood how and why in the kingdom of heaven the first can be last and the last first, how and why Christ presented the child as a model to us, and how and why he that seeks to save his life will lose it.

It was of a piece with the developments I have portrayed that I left the Protestant national church in 1928, having, previously, still outwardly belonged to it. I belonged only outwardly; inwardly, it meant nothing to me. So there was no particular stimulus to, or effect from, my departure in my heart. At most, it gave me satisfaction because of the spiritual decision that had preceded it.

The usual reason why people leave the Church, and why they left the Church in those years, was because they had grown distant from Christianity. My case was, in principle, quite the contrary of that. Through Anthroposophy and through the Christian Community, Christianity had come into my life in a newer and more inspiring way, and above all, in the only way that seemed objectively productive at that time—the task of the church I used to belong to had had its day. In the Christian Community, I became familiar with a hierarchically ordered religious movement furnished with all seven sacraments and whose services of worship contained a celebration of a mystery. From this starting point I was able to become aware of what I had missed by spending my childhood and youth in the Protestant church. My view of Protestant Christianity was more or less that which Goethe imparts very clearly in his account of his first (and only?) visit to the confessional in *Truth and Fiction* (part II, chapter 7). There Goethe speaks of the dangerous lack of sacramentalism in Protestant Christianity. Everyone, whether Protestant or Catholic, who possesses a set of Goethe's works, should read these pages; they are among the most significant in all Goethe's prose writings. However much the Mass had by the sixteenth century become a mismanaged and external affair, doing away with it tore out the heart of Christian worship, objectively speaking. Preaching and the liturgy of the word can never replace the objective and solemn celebration of a mystery. One can or could see many signs of this. Let one suffice here. Protestant churches, when compared with Catholic ones, are in general merely assembly halls, even when they are architecturally as noble as, for example, the Elisabethkirche in

Marburg, or the Naumburg cathedral. They lack objects of adoration, the monstrance, or the holy of holies.

I also objected to Protestant Christianity's close connection with the state. The Christian Community kept itself going, as it still does today, from the sacrifices made by its members alone. A Christian church, I thought, ought to be completely free from state power. I could not imagine myself then as a member of a "national church," any more than I can today. This is said as a profession of faith, and needs supplementing and deepening. At this point, though, where it is a matter of accounting for a personal decision, enough has been said. I got to know many fine and venerable people and clergy in the Protestant church. Many of them won my admiration and reverence. It was for the sake of many of them that I went to church. It was always their sermons that I went to hear, however, rather than going to "church." When Dr Rittelmeyer preached from the pulpit in Berlin, the "cultural world" from all parts of the city and its suburbs came to hear him. But it cannot really be said that they had "gone to church," for there were also churches in Dahlem and Stieglitz, in Charlottenburg and Lichterfelde. The last time I went to a Protestant church, I heard the pastor say, "after the service, communion will be celebrated, and you are all warmly invited to come along." Now there are certainly many pastors who would never utter such a sentence, and for whom communion is itself the chief service of worship, while there are doubtless even some Catholic priests who could speak such words. In 1928, however, I did not trouble myself with the question "What is the Church, and how should I fit in with it?" Nor did the Christian Community bring me any closer to this question. And the Anthroposophical Society certainly did not.

6

On the Way to the Priesthood

IN THE FOREGOING SECTIONS I HAVE TRIED TO DEPICT the spirit of Anthroposophy and the Christian Community *in general*. It seems right to me now that I should also try to invoke it in a quite *particular* form. I mentioned that all the "systematic" elements of the anthroposophical worldview were meant to be at the service of the "methodological" aspects. What that means will most easily be shown by giving a view of anthroposophical *practice*, upon which, for Anthroposophy's adherents, everything depends. In the following, therefore, I set out the text of the first exercise given in the book *Knowledge of Higher Worlds*. It should be noted beforehand that the "higher worlds" there spoken of are sites where the angels and those who have been resurrected exercise their powers, and that the expressions "student of the spirit" and "spiritual science" mean nothing other than people who seek to elevate themselves to these sites and who are able to say something about them from their own experience. Rudolf Steiner presents the first exercise in the following way:

> He must begin with a certain fundamental attitude of the soul. In spiritual science this fundamental attitude is called the path of veneration, of devotion for truth and knowledge. Without this attitude no one can become a student of the spirit. The disposition shown in their childhood, by subsequent students of higher knowledge, is well known to the experienced in these matters. There are children who look up with religious awe to those whom they venerate. For such people they have a respect that forbids them, even in the deepest recess of their heart, to harbor any thought of criticism or opposition. Such children grow up into young men and women who feel happy when they are able to look up to anything that fills them with veneration. From the ranks of

such children are recruited many students of higher knowledge. Have you ever paused outside the door of some venerated person, and have you, on this your first visit, felt a religious awe as you pressed on the handle to enter the room that for you is a holy place? If so, a feeling has been manifested within you that may be the germ of your future adherence to the path of knowledge. It is a blessing for every human being in process of development to have such feelings upon which to build. Only, it must not be thought that this disposition leads to submissiveness and slavery. What was once a childish veneration for persons, becomes later a veneration for truth and knowledge. Experience teaches that they can best hold their heads erect who have learned to venerate where veneration is due. And veneration is always due when it flows from the depths of the heart.

If we do not develop within ourselves this deeply-rooted feeling that there is something higher than ourselves, we shall never find the strength to evolve to something higher. The Initiate has only acquired the strength to lift his head to the heights of knowledge by guiding his heart to the depths of veneration and devotion. The heights of the spirit can only be climbed by passing through the portals of humility. You can only acquire right knowledge when you have learned to esteem it. Man has certainly the right to turn his eyes to the light, but he must first acquire this right. There are laws in the spiritual life, as in the physical life. Rub a glass rod with an appropriate material, and it will become electric, that is, it will receive the power of attracting small bodies. This is in keeping with a law of nature—it is known to all who have learned a little physics. Similarly, acquaintance with the first principles of spiritual science shows that every feeling of true devotion harbored in the soul develops a power that may sooner or later lead further on the path of knowledge.

The student who is gifted with this feeling, or who is fortunate enough to have had it inculcated in a suitable education, brings a great deal along with him when later in life he seeks admittance to higher knowledge. Failing such preparation, he will encounter difficulties at the very first step, unless he undertakes by rigorous self-education to create within himself this inner life of devotion. In our time it is especially important that full attention be paid to this point. Our civilization tends more toward critical judgment and condemnation than toward veneration and selfless devotion.

Our children already criticize far more than they worship. But every criticism, every adverse judgment passed, disperses the powers of the soul for the attainment of higher knowledge in the same measure that all veneration and reverence develops them. In this we do not wish to say anything against our civilization. There is no question here of leveling criticism against it. To this critical faculty, this self-conscious human judgment, this "prove all things and hold fast what is best," we owe the greatness of our civilization. Man could never have attained to the science, the industry, the commerce, the legal advantages of our time, had he not applied to all things the standard of his critical judgment. But what we have thereby gained in external culture we have had to pay for with a corresponding loss of higher knowledge of spiritual life. It must be emphasized that higher knowledge is not concerned with the veneration of persons, but the veneration of truth and knowledge.

Now the one thing everyone must acknowledge is the difficulty for those involved in the external civilization of our time to advance to the knowledge of the higher worlds. They can only do so if they work energetically at themselves. At a time when the conditions of material life were simpler, the attainment of spiritual knowledge was also easier. Objects of veneration and worship stood out in better relief from the ordinary things of the world. In an epoch of criticism, ideals are lowered; other feelings take the place of veneration, respect, prayer, and wonder. Our own age thrusts these feelings further and further into the background, so that they can only be conveyed to man, through his every-day life, in a very small degree. Whoever seeks higher knowledge must create it for himself. He must instill it into his soul. It cannot be done by study. It can only be done through life. Whoever, therefore, wishes to become a student of higher knowledge, must assiduously cultivate this inner life of devotion. Everywhere in his environment and in his experiences, he must seek motives of admiration and homage. If I meet a man and blame him for his weakness, I rob myself of power to attain higher knowledge, but if I try to enter lovingly into his merits, I gather such power. The student must continually be intent upon following this advice. The spiritually experienced know how much they owe to the circumstance that in face of all things they ever again turn to the good, and withhold adverse judgment. But this must not remain an external rule of life. Rather, it must take possession of our innermost soul. Man has it in his power to perfect himself, and, in time, completely to transform himself. But this transformation must take place in his innermost self, in his thought-life. It is not enough that I show respect only in my outward bearing; I must have this respect in my thoughts. The student must begin by absorbing this devotion into his thought-life. He must be wary of thoughts of disrespect, of adverse criticism existing in his consciousness, and he must endeavor straightaway to cultivate thoughts of devotion.

Every moment that we set ourselves to discover in our consciousness whatever remains in it of adverse, disparaging, and critical judgment of the world and of life—every such moment brings us nearer to higher knowledge. And we rise rapidly when we fill our consciousness in such moments with thoughts evoking in us admiration, respect, and veneration for the world and for life. It is well known to those experienced in these matters that in every such moment powers are awakened that otherwise remain dormant. In this way the spiritual eyes of man are opened. He begins to see things around him that he could not have seen before. He begins to understand that hitherto he had only seen a part of the world around him. A human being standing before him now presents a new and different aspect. Of course this rule of life alone will not yet enable him to see, for instance, what is described as the human aura, because for this purpose a still higher training is necessary. But he can rise to this higher training if he has previously undergone a rigorous training in devotion.

Noiseless and unnoticed by the outer world is the treading of the Path of Knowledge. No change need be noticed in the student. He performs his duties as hitherto; he attends to his business as before. The transformation goes on only in the inner part of the soul hidden from outward sight. At first his entire inner life is flooded by this harmony of devotion for everything that is truly venerable. His entire soul-life finds in this fundamental feeling its pivot. Just as the sun's rays vivify everything living, so does reverence, in the student, vivify all feelings of the soul.[6]

Thus far Rudolf Steiner.

6. Rudolf Steiner, *Knowledge of the Higher Worlds and its Attainment* (New York: Anthroposophic Press, 1932), 4–10. See the Appendix for further on this subject.

This exercise is obviously not provided for people who live in worship as it is practised by the Church, but for those who have to seek it elsewhere. Whence should a person in whom the sense for the divine world, for the plenitude of everything that is worthy of adoration, has atrophied, or has died altogether, acquire adoration once again, and how can he strengthen it? Who or what can guide him in this? I have never found exercises that can even distantly match up to the one quoted, and those that follow it. Here the "modern" person is addressed without preconditions that he cannot (precisely because he is "modern") fulfill. Not only I, but all seriously dedicated anthroposophists owe it to Rudolf Steiner that they have learned, to the extent that Anthroposophy has entered their lives, to worship again, or to worship more strongly; that they have found a way out of a spiritless bondage to apparently spiritless matter, and into "higher worlds."

For Anthroposophy is aimed at the *whole* person, not only at the ethical or religious consciousness, and it leads to a transformation of one's being, which helps to overcome the fragmentation in which we all live today—even those of us who are churchgoing Christians. How often do we see it happen that the impulses and ideas with which people are filled in church fail to have any effect on their lives as a whole, like a ship that is divided by its bulkheads into water-tight compartments! Here I am not referring to the power of original sin, which trails us everywhere, but to the fact that the religious and secular parts of ourselves so often fail to be organically connected with each other, so that no light at all falls from the religious part of ourselves into many of the other parts, and so that both how we act and what we do often conflicts with the best thing we have within ourselves. Wherever Anthroposophy is received and realized in a living way, the different parts of the person do not simply sit alongside each other; instead there is a striving that comes from the heart of a person's being and relates to everything he thinks, feels, and wills, as well as not only to what is divine and invisible, or to what is human and spiritual, but also to what is visible and natural. From this it can be gathered how and why Anthroposophy had a curative effect on my being, which was distant from God. It did so for a second reason, too.

Anthroposophy and all its driving impulses—and therefore the Christian Community, too, as well as everything they provided and to which they appealed—were intended transpersonally, for the whole of mankind, "cosmically." All the beings and stages of development as a whole are looked at and thought about as a whole here, or can be so thought about. Man today, according to this doctrine, also has a living relationship to everything that exists, everything that comes into being, and everything that has effects. The individual person may not and ought not to feel responsible only for himself and for those close to him, for his people or his race alone, but for humanity as a whole, and, beyond this, for everything that is and that is coming to be—an enormous extension of the spirit and feeling of life! All I can do here is bear witness to this.

At the start of my time as an anthroposophist, I once heard a lecture in which the speaker compared humanity to a giant cube composed of innumerable very small cubes. These very small cubes were an image for the individual people. Just as the form of the huge cube would lack something essential if even one of the tiny cubes were not present, so with humanity: here, too, not even what was small, not even one individual, could be imagined as absent without the whole suffering a decisive disturbance. One could and should therefore take oneself as seriously as this fact implies, and in the ideas mentioned there can be a strong motive selflessly to perfect one's being. Perhaps many Catholic Christians may think that the image of the cube is too mechanical, and reproduces the idea of catholicity in a way that is all too human as well as too demanding; but just because of its clarity, the idea can have an effect on people who are distant from the idea of Catholic universality and are thus not able to hear it proclaimed.

During the First World War, the first "Goetheanum" was built in Dornach, near Basel, Switzerland, as a headquarters for anthroposophical life. Members from various nations, including precisely those nations then at war with each other, took an active part in the building of the site at a time when almost all people's feelings towards each other were determined by national antagonisms. This peaceful collective work at a time of general mutual hostility is a fine and telling example of what Anthroposophy was working towards.

It was and is intended to have an international effect. For me, as someone who knew nothing of the trans-national character of the Catholic church, but was familiar only with the Protestant church with its national ties, it was deeply pleasing and promising.

In the Christian Community, too, the being and becoming of the individual, as well as that of our Lord Jesus Christ, was thought of as being in relation to everything that is, and is alive, and was appealed to accordingly. It is telling that one series of texts edited in the spirit of the Christian Community bore the title *Christus aller Erde* (Christ of the Whole Earth). What one did as an individual, whether one brought about good or evil, had significance for others, for humankind, for the whole world. Christ, too, for this doctrine, affected not only human souls, but also the whole cosmos. That for which and on account of which the "creature," in Paul's famous expression, "sighs," could be intimated and imagined here by means of simply believing. The scope of this idea, so far as I understood it, filled me with satisfaction and hope.

But a third thing was important here, too. Through Anthroposophy and the Christian Community, the idea of the community of the living and the dead became clear to me—intellectually, that is, rather than through personal experience. In the Protestant church I had never heard a word about this. Books from the field of "occultism," which dealt with "spiritualism" and phenomena of "materialization," did not get as far as the seriousness and the nature of the world of the dead, and I knew nothing of the Catholic teaching of the Church "suffering" and the Church "triumphant." Anthroposophy, however, speaks of the continuation of life beyond the gates of death over and over again, in ways that are quite visualizable and specific. By this means, too, there came into my life a deep current with a purifying, strengthening, and broadening effect. Yet Anthroposophy can provide not only a living connection with the dead and with the divine hierarchies, but also with the whole of "Nature."

The all-embracing character of the anthroposophical worldview, however, is expressed by the fact that it has effects on every individual domain of life's tasks. Along with the Christian Community, which can be described as a field of anthroposophical work, there are the most diverse artistic efforts—for example recitation and

eurythmy, the only form of modern dance in which nothing uncon-
sidered or unfamiliar can come from the human body. Waldorf
education, too, is a field of work in which absolutely wonderful
things are achieved when compared with state education, and from
which there is a very great deal to be learned. The work of the communities for children in need of special care should also be mentioned and celebrated, communities in which co-workers selflessly
and with great self-sacrifice and strength of belief dedicate themselves to children who "have been lost to life."[7] I have always seen
these communities as an especially fine sign of the anthroposophical spirit. Beyond this, there is also an anthroposophical approach
to agriculture, anthroposophical medicine, and even, although
existing conditions have so far prevented it from having an effect on
a large scale, anthroposophical ideas and efforts towards the healing
of the whole national and human organism—that is, of political
and social life.

All these fields of life are seasoned with the spirit of Anthroposophy, and do not draw upon people who are adherents of Anthroposophy on the one hand, while working in such a way on the other
as though they had never heard of Anthroposophy. Whereas, for
example, the best Catholic doctor will be Catholic only in his ethical
and religious life, while as a doctor he uses all the means of contemporary medicine (which has no connection with the Church), the
anthroposophical doctor's activity grows directly out of the anthroposophical intellectual legacy; furthermore, it does not merely grow
out of that legacy, but also in the longer term represents its *realization*. This is how it is in principle in all fields of anthroposophical
work.

The individual groups of tasks are thus spiritually and organically
connected with each other. Anthroposophical agriculture, for
example, is not unconnected to anthroposophical pedagogy. The

---

7. In the intervening years, such communities, best known as "Camphill Communities," have expanded into an international movement of more than a hundred
such communities in twenty-two countries, in which not only children, but also
young people and adults with developmental disabilities can live, learn, and work
with others in healthy social relationships based on mutual care and respect. ED

connection between farmers and educators is not of such a kind that they share common basic ideas, but in everything else get on with their own particular task using means particular to it. Instead, they live from the same foundation and source, just as the same stream can turn a mill, feed a fish pond, and water a large garden. Universality is not merely thought about or demanded here, but, as far as possible, is actually brought about. Even if one had made a wretched start in life oneself, and had nothing in the way of visible achievements to one's name, one could still feel oneself to be a member of a spiritual organism in which healing powers were at work for the life of the whole, and in which these powers could also have a healing effect on the personal existence of the individual.

With the help of Anthroposophy, therefore, I began to believe that the modern, godforsaken, fragmented world could be healed, as there was a cure for what had deeply harmed it. The thought that all the sickness and the objective distress of the age could be overcome and transformed was itself an essential medication. The individual cannot be healthy if he does not think of the whole. The healthy spirit, or the spirit longing for health, needs ideas that go beyond him personally. He wishes to serve the whole, not to gain something for himself. In the outside world there was no longer any universality. The anthroposophical impulse, and our service in, for, and from it, was supposed to restore the whole world of lost universality and to overcome its godforsakenness and fragmentation. This is roughly how I would summarize the ideal will that I wrestled from out of the chaos of my soul, a will that became ever more decisive, so far as anything at all could be decisive for me at that time. Anthroposophy was able to be spiritually nourishing, and it saved from starvation many people who were not strong enough to receive any other nutriment.

It cannot be left unsaid that my later illuminations go hand in hand with what I experienced earlier, and with what I am setting out here. I must therefore admit that the ideas I have set out in overview here became clear to me only in the course of time. It took a long time before I was able to see the nature of Anthroposophy and the Christian Community clearly, and thus before I could even begin to be capable of serving them. When I was introduced to them I was a student in the early stages of my course, in which I was having great difficulty in achieving even the minimum standard. I had little ability to learn. No one could quite understand why, but even in my schooldays I had found it increasingly difficult to master the material to be learned. Despite a certain gift for music, I was unable to master the viola, let alone read musical scores, and despite my practising keenly for more than a decade, my piano playing never progressed beyond a certain level, once I had reached it. For two whole semesters I was a pupil at the "Odeon," the secondary school for music in Munich, and practised four hours every day. I did not come close to progressing in the way that this might have led one to expect. I had to recognize that even this much diligence could not remove the basic problem, and had to give it up. Here and in many other things I was taught humility by bitter experience. It was a long time before I understood this humility, and could fully affirm it.

It was a similar story with German studies. Old High German, Middle High German, and Gothic letters would not stick in my head. Years flew by like snowflakes: either I could not catch them, or they quickly melted, leaving me without hope. During the whole period of my "studies" I could not even learn one small and pleasing poem by heart. If the spirit has mastered little material, then it has little to work on. The split mentioned here also determined my later life, and only became bearable as the idea of "karma," and later that of sacrifice, began to dawn on me.

I was in need not only of knowledge, but also of the formation of my whole being—and my soul, compared with those of most other people, was a seismograph, with very sensitive responses. I believe that it is just because of my being so sensitive that I felt so strongly the damage done by the system of higher education we have today, although I do not think it was good that most people suffered so little from it. What does it mean to suffer from something? I have come to know many people in the course of my life who have in their own way "suffered" from the world of today's culture, and who saw and lamented this and wanted to do something about it, but they did not carry any really detectable or conscious damage caused by this "culture" in their souls. Because of that they hardly thought about the reasons that lead certain fields to cohere or not to cohere, that lead divine inspirations or their opposites to be at work, and from which good or harm results. Whoever does think about these reasons comes, for example, among other things, to the realization that if the spirit of our higher education had been different, Adolf Hitler would never have come to power. Research and insight had, on the whole, retreated into the domain of ideas, of mere theory, and exerted no influence on the actual course of reality. Good and correct ideas could have been thought in countless fields and by countless scholars, but they lacked the relation to life that shows in life's being itself determined by those ideas. The course of history shows ever more clearly that the absence of God from university life, and its secularization, like that of all modern intellectual life, were and are dangerous. Even if the reason why I felt this more strongly than most others, and was more helpless in the face of it, was because of my own illness, this illness produced a will to healing. One could say that it might have been better if those who are naturally healthy had also known such a will to healing. It seems to me justified to measure the spirit of higher education against the God-inflected universality of the universities of the late Middle Ages, a spirit that still shines through today, despite everything.

My main field of work, German studies, was governed by an essentially burdensome historicism, from which other students evidently suffered too, for I seldom or never saw their eyes light up as a result of what they heard in their lectures. But shouldn't and wouldn't one's eyes light up when insights are communicated and awoken, insights that concern the whole person, and not merely the part of his intellect that understands the past?

In German studies itself we were taught historical philology as it had been developed since Jacob and Wilhelm Grimm. The derivation of words from "the Indo-Germanic," the laws of the "sound shift," the laws governing the relations between Gothic, Old High German, Middle High German, and New High German: all these had to be learned, as well as the branches and relations between German dialects from High German to Low German. All this happened without any spiritual penetration, in as natural-scientific a spirit as possible. There was no trace of the fact that even this transitory material is a likeness and an expression of something spiritual

131

(but of what?), that it is part of an essentially human history. German studies still lived on the pleasure its founders had taken in the discovery of the laws of the development of language, but it no longer conveyed this pleasure. I never met a single student in these realms who was joyful in the basic sense of the word; not one who would have been able to give any other reason for this philology than that this sort of thing was stipulated by the curriculum. One of our number was already almost at a research standard in his work, and yet there was no question that he found a climbing trip much more exciting than working on a text in Gothic.

A little more "life" could be detected in modern literary history. Here we were dealing with more or less imaginable human beings, with their spiritual development and how they had expressed it. Here one could not work in a purely natural-scientific way. Captivated by the idea of "objectively rigorous research"—since the living thought of Anthroposophy filled me only very slowly, very gradually, and had to displace something else when it arrived—I once opined to my professor that a method must be found by which the history of literature could be mastered as exactly as physics or biology. He observed that this was not really possible, and he was doubtless right about this. But he was not able to offer any valid or even any inspiring idea with which to counter my suggestion, which I really had expected he would be.

"Intellectual history," which meant, for example, recording, conserving, and labeling every discoverable ancient urn, which concerned the most isolated pure facts, and which stacked up knowledge for "Scholarship," had no sort of blossoming or inspiring relationship to a living present, even though many hearts warmed themselves on poems and poets, and even though insights were still communicated that could have stimulated a spirit with strong ideas in many ways. It was a public joke with some justice behind it that one student had suggested "Goethe and the dentists of his time" as a dissertation topic.

Friedrich Gundolf, the author of a widely-read book on Goethe, once spoke at the University of Munich. He read out his lecture without honoring his audience with a single glance. What that means, though, is that there was no inspiration from Goethe really at work within him, an inspiration that it might have been worth his traveling to impart to others. Instead, he was only really able to write down what he had to "say." Even if "reading something out" has unfortunately today become a recognized academic style of teaching, it is also a sign of the fact that purely historical, intellectual, dead thinking has smuggled itself in. In Plato's Academy, or in the School of Chartres, teachers did not just recite lectures, but actively presented their thought. Recitation never allows for an immediate connection between speaker and listener. No one ever wants to hear a "lecture" from a speaker in the pulpit. Where there is enthusiasm, where ideas are to be communicated that are really worth hearing, there the corresponding form of delivery is found. If we want to wrestle with another person in a conversation about truth, we form our thoughts directly, and while we might sometimes read out quotations, we never read out what it is we want to say ourselves.

A complete contrast with Gundolf was provided by one of the professors at Munich, who always spoke quite freely, without having even the briefest of notes in front of him. He thus represented the opposite pole of intellectualism: he was able to bring any sentence, even one that had already become intricate and involved, to a close with a flourish, and in a grammatically correct way. But his lectures, which lasted four hours and were given throughout the semester, were really only a form of acrobatics, a display of sporting prowess, effortlessly delivered. I think he could have talked for three hours without a pause and without any notes, but also without uttering a single sentence informed in any way by his own experience. I can still see his genuinely touching, harmless eyes and remember the difference in the impression they made on me before and after he had spoken. These examples summon up the core of the "intellectual history" of that time and place. There is no healthy intellectual or spiritual life, no life that brings healing, without the detectable presence of intellectual and spiritual effort; nor can that effort be contained in a manuscript that has been written in advance and is now to be read out. Goethe observed: "Have something to say, and you will say it"; and Rudolf Steiner once remarked that thinking needed once more to become work as hard as chopping wood. In my view it is inconceivable that an anthroposophist would ever read his lecture out from a manuscript.

Gundolf was an intellectualist. He threw light on the figure of Goethe from every conceivable angle, described the poet with a flood of foreign words, and succeeded in providing, so to speak, a complete anatomy of his spirit. But this way of looking at Goethe is un-Goethean. Bielschowsky, even though he is too much of a materialist and is too conventional really to grasp Goethe's essence or his greatness, is still much closer to Goethe's spirit. At least he worked in a spirit of reverence and allowed his book time to mature; Gundolf's book, with its nine hundred or so pages, comes across instead as having been tossed off without any effort, and is as far from the spirit of Goethe as is the historical and liberal Protestant theology of the turn of the century from the divine figure of Jesus Christ. How distant had the spirit of the age not already become, in the course of a couple of decades, from that of Hermann Grimm, in which love and reverence still shone through? Are we not permitted to point out the lack of a spiritual life, when something better is hoped for in the future? And did not the age have need of universities that would immediately refresh their students, strengthen them in what is essential, and fill them with the power of truth? We certainly cannot do without specialists, but they have no place in the authentically spiritual realm. Just as one can only understand the circulation of the blood or the operation of the nerves if one is familiar with the whole organism, so everything that belongs to intellectual and spiritual history (and what does not belong to it?) can only be observed illuminatingly if the light of the whole, the light of the world itself, is thrown upon it—only when "light shines in the darkness."

Amid these and similar impressions, exertions, and initial studies, I found myself looking for a dissertation topic. I fell first upon Rainer Maria Rilke, whose powerfully tragic *Duino Elegies* had appealed to me, and that I believed I was able to grasp with the help of some of my own experiences. *Wer, wenn ich schriee, hörte mich denn aus der Engel Ordnungen?* "Who, if I cried, would hear me, from among the orders of the angels?" That is the beginning of the first elegy. This deeply sad confession corresponded in its essentials to my own situation and my own view. But I thought I also knew from my own experience something of the way in which the poet picks himself up. I sensed truth in, for example, the beginning of the sublime tenth elegy:

> May I some day, at the exit of grim understanding,
> sing out jubilation and praise to affirmative angels!
> May none of the clear-struck hammers of the heart fall on loose,
>   uncertain, or breaking strings.
> May my streaming face make me more shining. May humble
>   weeping bloom.
> O nights, how dear you will be to me then, nights of grieving.
> Alas, that I did not on my knees, kneeling more, accept you,
>   more kneeling lose myself, disconsolate sisters, in your
>   loosened hair. We, spendthrifts of the sorrows.[8]

What experience, what tragedy, what an exhortation lies in the words "We, spendthrifts of the sorrows"! Yet I had the impression that Rilke was a spirit who stood outside the authentically Christian world—which in no way affects his greatness. He seemed to me to have been blown in as if from the Far East, as a wondering, suffering, foreigner. How close I often felt myself to be to him! I too was in some sense "blown in," not from a non-Christian East, but from warm tropical native realms into a cold and deadening North. The dissertation, however, had the aim not merely of schooling the understanding, but of fostering my being. I sensed that it would be better to occupy myself with a purely Christian spirit, and gave up Rilke, all of whose works I already had in my room.

So I hit upon Christian Morgenstern, whose work culminates in poems that can stand as a symbol for the good name of the poet.

> Give me the sight of what you are, O world,
> Let sensuous appearance fill me slowly.

Or:

> O give me joys that are not bound
> To that unworthy lower "I,"

---

8. Rainer Maria Rilke, *Duino Elegies*, with English translations by C.F. Macintyre (Berkeley, CA: University of California Press, 1961), 74–75.

But those where soul with soul is found,
Spirit to spirit draweth nigh.[9]

Or:

A very Grail I elevate
To thee this heart of mine,
The which doth all its blood abate
The thirst for thy good wine,
O Christ, for Thee!
        O CHRIST!

O fill it new until it flood
With flame of roses of Thy blood,
That Whom I bear henceforth
Through nights and days of earth,
O Christ! Thou be!
        O CHRIST![10]

This was the Morgenstern "on" whom I wanted to work, as they put it—the poet of Anthroposophy, and the person who had most intelligibly and warmly carried its spirit forward. The professor to whom I suggested this plan picked it up and set me the topic of "The Mystical Element in the Poetry of Christian Morgenstern." With this suggestion he had seized on what was essential in Christian Morgenstern's work, although he had, alas, expressed it in a very "academic" language. So I set to work.

Work proceeded, like my whole life at that time, on two levels that were alongside each other, and overlaid and interwoven with each other. On one level I tried to serve everything that had been presented to me by Anthroposophy and the Christian Community as an obligation and an opportunity, everything that increasingly gave my life meaning and support, and that was to prepare me for a dimly hoped-for vocation—all this still only in an initial way, and one that was still full of confusion and weaknesses. On the other level I attempted to participate to a sufficient degree in the spirit of

9. Trans. Eileen Hutchins and Ursula Grahl, in Angel Flores, ed. *An Anthology of German Poetry from Hölderlin to Rilke in English Translation* (New York: Anchor Books, 1960), 316.

10. Trans. R.G.L. Barrett, in Flores, ed., *An Anthology of German Poetry*, 319.

"scholarship without preconceptions," to achieve philological precision, and to satisfy the spirit of the university as it then was.

These two efforts lacked any organic connection to each other, but my study still needed to find an objective form it could take. Unfortunately, I did not have the courage to provide that form by means of the first set of efforts I mentioned. I thought I was obliged to commit myself to what was "strictly scholarly" alone. I kept to myself everything I had learnt from my own budding faith about what the poet had experienced and borne witness to, and I wrote "without preconceptions," i.e., in reality, *with* the preconception that it was possible to get at the truth by means of philology and psychology. Indeed, perhaps just because of this, my study was judged "very good," and was at once printed as a book. Not many people have read it, however, so it has not done too much harm.

There was only one good thing about my study. A fatherly friend read the first draft and objected to the number of foreign words it contained. I thought the objection justified, for it was aswarm with *-isms* and *-ions*. The criticism led me to rework the whole dissertation ("scholarly study") so that not a single foreign word any longer remained in it, apart from words like *Kultur, Religion, Mystik, Anthroposophie*, words that could neither be translated nor rewritten. This revision of my draft was not easy. It is much harder to think in pure German than to indulge in abbreviations for intellectual terminology. The revision was thus, more than anything else, an intellectual exercise, and it also gratified a certain playfulness in me. The effort to keep the language pure or to purify it can be a purely intellectual concern, and it is strongly to be recommended as an exercise.

In my academic exams (in the language of that time "in the final higher education examination") the examiners amicably took it as quite certain that I knew a lot, or at least enough. The examinations were only discussions (an "exchange of ideas") between the professors ("higher education teachers") and the candidate ("the examinee"). "My" professor discussed with me only dramaturgical questions in Schiller, and the professor from Education confined himself to particular works by Natorp and Kerchensteiner, which I had been assigned to read and think about. In music history, however, I almost failed. How could I keep in my head what the first opera produced in Naples was called, or who had worked as a choir-master in Milan in the sixteenth century, or how homophony had evolved in detail from polyphony? Nevertheless, everything went all right. I was a *PhD*, and so far as I can remember first acted as a server in the Christian Community the very next day.[11] So it was solemnly confirmed that I had now left my university days behind me.

Something, however, must be said about the course of my studies, because it shows how and in what way Anthroposophy and the Christian Community brought healing into my life. It was not a question of a change of attitude having been brought about in me by accepting different ideas and motives, but of the formation and shoring-up of the core of my being—about a series of events, there-fore, that were not to lead me from a false path (or from a standstill) to the right path, but were to provide me with the very strength to walk. I do not know whether, if I had encountered the Church too early (and had I not had encounters with it for many years, which were not, however, truly encounters at all?), this would have been able to bring me out of my resistance, unbelief, and doubt. The sense with which I was later able to understand the Church was awoken in those years and by those means.

After my studies came to a close, I had the task of immersing myself, and the right to immerse myself, in the spirit of Anthropos-ophy and the Christian Community. This always happened within a circle of friends and acquaintances who were pursuing the same basic goal, whose members were, however, as I shall always grate-fully admit, far superior to me in their powers of life and vision, and in their power to have an effect on the world. It was the time when Adolf Hitler was preparing to come to power, and we saw the world around us as outwardly and inwardly afflicted by evil, in need of

---

11. In the Christian Community, it is always adults, never children, who act as servers. Children may not take part in the Act of the Consecration of Man, in con-trast to the Holy Mass, which works in so many different ways and on so many dif-ferent levels.

redemption; and we were determined to do our part in bringing this redemption about. I believed that all "outsiders" must sooner or later either arrive at zero, or open themselves to the spirit of Anthroposophy. All other Christians, whatever their confession, were living in an "only just Christian" state, and still had to climb to the level on which we ourselves stood, or sought to stand. There was one good thing about this belief, but there was also a risk in it.

From one point of view, this belief had the effect of obligating us. A task of importance for the whole world had fallen to us, we few. Rudolf Steiner had particularly described and marked out our age as "the age of Michael," that is, as a time at which what endangered humanity was, as seldom before, to be combated by means of powers unfolded in the service of the archangel Michael. Anthroposophy had been given to us and developed so as to serve as the principal means to this struggle. We were thus called to something of supreme and decisive importance. Un-Spirit was to be defeated by Spirit, the sub-sensible by the supersensible, the host of Satan by that of the angels, and this was to take place essentially by means of the development and realization of the "science of spirit." Each adherent had to take the task as seriously as possible, and to take himself—while remaining modest—as seriously as possible. All that was overlooked was the multiplicity of God's ways and the multiplicity of the ways in which people could serve the archangel Michael.

This hints at the other side of the question from today's standpoint; that is, a certain danger of self-overestimation. For now the small band of anthroposophists stood as a decisive group of fighters within a world with which it was difficult for them to feel in their hearts that they were in any simple sense at one. Rudolf Steiner called, it is true, for "selfless self-consciousness," which is a rewriting of Paul's idea that "by the grace of God I am what I am." On the other hand, something like the following idea was in the air: just as Christ recognizes the greatness of John the Baptist, but ascribes greater significance to the "least in God's kingdom," so all human greatness and achievements were indeed to be recognized, but the "least" of the anthroposophists was more important. For everything that was outside the anthroposophical movement, whether historical or present, was, when looked at closely, taken in a merely historical sense. It received its place in the anthroposophical worldview, and was thus relieved of any obligating influence. Rudolf Steiner himself, certainly with justice in his own case, often ran the risk of describing historical people and facts in an outrageously bold manner, as if he were dismissing them. Thus, for example, he described the church father Tertullian as being "not even a particularly cultured writer." He may not have been, when compared with Rudolf Steiner. But what if this evaluation were passed on to people whom it would better befit to admire the level of culture reached by the Church Fathers, and to learn "devotion" from them here too, so as to be able after all to make their own judgment? Among the things I have always found hard to understand about Rudolf Steiner is that he expected his readers and listeners to entertain ideas that are far beyond the capacity of average people to understand on the basis of their own efforts. Yet he was writing and speaking for average people, not for a small society of illustrious, independent spirits. Many anthroposophists thought it was no longer relevant to read the New Testament. For them, Rudolf Steiner's lecture series had replaced it. In later years, many of them even regarded Rudolf Steiner's lectures on the gospels as out of date, and now only wanted to—what shall we call it?—"do Anthroposophy." Many of them could only now "understand" the texts of the New Testament if they had a "translation" in front of them that barely recalled any familiar and literal translation.

The books and lecturers of our Teacher were read over and over again, on our own and in reading groups. To accept them meant not only expanding one's insight, but also nourishing our very being. I well know, even today, that I am not mistaken in this opinion, but that it corresponds to the truth, as well as to other people's experience. The exclusive dependence on Rudolf Steiner harbors, admittedly, the danger of exploding any Christian consciousness of unity. But I did not notice this at the time.

Rudolf Steiner wanted to lead his followers to freedom and spiritual independence in the deepest and most comprehensive sense that I have ever seen outside the Catholic church. Each person was to know for himself, to think for himself, to take his own spiritual steps forward. He also said very clearly that no progress can be made in knowledge without corresponding progress in morality, and that, for example, a positive alteration of one's character and habits is more important than the acquisition of any amount of knowledge, even if it is knowledge concerning the "higher worlds." In his lecture on the Lord's Prayer we find this sentence: "It has already often been emphasized here that secret instruction (let the stranger not stumble at this word: it means something good) does not consist in theoretical learning, but in subjecting the otherwise stationary objects of the etheric body to development" (by which is meant an alteration of the moral character of one's life). And in the book *Knowledge of Higher Worlds* the "golden rule of the true secret sciences" is given as follows: "If you would try to take *one* step forward in the knowledge of secret truths, take *three* in the perfection of your character towards the good!" Anyone who not only listens to this, but follows it, lives in a pure and Christian spirit, even if, of course, not in a churchly one.

Hand in hand with anthroposophical work went preparation for the priestly vocation towards which I was working. I was permitted to attend several theological courses at the Stuttgart Seminary of the Christian Community. I not only worked through the available literature of the Christian Community, but also began to write in this area. For a long while I was a parish worker and a server at the Act of the Consecration of Man, was able to participate to some extent in the care of souls, and gave courses on the gospels and other topics, including, for example, on Richard Wagner's *Parsifal*.

On the whole I had taken on too much of a certain intellectual idealism. Idealism befits young people and is always a sign of youthfulness, irrespective of the time of one's life at which it is cultivated. Christianity, however, is—in the literal sense of the word—realistic. It is addressed to reality, through and through, because it is related to and seasoned with the most "real" thing there is or has ever been on earth: the cross on which Jesus Christ hung at Golgotha. Certainly an attitude towards this that could be called "idealistic" can be nourished and inspired precisely by the cross. What I meant by "idealism" earlier was a striving towards higher things that breaks out from one's inner being, but that lacks a full connection to earthly reality. I spoke too "idealistically" about Richard Wagner,

about Hölderlin, about Mozart, and so on. What I said was probably not false, but it went beyond the degree of maturity I had actually reached. It would have been better if we had let the darkness of
our own being be illuminated by the light of Christ than to enjoy
what is expressed and summoned up by the darkening of the Temple of the Grail before the sacred fire: objective observations can
also contribute to the good.

I once submitted an essay to Dr Rittelmeyer with the title "Faust's
children." It was about Gretchen's child, about Homunculus, and
about Euphorion, and these three characters were interpreted as
symbols of human levels of consciousness. Dr Rittelmeyer's view
was that my ideas were probably quite right, but that I should wait
ten years before publishing the essay, until I had been able to go into
things a little more deeply. Luckily, I was able at once to recognize
the wisdom of this judgment. I saw that I had gotten ahead of
myself in an "idealistic" and speculative direction, did not give the
essay to anyone else, and later concerned myself increasingly with
what was "realistic," with the moral and spiritual harmony between
what I said and my own state of being and level of maturity.

Even in the Christian Community, however free and unobligated
it left its members, and however free-spiritedly they behaved in
public, there was a certain spirit of exclusivity. The Catholic church
was held to be obsolete. A leader of the Community once said that
something as rigid as the Catholic church would have to be "shown
how to die." Protestant Christianity was said over and over again to
be a "Good Friday Christianity." The Christian Community, however, wanted to provide an up-to-date "resurrection Christianity."
Today such descriptions seem superficial to me. At the time I
thought them profound. They lacked a substantive relation to history and to a knowledge of everything that has happened in it
("who can think of anything clever or new who has not already
thought through the world which precedes him"). At the extreme,
Goethe describes the spirit of a person who takes everything that is
merely new to *him*, personally, as though it were new as such, in the
words of the "Baccalaureus" in the Second Part of *Faust*:

The world was not, till I created it;
I brought the sun up from the sea;
The moon began its changeful course with me; [...]
Who, if not I, delivered you and brought
You out of cramped Philistine thought?
But I am free to follow on the track
Shown by my inner light and my mind's voice,
I swiftly go my ways and I rejoice,
Brightness before me, darkness at my back.[12]

These verses do not describe the Christian Community as such, but only one of the dangers inherent in it. At that time I did not wish to share anything with Christians living in the existing confessions. Today I do not know how the Christian Community could even do so. In order to do so, it would have solemnly to revoke its declaration that all other forms of Christianity were obsolete. But can this, or anything corresponding to it, come about?

I lacked the necessary health to serve as a priest, and it was indicated to me that I should withdraw. Inwardly, I had, despite this, been regarded for a number of years as really belonging to the group of priestly workers. This was said even in one of the last letters I received from licentiate Emil Bock, Friedrich Rittelmeyer's successor as the Arch Guide. In 1933, when the decision mentioned was made, I found it hard, and dispiriting.

12. Johann Wolfgang von Goethe, *Faust Part One and Part Two*, trans. Charles E. Passage (Indianapolis: Bobbs-Merrill, 1965), 236.

7

Years of Transition

SINCE THIS ACCOUNT IS MEANT TO DESCRIBE THE development of my worldview in the sense specified, I must not speak only about what I was thinking, but also, repeatedly, about my own life. In the first place, it is not life events, the people I met, experiences of nature or of books that are to be portrayed, but, as far as is possible, their effects on the core of my soul, on my being. In what follows, therefore, even less will be said about external events than has been said up to this point. The narrative will be still less a series of actions, and still more a chain of reflections, than it has already so far been. My transition from Anthroposophy to Catholicism had a long gestation. It would hardly be possible to be aware of every aspect of this gestation. I have to try to get inside what was—previously, and for many years—unclear from the perspective of the clarity I acquired only later. I will therefore describe what was not then conscious, yet was indeed decisive, with the help of what I later became consciously aware of, so that these earlier elements can be understood retrospectively. Only a few characteristic details can be selected from the wealth of material at my disposal. For long periods I lived on Anthroposophy—and lived, so far as I was able, *for* it, too. Yet I still had questions about it, and had some reservations, unlike those who were at that time my friends.

For the sake of clarity, in what follows I will first consider my ideas, and then the external events of my life.

Spiritual life does not consist only in ideas or only in what a person is conscious of, but also, and essentially, in the impulses of the heart, and in everything that lies behind and within a person's deeds. The soul is, on one hand, nurtured by what is spiritual, but on the other it is bound to the body and determined by the body.

The soul lives between "higher" and "lower," with the task of ensuring that what is higher increasingly transforms the lower (ascesis). Whether ideas can become decisive for the soul, and, if so, which ones, depends not only on the nature and content of those ideas, but also on the soul's connection to the workings of nature, to habits, and to its own peculiarities; and this connection is very strong in most people. We become receptive to new ideas insofar as the rule of nature, in the broadest sense, retreats. A struggle for truth, a struggle over one's worldview, thus consists both in a receptiveness to ideas (whether these derive from other people or from the eternal) and in the cultivation of the organ able to receive these ideas.

Anyone who has not been reading with close attention, or who does not keep in mind what was said in previous sections of this book, and who now does not pay attention to what is said here and in the following chapter (all the way through to the closing observations), could easily have the impression that the author wavered in a rather murky way between pious reverence for the founders of Anthroposophy and a rejection of them. So it is right to add the following here. First of all, the course of a person's development has to be retold as it was. During that time, the author was in no way influenced by the value or the truth of the Church's dogma. Second, however, the author never simply rejected everything anthroposophical, but instead arrived at the knowledge that the core spirit of Anthroposophy (Rudolf Steiner was born and brought up a Catholic, and constructed his worldview in conscious opposition to the Church) as well as many of Anthroposophy's individual teachings are to be rejected if one follows the Church's dogma, but that others can be acknowledged, and that much of Anthroposophy does not fall within the domain of dogmatics at all. Here, the Church's thinking does not face the simple question "Yes to everything, or No to everything?" Instead, it faces the more difficult question "what is and ought to be affirmed, and what must unfortunately be denied?" Here, only one who has engaged very thoroughly with the rich and multifarious details of Anthroposophy can arrive at a clear answer. It is also the intention of the present study to incite those who are looking for a valid judgment of these questions to undertake a correspondingly thorough engagement. Prejudices rarely conform to the truth. Judgments can only be made, here as elsewhere, by virtue of serious work.

Thus, for example, many are content to hear Anthroposophy described as "a kind of gnosis." But what work is such a word doing? Who knows what gnosis actually was like? To whom does the sentence "Anthroposophy is a kind of gnosis" convey a meaning as vivid as the sentence "there is an apple tree"? But even if we all knew exactly what we meant by gnosis, the comparison is simply not accurate. Speculation is endemic to gnostic systems. Anthroposophy, however, did not originate in speculation, but as a science of experience. It wishes to extend modern materialist natural science into the spiritual domain. Rudolf Steiner only ever wanted to speak from experience, and about what could be experienced. It is this, rather than anything else, that explains, for example, the fact that in his portrayal of the creation of the world he speaks only of the workings of the divine hierarchies, and not of God the Father or the Son. It is, however, a completely different thing to leave God unmentioned because God, as the creator of the world, stands beyond anything that can ever be experienced by human beings, than it is to leave Him unmentioned because one does not believe in Him. You can see that it is extremely difficult to do justice to Anthroposophy. But it is always better to decline to judge something than to label it without having a full understanding of it. "The truth will set you free": this sentence goes for the field of discussions about worldviews, too.

Even the path of Christian faith and the method of anthroposophical knowledge are not simply opposite to each other; or at least, they do not need to be so. The anthroposophical method of knowledge could, instead, lead to faith, in the Church's sense, and ought to do so; and it certainly is never able to replace faith. The greatest and most vital anthroposophists have arrived at faith through "knowledge," in the basic sense of the word faith (*pistis*), just as the Church teaches that thinking can be and ought to be a preparatory stage before faith. It is true that anthroposophical research entirely fails to subordinate itself to the Church's teaching, and so Rudolf Steiner's statements take that place for anthroposophists which, for Catholics, is held by the dogmatic decisions of the

Church. The *ought* mentioned above in connection with Anthroposophy has therefore not become a reality everywhere, for understandable reasons. Yet this does not prove that it could not do so. Here too it becomes clear how difficult it is to see and judge "Anthroposophy" correctly. It is comprehensible and necessary to see Anthroposophy in the light of the doctrine of faith as a whole— in which light it must appear as an erroneous teaching—but it is also possible and necessary to reflect on the fact that, as a "science of experience," Anthroposophy is a many-layered phenomenon that produces many fruitful outcomes in life. After these remarks, I can now continue with my narrative.

My "yes" to Anthroposophy, my belief in it, and my enthusiasm for it were based above all in what can be called anthroposophical practice and the anthroposophical method. Everything Anthroposophy provides, through Rudolf Steiner himself or through his students, is directed towards the reader's or listener's own thinking. It does not provide any dogmas that are to be accepted upon authority, without being tested. Even its ideas about the supreme being are developed and communicated in such a way that the person who follows and accepts them is someone who "has knowledge" himself. To take the supreme example, the fact that Jesus Christ freed us by his blood from the curse of original sin was something that I came to understand through its proclamation in Anthroposophy—to the extent that one can speak of "understanding" this. Even this knowledge is self-evidently, at the deepest level, a faith. Yet the word "knowledge" is not wrong: it was through pure or mere thinking that I arrived at the certainty of faith. It was the same with everything concerning essential matters. The world teems with appearances and beings. To listen to their existence, their effects, and the way they work together with each other, in a way that is both well-structured and awakens knowledge, can be inexpressibly fruitful. Catholicism stands, works, and bears witness to itself in a world that must be taken as a whole. There is no such thing as a Catholic natural science that could be conceptually and methodologically deduced from theology. There is no Catholic science of the nature of rock strata, of the life of plants, of the peculiarities and distinguishing features of animals, of the stars, of the sun, of the moon; there is only one, universal natural science. But from Anthroposophy one can find out enormously productive things about how beings are at work in all of nature's realms, and how those realms are constituted. The most important physicists of the age leave a "free space" for the divine spirit in their world-picture. Those who testify to the divine spirit, and communicate it, speak only of this spirit, only of the religious and ethical world, without setting out how it enters into the material world. Anthroposophy, however, speaks of a living connection between spirit and matter, between God and world, between the hierarchies and nature. It can thus, if I can put it like this, help to overcome practical deism. For its teachings are not only teachings, or rather they are not really teachings at all, but are stimuli and forces. They unleash in the person who actually opens himself up to them, and not just as a fellow traveler, capacities and achievements that previously slumbered, but that can be very present, even if they do not yet have to be Christian and even if they certainly never become churchly. Serious reading of Rudolf Steiner's books and lectures can nourish the being of the reader, just as Thomas a Kempis's *Imitatio Christi* can nourish one's being more than any doctrine, even if for a quite different type of person than the anthroposophist.

Practice and method, however, also determine anthroposophical life quite directly. I have quoted the first exercise from the book *Knowledge of the Higher Worlds*. This is followed by a series of further exercises that serve the natural environment, relations to one's fellow men, and ethical and spiritual perfection.

Devotion and concentration are the first tasks, at the beginning of the training. The "spiritual student," i.e., the person who strives towards the essential, is to learn, for example, to look at himself "as if he were a stranger." He is to rise above his personal wishes, habits, and truisms, and to acquire an awareness of what would be important to him if his situation in life were quite different—and not only to him, but to everyone. Anyone who carries out this exercise is able in the course of time both to overcome self-seeking and also to achieve insight into his own sins. The expression "to look at oneself as a stranger" sounds much more harmless and non-committal than it really turns out to be for anyone who performs the exercise suggested. If I look at myself "as a stranger," then that is the end of all vanity, of all overvaluing myself, and of all purely personal pre-tensions. Moreover, this exercise prompts us to see ourselves with the eyes of our guardian angel and of Jesus Christ himself—and what sort of a picture do we get then? The exercise is, among other things, a preparation for repentance and penitence, which the "spir-itual student," when he follows his course, experiences more fully than people usually do. That a deeper self-knowledge and knowl-edge of one's own being leads to a mortally terrifying, almost anni-hilating result, is written with utmost clarity in the book *Knowledge of the Higher Worlds*.

The content of one of the other exercises, for example, is to reflect upon the fact that ideas are forces, and that they are more essentially real than anything material and sensuously perceptible. Even this perhaps sounds obvious or, once again, harmless to the outsider. But through this exercise the materialism that habitually sits uncon-sciously, so to speak, in the basis of our being, is overcome. Here the organ for being and for spirit can be built up. Here, too, it is a ques-tion of a training or a preparatory training in what is called *faith* in Christianity, but that is not described and named as such in anthro-posophical instruction. Our priests appeal to faith essentially by portraying the objects of faith; anthroposophical instruction does not *talk* of faith, and still less of its objects, but it helps to build up the *organ* with which those objects of faith can be perceived and entered into. Yet it deals, as has been said, not only with fields and with facts that are discussed by theology, but also with the world as a whole, and first of all, methodically, with facts about nature, which for people today is of course what they encounter first, and behind which are hidden the effects of spirit and of spirits.

Even someone who does not attain to the summit to which these anthroposophical exercises are intended to lead nevertheless gains richly from Anthroposophy, depending on how seriously he takes it. The smallest serious striving can be significant; the mere attempt actually to concentrate is already a fight against the spirit of distrac-tion, to which we are so terribly subject today; and for many people the anthroposophical method "without preconceptions" is the only one they are at first capable of following. It can certainly be said that there are plenty of devotional exercises in the Church, but it cannot be said that churchly practices of devotion are readily accessible to all our contemporaries. In those years, an image of the Mother of God, for example, or an hour of devout meditation in church, the stations of the cross, or a reliquary, did not signify anything that could actually be named. True, through the image of holy Mary one could seek to breathe in purity; I was quite willing to accept that some people might need an hour of devout meditation; the stations of the cross recalled old and pious times or reminded me of the artists who had fashioned them; and the reliquary (in Fritzlar or in Nuremberg) was to be venerated for the sake of art and history. Nothing that directly obligated me here and now, however, resulted from any of these. It was Anthroposophy that kept me going when practicing devotion, which is a precondition of living participation in the Church. I began from the start over and over again, and never noticed any progress; and I read over and over again the guiding words that called on me to have trust that none of my work was in vain, and that even if I had given up a hundred times, I should strive for confidence, and that the hundred and first time it might work and I might achieve what I was striving for. What I owe to Anthroposophy here, and what is in this respect essential in Anthroposophy, must not be underestimated.

Second, I might mention that the anthroposophical picture of history, as a picture of the whole of human history, is of a unique grandeur and unity. All the great currents of the pre-Christian and Christian eras have recognizably meaningful places within it. Since details would exceed the framework of this book, perhaps the following comparison may at least indicate what I mean in a general way. Just as a harmony of the gospels has been produced from the four gospels, and the life of Jesus described by fitting the parts together, so in the anthroposophical picture of history the "parts" of human history, e.g., Buddhism, Chinese culture, Islam, have been arranged into a meaningful structure by means of a vision of the whole. The anthroposophical picture of history can be compared to the biography of a human being, which portrays the development of a single being, not by putting together individual traits and individual experiences, but by grasping the core in the ways in which it is expressed and the ways in which it changes. Anyone who lives within this picture of history knows and feels himself to be an organic part of a powerful, human-divine stream of becoming. This can powerfully further one's whole feeling of life, one's comprehension of the meaning of life, and the strength to strive for what is right in one's own station in life.

It is true that in this picture of history, which represents human development as the history of consciousness, there is the danger that earlier periods will be looked back upon from the perspective of later ones as belonging to a "stage" of consciousness that has been overcome and is no longer appropriate. Earlier "states of consciousness" are held, strictly speaking, to be almost unintelligible; the greatest figures, such as for example the legendary Zarathustra or the prophet Moses, thus become pioneers of the current state of humanity, but for people today they have nothing to say that can stand without qualification. From our current standpoint we are (or we think we are) capable of judging as an adult judges the achievements of a child. What awakens reverence from one point of view threatens from another to destroy it. How can anyone who regards the Psalms of David as the sign of an earlier "stage of consciousness"—one that now lies far behind us—unreservedly plead: "Out of the depths have I cried unto thee, O Lord"?

But every figure who prepares the way for the "science of spirit" is fully and unreservedly revered within the anthroposophical picture of history. This includes, above all, Goethe—whose natural science and whose methods were directly followed by Rudolf Steiner. Here it is not so much a matter of celebrating Goethe as a great poet, as it is of continuing his way of practicing botany or zoology. Just as Goethe sought the "archetypal plant," and found it in the garden in Palermo, one could almost describe this as the beginning of the anthroposophical method of gaining knowledge. It is with profound justice that the headquarters of anthroposophical life in Dornach near Basel is named after Goethe, and a great portion of Rudolf Steiner's work is devoted to Goethe's natural science. Steiner even wrote an "epistemology of Goethe's worldview," a very fruitful book, which gave me essential assistance in overcoming my doubt and in believing in the power of insight. I have also been deeply occupied with Goethe, over and over again, in the course of the years. The little volume I was able to write on him in 1943–1944 was long in the making, and would not have been possible without the stimulus and insights provided by Anthroposophy. I would like just to add here that Anthroposophy teaches us to regard all human testimony—I am thinking of legends and tales here, in particular—in a living way. Anthroposophy forms the organ with which one can comprehend the language of images livingly ("The Star Money," "Little Red Riding-Hood," "Snow White"), and use it, if one has the necessary skill.

Third, let it be said that to Anthroposophy I owe a certain suprapersonal humanitarian thinking. Anthroposophy is by its nature entirely supra-national, and awakens each person's responsibility for everyone and for everything. This met a deep need within me. Yet a merely general appeal would never, in those years, have touched me. The structure of meaning that Anthroposophy represents, the possibility of understanding how, why, and that we all belong together, had a decisive effect on me. My decision to contribute to the work of the priesthood in the Christian Community was indeed connected to this.

In the priest I saw the person who must work in a supra-personal way. The priest is not to become involved in his own sufferings and joys, but to serve those who still are so involved. He is already to realize today that which would, at root, be everybody's task. Anthroposophical instruction also holds us to standing "above sympathy and antipathy," and to strive for the greatest possible intellectual and practical selflessness. Everything that binds us to a narrow circle of our own is to be overcome. If I can put it like this, *we are to become pure organs of the world-spirit.* This effort or stance is represented in an exemplary way in the activities of the priesthood; and its archetype is the governance of the God-man on earth, who never anywhere pursued ends of His own, but who was always in all things a servant. This is said in the spirit of that time, and is not intended as, say, an exhaustive description of the Catholic priesthood. Before I got to know Anthroposophy, I stood in the world without a goal or any counsel. Life seemed meaningless and cruel to me, and at bottom I could do nothing with it or with myself. Anthroposophy worked upon me like a magnet attracting me towards the good.

Although I had first to absorb it intellectually, and could only accept it very gradually, it worked upon the depths of my being—where receptivity can either slumber or be awakened, where it can either remain dead or come alive.

I wish also to state that I understood the priesthood of the Christian Community as a help to my approaching the goal of all-humanity. I thus sought, in striving for this vocation, to provide myself with a stimulus to my own maturation. In this there still remained something of an unexamined and unjustified self-centeredness, even though it can hardly be called dishonest. The distinctiveness of the priesthood as an office ought to serve the goal of the universal priesthood. That this can be made to happen in any and every situation, that it has no preconditions, nor can endure any, is something I have increasingly come to understand over the course of the years. At that time I was also still entirely under the spell of anthroposophical thinking, for which the "path of knowledge" was the "highest path," and for which only the anthroposophist could truly provide what the age demanded. Even though what I am about to say will be largely familiar to the Catholic reader, I should like to add this, and then support what I say: my decision to work as a priest showed that the process of spiritual healing had really begun. I knew, of course, that the priest's role chiefly concerned serving at the altar, and that the essential point about this was the transformation of the elements. Anyone who takes the decision to work as a priest must possess the belief that this transformation happens, that Christ becomes present in the substances of bread and wine, and that God's power can operate directly upon the physical world. Once I could begin to believe this, the damage wrought by doubt and godlessness was already in good part overcome, and a readiness to serve the good was awakened.

I grew up as a Protestant Christian, and later on (apart from a few years) I never lost my connection with Protestant life and writings. I had never heard a word breathed about *how* it might be possible that we could consume the body and blood of our Lord. Zwingli's doctrine, according to which Holy Communion was only an analogy, had never had any meaning for me. Even though my parents were originally of the Reformed faith, I grew up within Lutheran Christianity, and Martin Luther argued passionately and without reservation that "in, with, and under the species of bread" we received the Lord's body. The pastor who confirmed me taught this doctrine, if I remember rightly, and my Protestant friends all held the same view. But *how* does it come about that we consume the divine body? At school we learned of the *Religionsgespräch in Marburg* [The Marburg Dialogue on Religion] in which Martin Luther expounded his belief in the reality of the sacrament of the altar against Zwingli; but neither Luther's assertion nor the convictions of my own friends could persuade me that a mystery took place during Holy Communion. Here, too, Anthroposophy gave me decisive help. I had become incapable of faith, and the faith or experience of supremely graced people was something I could take only as personal lived testimony, not as a surety of the truth. Anthroposophy, however, makes possible certain insights into the fact *that* this "transformation" takes place, and into *how* it does so, even if, obviously, the original reason for grace will forever remain unfathomable. My participation in the Act of the Consecration of Man became increasingly fruitful, not only because my heart had become, to an unrecognizable degree, better prepared for it, but also because of certain theological ideas resulting from Anthroposophy. I cannot go into detail here, but I must bear witness to the fact as a whole.

The priesthood of the Christian Community, a community that was founded "directly out of the Spirit" and therefore possesses no connection to the tradition, obviously cannot be recognized as valid by Catholic theology. At that time, however, I arrived at the idea of the priesthood by way of secularization and materialism. So it is to be remarked upon as significant that my certainty was growing that there was a task justified before, and willed by, the "spirit world"—a task that consisted in selected people bringing about this transformation with Christ's help, people who created the preconditions for the body and blood of the Lord to be consumed. "Do this in memory of me": these words are taken in the Protestant world as a demand to consume bread and wine in the belief that, in them, one is receiving the body and blood of the Lord. Catholic theology, and indeed the Christian Community (to the extent that one can speak of a doctrine in its case), relate this above all to the action of Christ himself. Protestant thinking, so far as I know, mainly derives the law of *communion* from Christ's words, while Catholic thinking and the thinking that influences the Christian Community mainly derives the idea of *transubstantiation* from them.

In the Reformation period, even the idea of the priesthood itself was attacked. It was seen—at least so I was taught—as something that placed itself between God and the individual soul, as something that compromised human dignity and freedom, and that needed to be got rid of. Probably there are differing and changing views about this in Protestant Christianity too, as there are on so many topics. The first doctrines one learns in the early years of life usually become deep-seated, and we were taught that the greatness of Martin Luther's Reformation lay in the fact that he fought for us to enjoy "self-government before God." According to this idea, Catholic Christians, apart from the priesthood, lack any direct relationship to God, an idea that crops up again in the Protestant aversion to the veneration of Mary and the saints. Fourteen-year-old Protestant boys lacking much experience were thus "self-governing before God," and mature Catholic Christians (about whom, however, we never heard in any detail) stood in need of emancipation from their tutelage, an idea that harbors a certain absurdity, but that I implicitly believed as a boy, and that displayed what I must now call a certain Protestant arrogance.

This, then, was roughly where I was starting out from, and only much later, when the questions connected with it had begun to raise themselves in my own life, did I think that there was a half-truth, a lack of consistency, in the Protestant view. If one were to be consistent, then all believers who were "self-governing" would be able to make the "do this!" happen at any moment and under their own steam. But in Protestantism, too, there is an office and a set order. It seems to me to stand midway between the idea of the Catholic hierarchy and the idea that "there simply should not be any spiritual offices." In the Christian Community, on the other hand, it was possible even for the idea of the priesthood to be made plausible, and to recognize it as essential in wider contexts. Even though the Christian Community would never have come into existence without Anthroposophy, and although objections against a life

156

under priestly direction can always be made on the grounds of anthroposophical thinking, the priesthood in the Christian Community can be seen to be necessary to Anthroposophy as a whole and thus to the world as a whole. How long and how full of blessings is a path that begins in doubt and in denial of the sacrament, and ends in a resounding and unqualified Yes! Anyone who takes communion in the Christian Community is doing nothing less than taking the being of the God-man into his own heart, and anyone who works in it as a priest wishes to do nothing less than to lead the souls of human beings to this point.

I must also gratefully mention here that in the Christian Community a sense for liturgy is built up in everyone who is receptive to it. It can be unusually productive that here so much is consciously thought of and consciously performed. Why there are steps to the altar, why there are candles burning (in the rites of the Christian Community there are always exactly seven of them), why the Act of the Consecration of Man and the Holy Mass ought always to be celebrated at sunrise, why the altar is situated at the eastern end of the building, why the priest's vestments are as they are, why the priest stands now to the right of the altar, now to the left of it, and now at its center, and so on—all this takes us into the realm of insight, and I do not know whether I would ever have learned to offer up my heart if I had not first of all been able to *think* of the meaning of all this.

Perhaps it will seem to this or that reader as though I have not mentioned politics at all in this portrayal of my spiritual journey. Politics made up no part of my worldview in the years during which I was developing. (This would certainly occur all too soon—and dangerously so!) I did not even consider the Center Party, since it was an explicitly Catholic party; the parties of the "Right" had purely "patriotic," and thus earthly goals, so were also ruled out for me; and everything of the "Left," as I then thought without further ado, was dedicated to a "class" (the working class) wedded to materialism, and that could not be my concern either. Moreover, I was prevented from taking an interest in politics by the increasingly urgent question of what I would do with my life; and the idea of what was universally human, of what was priestly and above partisanship, created within me from an early stage (even if deep within my unconscious) a resistance to signing up for special interest groups, and a need to serve only what was highest and what was universal. As things stand today, not everyone can take this approach; there have to be people available to carry out the specific tasks of economic, national, and intellectual life (and who knows how much of an effort of will is required for those who work in the public sphere to do this?), but there may and indeed must also be people who see their task as lying on the level of intercession rather than in the world of external deeds, and everyone who works as a priest ought in my view to be above party politics, and not belong to any political party. Otherwise, how can he become close to those who belong to another party? Even in my childhood I thought (rather precociously, but already anticipating my later views) that a number of pastors in our city who had joined the Social Democratic Party in order to minister more effectively to the workers, had unfortunately thereby given up their non-partisanship. I would not have been able to put this in that way then, but what I mean by saying it now accords with the actual state of my soul at the time. And the "conservative" pastors provoked similar reflections on my part.

But the National Socialist Party of Germany, the Nazis, faced me with a serious political decision, one that pressed itself more and more on my field of vision at the beginning of the 1930s, and that claimed to be serving the interests of the whole. In truth, however, it was not difficult to decide, since three things sufficed to show me the spirit of the party, or rather the lack of spirit in it. First, the red election posters, full of hatred, that one saw everywhere in those years and were always very clearly inciting hatred of some kind, spoke a very clear language. They showed that it was by no means a question of the whole here, but rather of a party. Second, the samples I had read of Hitler's *Mein Kampf* and of Alfred Rosenberg's *Myth of the Twentieth Century* allowed me very readily to see what the spirit of the "party" was. There was no need for more detailed explanation, and I had neither the inclination, the strength, nor the time to explore them further. Third, at the beginning of the thirties

I once attended an election meeting that had hardly begun before it became very clear that inhuman or subhuman powers of the will were at work here. When, today, or (seen from the standpoint of that time) later, it was so often said that "one" could not have foreseen the spirit of what was to come from the beginning of the party's work, in its program and its promises, this seems to me to tell us more about the person speaking than about what the party's expressions of its will were at that time. Certainly, what later happened was still hidden at first. But the oak-tree is already present in the acorn, the predator in the charming little lion cub. The strength "to discern spirits" was too small; for if I only see what spirits are from their deeds, then I have not recognized the spirits, but only their expressions. In any case, there are a great many people alive among us who, each in his own way, recognized the pernicious nature of the National Socialists in time. Thank God that I was in no way an exception.

It is true that I should not have been content with understanding what the party's intentions were, but should have worked much harder than I did to counteract the darting tongues of the triumphant demons in a purely spiritual way on the level of prayer and meditation. The real responsibility does not fall on those naive people who were perhaps really able to do nothing other than be taken in by words, and to believe in a "good future for Germany." Instead, it falls precisely on all those who saw the approaching spirit of destruction. Now, I was at that time completely at the end of my tether, and hardly had any spare strength to put to use in the civil service in this way. I could thus have regarded myself as excused, given the state of my life as it was. But the more one's awareness of responsibility grows, the more all reservations disappear, and one must stand accused before the eternal even of those things for which there may perhaps have been sufficient excuses at the time. So, not: if my education had been different, if universities had been different, if other people had been different—but: if *I* had been different!

When the Nazis came to power through Hindenburg, and the Third Reich was founded, I shuddered. I still well remember the crossroads at which I found myself when I examined the meaning of the victory of the "Party" as if with eyes of the spirit. It was a day of heavy, menacing clouds, sunless, with high winds. Rapidly, I wrote down in verse what I "saw." Later, when there was the threat of house-to-house searches and there was no point in getting arrested for a couple of lines of verse, I destroyed them. But I still remember the line: *Those who can see, watch the spirits departing*; and the meaning of the line: that the good and divine spirits were leaving Germany and going away into exile somewhere abroad. Yes, they emigrated then, and others came in their place. There is not only a human emigration, but one of more than human spirits, too; and the latter is much more dangerous than the former. But the good spirits can also be called back—asked to come back, that is, not compelled to do so—and today it is up to those who are *bonae voluntati*, of good will, in what numbers and how powerfully they return…

One of my fellow workers in the Christian Community once said to me "there is spirit there, but we still need courage in the breast and marrow in the bones!" It is however precisely the nature of "courage" and "marrow" that they cannot be created by an act of conscious will, and that they can only be increased under certain conditions. One cannot demand of anyone: "you have a sense for colors: now add a sense for mathematics and for music to that!" I had to endure a split between my knowledge and my ability to act not only at that time but also later—again, a school of humility. How things were with me then can be shown with the help of two examples, a poem and an essay from 1933. The poem is called "Path of Fate," and reads as follows:

You know the heavy hammer blows of fate,
Often you have felt as though a form almost
hammered into shape by a divine hammer;
and do you seek in vain its deep meaning?

My friend, once long ago I saw
a silversmith in a sacred workshop.
With great strokes he shaped a golden chalice
that became more beautiful with each blow.

The wise smith's pure eyes beamed.
The image of the chalice stood before his soul,

the chalice that was to bear Christ's blood
and so bring heavenly nourishment to men.

Do you know the heavy hammer blows of fate?
Look then upon the gods, who wish to shape
you too into a chalice, and upon HIM
who wishes to fill you, as once he filled us.

Here one must bear in mind that the word *gods*, in anthroposophical parlance, means in many ways the same as angelic beings. It is subjective and distracting to object "but what *I* mean by *gods* is this and this." The word *gods*, in this poem, and, in many ways, in anthroposophical texts, is neither a figure of speech nor a sign of un-Christian thinking, and any outsider who wants to do justice to what has been communicated to him just has to accept that. It is another question whether it is felicitous to use in a different sense a word that already has a specific meaning.

The first essay I submitted to Dr Rittelmeyer had the title "The riddle of Konnersreuth in the light of a new case of 'stigmata.'" A Protestant doctor had conducted hypnotic experiments with a highly suggestible patient, and had suggested to her, at first without her knowledge, that she had wounds in the same places of her body as those of Jesus Christ at Golgotha. The signs of stigmata did indeed begin to appear; and in the course of several months, during which the experiments were continued, the "stigmata" also bled. Now the doctor published a book as a polemical tract against Catholicism that purported to demonstrate that Therese Neumann of Konnersreuth's stigmata were also the consequences of auto-suggestions and therefore of no religious significance. I recounted these facts and took a position on them. I acknowledged something that is not self-evident for a non-Catholic, which was that it is the height of blasphemy to carry out experiments concerning the most sacred thing on earth, namely, Christ's passion, irrespective of the fact that even a "successful" experiment of the kind mentioned demonstrated nothing at all about the religious authenticity or significance of Therese Neumann's stigmata. The essay culminated with the sentence "Christ's passion has become an accessory to psychological experiments; this is still more pernicious than any vivisection of animals, a *crime against the spirit*." If one compares the previously quoted poem with what has been said above and what was said in the essay, which provides an unequivocal confession of the Spirit and also of Christianity, with my 1930 study of Christian Morgenstern, which was still unclear about these matters, then progress can be seen—progress for which I have Anthroposophy and the Christian Community to thank, after God Himself. How dubious and mistrustful I felt towards all Catholicism at that time is admittedly also shown by the sentence preceding the one I have quoted: "It is impossible for modern intellectual life and past religiosity to meet in the concepts of suggestion and the unconscious." That is completely correct, but how bold, one-sided, short-sighted, and false it was to describe Catholicism as "past religiosity"! Within the Christian Community, however, this was an entirely usual way of seeing Catholicism. No one objected to the arrogant expression "past religiosity." We all considered that, both as a matter of objective spirituality and as a matter of personal spirituality, we stood on a higher "level."

Now, however, I must speak of the second point. I was never quite able to get rid of a small reservation with regard to Anthroposophy. Since this cannot be shown exhaustively, I will pick out one example that can serve to indicate what I mean.

Rudolf Steiner, whom I also considered, and still consider, to have saved my life, enjoyed a degree of veneration that not only induced gratitude and discipleship, but in many ways seemed to lead to a new, very hidden form of spiritual unfreedom. His words stood high above any doubt and were thus, among other things, taken by many people as ultimate solutions of questions that did not seem to me personally to have been solved. Over the course of the many years during which I belonged to the anthroposophical movement, I found over and over again that a conversation would come to an end when anyone said "this is what Rudolf Steiner said about it." Indeed, even asking questions could be seen as a sign of an insufficiently anthroposophical spirit. The task seemed to be to live out and work with the materials "provided" by Rudolf Steiner, without reservation. The friend who introduced me to the movement once said to me, "Everything that is done by anthroposophists is only putting into practice what was communicated to us or prepared for by Rudolf Steiner." Now, one should not hurry to laugh disrespectfully at this, since the value of every lesser person is shown in his knowing how to serve a greater.

Nevertheless, Rudolf Steiner's authority always seemed to me, for all this, to be somewhat oppressive, and I was never able to join in with or to champion anything I could not understand reasonably enough myself. Granted, this was not much, but who can be completely certain of or prove where his own knowledge begins and where he is only following someone else's lead and has not worked things out carefully enough in his own mind? Rudolf Steiner was and remained an authority to me, but I still had to walk my own spiritual path, and that could never be limited simply to agreeing with whatever Rudolf Steiner had said and written. I once said to one of the priests in the Christian Community, "I would rather make my own mistakes than be right by following Rudolf Steiner." Yet it was pointed out to me that this was a dangerous principle, and that whoever knew the truth must also follow it. If I had accepted this, my principle would also have been always to submit myself ever more fully to what Rudolf Steiner had provided, on the grounds of the great trust of which Steiner was deserving. It seems that I was never to become so capable of doing this as those who were then my friends. The Catholic church can indeed demand faith and obedience; in the anthroposophical movement, however, they are not appropriate.

It is understandable that the power of the soul that we call faith should have focused on the truth communicated by Rudolf Steiner. This is not what seems questionable to me. Instead, it is the fact that this faith is not *called* faith, but is too often wrongly called "knowledge." When does a person have knowledge in the full sense of the word? Rudolf Steiner explained this very precisely and in a way that can be methodically followed. As long as I stuck to the method, once I had understood it, all went well. But the authority of the "teacher" seemed to me not only to illuminate matters, but also to cast a shadow over them—not only to free us, but also to burden us.

When I wrote a short book about "imitation" many years later, one of the chief authorities of the Christian Community (whom I had not mentioned) said to me that without Rudolf Steiner "we" would not have known what imitation was. He was right, doubtless, for many of our friends: they did indeed not know that their imitation of Christ was not called forth by looking directly at the God-man, but through Rudolf Steiner. It was really Steiner whom they were imitating, not the master whom Steiner himself, as I know and must testify, confessed and represented as his own. Later, a wise man gave me the following advice: "One ought not to see Jesus Christ through Rudolf Steiner, but to see Rudolf Steiner through Jesus Christ." I was not able to do so in those years, but the need to do so must already have been alive within me. This alone seems to me to be a sufficient explanation for the fact that I did not so fully submit myself to Rudolf Steiner's authority as my friends did.

Everything in Anthroposophy which points beyond the territory of a history we can grasp or perceive was difficult for me, and even unacceptable. Anthroposophy portrayed the development of the earth from the earliest times, and so there is talk of the "evolution" of Saturn, the Sun, and the Moon. Rudolf Steiner even sets out in detail the fact that the hierarchical beings take part in these developments, as well as how they do so. If I could form for myself a *distant* idea of the distinction between thrones, cherubim, and seraphim, I had no personal experience whatever of them. I neither believed nor denied what Rudolf Steiner said about their deeds, but left it open, without engaging with the matter in more detail.

Difficulties also arose for me as a result of the strictly natural-scientific language in which Rudolf Steiner set out his insights so as to communicate them. At first I saw it as a sign of irreverence that Jesus Christ could be talked about here in a way that hid any personal movement behind a completely objective form of expression. Later, I understood Rudolf Steiner's style. It is not a good style, in the usual sense of that term. It has something of the power of erratic celestial objects, of meteorites or lightning—but nothing of the power of form in an ice crystal or in the dearness of a flower. Only someone who can supply the power of enlivening the material from their own heart can extract the intended nourishment for the soul from Steiner's often powerful oratory. But the little doubt within me never fell completely silent. "Is it permissible to speak of the most sublime events, in the face of which people ought to fall to their knees, in exactly the same sober way in which one would speak of stones, plants, and animals?" I accept that Rudolf Steiner expectantly calculated that the reverence I have referred to would emerge, but on the whole it does not seem to have emerged very much. There can be no dispute about this, only supposition. In the first place, no one can know what is happening in the heart of another; in the second, different people can mean different things by "sufficient reverence."

A not yet burning, but at least smoldering question was posed to me by the Act of the Consecration of Man. It was intended as a celebration of a mystery, as a divinely real and efficacious event, for which the human being provided only the site, not the final cause. Yet in many ways it was nevertheless regarded as something that we human beings had to perform. It was not accidental that we were supposed to celebrate it "as consciously as possible." I have often heard people speak of "stronger" or "weaker" Acts of the Consecration of Man, but not of, say, more or less beautiful Acts—and the "stronger" ones were those in which human strength had been more successfully applied. This has not been sufficiently well expressed, but I do not how to put it more satisfactorily. I myself was, in addition, told that my presence had "strengthened" the whole event. Still more than that, however, it was a matter of the priest's attitude. He too was called to celebrate the Act as consciously as possible, but if he should "fail" to do so, one ought to be able to trust that the "spirit world" would lend its assistance. But if there can be any question of *failure* at all, then one might ask *when* this occurs and when it does not, and how a human being is ever supposed to suffice here. Who brings about the transformation? The Christian Community's doctrine of the transformation picks up in the end from that of Catholic theology, but unfortunately without Catholic theology's consistency, and unfortunately not without disparaging Catholic teaching. The Christian Community has no firm doctrine, and demands from members only that they "affirm" its worship. But how many unreliable or erroneous ideas may yet remain within the heart of someone who "affirms the worship"?

Over the course of many years I was deeply concerned with and disturbed by the question of the forgiveness of sins, which I could not with the best will in the world resolve with the help of the resources present in anthroposophical thought or in the life of the Christian Community. According to anthroposophical teaching, man does not live only once on the earth, but repeatedly, and he creates his own future destiny by his conduct in his individual life. If he has taken guilt upon himself, then it cannot really be taken away from him. It necessarily has consequences, and it is part of the dignity of the human being that this is so. Forgiveness cannot remove responsibility for one's own actions. The human being who has awakened to himself—so I often heard it said—does not wish the consequences of his guilt to be taken away from him. He wishes to make reparation for them himself, in the *karma* that is to come. In the "confession" of the Christian Community, therefore, there is no absolution; the person making confession is merely left with some promising-sounding sayings, and I have never understood why he could not just say these to himself. How does this relate to the fact that the fifth petition in the Lord's prayer asks Him to "forgive us our trespasses, as we forgive those who trespass against us?" Indeed, what is it to be guilty of sin at all? Why are we guilty? And are we guilty before a divine being, or only, as it were, before ourselves?

All these questions are hard to master with the resources of Anthroposophy. Rudolf Steiner, for the reason given above, set out the development of mankind, of the earth, and of the world from its first beginnings without using the word "God" at all. He speaks only of the creative hierarchies. Can the human being derive from this a relationship with the "foundation of the world," as a relationship to a Thou? In Steiner's account much is said about the Fall into sin, but in a completely natural-scientific language, and in a way that can give the impression that the Fall was really a good thing for human beings, because it brought them freedom and independence. If that is really so, then there is, if one is consistent, nothing to regret about the consequences of original sin, since every seed always gives rise to more than itself. If the seed of sin "had to" be present, then it is hard to see how the consequences should not also have followed. The Church's teaching is that man could also have been independent and free during the temptation in paradise, without giving in to the influence of evil, and thus that the original sin at work in every mortal is damnable or at least regrettable, but in no way justifiable. But of this I never saw any sign in the anthroposophical intellectual heritage.

But on the other hand I sensed that there *must* be forgiveness, and that it must not only be possible to experience and believe it, but also to think it. How was it to be thought of? In his lecture series, Rudolf Steiner distinguishes between the objective and subjective "aspects" of guilt, and says that objective guilt (that which concerns the earth as a whole) has been removed by Christ, and that this is what forgiveness consists in; and subjective guilt, individual "karma," must be borne by the human being himself. I never fully understood this, nor did I ever find anyone who was able sufficiently to explain it or even to testify to his own experience of it. What is the use of ideas about forgiveness that are not linked to any experience of it? The idea of karma stands in the way of any experience of the forgiveness of sins, and easily misleads one into overvaluing the realm of human possibilities. And if I really develop myself in a higher and higher way, can I really make reparation for my guilt by my own efforts? Is there a normal level of human obligation that one can have or get back, so as to be happy with oneself? Today I would say that only where sin is seen and confessed without being minimized is there forgiveness. Only where man becomes nothing—and Rudolf Steiner also spoke about this elsewhere—does Christ come to dwell within him. I was unable to see this or to say that at that time, however. All I thought was that there *must* be forgiveness, real and unreserved forgiveness. It is promised to us, but how does it become a reality?

In his lectures on the gospel of Matthew, Rudolf Steiner said

> Just as it does not contradict the idea of karma if I give something to a poor person, so also does it not contradict the idea of karma if a person is relieved of his individual karma by a congregation. The congregation can bear the individual's lot with him. . . . If one wishes to call the congregation a "church," then the church lays on

itself the obligation of taking the individual's sins upon itself, in order to help him to bear his karma. It is not a question of what is called the "forgiveness of sins" today, but of a real bond, a taking of these sins upon oneself. And it is a matter of the congregation's taking this *consciously* upon itself.

Here we are quite close to the Church's doctrine of forgiveness. The "congregation," the church, is not an organization called into being by human will, but an organization founded and animated by Christ; and the "consciousness" of the congregation or church is precisely the consciousness of Christ, to whom we may say *Agnus dei, qui tollis peccata mundi, miserere nobis* ("Lamb of God, thou that takest away the sins of the world, have mercy on us"). What other sort of "consciousness" can a "congregation" have of itself?

Only much later did the second part of the fifth petition of the Lord's prayer become a key for me to the question of forgiveness. If I forgive a person who has done me wrong, I voluntarily, consciously, and completely renounce any consequence his guilt is to have for me, or could have for me in the future. By means of a spiritual decision, I transform his guilt into nothing. He is no longer to be obligated to me, and I myself do not wish there to be any further consequences from his guilt. Must I now, because there is a law of "karma," become, against my own will, the subject of a future reparation? As Rudolf Steiner put it, I "help to bear his karma." Every act of forgiveness, admittedly, means a "real bond," a "taking-upon-oneself" of sins, even in the case of people who do not reflect upon how forgiveness happens, but simply and honestly grant it.

So developed is human authority or human consciousness, that every Christian finds makes the discovery that he himself can forgive. The forgiveness our Father in heaven grants us, however, is no different *in principle*; that is, it is the cancellation of a debt. Just because this is the case, the fifth petition of the Lord's prayer provides the moral and legal connection between human and divine forgiveness. Christ has the authority, but also the will, to cancel debts. This is precisely what he "consciously" does. And just as God created the world out of nothing, so He can also return whatever He will to nothingness. The idea of "karma" transfers the notion of legality into a sphere that stands above all legal claims. "All things are possible with God." "For God so loved the world, that He gave His only begotten Son, that whosoever believeth in Him should not perish, but have everlasting life." One can never attain to the experience of the love of God by reflecting on it; but through the experience of the love of God one can indeed come to an altered sense of the possibilities of one's fate. I came to these ideas and experiences only late in my life. I had to discover them for myself, and it is not easy for an anthroposophist to discover something that Rudolf Steiner had not already thought of. Only what moves directly, visibly, and demonstrably in the direction of his own statements is easy, or, as it were, permitted.

It can seem strange to faithful Catholics that a person should have thought so searchingly and so long about something that Christ's revelation and the teaching of the Church so unambiguously provide. If, however, one lacks any living relationship to either of these, then thinking can assist, and sometimes has to do so. Experience, in my life, has always come after thinking. Even my entry into the Church was (much later) opened up for me by thinking; and many of my fellow Catholic Christians who have known something of my path have found it entirely felicitous that someone who has long been grown up should have reflected about everything they were used to living with, on the basis of what they had learned earlier in life…

I once rashly joined a course for the training of priests, and was then compelled to see that I was not suited to my chosen profession. An inauspicious period of transition followed, a hard school of humility, in which I first worked for some time as an assistant gardener, and then made various efforts to attain some earthly "profession." None of them were spoken for by any inner voice of mine, and the possibilities were alarmingly limited. The longest of these efforts was devoted to being a public librarian; but this profession had been incorporated into the "popular education" planned, recommended, and ever more fully realized by the leadership of the Third Reich. This did not sit comfortably with me, and in the long term I would have preferred to work in a purely commercial job than in this sort of secular "cultural" occupation. For a period of time I was the literature librarian at the public library at the City Book Halls in Leipzig; but then the director explained to me that I was "not the right type." He was certainly right in this, but he still brought difficulties and distress into my life.

At that time a kind of employment as an author became possible. I had compiled a book for a doctor out of a large stock of papers, lectures, and essays. It set out what he had intended in a systematic way, something he did not feel in a position to do himself. I was able, as I have already mentioned, to visit Martin Rade, who was then already more than eighty years old, and he threw open to me, youthful as he then still was, his old periodical, the *Christliche Welt* (Christian World), which had under his editorship been of no little significance in the Protestant world for half a century. He smoothed the way for me to meet a respected editor in Berlin, who gave me help and who suggested that with my "wealth of ideas" I would easily be able to make a "literary existence" for myself. If I had indeed had a "wealth of ideas," that might have been possible. Two things, however, stood in the way of exploiting this "wealth" correctly in the sense meant by the editor. The first was the fact that I was never the independent master of my own mind and its "ideas," but was reliant on notions whose extremely small breadth I was not able by my own willpower to enlarge (despite the appearance of "wealth"). The second was that the idea of working as a priest (in the sense mentioned) was still alive within me, and this idea prohibited me from "writing" for money. My "existence" could never be based on "literary abilities." Journalism was completely contrary to my nature, and the very idea of *having* to write drove away any good ideas I might otherwise have been able to come by.

At the end of 1936, Karl Vötterle, the founder and proprietor of the Bärenreiter company in Kassel, asked me to come and work with him. I took up the invitation and found a job in his company that suited my talents and abilities. It neither demanded nor permitted any more writing than I was able to provide, and it was a kind of writing that corresponded to my idea of a "universal priesthood." There I was able to use many of my own not altogether easy experiences for my own and others' benefit.

8

A Critical Period

WHEN I BEGAN WORK AT THE BÄRENREITER COMPANY on January 1, 1937, there had already no longer been an Anthroposophical Society in Germany for more than a year. At the end of 1935, it had been banned by the Gestapo. The ban was consistent on the part of those in power and who controlled us. The Anthroposophical Society supported a concern that was in principle working against the will of the Third Reich, and that could therefore not be tolerated by that regime. This much can be said as an overview; but what was expressed by the ban itself? It was not only the Anthroposophical Society that was prohibited, but any movement that wished to serve the good. It was only a matter of time, and at the end of the Third Reich only the large churches were left, since those in power did not dare touch them during the war. Every thoughtful person experienced the horrors of that period in his own way. For each, the prohibition of what was especially sacred to him was perhaps the sign that spoke most clearly of them. That was how I experienced the ban on the Anthroposophical Society at the time, and it was the Society alone which concerned me.

However terrible the ban objectively was, then—and even those who had recognized the "little seed" of the Third Reich in time had no intimation of what the fully grown "plant" would be like—it did not affect me too drastically in a personal capacity. I had always had a personal or spiritual relationship to Rudolf Steiner himself rather than to the Society as such. In those years I had to deal with so many personal difficulties that I was unable to do anything external for Anthroposophy at all. Nevertheless, Anthroposophy was my spiritual homeland, the source of my recovery, the provider of my goals in life. How was it possible that I was able to receive the victory of the Third Reich over the Anthroposophical Society without a tremor?

With respect to what I am about to say, it should be borne in mind that ideas are often brought into the light of day only with great effort, and that it is often only later that something which has already been at work in an earlier period becomes completely conscious. Anyone who attentively searches retrospectively through his life will always find many things that were at work then, but can only later be adequately put into words. Anyone who seeks to provide reasons drawn from later experience for his earlier behavior may be in error, but is not necessarily so. It can happen that it is only at a later period that the ideas which previously had an effect on him can be grasped. A friend of mine, a Protestant theologian, once wrote to me later, on the subject of my conversion, to say that, in the end, reasons could be given for anything, and that in the case of my conversion it was at bottom not really about "reasons." What I had told him showed him that there was a personal necessity involved, and that was enough.

This idea has something captivating about it, but also something dangerously seductive. There is within it the view that the conscious life of the person arises essentially from the unconscious. If what my friend thought were true, then we would, if we were being consistent, not need to reflect any further on our worldviews and professions of faith, but simply listen to the needs rising up from the unconscious. Human spiritual life can only prosper, however, if it is given certainty that it is decisive or that it can be so, and my friend would certainly have rejected the idea that he was a Protestant Christian only because it accorded with his "needs." For a great deal of what is called conscious spiritual life, such an objection is certainly correct. I myself know only too well how often people erroneously declare that this or that idea is the motive for their action, when in reality they are led by another motive of which they are not conscious. Anyone who develops a sense for when this is the case and when it is not, however, and under what conditions one may speak of a conscious decision or of its opposite, is able to give the life of ideas its correct weight in each case. He can know in his own case whether he "thinks" something because he "had to," or whether he is acting in accordance with something he has thought, whether before or afterwards. I did not "have to" convert because of "needs" that had come to me from somewhere (from where, after all?) in some way (how and by what means, after all?). I simply had to do it because I thought it was right. More of this later, however.

It was often put to me later from the anthroposophical side, too, that I had been a victim of my own unconscious. According to this line of argument, I had fallen prey to the impulses of a "previous incarnation"; I had carried unawares a need within me to submit myself to an authority; I had lacked the strength to make conscious progress and had been ruled by a longing for a religiosity more in accordance with my feelings. Such ideas are to be explained by discouragement and disappointment over the step I had taken. They by-pass the reality. There *is* freedom in spiritual decisions; but the person who is making those decisions stands alone, at first.

People are certainly not free in all the ways they think they are. For example, almost everyone belongs to the confession and to the church into which they were born or in which they were brought up, and are influenced by motivations that stem from their own early years. But anyone who, in whatever way, makes a decision reflectively, after excluding other possibilities, and for reasons that are consciously understood, is not a "victim of the unconscious." Moreover, it is possible that, as has been said, the ideas that have influenced him become comprehensible only later. I am attempting, therefore, with the help of a clarity I acquired only later, to portray something I would not have been able to express so clearly during those years themselves.

When depicting my schooldays and my further studies, I discussed the secularization and fragmentation of intellectual and spiritual life, and its consequences. The anthroposophical worldview helped me to begin, at least in principle, to overcome the damage inflicted then. As far as the outside world was concerned, I was in the same position I had always been in—neither Anthroposophy nor I myself had been able to change that—but this became bearable, because I had found a place and a source from which and with whose help I could gather meaning and redemption in an apparently meaningless and ruinous world. This is connected to the fundamental question: for what reasons did Rudolf Steiner found, develop, and champion Anthroposophy?

Without going into detailed proofs, I would like to suggest that he did it not for his own sake, but for that of the world. The situation in which humanity found itself must have seemed to him so menacing and dangerous, so close to the abyss, that he wished to do whatever he could to rescue it. The Catholic reader, and certainly the Protestant reader, too, may ask here why he did not therefore turn to Christianity. Would this not have been a more obvious way than working within a group of people who had fallen away from tradition? Many people, too, who are only familiar with fragments of the anthroposophical intellectual heritage and of the life story of its creator, understandably doubt whether a truly Christian life was intended here. Rudolf Steiner once contended appreciatively for Friedrich Nietzsche and Ernst Haeckel, and admitted to being a monist. Did he really intend, through Anthroposophy, to serve Christ? It is hardly possible for an outsider adequately to answer the question, but it is also very difficult for a participant to provide clarity here. I will do what I can.

As far as I can discover, Rudolf Steiner was of the opinion that Christian and church life was suffering from an irresistible loss of its substance, was incapable of recovery, and was certainly heading towards its demise. The believing Christian will be astonished at this, and will regard the idea as being absurd and rash. Here, however, we are not concerned with what outsiders think or with, say, what the course of history has or has not shown, but with what Anthroposophy was when it began; and when it began it can only in my view have been with the idea that has been mentioned. Amid an ever more unspiritual and unbelieving world, the "science of spirit" was to work towards rescuing and benefiting the whole human race, including rescuing Christianity (but not the Church!). Since Rudolf Steiner evidently expected nothing from the Church's Christianity in any of the traditional confessions, he left the Church and everything Christian that came from history to one side, and turned towards groups of people and towards a disposition that had literally nothing to do with historical Christianity. What he did in the life of spirit can be compared to what a farmer does when he leaves fields whose soil has been exhausted and begins all over again in virgin soil. He left the historical forms of Christianity behind not out of thoughtlessness, but as a result of a fully conscious judgment, so as to turn towards groups that seemed to offer "untilled territory" and could precisely for this reason make a decisive contribution to saving humanity. Thus far I believe that those with whom I previously shared a worldview are still in agreement with me. The enthusiasm that the true anthroposophist carries within himself derives from belief in the significance of the anthroposophical spirit. It is a bad anthroposophist who does not wish to serve the anthroposophical movement with all the strength at his disposal, but treats it merely as a source of assistance in his own life. Two different judgments can be made, however, about the history of the movement.

Anyone who shares and keeps to the presuppositions outlined above about the origin and meaning of Anthroposophy, and anyone who is still, amid all conditions, even those pertaining today, of the opinion that "everything else contains the seeds of death, only Anthroposophy unleashes the forces of the future," will regard service in Anthroposophy and from Anthroposophy and for Anthroposophy as the most important thing on earth. He will remain an anthroposophist, however the face of the world might change, and whatever it might come to show as it continues. Anthroposophy is for him a stimulus for the centuries, if not for the millennia—and the less contemporary humankind accepts Anthroposophy, the more he regards himself as a pioneer of the future.

Anyone, however, who notices the changes in the face of the earth and thinks, on the one hand, of the chaos into which the world has fallen despite the "saving" impulse of Anthroposophy, and, on the other, of the world's inability to open itself to Anthroposophy—as well as anyone who notices the deepening of the whole life of the Church—may come to a different conclusion. For anthroposophical life does not wish to be seen only in accordance with its own idea of itself, but also as a reality.

In my view, when Anthroposophy came into being at the start of the twentieth century it was by no means so that a few hundred, or a few thousand, or tens of thousands of *people* should personally learn to lead better and more spirit-filled lives, but so that the endangered *West*, and, indeed, the endangered *world* should be saved at the last minute. A person with a wider view of the situation later told me: "The world war would not have broken out if the Anthroposophical Society had reached the heights it envisaged reaching." The idea is as justified as that which is repeatedly emphasized in the Catholic church today, that peace would come about and would continue if we were able to pray hard enough for it. Rudolf Steiner, however, who always appealed in principle to people's freedom, and must have expected the results mentioned from his "movement," himself noted in a lecture he gave in 1917 or 1918 on the "changed times" that human beings had already lost the power to choose what would happen in history on a large scale. This loss must, so far as I can see, have happened between the beginning of the century and the year when he gave the lecture. But if that is the case, then Anthroposophy has either never acquired the world significance it envisaged having, or has lost it once again. It is by no means a matter here of the deeds or omissions of any individual persons. I myself got to know many high-ranking anthroposophists, and am in no danger of undervaluing them (or the many experiences that I had myself) simply in order to make points against the movement.

What is said here is meant *supra*-personally. I did not seek out the question touched on here, and dealing with it has cost me a great deal of pain. In the years that I am presently recounting I shuddered even to think of ideas such as these, but they were nevertheless working away within me. I can also explain what I mean from another point of view.

Before I ever possessed the slightest relationship to the Catholic church, I was of the opinion that when seen as a whole there were only two great powers in the present Western world that were capable of having a deeper effect, namely the anthroposophical movement and the Catholic church. The expression "great power" here is not a quantitative one, but an ideal one, meant as a matter of principle, for obviously the position within the world held by the Catholic church, consisting as it does of hundreds of millions of people right across the globe, is outwardly quite different from that of the anthroposophical movement, which comprised only some thousands. Here it is a question of the spiritual force that flows into life by means of mystery alone. By giving up a mystery-based worship, the non-Catholic world had, I believed, largely or entirely lost this force. I had nothing to do with the non-Catholic Christian world, so far as seeking for a worldview went. My only connection with it was through friends and sympathizers, none of whom was, however, in any position to offer any help to me in solving the central questions of my life. The anthroposophical movement, however, is—and this I must say even today—not without a force of mystery. At that time this force seemed to me to be of a unique strength; that is, I did not then dare to think about the doubts that I am now expressing and that were nevertheless already at work within me. As far as my conscious life comes into consideration, it was from the anthroposophical movement alone that I expected any benefit to come for the future. The good things it brought into my life, the clarity and steadiness it had brought me, the good it had also released within me, rests (and I do not know any other way of putting this) not on personal satisfaction, but essentially on the belief that the spirit of salvation is objectively given in Anthroposophy, and that I was permitted to participate in this spirit. What I did and wished to do, with my limited strength, and in a limited field of action, was not to serve particular people, but the whole. The consciousness of being permitted to serve the whole was the main source of and basis for personal satisfaction.

It was certainly neither soon nor rapidly, and certainly not easily, that doubts about the *world* significance of the anthroposophical impulse entered me. Did not we few thousand people stand amid a world whose progress on the whole showed itself entirely unaffected by a movement that was supposed to save the world? Could one really, amid Adolf Hitler's Reich, and during the sinister and ungodly course of the Second World War—which appeared, as it unfolded, to be a law unto itself—still believe that service to Anthroposophy was going to save the world? If estimated by its actual objective effects, rather than its intellectual content, its task, or by that which provided blessing in individual cases, the anthroposophical impulse seemed to me more likely to save *individuals* than to save the *world*. This was a consequential failure, in which I myself(!) had a part, and it seemed irrefutably to be the case. Thus, a burdensome sacrifice came gradually to replace enthusiasm and belief. But this does not express my point adequately. The words retrospectively convey what I felt during those years in the bottom of my heart, but could not yet become fully aware of. How, though, was the "failure" of the anthroposophical movement to be remedied? Be mindful that I am recounting the experiences I had then with the words I have now.

This does not mean that I was illustrating the limitations of the anthroposophical movement in the light of the Church's dogma, for I had nothing at all to do with dogma at that time. It means that today I am aware of what was then at work within me, but was not yet completely conscious. Anthroposophy stands opposed to every form of dogmatically determinate Christianity by virtue of its foundational "how": its idea of freedom (there will be more to say about this later). At that time, however, I believed dogmatic Christianity, especially Catholic Christianity, to be obsolete, and not worth any attention. The reader is also not to expect that I shall bring forward here the desired objections to Anthroposophy. I must mention those that filled *me*, the anthroposophist, *at that time*—objections that sprang *only* from the nature of the case itself and *my* own world-picture at that time.

Rudolf Steiner set an unusually high degree of importance on human freedom, and refrained from any sort of attempt to sweep people along. He placed absolutely no obligations on his readers and listeners, only ever spoke of possibilities and tasks, and presented Anthroposophy to people as a "science of spirit." He left it completely up to them what consequences they wanted to draw from this. Within anthroposophical life there is no sort of "ought," not even in respect of any of the divine commandments. Probably the most important of the books Rudolf Steiner published in his pre-anthroposophical period bears the title *The Philosophy of Free-*

dom, and puts forward the following idea: "the individual must acquire his concepts through his own intuition." Against any sort of obedience, Steiner appeals to the "moral imagination" of the individual person, describing thus one of his supreme values, and one that negates any form of authority. Even the whole of the later, authentically anthroposophical, work is directed to the independent human being who decides only on his own grounds. How many people, however, or how few, possess the strength for this "moral imagination" in the grand style? How many or how few are, in the grand style, capable of acquiring concepts for themselves "by means of intuition"? I believe that Rudolf Steiner greatly overestimated the strength of human beings as it currently stands, apart from a few exceptions. Or did Rudolf Steiner perhaps mean something less significant than I am assuming? Have "our" achievements really matched his expectations and the demands of the age?

What is more, Rudolf Steiner developed Anthroposophy from modern natural science. For reasons already explained, he started out from the secular science of the second half of the nineteenth century. It was from just this science that the "science of spirit" was to be developed. Rudolf Steiner's own words were typically of a scientific character; he spoke in a sober and objective way even about the most sublime facts and beings of the religious and spiritual life, just as if he were speaking about questions of biology or physics. In his mouth, the expression "the Christ-impulse" was without question a solemn, deep, and serious one. Is it surprising, however, that this expression—it is only one example of many—impeded many people from entering into a personal relationship with Christ, rather than awakening such a relationship? My children, for example, do not have a father-impulse or a mother-impulse or a teacher-impulse in their lives; they have a father and a mother and have teachers. The expression "Christ-impulse" harbors the danger of its being misunderstood in a neutral sense. No one prays to an "impulse," but only to a person.

It is symptomatic—and this too is just one example—that in anthroposophical circles the following saying of Rudolf Steiner's is often used as a "grace" at table:

The plants germinate in the night of earth.
The stems and leaves shoot up through the power of the air;
The fruits ripen from the power of the sun.
So the soul germinates in the shrine of the heart.
The power of the spirit springs up in the light of the world.
The strength of the human being ripens in God's radiance.

The inner being of the person, as to its essential nature, does not, however germinate, spring up, and ripen, as a plant does in outward nature. It goes through tests, sufferings, and transformations which are absent from these lines. Rudolf Steiner knew this better than most people, of course. A great creative spirit expresses itself in many ways, and one would do him an injustice if one were to seek the essence of his thought in the least of his expressions. But the fact that this saying has achieved such wide dissemination seems to me a sign of the way that Anthroposophy has largely been received—a way that is too natural-scientific, and not sufficiently religious and Christian. What I did not dare to think for many years, and what I would perhaps never have dared to think on my own, was once expressed to me by someone with an overview of the movement in the following words: "the whole of Anthroposophy was launched on moral credit, but the loan has never been paid back."

Furthermore, Rudolf Steiner essentially championed and invoked "spirit" and the "spiritual," emphasized the significance of "consciousness," and appealed to human "thinking" alone. The figure and the works of Christ did indeed play the principal role in the world-picture he developed, but they can all too easily (although this too is not developed explicitly enough) become components of human thought, because they are not put forward as being authoritatively obligating. In the struggle against the unspiritual and the anti-spiritual elements of our age, the "spiritual" as such was often taken as something sufficiently essential, and as something definitively Christian. It is indeed *very* important that materialism be not only "refuted," but overcome, by forming an organ for the spiritual; no one, however, becomes a Christian by means of "the contents of consciousness"—even the most "spiritual" among us—but by means of their fundamental stance towards life (1 Corinthians 13). The "spiritual" is not the purpose and the goal, but a means. I shall never forget the look of surprise on the face of someone who was a well-known anthroposophist, not just any old follower, when I said to him, "but the spiritual is not the Christian." According to the will of its creator, however, the anthroposophical movement was supposed to be Christian. Perhaps the movement would have been stronger if Rudolf Steiner had said this more strongly.

Thus, it was not really possible wholly to banish the risk that the anthroposophical impulse might often be taken in the sense of what the Church would have to describe as "self-redemption," even where, and indeed precisely where, this was of course not its conscious intention. Wherever such a strong appeal is made to human responsibility and to the development of thinking, wherever the significance of human consciousness and of human insight is so strongly expounded, it is easy for people to overestimate their capacities, especially when they are not really required or invited to pray, but only to meditate. When the Anthroposophical Society was banned in Germany, while the Waldorf schools it had set up nevertheless continued, one of the teachers once said to me enthusiastically and triumphantly that "they can't touch us, because we (the teachers) have stuck so close together!" I was deeply horrified by the critique of the Anthroposophical Society here expressed, but still more by the inappropriateness of such a remark. To this man, human achievement was everything, trial and grace nothing, even though he quite certainly (I knew him well) wished to serve the "Christ-impulse." But this did not last: the Waldorf schools were banned too. True, I do not know whether, and if so how, the teacher I mention managed to solve the problem once that had happened. This anecdote is an example of the risk of "self-redemption" that Anthroposophy poses. It must be testified, however, that Rudolf Steiner strongly, if seldom, emphasizes the importance of grace (in the usual sense in which the Church uses the word). But words such as grace were drowned out in his work as a whole by other, louder ones. It is no wonder they often failed to be heard and remained without effect.

The "failure" of the "movement" as a whole, however, as far as I can make out, goes back to the fact that Rudolf Steiner appealed to people who were far removed from the historical Christianity of tradition. These people were not guided in any way to seek out those values which were without question still very much alive in the churches, even if they were not sufficiently emphasized, but were able, indeed compelled, instead to seek the development that was to come as the only thing that mattered. How could the seriousness of the core Christian attitude become real for all these people when it was introduced only with preparatory and optional expressions, and when historical Christianity was, one can truly say, undervalued? Some of the leading spirits embodied this seriousness in a way that instilled respect and served as an example to many. Christian Morgenstern, Michael Bauer, and Friedrich Rittelmeyer were a venerable triad, to whom I shall always look up. But every anthroposophist will admit even today that they were exceptions. Thus, the causes of the movement's eventual fate lay not in the kernel of its doctrine but in the kernel of the movement. This fate was in many respects questionable (by which I do not intend *any kind* of personal criticism of other people). I could support this judgment, since, as a member of the Anthroposophical Society, I aware of much, if not of everything, that was going on. Let the outsider understand, however, that I do not wish to speak publicly about events that occurred in secret... The following, however, may be mentioned, since it happened in plain view of the world, and raised questions, to my knowledge, in many people's minds.

Rudolf Steiner's first collaborator, and his literary executor, was Marie von Sivers. She was not only a member of the board of the Anthroposophical Society, but was also the editor of the subsequent publications of Rudolf Steiner's works. She often wrote prefaces to these works, prefaces that, when I had the chance to read them, I considered highly questionable. They were purely intellectualistic, and in open contradiction of the spirit of Rudolf Steiner's own work. I often found it incomprehensible that a person who had been so closely associated with Rudolf Steiner could be so unspiritual. Only later did I dare to see in this a sign of the spirit of the movement itself. For the ways in which Marie Steiner (who died early in 1949) acted, and the ways in which she expressed herself, manifest something that is more than merely personal. I never heard in the anthroposophical movement, which so strongly emphasizes freedom, any objection to Marie Steiner's "spirituality," so she must have been approved of, and people must on the whole have been in solidarity with her.

In the preface to the lecture series on Luke's gospel we read that

> the precious images and parables of the gospel of Luke were indeed given as the content of faith and as sustenance for the souls who were obliged obediently to subject themselves to authority, and the magic of the art inspired by them poured warmth and devotion into their hearts. But direct study of the gospels was forbidden to lay people. The breaking of this command or of any dictum of faith dictated by dogma was heresy.

Now, anyone who can write like this has assuredly failed to understand the history of the Church, and is obviously speaking not from their own knowledge, but as a champion of the work of Rudolf Steiner, as he understood it. What, incidentally, is "a dictum of faith dictated by dogma"?

The preface to the lecture series on the gospel of Matthew brings with it the remark that

> even if European humanity went astray in its thousand-year-long unfreedom and blindedness of spirit [one can hardly believe one's eyes reading this sort of thing—*Author*] under the impact of Church and academic dogmas [!], and even if it was pushed away from the divine freedom-bringer and redeemer of mankind [!]; even if it was dead in spirit and soul [!], it longed for the emancipating act that would lift the stone from the tomb for the redeeming word that would transform its fetters into rays of light [!].

In the preface to the series on John's gospel Marie Steiner speaks of the origins of the Christian Community in the following way:

> A number of theologians came to Rudolf Steiner and said "our churches are withering away; our seminaries are not giving us anything we can offer as the bread of life to hungry souls. You alone can help us. Will you give us the things that will make us able to help others in the exercise of our offices? Otherwise we must give up our posts in the religious orders."

And Rudolf Steiner gave them what they asked for: the key to the gospels, to the living Christ, the word that became the Act of Consecration. He said to them: "You asked me for something you could offer to those who are not strong enough to work through the science of spirit or for spiritual communion. You wish in this way to lead them to the source of knowledge that makes people awake and free and fully conscious, in accordance with the demands of the age. You may be able to help in the work in this way, if your own action is not an end in itself to you, if the idea of the Church does not triumph over that of the spirit, and if the path of the care of souls gradually leads to allowing man to become strengthened in his 'I,' so that he may connect in freedom and wakefulness with the divine worlds and with the heart of Christ that shines in the sun and pulses through the earth. You have wished for this and have spoken it. Act accordingly, and be true to your words!"

They went and founded a community for Christian renewal, to the salvation of many souls. The knowledge of the gospel is eagerly pursued there, a knowledge to which Rudolf Steiner provided the key.

These sentences require no commentary. But truth obliges me to say that they contradict the very nature of Rudolf Steiner's spirit. Rudolf Steiner was, for example, benevolently, tenderly, and lovingly disposed towards the Christian Community, and would never have said that *he* brought the "living Christ" to other people. For Christ Himself alone gives Himself, always and everywhere. Would not the colleagues working in the Christian Community have had to make public and universally noticeable objection to this apparent depreciation of the value of their work? Or did they approve of it? But in that case, how would they have been able to represent the meaning of the Christian Community in the way that they did?

Rudolf Steiner's words, which always called his readers to spiritual deeds of their own, have largely been turned into doctrines ("dogmas"), which is not in accordance with his spirit or with what he wanted, if I have understood the latter correctly. What he "said" and "gave" is taken within the movement, so far as I was able to see, as unconditionally true in the sense that the individual's task is only to grasp its truth. Most of the anthroposophists I got to know had a relationship to Rudolf Steiner's work resembling that of the believing Catholic Christian to the dogma of the Church; for this relationship too rests on a trust that the Church propounds and communicates the truth. While the believing Catholic confesses his faith, however, the anthroposophist is bound to his "free life of insight," and, unfortunately, what "he himself believes" is strongly remarked upon, while the faith that lives within a member of the Church is all too readily undervalued (see Marie Steiner's words!). Unfortunately, however, the undervaluing of dogma may be traced back to Rudolf Steiner's own way of teaching. Here is an example.

In his account of his life, Rudolf Steiner recounts a conversation he had as a young man with a Catholic theologian in Vienna. He concludes by remarking that

> this conversation remained deeply imprinted on my soul. It kept surfacing, for it was deeply significant for me. Three of us were actually talking together at the time, Professor Neumann and I, and a third, invisible, interlocutor, the personification of Catholic dogmatics, who, as if menacingly visible to the spiritual eye, showed itself behind Professor Neumann, and tapped admonishingly on his shoulder whenever the scholar's acute logic brought him into too much agreement with me.

In a similar way, I could myself say not only of one but of many conversations I have had over the course of time with anthroposophists that there were really three people in the conversation: the person to whom I was talking, I myself, and a third, invisible interlocutor, who could be seen behind my conversation partner, telling him what to think and what to say. Even at the time, I once said to someone who was close to me that "along with other dogmas, we also have the dogma that 'we have no dogma.'" I was certainly not entitled to express this thought publicly, but it would perhaps have been good if it had not been completely dismissed. I mention it here, along with everything else I have quoted, because I am writing the prehistory of my own conversion.

It is obviously very difficult to be completely objective where matters of one's own worldview are concerned. It is easy to be suspicious of someone who thinks or believes something different from what one thinks or believes oneself; and it is easy, even, to sketch a caricature of someone else's intuitions and spiritual forms while using words that are correct in every detail. Every anthroposophist will read the just-quoted words of Rudolf Steiner's to self-evidently mean that here the dark and coercive spirit of the Catholic church is strikingly illustrated, whereas in the anthroposophical movement a quite different spirit, namely the spirit of freedom, holds sway. That is, from one point of view, or even in principle, quite right, as I judge the matter today, *if* by freedom one understands the absence of authority; for Anthroposophy appeals to the individual's thinking without preconditions, and is to this extent opposed to the teaching of the Church, which makes such an appeal only in the light of the doctrine of faith. It is therefore important here to pay attention to the specific point of comparison. It is a question of the way in which one ultimately relates to a doctrinal legacy taken to be binding, a legacy that, precisely, one has not always oneself understood.

Rudolf Steiner himself probably found it very difficult that such faith was placed in him and was mistaken for knowledge. How, though, could he have prevented this from happening? Complete spiritual independence *is* rare, and *is* only to be encountered where a person is in a position (so Rudolf Steiner's exposition suggests) to approach the observed world with sufficient conceptual penetration. But who has strength of this kind at his disposal? It is easier to demand it than to supply it.

Anthropological instruction must, if it is to gain the significance intended for it, bear the stamp of sacrifice, of self-overcoming, of pain. The intellectual appropriation of what was given by the teacher is only the first and so to speak harmless step; but no further progress can be made without harm, just as any ascesis in the Church must bring with it inner sufferings, as a substitute for or an anticipation of outward ones. The path to perfection leads through pain, and not without reason did Rudolf Steiner himself bear the venerable marks of suffering. Who, though, is in a position to progress under his own steam through levels of suffering that in their gravity and their power to transform us are like heavy blows of fate? In *Führung und Geleit* [Leadership and Escort], Hans Carossa recounts, among other things, his meeting with Rainer Maria Rilke. He speaks about Rilke in general and reports in addition that he had learned from Rodin to look so often and so penetratingly at a tree, an animal, a statue, a person, or even a historical figure, that in the end the essence of the phenomenon contemplated emerged within him. Now, this way of proceeding was not completely unfamiliar to me; a short anthroposophical essay I once came across said the same thing. Yet I regarded such spiritual instruction as too difficult and protracted for me to dedicate myself to it. I also imagined that this could only work for static objects, less so for those subject to strong movements, and least of all for human beings. The latter would of necessity have been afflicted by destinies that would bring them into situations of great disorientation, situations that would then force from them the unforgettable gestures, the compulsive words, the deep, tender touches, that would bring their most secret feelings to expression.

I still remember well that at that time these sentences prompted me to think that Hans Carossa had avoided an essential task of his life, and had sentimentally attached great importance to the field of poetry at the cost of what I would roughly speaking have called "the spiritual." I cannot therefore by any means say that I then had the least doubt in my mind of the absolute seriousness of anthroposophical practice. Yet such a doubt must nevertheless have been at work in my heart. Where were there people who had gone through burning and life-changing pains, pains that were voluntarily incurred through practice? What I then only dimly sensed was later clearly shown by the course of events. Apart from a few exceptions, truly powerful fates had to befall people before they were really able to change. It is obvious that only a *very* few people are able to achieve by means of a spiritual deed carried out "of their own free will" what can be brought about by the death of a child, by going blind, or by a life-threatening illness. It is just *this* that anthroposophical practice aims at, however, and it is from this that a strength sufficient not only to fortify an individual person, but to save the world, might come. It cannot be demanded of anybody, and Rudolf Steiner did not demand it of anybody. If it is a question, however, of a knowledge of the situation of the anthroposophical movement as a whole, then I think I must mention that before 1944 I only got to know *one* anthroposophist who had arrived at mastery through training: Michael Bauer. Often, however, I saw my friends expecting the salvation of the world from this "new thing" (or however they put it), without their having seemed to me sufficiently to have reflected on the fact that this "new thing" could only become a reality through human effort. It can only have been because I already had a sense of this that the banning of the Anthroposophical Society did not create any personal horror in me, and that I could carry on along my own path exactly as I had done before.

These ideas may roughly describe what then moved and filled me. *Perhaps*, in the depths of my being, an intimation was already taking root that the denial or exclusion of all ecclesiastical Christianity, a denial or exclusion which is native to anthroposophy, signified an all too bold and excessive demand of human beings; that "dogmatic Christianity" is, *despite everything*, the place where truth and salvation are most strongly imparted and realized. *If* such an intimation was taking root, then it was happening at a depth of which I was quite unconscious, and it would be false at this point in my account to mention the doctrines and the life of the Church and to measure anything anthroposophical against them…

The Christian Community was for many years the only place in which the anthroposophical spirit could still be publicly and purely championed within Nazi Germany. It was able to resist being banned until 1941. Then it too was prevented from continuing by the state authorities. But even with the banning of the Community, nothing essential or indispensable was taken away from me. My relationship to it had at bottom always been determined by my relationship to Anthroposophy. I was increasingly preoccupied more with the way in which the work of the priests should be carried out than with what was believed by the actual congregants. It was indeed by no means, as Marie Steiner put it, only for people who "were not yet strong enough to work through the science of spirit and for spiritual communion." It is an anthroposophical ideal to work through the science of spirit and to seek spiritual communion. This ideal was mine too. I could not at that time ask myself whether "spiritual communion" should be the rule or the exception, for this question can only come up in the Church, not in the anthroposophical movement. For me, too, the idea of "freedom" and the idea of "the development of consciousness" were decisive. That one could, for the sake of the community and of Christian order, go along with the forms of a universally valid worship even if one happened to be capable of "spiritual communion," was something that still lay entirely outside my field of vision. I was the "ideal type" of the anthroposophist who regards himself as "progressive," or as obligated to follow "progress." In my conscious mind I still hoped that all schisms from the spirit of Anthroposophy would be overcome. It became, however, ever harder to hope for this, given the increasingly grave historical situation. I had, indeed, often and gladly taken communion in the Christian Community; yet I could not say that I had ever experienced anything different, or believed I would experience anything different, from what was called "spiritual communion" in the anthroposophical movement (a communion of which one could of course speak only, in my case, of the beginnings, rather than a full experience). I knew the Act of the Consecration of Man by heart. One could also consistently "meditate" on it, or on parts of it, alone. In any case, no meaningful objection could be raised to it from anthroposophical quarters, even by anyone who thought they themselves were able to renounce worship altogether.

Although, as will readily be understood after what has just been said, I was easily able to keep going in the period without public worship (from June 1941 onwards), and was not deprived of any inner resources by the banning of the Christian Community, the ban was nevertheless, objectively speaking, a sign of horror of the worst possible kind. What had we come to when a Christian congregation in which not a syllable had ever been spoken about anything political or military was condemned to disappear because it represented a Christian world-view and a Christian life?

Seen spiritually and objectively, however, the state authorities were from their own point of view quite correct in enforcing this ban. What is surprising is not that the Christian Community was banned too, but that it took so long to happen. The Community, too, belonged among the "resistance movements," even if it was at work in a purely spiritual domain, and thus "only" strengthened souls for spiritual combat or for combat concerning the fate that was to befall us.

Outwardly, the ban had to be accepted, especially since it was accompanied by the confiscation of all the lands and possessions of the Christian Community. More difficult was accepting it inwardly, that is, understanding that the priests were not celebrating any rite even in private, while worship was nevertheless declared to be unconditionally necessary to life in countless speeches. I was never invited to take place in a forbidden service of worship. Only once was I invited to attend when a priest wanted to read the text of the Act of the Consecration of Man aloud. It was not an attractive prospect; and I know very well that I was too proud to put myself on the same level as members of the congregation, so that I would rather speak the deeply familiar words to myself alone.

During the time when the Christian Community was banned, my second child, Christiane, had to be baptized. One of her sponsors was a well-known priest in the Christian Community. The baptism was to be performed by me, her own father, as an "emergency baptism." We were together in our flat: the child, we parents, and the two sponsors, in a small, entirely reliable circle, five people altogether. Why could the priest who was present not have baptized the child "correctly" in the spirit of the Christian Community? Yet this was not all: I completed the emergency "baptism" (the inverted commas are unfortunately justified) in the presence of the priest mentioned without any external element, merely speaking the baptismal words. Later this "baptism" was declared to be invalid in the sense required by the Christian Community, and Christiane had to (and was able to!) be "baptized" a second time, this time correctly. So we had really only been playing a game with the first "baptism," the one performed by me—and that in the presence of a priest, who should either have performed the baptism himself, or should have seen to it that the "emergency baptism" was valid, i.e., unrepeatable. The more I looked into theology, the more this experience gave me pause for thought. One can overlook a lack of knowledge in the performance of the sacrament of baptism in the members of a congregation (in me myself, at that time), but not in a priest whose task it is validly to represent the movement.

Once the Americans had marched into Germany, and Hitler's rule was overthrown, the Christian Community began its work once more. It was beautiful to see how the members of the Community, separated from each other for years, found each other again, and how the public worship showed something of its first freshness. Not only, indeed, did it seem to have this freshness, but there seemed, for a short while, to be new life in the whole Community. It was possible to have the impression that the movement had received new possibilities. I soon felt this impression extinguished, however. As time went on, it was unmistakable that the Christian Community was essentially at home among the educated citizenry, and that that was where it would remain for the foreseeable future. Among those who lack anything more than basic education, it has only vanishingly few members.

The Anthroposophical Society, too, began work again in the summer of 1945, but only once was it given permission to do so by the military government. Any other course of action would have been impossible under the circumstances then prevailing. But the fact that it was impossible seemed nevertheless to me to be a sign of the situation in which the Society found itself. The state authorities, or rather the occupying powers, stood above it, and it was permitted because it was not thought to be dangerous. Accordingly, the anthroposophical movement was not, as I had once hoped it might be, something that was going to be able to lift today's world off its hinges or bring fundamental healing to it. It was directed towards the sphere of private life, a field for individual achievements and for undertakings that could only be significant to individuals and groups, but lacked the strength to "move the world." When Rudolf Steiner began to work anthroposophically in public, he did not ask the permission of a state authority or of an occupying power, and if that had been necessary he would, from what I have understood of him, have given up. When the Anthroposophical Society began work again in 1945, it could only happen upon receiving such permission. The history of the last five decades, so far as it concerns either Anthroposophy or the state authorities, can be seen in the light of this fact. There are, in any case, menacing signs aplenty in contemporary life.

To take a couple of great examples: Jesus Christ did not ask any state power whether he might start work. Islam did not secure its victories after receiving permission. Martin Luther and the Reformation did not shake the world after being approved by a board of censors. That history is made only by a movement in command of itself, and how this happens, is shown to us today by the Soviet state. It is indeed *immensely* painful to have to express such ideas— for not only do I owe a great deal to Rudolf Steiner, but I also very much admire many anthroposophists.

In the Bärenreiter company, and in the work that fell to me there, being an anthroposophist was irrelevant. Here there was no possibility of any sort of calling to "spiritual apprenticeship." Instead, all one's work had to be justified before a wider circle of people. For a long while I still retained a certain anthroposophical self-consciousness, and, despite what I have already said, regarded all those who were not anthroposophists as "outsiders." So it was healthy for me to have to complete work that was destined not for a small group of people, and with a narrowly-defined content, but for a large circle composed of different sorts of people. My work in the Bärenreiter company, whose outlook was and is Protestant, but which was and is also to a certain extent supra-denominational, meant at once learning about Protestant Christianity and training in an ecumenical approach. At that time I was able to publish a small monograph on the artist Karl Thylmann, who had died in 1916; a number of issues of the art calendar *Über den Zeiten* [On the times]; a little book of meditations on "the twelve months"; and a series of "war articles," in which I attempted to strengthen the readers of the *Neue Schau* [New View] in their faith in increasingly difficult times.

During the Second World War, I lived at home with my family, apart from during the days, when I was in a calm and satisfying workplace; and I was able to keep or at least salvage my flat even in the final heavy bombing raids. I thus found myself in a position that all too many people would have envied at that time, and that might not seem to be a good one from which to be invigorated to survive the trials of suffering. I wondered again and again whether I would be permitted to do so, or whether my own situation in life would inevitably produce only words, without sufficient depth. Perhaps I may admit—so much has already been admitted in this book, and it is true in relations among people, too, that only the truth will set us free—that, in my hometown and in the area where I lived, I felt the threat of death to be almost unbearable, and always wrote in the first instance simply to cheer myself up. It became evident that the essays that meant most to others were those meant entirely for my own use, at least when they were first written, but also when I re-read them, when attacks were underway. Many people copied out the aphorisms "On the Ruins of the Destroyed City" and the "Hymns to Michael," and read them in the shelters during the terrible air raids. I had written them, however, to console and strengthen *myself*, when my hometown was reduced to rubble and ashes in a single night and thousands of people lost their lives (October 22–23, 1943).

At bottom, it is not decisive where or how one has experiences, but *that* one has them. The "lines of life," as Hölderlin put it, vary. Everyone has his own destiny, peculiar to himself, which cannot be exchanged with that of anyone else. Suffering and its overcoming are learned not only in outward and visible distress, but also in distress that cannot outwardly be seen. There is an inner Stalingrad, as well as an outer one.

I owe it to Rudolf Steiner and to Anthroposophy that I was able to contribute to the good a little in those years of horror. Anthroposophy not only gave me a certain overview of the world and of history, but also, much more importantly, and connectedly, allowed me to strengthen my own being and to gain an adequate understanding of myself. Despite the questions about Anthroposophy that I have inevitably had to express in this account, and despite a distancing both in public and in private from Anthroposophy and the Christian Community as the highest values of my life, Rudolf Steiner was and remained my teacher. Through him I was freed from perplexity and doubt; through him I was protected from the many "worldviews" that are not really worldviews at all; and through him I was also later put in a position to understand the Church and to convert.

In those years, as they became ever more difficult, my lot had an essentially awakening effect on me towards the good—a divine education by means of horror and distress. Seen from one point of view, it was good that we came into the greatest peril. We experienced what we had previously only known intellectually, the questionable nature of the world. We were sent back to the sources of life. Slowly, we came to understand the meaning of each Passion: we began, at last, to imitate Christ. European humanity had involuntarily to undergo that "apprenticeship" that Rudolf Steiner had called on it to undertake of its own free will. This is how the catastrophes came, and they came most of all to souls who were helpless or lacked courage in the face of them. These catastrophes are, in my opinion, the "proof" that Anthroposophy, as a matter of *historical* fact, did not become what Rudolf Steiner expected it to become, an idea that may perhaps seem to many anthroposophists to be an unmistakable sign of incomprehension or presumption on my part. I can say nothing better in my defence to my former friends than the famous request: "allow me to think as I choose."

9

Catholicism as Problem

IN THE COURSE OF THE LAST FEW YEARS (1942–1944) I
had now and then caught sight of the writings of a man who seemed
to have come to grips with the anthroposophical spirit in a deeper
and more individual way than I had ever before seen, even in the
work of those figures worthiest of respect. One can tell a person's
significance, strength of vision, and breadth of experience from his
style. Only at the level of abstract thinking, and if one looks only at
the surface, can one be deceived about this. A person's style is as
unequivocal as his gait, how he looks at things, his gestures. Among
its other merits, for example, the *Imitation of Christ* announces its
lofty standing through its style. Or again, no connoisseur of style
who looks at Rudolf Steiner's works impartially can doubt that he
was speaking and writing from personal experience when he discussed human nature, "higher worlds," the workings of the hierarchies, or the development of the cosmos. It was the same thing in
the case of the man whose writings I mentioned. The style (though
this was, incidentally, by no means "fine writing") showed me that I
was in the presence of the utterances of an "initiate."

Unfortunately, I only caught glimpses of these writings in another
house, a house I only rarely had the opportunity to visit when I was
traveling on official business, and where there were always urgent
matters to be discussed in the precious little time at my disposal. For
this reason, I could not read these writings with the attention they
deserved—and that I would gladly have devoted to them. Nor were
they lent to me. But even so, I was as attentive and receptive to the
writer's spirit as I could be, and his name began to resonate, as it
were, ever more strongly within me.

Then, as a result of a strange and most fortunate opportunity early in 1944, I was able to spend several weeks on holiday in another house in which almost all the most important writings of the man I have mentioned were available to me, and straightaway given me to read. It was at once clear to me that reading this work would have to be more than mere reading, that it would have to be the real meaning of this holiday. And indeed, the impression I had previously had was ever more deeply confirmed. I found myself face to face with the mind of one who had not only continued consistently and painstakingly to think through the work done by Rudolf Steiner, but who was himself a gifted and independent thinker (here, those two qualities coincided). He was not subordinate to Rudolf Steiner, but was Steiner's equal, capable of "discerning" him as his peer. This fact moved me deeply.

Up until this point I had only encountered anthroposophists who, even if they were for the most part far more distinguished than I, could strictly speaking only be described as pupils of the master. This man whose works I was now reading, however, had long outgrown his pupillage. He was writing *independently* (or, more precisely, he had written independently and, even earlier, had often spoken independently) about those matters and questions that Rudolf Steiner was the only other person to have written and talked about in this way. He was moving, from personal knowledge, within "higher" or "supersensible" worlds. For me, this was indescribably beneficial, calming, and promising. The author had, like me (except in an *incomparably* more significant way) become what he now was through Rudolf Steiner. He had worked through the exercises in the book *Knowledge of Higher Worlds* to a point of supreme and undoubted mastery—like a pianist who has once been the pupil of a significant teacher, but who does not, like many ordinary music pupils, always remain at a level of artistic capability below that of his teacher, but instead attains the rank of a teacher and master himself. No one who does not have a close acquaintance with Anthroposophy can really imagine what this fact meant for a heart like mine, hungry as it was for knowledge.

At this point in writing the present study I became especially aware of one of the difficulties attending it. For which people should I be writing? I would be glad to give an account for my earlier anthroposophical friends, and yet much experience has shown me that anyone who dares to think in a way that no longer fits within Rudolf Steiner's legacy, but instead goes beyond it, is "yesterday's news" with them. Nor, essentially, will the people for whom I must write be those Christians who live outside the Catholic church, although I hope nevertheless to reach some of them. The present work is thus chiefly aimed at Catholic Christians who are seeking to make up their minds about Anthroposophy, in the hope that this book will perhaps enable them clearly to answer any questions that may have come up for them through their encounters with the spirit of Anthroposophy. To this group, everything anthroposophical is on the whole *terra incognita*. The ideas, concepts, inclinations, and tasks found in the anthroposophical movement are all different from those found in the Church. Can this unknown land be spoken of with sufficient clarity?

The reader must try to make himself a picture of anthroposophical spirituality using what this book says about Anthroposophy, so as to try to understand it. He may also wish to treat what is personally alien to him not merely as absurd but instead as something that is in itself at first (at least provisionally) to be acknowledged as substantive and as worthy of respect. Is it meaningful or productive to dismiss an "opponent" with theoretical refutations? This does not make him disappear from the world; all that happens is that one loses the chance to have a substantive dialogue and to profit from what is valuable in him. I must therefore ask for the reader's patience, and report on matters as truthfully as I am able.

For anthroposophists, "spiritual knowledge" and the life deriving from and according to it is the most important thing in life. It is the "term of art" by means of which this most important thing is to be expressed. Any belief in authority and tradition is mocked. The person who knows himself, and who acts on his self-knowledge, is free. Now, I myself had accepted with an open heart and with sufficient reason what Rudolf Steiner had "said." I had applied it to my own life, and particularly to my personal efforts to acquire knowledge. But I had never prematurely regarded anything I had heard from him (or indirectly, through his students) as knowledge *of my own*. It was enough for me that, through Rudolf Steiner's works, direct "spiritual knowledge" of any kind at all seemed possible in our own age.

Unfortunately, there was among anthroposophists a phenomenon that I quite early on (and certainly too uncharitably) called vicarious perception,[1] meaning you read something, tried to make it your own through meditation, found it convincing, then passed it on *as if* it had been discovered in your own cognitive work and were already your own possession. It is, of course, not so easy to decide where the border lies between what one has personally experienced and what, strictly speaking, one has only adopted. It is difficult to note where one is really believing, even when one speaks of "knowing" and considers that one is permitted so to speak. I once heard, for example, a "Michaelmas sermon" to a Christian congregation in which the speaker expressed very surprising ideas that deeply astonished me, indeed put me into a state of the greatest personal perplexity. It later emerged, however, that he had read these ideas in Rudolf Steiner's works, and had simply repeated them without mentioning their source. This is what I called "vicarious" perception. It came up quite often, and went together with an idea of Rudolf Steiner as the supreme, sole, and absolutely reliable master, whose words and instructions one only need follow to be assured of invariably knowing what to do and what was right—as a spring from which the "water of life" was at any time to be drawn.

As regards Christ, Rudolf Steiner said to his students that Anthroposophy would develop further, and that, in due course, new and deeper knowledge would be acquired, for which he was only preparing the way. But in the anthroposophical movement it seemed to me that there was a widespread mood to the effect that greatness lay behind us. All we had to do was carry the "stimulus" we had been given out into the world. Although this mood was an expression of deep respect for the master, and was certainly reasonable for all the "lesser" spirits, it sometimes appeared to me to be a dark cloud

---

1. The expression "vicarious perception" here translates the term *An-Empfindung*, which is itself a coinage, presumably from *anempfunden* (artificial, spurious, false) and *Empfindung* (feeling, sensation, impression, perception). Other workable translations could have been "pseudo-perception" or "presumptive perception." Tʀ

overshadowing my life—and this despite the enthusiasm that was alive within me.

Now I found myself faced with a person who awakened in me the impression that greatness did not only lie behind us, but also lived among us. The Catholic reader can perhaps picture the effect on my soul by imagining what it would be like if a Doctor of the Church of the stature of St Thomas Aquinas were to appear among us today. I cannot sufficiently emphasize how deeply happy the experience made me, how greatly I had thirsted for such "originality." In my early days and in my youth, one reason I turned away from Christianity and from the Church had been that I had the (certainly mistaken, as well as insufficiently thought-through) impression that we who in the present day were living without any core experiences ought simply to accept and believe what had once been a really present, living experience, rather than something merely accepted or believed. I became an anthroposophist because Anthroposophy did not come from tradition, but from experience and from revelation (in a non-dogmatic sense).

Despite this, I always came up against a comparable difficulty, a comparable question, within Anthroposophy itself. This difficulty, this question, could be summarized roughly as follows. If it is impossible for anyone else to "catch up" with Rudolf Steiner, the great "initiate" (a *terminus technicus* that must be taken in an unqualifiedly positive sense), and if we have in him not merely *a*, but rather *the* Teacher, then we are at bottom only epigones, since we are living off something that strictly speaking is already in the past, even if that past is not so very many years behind us. I could not deliberately abandon this perhaps presumptuous, yet honest, need not to set my stall in the past. (The reader can see here how distant I then was from faith.) I could express as follows the happiness that filled me at this new discovery: Anthroposophy is not something that only *was*; it *is*. After all, my need for "originality" did not consist in a foolhardy wish immediately and in person to be endowed with supreme knowledge, but only in the more modest wish to set eyes on such a gift.

Henceforth, then, I devoted the greatest possible attention to the spirit concerned. By no means did I wish to repeat the mistake of passing by a great spirit or event without noticing them, as Parsifal had passed by the miracle of the Grail, and as I had carelessly passed by Rudolf Steiner. I was twenty-five years old when Steiner died, and so could easily have gotten to know him in person. True, the fact that this did not happen was a result of circumstances that make it entirely understandable, and certainly from an earthly point of view excuse me. Despite this, however, it certainly appeared to be a significant omission (in the deeper sense), even if one cannot speak of guilt.

After reading these writings, there sprang up within me an urgent need to be permitted to speak to their author. I was so bold as to ask him for this permission, and although he was living in seclusion from the world, he invited me in for a conversation. The first encounter (which was not to remain the only one) was solely concerned with anthroposophical and personal questions. We talked about "spiritual direction." But this phrase points to much more than a solely religious matter, as it might seem to anyone who lives only in the world of prayer, or who only knows the phrase "spiritual direction," rather than the thing itself. I hardly dared come into the room in which the conversation was to take place. And I know even now that at its end I was filled with the thought: "Master, we have toiled all night, and taken nothing: nevertheless at thy word I will let down the net." I let it down, and it was not in vain that I did so!

Not long afterwards I learned, to my great astonishment and regret, that this man with whom I was now, blessedly for me, acquainted, was close to the Catholic church. I simply could not understand it. The Catholic church was in my view spiritually obsolete, a power opposed to "progressive thinking," in which people lived on in a "purely emotional" piety, dependence, and unfreedom. Although I was perfectly ignorant of the Catholic church, I bore deep within myself, even in early 1944, all the prejudice and revulsion towards everything "Catholic" that could have been instilled in me by the Protestant thought of the turn of the century, and that had only been strengthened by my membership in the anthroposophical movement. I was truly a real "Protestant." I do not use the word in a denominational sense here (since I had strongly distanced myself from Christianity and the Protestant church), but as a description of a type. Thus, for example, I had an implicit belief that there was infinitely much to be learned from Goethe, Schiller, and Novalis, while to me Thomas Aquinas, the Jesuit order, and the institution of the papacy, of which I knew more or less nothing at all, did not seem worth consideration. They belonged, of course, to the Catholic church, and it was obvious what one should "think" about the Catholic church. I had never become aware that the anthroposophical theory of knowledge (knowledge is only present when "perception" and "concept" meet in a living way in an individual person) was to be applied not only to nature, but also to the history of religion. And all my friends were at that time quite content with the generalizations produced by anthroposophical thought. Could this spirit then, who seemed to me unconditionally strong in his knowledge and worthy of trust, really be close to the Catholic church? For he seemed to me to be strong in knowledge and worthy of trust precisely *because* he embodied the spirit of Anthroposophy in his thinking, and in a way I had never before encountered. I could not be in the slightest doubt that there were the most serious fundamental tensions between Anthroposophy and the Catholic church. In Protestantism it is much easier to acquire a truthful picture of the Catholic church, and this picture is becoming increasingly accurate. But it is hardly possible to acquire such a picture from within Anthroposophy, for here judgment has already been passed by Rudolf Steiner. Within Anthroposophy, no living development is any longer attributed to the Catholic church.

"Anthroposophy is not just something that *was*; it *is!*" And this apart from the fact that I have already reported what doubts had developed in me over the years about the universal significance of the whole movement, even though I had not become fully aware of those doubts. But this is precisely the point: these doubts had not yet, by a long way, come so far into waking consciousness that I could have spoken about them, or even that they could have influenced my actions. From everything else at work in my worldview, I received ideas that did not admit of an explanation, or even of a connection. Through Anthroposophy, however, I had recovered my health. I had an exact knowledge of the basics of Anthroposophy, even if not of all its branches. I did not have the choice between

Anthroposophy and other worldviews, between Anthroposophy and the Protestant or the Catholic church, but only the choice between Anthroposophy and the void. The doubts (if one can describe them so) that had emerged by no means brought with them an openness to anything else, nor any seeking or longing, but only a certain impediment to my cheerfulness and my faith. The doubts deprived me of something, without directing my gaze towards anything else. My heart had, therefore, to be warmed indeed by the idea that "Anthroposophy is not just something that *was*; it *is*." Perhaps I can explain it this way: A wagon can go forward thanks to a push it *has* been given, but that is no longer *being* given; or it can go forward thanks to a push *still* being given. In the former case, one can calculate in advance when it will stop moving; but in the latter, one cannot know whether the journey might not soon get a great deal quicker. So long as someone with a special gift from God is at work in a spiritual movement, something different can always become of it than is the case if it is only carried on by people who lack these supreme gifts. The operation of this law can be seen from a whole range of examples in Christian and non-Christian life.

But here one could ask, "If this spirit of whom you are speaking was so powerful, why did he not work openly in the public sphere, recognized by all the friends of spirit?" This question I can only answer here in part, not fully. A partial answer seems to me to be this. In the Anthroposophical Society, Rudolf Steiner's authority was so powerful that original work by anyone else on the same level as that on which Steiner himself worked was hardly recognized or tolerated. As far as I can tell, something has happened in the field of anthroposophical life of that tragic kind which Dostoyevsky relates in his celebrated tale of the Grand Inquisitor of the Catholic church. Christ comes back to humanity, but the Grand Inquisitor has him taken captive, and gives him to understand the following. *You* must keep quiet; *we* are carrying out your work, and we do not wish to be disturbed in any way. Now, nothing need be said here about Dostoyevsky's wisdom as a writer. It will suffice to say that (so far as I can see or guess) the leadership of the Anthroposophical Society wished not to be "disturbed." So that the man I am writing about had already, by the time I first met him, lost the influence within

Anthroposophy that he had had in earlier years. In him I met a model of someone quite free from ambition, whose spiritual influence is so certain that he could renounce any other kind of influence, and whose silence, moreover, did not trouble him for his own sake, but for the sake of others.

But the fact was that this revered man stood close to the Catholic church, and this threw a new burning and disturbing question into my life. Someone had whispered to me the suspicion that—how shall I put this—this man had been overrun, taken prisoner, and overpowered by the Catholic church, and that he was now being "used" by it. Many foolhardy and nonsensical things were then attributed to the Catholic church. Catholic theologians were supposed to be sitting in cloisters and in secret hideaways reading Rudolf Steiner's lecture courses, so as to make use of them in the struggle against Anthroposophy. I can attest from my own case how much mistrust, as well as how much delusion, there was here. An acquaintance of mine, who later became my friend, and who had been a member of the Anthroposophical Society for many years, spent some time in the abbey of Maria Laach. At the time, I was firmly convinced that he was working against Anthroposophy, that he was having meetings with "leading Catholics," meetings in which foul plots were hatched against the non-Catholic world. I also imputed to the Catholic church the possession of "black magic," and, to its leading minds, the recklessness to make use of that magic. In the case of the spirit whom I had just met, however, I could not with the best will in the world imagine that he could have been the victim of such magical practices.

I asked for a second interview. This too was granted to me, and we spent almost a full day in conversation about the question of Anthroposophy and the Church. During this, my impression of the spiritual eminence of my host was confirmed. Moreover, the firm wall of my prejudices against the Catholic church was now for the first time pierced, and pierced deeply. What I had previously examined only through the spectacles of deep-seated prejudices (or had not examined at all) was now illuminated for me in its true nature and—so far as this was possible in a single conversation—clarified. True, no questions were answered; rather, more were raised. I have never been able to accept opinions and judgments simply on the authority of another person. The spirit with whom I had been led further along had his reasons for having left his anthroposophical activities behind him, and it must have been at around this time that he entered into the Catholic church. Whether his reasons might ever become mine was at that time completely unclear, and I would then have held it to be impossible. In our first interview, he had rightly thought it appropriate (since I was of course very distant from the Catholic church) to speak to me only in such a way as my power of comprehension and my concerns permitted. He did, on his level, what I would always do on mine, following the phrase, "what matters is not conversions, but Christ."

I was able to speak often and at length to my "spiritual director," as I may call him (at the risk of being abandoned by my fellow travelers). But I was still not done with the questions that had so disturbingly broken in upon my life, and the greater man put himself again and again at my disposal. Thus I received many ideas I could hardly have stumbled upon if left to myself, and my courage to think about many things before which my soul had at first trembled was strengthened. To this source belong, on one hand, the ideas I set out earlier about the situation of the anthroposophical movement, and on the other, those that helped prepare my path towards the Catholic church. Many things concerning the former were, so to speak, ready at the bottom of my heart, and had already then been received, if not given birth. But most of what concerned the latter was foreign in its nature to me, and could only be comprehended in supreme spiritual selflessness—a selflessness such as could not be conjured up overnight. A person can be midwife to another person, a spirit to another spirit. My spiritual eyes were opened to many things I had previously been able only to sense, not to see. What I saw with these opened eyes, however, I saw for myself. And just as little as before—when a pupil of Rudolf Steiner—did I here allow life's spiritual guidance to pass me by.

Even elsewhere, and in everyday life, we draw upon each other in our lives. The history of spirit is a stream whose waters flow into each other at many places. In Goethe's *Tasso* we find the words *Und was wir sind, das sind wir anderen schuldig* [And what we are, we owe to others]. I became in my nature the "pupil" of my new teacher in no other sense than that founded and methodically developed by Rudolf Steiner—that is, the same sense held to be right and fair by other anthroposophists. Rudolf Steiner himself wrote the theory of knowledge that was to be applied in this case too. The question, however, was whether the method of spiritual striving that Steiner had created, realized, and mediated had to remain within the intellectual legacy he developed and the idea of freedom he set out, or whether it might be possible to go beyond that legacy and that idea of freedom. Can Anthroposophy, in the sense given it by its founder, be contravened, and applied to fields that Steiner himself described throughout his work in a particularly unappetizing way? Anyone who has not paid heed to the anthroposophical movement, who knows it only from hearsay, will find it hard to take these questions seriously. To me, however, they were urgent, burning questions full of meaning. They stood menacingly above the soul and almost overtaxed it. They brought my whole existence into question. I used all the strength at my disposal to wrestle with and solve them. And with them came a second set of questions just as menacing: the questions about the Church.

If I have left the name of my teacher unmentioned, this is not out of ingratitude, but rather in his own spirit. I am defending only the ideas put forward in this study; the proper name is quite irrelevant in the present context. But one thing does need saying. Now and again in my life I had noticed traces of the activity of my guardian angel. But this was hardly ever so clearly to be seen as in the fact that at the "last moment" I was permitted to meet an outstanding spirit, who helped me to go on. What he brought into my life was not anything like a garden, in which I might have settled down—instead, it was like the beacon of a lighthouse directing ships where to sail. Even so, however, shipwreck is only avoided if the sailors and the pilot do their part.

Only now did I dare fully to admit to myself that the anthroposophical life, when measured against the situation it was in when Rudolf Steiner was still alive and that must have been intended by him, had failed to progress. I had met many anthroposophists in whom Rudolf Steiner's prolific communications were bread by no means as nourishing as they believed it to be. Only a few of them seemed to have worked patiently through the vitally important exercises in Steiner's basic work, *Knowledge of the Higher Worlds*. The leadership (in which significant, dedicated, creative people were often to be found) stood out from a circle of rather different folk who enjoyed the fruits of a struggle for a new consciousness but were not themselves really engaged in the struggle, which can be very bitter and trying. It was also the case that what had happened within the leadership of the movement in the years after Rudolf Steiner's death had not been without consequences for the whole life of the Anthroposophical Society. But in the end, even as today's Protestant Christian cannot call on the experience of Martin Luther, neither can the anthroposophist call on the experience of Rudolf Steiner and his "legacy." When Anthroposophy becomes a denomination, it loses its vital force. It is painful to me even today to have to point this out.

For the sake of clarity I must say that, in the spiritual struggle, one ought always justly to weigh idea against idea and reality against reality. In any "camp" of those supporting a particular worldview, significant and noble spirits are to be found as well as those less significant or failing. Reference to failures is no more a refutation of the group to which they belong than reference to the great figures is proof that they are in possession of the truth. Is it permissible to say something to the detriment of Anthroposophy by referring to many of its adherents? The answer is first of all no, and then yes, as follows. The answer is no insofar as here, too, the idea stands above reality and can never be disfigured by the latter, whatever it is like; and the answer is yes insofar as in order to verify and demonstrate its significance, the idea depends on reality. In other words, a single significant work of art can be praised, a given gifted artist can be celebrated, even if the whole world were to receive them with disrespect and misunderstanding. Anthroposophy, however (if I have understood it correctly), is not intended as a help to the individual life, but is intended as a means to prevent an epochal catastrophe—as a direct stimulus towards the future. If the epochal catastrophe has nevertheless occurred, this certainly does not speak against the idea that was originally expressed, but rather against the significance that idea possesses in contemporary life. An Anthroposophy that does not prevent any epochal catastrophe, but is only cultivated in small circles, is to be praised solely from an ideal perspective—and is not to be described as an essential component of history on a *large scale.* My anthroposophical friends would value Anthroposophy at its true worth if it had in fact had as great an influence on the historical course of the last half-century as its creator expected of it. Rudolf Steiner *must* have been reckoning on "more" than what has come about. And, to our knowledge, none of those who publicly represent Anthroposophy have ever come forward with a claim that they can speak of "higher worlds" from their own perfect knowledge of them.

Now that we can look back at the history of the first half of the twentieth century,[2] it can seem almost inconceivable that such a great and powerful spirit as Rudolf Steiner could have thought fifty years ago that there was no future in the Christian churches, and that the flame of "Christianity" should be fanned anew in the ranks of the unbelievers, whence it should be brought home to set all people's hearts on fire. At the beginning of the twentieth century, so far as it had a public effect, Anthroposophy must have been thought of otherwise than it is today. The non-Catholic realm, at least, might have seemed seriously endangered to people outside the Church. Speaking of God and matters of faith in "society" invited mockery. Christianity was largely interwoven with politics. The "progress" of the "world" and of the "life of the spirit" was in the hands of those who kept up with the latest research. It was the age of liberal theology. The nature of the God-man was largely forgotten. Jesus, the "simple man of Nazareth," was put in his place. Anthroposophical thought, however, always leads to seeing things as a whole, however this may be done, and to this extent we can indeed say with Rudolf Steiner that as a whole (one need not think of the exceptions to such a view, nor see such a view as ignoring those exceptions) Protestant Christianity *has* followed a path of decline in the course of the four centuries of its existence. When seen as a whole, the relationship of human beings to the divine truth *has* become weaker in that time,

---

2. This work was published in German in 1950.

and a purely secular spirit stronger. If one draws a line from the strength of truth in the century in which the Reformation took place to the strength of truth at the outset of the twentieth century, and if, further one imagines this line protracted into the future, one could and can have but very little hope for the future of Christianity. From the *Confessio Augustana* (who now knows it by heart?)[3] to liberal theology is really a decline of a dangerous order. How should development go forward? Secular and natural-scientific thought alone seemed more alive and to offer, if anything did, the first signs of a possible good progress. All this is said here in the spirit of the anthroposophical worldview (which indeed did not originate in faith but in the scientific spirit of that age) as a way of explaining its emergence. That goes also for what follows.

It was not only within Protestant Christianity that an outsider could have observed such a decline, but also (leaving aside for our present purposes some exceptional figures) within Catholic Christianity. Despite the Catholic church's powers of conservation and probation, such an outsider, if he were not concerned with the content of the faith but with making an overall estimate of its dissemination and strength, might have observed here also a decrease in the sense of truth. Would the *Syllabus of Errors* and the *Oath Against Modernism*[4] have been conceivable in the sixteenth century? In that period, the questions were essentially religious, rather than scientific. Materialism has, however, taken hold only too powerfully even of the faithful—if not in theory, then in their lived experience and in their practical thinking. Here too, from a *human* perspective, one could draw a line from 1500 to 1900 and on into the future that would seem to show the Church at risk. One might object that reli-

---

3. The Augsburg Confession, also known as the *Confessio Augustana*, is the primary confession of faith of the Lutheran Church and one of the most important documents of the Protestant Reformation.

4. The *Syllabus of Errors* (1864) is the name given a document issued by the Holy See under Pope Pius IX that condemns eighty of what the pope considered as errors or heresies, articulating Catholic teaching on a number of philosophical and political questions. *The Oath Against Modernism* (1910) marked the culmination of Pope Pius X's campaign against the theological movement of modernism.

gious and spiritual history is here seen too much from a human, and not enough from God's perspective. It is a question here, however, not of the objections of the faithful, but of explaining the emergence of Anthroposophy, whose founder was not in the Church's sense one of the faithful, but rather saw the Church from the outside, even though he was born and raised a Catholic. Let the thoughts presented here, then, be taken as they are intended.

In the wake of the sinister and yet salutary catastrophe we have lately undergone,[5] even those distant from the Church can see (if they look at all deeply into things) much more strongly than they could fifty years ago that history belongs to God, not to man, and that "God is able of these stones to raise up children unto Abraham."[6] Who today, now that "civilized humanity" may possibly have been summoned to its own and to the whole world's demise, believes in "development" and "progress"? But was the knowledge available to us today possible for those who believed in progress in 1900? Evidently, Rudolf Steiner did not believe the promise given to the Church at its birth by Christ ("the gates of hell shall not prevail against it"). Certainly, it is good Christian churchmanship to believe God everywhere and at all times capable of "the impossible." Anthroposophical thought, however, conceives of human development more as something predictable. Man and his development seem for Anthroposophy to be ordered according to laws that, strictly speaking, do not permit God at any moment to interrupt what is predictable. Nevertheless, it has become clear in the course of events that the life of the Christian Church is not dead. In the danger that has menaced it and in the assistance given to it by the most recent catastrophes (at once dangerous and beneficial to it), it has shown itself (unexpectedly to many) to be very much alive. Once again, if in hideous fashion, it has been shown that the Church lives upon the blood of its martyrs.

Unquestionably, one can and must say that in its delight in progress during the nineteenth century, "civilized" humanity went further away from God. Man has always behaved arrogantly on

5. The World Wars and their aftermath. ED.
6. Matthew 3:9.

earth, and fallen victim ever more seriously to the "serpent's" old promise, "you shall be as God." Modern consciousness is no longer connected to God. It no longer subordinates itself to God's or to the Church's commandments without questioning them. It has rashly and unhappily dared to place their validity in question. It was to this type of person (godless in the sense we have described) that Rudolf Steiner turned. It was just this type of person whom he wished to lead to new spiritual experience—and thus to new faith. True, this estimate of the strength of human nature is so high as to make it unlikely that it can learn to subject itself to God's will. There are not many people whose "moral imagination" suffices to beckon them, on the basis of their own inner resources, to live an exemplary life in accordance with God's commands. But there certainly are very many who would do better simply to resolve to keep God's commandments rather than to develop a "moral imagination." The drive towards "freedom" that has increasingly dominated the last few centuries has led to orgies of caprice and subhuman behavior. Who will call an end to this chaos? The subhuman person? The individual person? The person who rejects any authority? A small reform movement, even should the noblest will pulse through its veins? A movement that only with difficulty can summon up full fraternal community with the general public, or not at all, and that nearly always detects only failings in that general public? A movement that can only ever reach those few who are capable of walking, and willing to walk, the hard path of "spiritual apprenticeship"?

In my youth, and later (for particular reasons) in my anthroposophical days, I looked upon "our classical authors" as the figures who would provide the most important impetus for the human and cultural future. Later, in 1944–1945, I thought: what would happen if we were, all of us, to adopt in practice the relationship that our classical authors had to Christianity—a relationship that is understandable in view of the age in which they lived, and that in any case cannot be changed? What if we *all* started wanting to take the same attitude towards baptism, church weddings, the Holy Eucharist, as they did, the great classical figures? If they scorn due decorum, can leading individuals, even the noblest and the most creative of them, be models for everyone? After all, the general public is not made up of geniuses, but of average people. What I mean here, as a reflection upon a great deal in modern times, but also upon my anthroposophical friends' belief in progress, is contained in Goethe's own words: "Everything that frees our spirit without giving us self-control is damaging." The enormous boldness of Rudolf Steiner's achievement, which could have grown only out of great trust, consists in his having "freed the spirit" without at the same time being able to give his listeners and readers "self-control." Certainly, he gave them the possibility of having it, and advised them to acquire it, but he gave them no requirement, no command, no unqualified directive to do so. In the anthroposophical worldview there is no divine authority. Neither God Himself nor Christ is represented in such a way that man owes Him an *account* of himself. The "Christ-impulse" is not a *thou* confronting an individual with absolute divine omnipotence. Never within Anthroposophy have I heard anyone speak of divine judgment with the *same* implacability with which the Bible and the Church do and must speak of it. This is connected to the fact that Anthroposophy is a science of *experience*. As such, it treats only of what can be experienced, and so must in a certain sense leave the highest values of faith undecided. But Anthroposophy's meaning is only fulfilled within an individual person when he manages faithfully—and obediently—once again to come closer to God and divine revelation, to the supreme power that cannot be scientifically known. Rudolf Steiner himself knew very well that everything open to experience derives from something that is at bottom unknowable. He wished to awaken the sense for this "Highest" through his science of experience. The outsider may find it difficult to discern, or even to acknowledge, this wish; but it belongs in this context because it helps to show why Anthroposophy is wholly outside the Church.

It is clear that at a moment of great need, God has once more shown himself to be close at hand with help. It is clear that the situation of Christian life and the life of the Church is more hopeful now than it was half a century ago. Indeed, in the Church, crucial testimony and probation were, if I may say so, never lacking, but these are certainly less impressed upon the public mind today than they were fifty years ago. Let me offer two examples of this, chosen almost at random (and which could easily be multiplied): one from Protestantism and one from Catholicism.

In Kurt Walter's book *God in the Concentration Camp*, we find these words:

> Christ descended for us all into those depths where all human greatness and glory and magnificence is long gone and at an end, where there is no fine and grand word spoken, no beautiful or blessed sound heard, no great and splendid thought, not even any "religious thought," perceived, received, or conceived; where man is nothing, nothing at all any more, other than needy humanity— the trampled worm, the creature writhing in pain and torment, who knows nothing at all any longer, other than *I am thirsty* and *Why hast thou abandoned me?* Christ descended for us and with us to this lowest depth of humanity when he hung on the cross, that he might become our savior and a "faithful high priest before God." And because, in the concentration camp, this lowest depth was a place in which we have often enough found ourselves, we have also, insofar as we listened to Christ, tasted the grace to meet him and to discover the trace of God on earth, and to follow that trace. For God's trace on earth was a trace of blood. And yet it is at the same time a trace of light, pointing out the path from earth to heaven.

And in the *Letters From Captivity* by "Brother Paul," the founder of the Una Sancta movement, we find a prayer that the author wrote in the Gestapo prison shortly before he was beheaded:

> Only one further prayer: Holy, all-powerful God, my Father, in the great crisis of my life I come to You, trusting the promise made by Your only Son, and the blood he shed for me. With Jesus Christ, my lord and master, I beseech you: "O my Father, if it be possible, let this cup pass from me: nevertheless not as I will, but as thou wilt." Yes, I believe that whatever your wise and beneficent providence decides for me will be for my salvation. Thus I say to it in advance the unqualified Yes of my obedience. In the name of Jesus I ask you: give me the strength of the Holy Spirit, that I may remain in this trusting obedience to you until the end. For I know that I am and remain your child, and that I will inherit your life of eternal blessedness. Amen.

Such voices were exceptions at the turn of the century, if they were to be heard at all. Today such voices are certainly not the rule, but they are nonetheless a sign that the spiritual situation is quite different now from what it was then. So far as I can tell, the Christian world has, from roughly the end of the First World War onwards (when the Baltic martyrs died for their faith) hearkened anew and transformed itself. At the beginning of the twenties, to take one example from many, the Berneuchener Movement was set up and very soon had a reanimating effect for the better on Protestant church life.[7] In the thirties, Protestant Christianity in large part rediscovered itself through the Barmen Declaration[8] and in the Bekennende Kirche ("Confessing Church")[9] it fenced itself off from the connection with state power that had previously been so dangerous. The Liturgical Movement[10] in the Catholic church had a similar effect, and with its help a large circle of Catholics acquired a much more living conception of the Church. (Romano Guardini was already speaking in 1925 of an "awakening of the Church in the soul.") All this became more and more visible to me. What I had previously only *known* about through Protestant friends, or (I think as early as 1922) had *read* about in the work of Romano Guardini, now became increasingly *important* to me.

Today, however, it is no longer the time to think about "evolution," or to represent the "second coming of Christ" almost as an event that could be predicted by natural science from which only a thin wall separates us ("wall" being a value-free term from the field of physics), as is done again and again in anthroposophical writings. But no anthroposophist will find it easy to celebrate the

7. The Berneuchen Movement was born in the 1920s, after the radical changes caused by the First World War. The founders felt it was necessary to give spiritual life a more concrete form in order to throw off the influence of liberal theology. ED

8. In brief, the Barmen Declaration (1934) gave a doctrinal basis for Protestant resistance to German nationalism. ED

9. The Confessing Church was a movement for revival within the German Protestant churches that developed in the 1930s from their resistance to Adolf Hitler's attempt to make them an instrument of Nazi propaganda. ED

10. The Liturgical Movement, spanning the nineteenth and twentieth centuries, was a scholarly project for the reform of worship. It began in the Catholic church and spread to many other Christian churches, including the Anglican Communion, the Lutheran, and some other Protestant churches.

reanimation of the spirit of the Christian Church in his heart. That Church was supposed to be replaced, in accordance with "evolution," by a "free" life of the spirit. Thus there are, remarkably or unremarkably, many opinions about the churches in the anthroposophical corpus, opinions perhaps not entirely false forty or fifty years ago, but that are no longer correct today, and strictly speaking are simply repeating what Rudolf Steiner "handed down" in his time. Yet I can only intimate this briefly. And what I mean to say, despite the fact that the life of the Church is eternal, may be summarized in this formula: "the hour of the Church has returned."

Thus I dared to examine in an unprejudiced way what the anthroposophical movement in the world *actually* was, rather than what its *task* was, what was expected of it, or what were the achievements of individual anthroposophists. And on the other side, I had to look towards the Church, and especially the Catholic church. What really was it, this Church to which I had never in my life devoted even the first inklings of genuine attention?

Although I did not know the Church, and therefore possessed no concept of it, I thought of it as an essential spiritual power, which (although nothing was said about it in the anthroposophical movement that did not reject or belittle it) was regarded as a dangerous opponent. And it is true: the Church cannot without reservations approve of the practice of the "free" anthroposophical life of the spirit. Rudolf Steiner spoke for those people who had fallen away from the Church, or who were falling away from it. Could one seriously expect the Church to approve when, for example, the creation of the world was discussed without any mention of God, or when the Church itself was represented as an obsolete power-center promoting unfreedom? Here I should like to add that it is part of the essence of anthroposophical thought that one condemns nothing, but tries to understand everything. To this extent, all anthroposophical thinking can be described as tolerant. But since everything is understood in the light of Anthroposophy and its doctrine of development, many of its "characterizations" become in reality equivalent to spiritual condemnations. Formally, no single anthroposophical idea about the Church is a condemnation, but in their effect on souls, almost all are so. I myself participated for many years in holding the religious life-forms of the people around me at that time to be obsolete. I also lacked any feeling for what the effect of that on other people's souls must be. After my conversion, there was one anthroposophist who sometimes thought he was playing a trump card against me when he cried, "What about the rosary?" He had certainly never prayed the rosary in his life, but his judgment was fixed. I myself held only too many such fixed judgments. So what *was* the Catholic church? Had *it* perhaps shown itself to be a spiritual power that could counteract modern secularization and spiritual fragmentation, and that could prevent catastrophes through the divine power dwelling within it?

This was not the case. No doubt was possible on this matter; the situation of the world clearly showed that. Anthroposophy, however, had become essential to my life particularly because it was supposed to prevent or obviate world disasters. What if even the Catholic church could not restore the old "universality"? Here I had to see something that is quite obvious to Christians: for the public collective life of humanity, "universality" has irrevocably disappeared. Humanity is split more and more into two camps (these have nothing *at all* to do with political camps). These camps can be called the Christian camp and the anti-Christian camp. The second camp can never entirely be won back; medieval "universality" can never be wholly restored ("my kingdom is not of this world"). The Church has to champion the good and the Christian spirit. Or, more precisely, through the Church, Christ himself champions the good, but champions it within a world that, according to his own words, is split into two camps.

In my early anthroposophical period I was an optimist in the sense that I believed in progress; slowly, I later became an optimist in the sense of believing in redemption. Since the previously hoped-for unity of the whole is irretrievably lost, it *could* be the essential task (so I then thought: I am here reporting how things were for me at the time) to join the "camp" that decisively championed what was good and Christian. But does this happen in the Catholic church? From what I had "known" or "thought" up to that point, I could not accept that it did. I could not do so even on the grounds that a man whom I respected had shown me the Church in a clear light. My only recourse, then, was to apply anthroposophical epistemology (according to which knowledge only comes about when a "percept" and a "concept" meet to form a whole within an individual person) to the Catholic church. My first efforts brought me to roughly the conclusion I shall truthfully set out next, although it shows that at that time I still had no inkling of the nature or the mystery of the Church.

First, the Catholic church is not an "evil power center" in which a priestly caste bent on domination keeps souls in a state of unfreedom. To the contrary, it is a lawfully ordered and hierarchically constructed (yet also living and organic) community—one that in no way infringes personal freedom. Naturally, anyone who rejects the binding acknowledgement of objective truth, and who experiences the requirement to live according to God's commandments as an "assault on freedom," must be of a different opinion. The following fact seemed to me to be telling. As things stand and have long stood, the Church is not able to keep anyone within its magic circle by force, nor to compel them to behave as it would wish. What can actually happen to anyone who does not follow the commandments of the Church? With what "tools of power" can the Church prevent people from denying it or fighting it? In reality, the members of the Church belong to it of their own free will. It is a spiritual power that remains alive on earth only thanks to the willingness of those who confess its creed to make sacrifices for it. No one can force me to join the Church. If I join the Church, I do it without any compulsion—that is, of my own free will.

Second, in the present struggle of the spirit, the Catholic church is the only power that has remained spiritual, without any compromise. The concordat with the Third Reich was not a spiritual compromise, but an attempt to protect Catholic and Christian life even in that state. Moreover, even on a small scale, what power or movement on earth defends God's commandment "thou shalt not kill" in respect of abortion and contraception as consistently as does the Catholic church? True, the Church wields no external power here, for how can it prevent the perpetrators from doing what they do?

Third, the Church is an important, indeed *the* important guardian of tradition. It makes what is past present, and develops (slowly and carefully, it is true, but in a living way) something that is to come from within what already exists, something in no way one-sided and without setting apart an "elite" such as the anthroposophical movement (in *one* respect) represents. The significance of tradition did not dawn on me all at once, for until then, like Goethe's graduate in *Faust*, Part Two, I had taken freedom from any tradition to be a distinguishing mark of spiritual authenticity. A wise man once said to me, "every form of Herostratism (Herostratus set a temple on fire) is damaging." I began to understand how much I had done this myself, and how often my friends had, too.

Fourth, I gradually saw in the Catholic church the chief site of a practice of devotion unparalleled in the West. No one who lives with this practice needs to have the significance of adoration pointed out to them. Here, adoration is objectively practiced and continued in a living manner, even if, unfortunately, it may not always be genuine in all those who practice it. In this domain, it goes without saying (given human nature) that the outsider notices the negative more readily than the positive. Nor was it any different with me, even at that time. I did not join in with the practice of Christian devotion. I just noticed it and pondered it. To me, the Church as a whole seemed comparable to an ancient tree: one person looks at it and sees only the cracked bark, another only a decayed fallen bough, a third the visibly living twigs, a fourth the leaves, blossoms, and fruit, while a fifth, perhaps, sees all these things at once.

At first, the conclusions I have mentioned (which still did not concern my inner life in any way) had not the slightest effect on my heart and soul. But in comparison with the attitude I had previously held towards the Church, they represented a progress not to be undervalued. How else, other than through the formation of my ideas, could I progress? What I knew or guessed about the Catholic church as a whole (and I was concerned only with the whole at that time) can be stated in the following sentences. They are to be found in Valentin Tomberg's book *The Art of the Good: On the Regenera-*

tion of Fallen Justice,[11] and say what I mean better and more clearly than I would be able to do myself:

> A community comes into being and remains viable thanks to the common *value* whose bearer it knows itself to be. These values can be in the *past*, in which case it is a common tradition that binds people together in a community; they can be in the *present*, for example, particular institutions and ways of life; or they can lie in the *future*, when for example they are concerned with a state that has set itself a programmatic goal of expansion.[12] The Soviet Union, for example, has a political goal that reaches into the future; China, conversely, had for millennia the political goal of the conservation of the traditions of the past.[13] The Western democracies see it as their task to work in the *present* towards the end of the safeguarding and dissemination of the democratic system. There is *one* community, however, which has the goal simultaneously of nurturing tradition, of developing a universal efficacy in the present, and of striving towards a distant universal goal in the future—namely, the *Catholic church*.
>
> What distinguishes the Catholic church is that it serves the goal of the conservation and nurture of tradition in a very intensive way, yet at the same time participates no less intensively to shape and contest all areas of contemporary life—and also strives towards an ideal of the future that embraces all mankind. Out of all known larger human communities, the Catholic church is the most perfect in this respect: it never forgets the past, it works and takes care for the future, and it takes an active position towards the events of the present day. It is also the most solid and enduring community, not only in comparison to political communities, but also in comparison to states (apart from those of the Far East)— indeed, in comparison to nations themselves. It has outlived all crises: the struggle with pagan empire, the barbarian migratory invasions, the encounter with Islam, the Reformation, the French Revolution and the Napoleonic wars, the wave of materialism in the nineteenth century, and finally, also, the storms of the present.

11. First published in German as *Degeneration und Regeneration der Rechtswissenschaft* (Bonn: Verlag Götz Schwippert, 1946). Citation is from the recent English translation as shown above (Brooklyn, NY: Angelico Press, 2021), 83–86.

12. Cf. G. Jellinek, *Allgemeine Staatslehre*, 3rd edition (Berlin, 1920), 242ff.

13. It is to be recalled that this book was published in 1946. ED.

In some of these crises, empires collapsed and dynasties rose and fell. Yet the Church remained standing and conserved its tradition, its hierarchy, its continuity, and its ideal. How is the fact of the super-eminence of the Catholic church to all other human communities in this respect to be explained?

In my view, the reason lies in the fact that it is the Catholic church which most corresponds to the requirements for a harmonious state of society as set out above. It is the most democratic community, since every son of a peasant can in principle achieve the highest station, the papacy. It is at the same time the most aristocratic community, since it is constructed in a strictly hierarchical fashion. It is arranged more plurally than any other community (one need only think of the many lay and monastic orders with their rules and regulations), yet at the same time displays a unity among all the different races and nations of the world, a unity that could never be attained or preserved by force, but could only be brought about, and *will* only be brought about, by virtue of a unity of values (of religious belief, for example).

Reason postulates the following, and the experience of the nineteenth century teaches us the same. If one wishes to bring about a durable, solidly based and harmonious community—that is, one that embodies *peace*—then either one must recognize that the Catholic church is such a community, or, if for any reason one is unable or unwilling to recognize this fact, one must found another community that is in all essentials modeled on the Catholic church: a community held together by a common ethico-religious ideal, by a common worldview, and by a common tradition, and which is nevertheless not national, nor confined to a single social class, but has a universally human character. Any attempt to form a community lacking these qualities will *eo ipso* be destined to collapse. To the extent that communities in part evince some of these qualities, however, they will be the more capable of possessing greater stability and permanence.

When I could think thoughts like those quoted here, I could already see more clearly that I had inwardly moved a long way from the Anthroposophical Society and the Christian Community. In the meantime, however, it was still the "postulates" of reason alone that I heard within me, and there were still powerful obstacles in the way of my germinating Yes to the Church.

10

On the Way to the Church

NOW THAT MY ACCOUNT IS APPROACHING THE DESCRIP-
tion of my conversion, perhaps many readers will be expecting a
portrayal of my feelings, of my experiences, of some visible transformation. But I have nothing of this sort to report. Before my conversion, I had no feelings for the Church, and no experiences of it.
Nor did I experience any transformation through it. The way to my
conversion was prepared by thinking alone.

This, however, is precisely why I decided to tell the story of my
conversion. Feelings and experiences are always bound up with the
particular nature of the individual, although different individuals
can have congruent feelings and experiences. Only thoughts are
objective, that is, suprapersonal. The same thoughts can be thought
in the same way by the most varied people. Indeed, if *true* thought
is actually *thought*, it will be definitive not only for its individual
proponents, but for everyone who receives it and lets it have its
effect. The Pythagorean theorem, for example, or trigonometry in
general, or the theory of gravity, are understood in the same way by
every consciousness to which they are disclosed. Truth is always
unequivocal. It lights up in different ways in different people, but it
always lights up as one and the same truth.

Admittedly, the capacity to absorb new cosmic and religious ideas
is not found so very often. Most people are tied to habits and inclinations with deep roots in the soul, which it is difficult to see past.
There is of course nothing wrong with feelings and inclinations.
Indeed, our world is becoming more and more desolate *because* the
life of the soul is becoming more and more feeble and people are
increasingly shutting off from one another—and woe betide us if
the armor-plating were to become thicker! But if we are to talk

about spiritual freedom, it must be said that it is possible to look at oneself "as a stranger" (as Rudolf Steiner put it). It is possible not only to believe the arguments for whatever one holds to be true, or follows as truth, but also to find the reason for the arguments.

This, however, comes at a price. One must be able to overcome oneself, to pick oneself up. One must be able to think things through to their foundation. Sigmund Freud, for example, whose psychoanalysis was discussed above, did not understand the deeper reason for his ideas, any more than did Ernst Haeckel, who exercised a powerful influence on modern materialism. In essence, each of them followed the interests that arose in the course of their lives. The same goes for the theologians who developed and championed liberal Protestant theology. Indeed, it goes for most of those, great and small alike, who have founded schools on their worldviews. Divine truth cannot be fragmented in the way one might suppose, given the appearance of so many different and incompatible tendencies all claiming to represent it. Even the reformers of the sixteenth century barely knew the reasons for the goals they pursued so ardently in their lives, but only the arguments for them. They "did not wish," for example, to blow up the previously unified Western church, but they *did* blow it up. This means that there were forces at play in their work of which they did not take account, and wherever that happens, one cannot speak of what is brought about in or by means of people as being *fully* intentional. It is easier, in any case, to be objective in the field of the natural sciences than it is in one's own spiritual life. I was only able to become a member of the Catholic church because I succeeded in *not* allowing feelings and habits to be decisive (or, perhaps, because the gift of not letting them decide was given me) and in overcoming prejudices. Let me at this point confess the following of myself.

Self-knowledge showed me that I was decidedly a loner. Through Anthroposophy, I had so completely absorbed the idea of personal freedom and an "evolution of consciousness" that all categorization and subordination seemed to me a shameful weakness. The "I" wanted to stand alone by itself rather than join with anyone else in a "We." But now, more and more, I was thinking "if everyone were to take this attitude and to behave this way, society would split apart, and the many people who are incapable of such 'independence' would be left alone, and would then certainly be much more at risk. Christian life, however—this is a truism—can only be achieved in community." Having come that far, the following thought gradually grew within me. "You must fall into line, however difficult you may find it!" This thought became stronger and stronger. But my pride held out against it. In the end, despite all my resistance, I wanted to make common cause with the small and the least, in accordance with the instruction of the *Imitatio Christi*: "Nevertheless thou must beware thou neglect not those [tasks] which are common, being more ready for what is private. But having fully and faithfully accomplished all which thou art bound and enjoined to do, if thou hast any spare time, betake thee to thyself, as thy devotion shall desire." But under which spiritual power could I fall into line?

At close quarters and from long direct experience, I was familiar only with the Anthroposophical Society and the Christian Community, and neither had sufficiently convinced me of its significance for and future in the world. Since the Orthodox church was completely outside my experience, only the Protestant and Catholic churches came into my reckoning.

After my conversion, a Protestant friend once offered the opinion that I had opted for "Catholic cake" in preference to "Protestant bread" without knowing enough about Protestant Christianity. The objection was understandable, but incorrect. In the first place, what one eats in the Catholic church is not cake but, likewise, bread; and in the second, it was not a question of my not being familiar with Protestant Christianity. On the contrary, before my conversion I was much more familiar with the Protestant church than with the Catholic church. I had spent almost my whole life with Protestant Christians, was open to Protestant theological works (apart from those from a certain period), and had repeatedly attended Protestant church services. There certainly are people who in later years, as a result of unhappy and one-sided experiences in their youth, are bold enough to "condemn" one church or the other; but such "condemnations" have never convinced me. In the Christian Community, for instance, people were always coming forward to recite certain experiences they had had in the Protestant Church as proofs of the value of the Christian Community. This method always seemed questionable to me, since it can be applied to everything. There is no community that cannot have certain experiences of it turned against it by someone or other. In essence, there were three things that prevented me from joining the Protestant church. Two of them (the absence of a hierarchy and the absence of the full complement of seven sacraments) I have mentioned above, and these objections were more strongly confirmed the more I thought about them. As for the third reason, I must now undertake to say more.

Protestant Christianity is irrevocably split into national churches and special interest groups. These do indeed give rise to a varied life, and can seek to establish connections and community with each other. But they do not immediately represent a visible unity. In Protestant Christianity, people not only speak of but also believe in "a" church. But for them, this church cannot really be imagined on earth, but only in the spirit. In the sense of Protestant Christianity, one can say that "Church" is everywhere that Christ is at work—a definition that even today I do not consider false, but only incomplete. In opposition to the "realist" Catholic conception of the Church, the Protestant conception can be called "spiritualistic." But as the Body of the Lord, the Church cannot be merely spiritual. It must also be *embodied* and *physical*. Through the multiplicity of churches and movements present in Protestant Christianity, the complete spiritual integrity of the Church, its spiritual power, is diminished. The power of the Catholic church (the Protestant reader is not, please, to think of earthly and political "power" at this point!) rests on its integrity, on its unity of spiritual and physical elements. Can schism within the Church be in the spirit of Jesus Christ, who called the apostles to be one, and who at the end of his life prayed for the unity of the Church? Does not the diminished power of Christianity in the modern world result from its lack of unity? And can an essential spiritual and bodily unity be restored in any other way than by bringing the original idea of unity back into being again? Like Christophorus, I was seeking the strongest master. If I was to fall into line, then it could only be by joining the Catholic church. If joining it were to succeed, this would not be on my account (I "could" remain alone), but for the sake of Christendom, of the Church, of Christ. I wanted to serve, but I could only serve even the "strongest master" if I had no misgivings whatever about him. My misgivings were, however, many; they sat on my heart like couch grass in a field overrun with weeds; and only thinking could show me the way forward. Of the necessary prayer I was—alas, but this is how it was—incapable.

As early as the summer of 1944, when the Catholic church had already entered my inner field of vision, I found to my surprise and delight that the "spiritual training" to which the book *Knowledge of the Higher Worlds* had led me called, at bottom, for something very like a churchly and ascetic training. All that is lacking, of course, is the idea of ecclesiastical authority, of dogma, of obedience to the faith. That was when I managed to write the essay that was perhaps most important of all to my own development. It bore the title "The Christ-impulse in Rudolf Steiner's book *Knowledge of the Higher Worlds And How to Attain It*."[1] It then became clear to me that here, in words and ideas in no way reminiscent of the Church, or tradition, or even Christianity itself, what is being spoken about is the process of becoming a saint, in a form that modern people can grasp. This discovery was essentially nothing other than my own becoming aware of what is already present in the anecdote mentioned earlier, of Rudolf Steiner and the two Catholic priests. But one has only ever really understood something when it has lit up the depths of one's soul, rather than the soul's surface alone.

In the book mentioned, the word "grace," for example, does not appear. After all, the book is written precisely for those people to whom the word meant nothing. However, Rudolf Steiner writes that "I must do everything I can to build up my soul and spirit, but I shall wait quite calmly until I am found worthy of a particular illumination by the higher powers." This fits with much, and at bottom with everything, that is said in *Knowledge of the Higher Worlds*. For me, this discovery was at first deeply delightful, but then also mind-expanding. For only then and by just this means did I become *capable* of opening myself, and very soon also *willing* to open myself, to the language of tradition. That language says nothing at all about

1. This essay may be found in the Appendix.

"eyes of the soul" and "ears of the spirit," but in its way helps to develop them by specially emphasizing the ethical and religious laws that are to be followed—laws to which Rudolf Steiner points only from a distance and while "leaving" the reader "perfectly free."

A little while later I came across the book *The Imitation of Christ*, which had been so important to my father, and which I had until then hardly looked at. In a crucial passage, Rudolf Steiner had earnestly recommended it, but I had never heard a single anthroposophist say a good word about it, and had for many years considered myself above such "medieval" forms of piety and devotional manuals. Now, as though making good an omission, I read the book at least ten times through in a short period. I sensed the nourishing power of the book, and learned (and wanted to learn) to share the feelings of those who spoke a different religious language than that which I had up until then been accustomed to myself. How greatly I lacked piety, humility, faith! How greatly I lacked the imitation of Christ! I stood as though helpless before the vocabulary in which, from the earliest times onwards, Christianity and the Church had proclaimed and handed down the truth! And I had myself, in part, imagined myself into this helplessness, by believing that everything "medieval" was "behind me." Thomas à Kempis (or whoever may have written the book) opened to me the temple of a common Christian language. I no longer thought that the only important thing was to extract an "up-to-date" message, but held it to be the highest task to perceive the language of truth in any garb, and above all in one that had outlasted millennia.

For the first time, sad to admit, I could have and seek for a spiritually open relationship with my fellow man. In all honesty, until then I had seen all non-anthroposophists (despite everything I have already said about my relation to Anthroposophy and anthroposophists) as "outsiders" who lacked the one thing that mattered. Now, for the first time, I became aware in the depths of my heart that the "evolution of consciousness" of which Rudolf Steiner had spoken by no means resided as much as I had thought in the area of mental alertness and self-consciousness, but that it embraced the ethical, and meant the transformation of one's nature by love. Thus the ground of one's soul was, so to speak, slowly worked over, and the beginning of a real sense of community was awoken. At last it became clear to me that whether one "evolves one's consciousness" depends not so much on speaking about it and consciously seeking it, as on how one lives. The consciousness of someone who understands only the latest and most up-to-date language cannot register what differs from that language. Now that I had become aware of this lack, I wanted to do what I could to overcome it.

At that time I also began to attend Holy Mass now and again. At first I did so quite presumptuously—that is, in a belief that it would soon disclose to me its secrets. But in fact I came up against things that were simply incomprehensible to me, and was obliged to recognize that I would only become acquainted with it slowly and with difficulty. I had spent weeks and months previously on Wagner's *Parsifal*, Goethe's *Faust*, Schiller's *Letters on Aesthetic Education*, and Rilke's *Duino Elegies*. Was I really to expect that the Holy Mass would give up its secrets in an afternoon, so to speak, just because I was at home in the The Act of Consecration of Man in the Christian Community service, and still retained a little Latin from my schooldays?

For a long time, an understanding of the Mass emerged only on an intellectual level, from individual passages. In order to grasp the whole, the mystery, I had need of an organ I had yet to develop. Only its rudiments were present in me before my conversion. Despite my many attendances at the Act of the Consecration of Man, I was incapable of understanding a different liturgy. Before my conversion, I had only arrived at an approximately correct understanding of Holy Mass, but had not yet acquired the strength to live alongside and within it. I "studied" it and said Yes to it for good reasons as the centerpiece of the life of the Catholic church— but *going* to it was not a personal need for me, and to take part in it was hardly a personal benediction. But perhaps what had once happened outwardly was now repeating itself: the catechumens cannot yet themselves participate in the mystery.

At first, many formulas in the text of Holy Mass were especially dear to me. For example, that indescribably humble and solemn expression, "Christ took the bread *in sanctas ac venerabiles manus suas* (in his holy and venerable hands)." The second prayer of the Eucharistic liturgy, *Deus, qui humanae substantiae dignitatem et mirabiliter condidisti* ("God, Thou hast wondrously created the dignity of human nature") struck me strongly at an early stage. The elevation of the paten at the beginning of the Eucharistic liturgy, which does not occur in the Act of the Consecration of Man, filled me with growing happiness, and I could at least begin to grasp the *Sanctus* ("Holy, Holy, Holy"), or the *Domine, non sum dignus* ("Lord, I am not worthy"). As a whole, the Holy Eucharist resembled a meadow full of flowers or a starry sky, but I had still to get to know the plenitude of individual blossoms and the multiplicity of celestial lights. When I converted, I knew at least a few "flowers," and, at least, this or that "constellation." But although my spirit began to be satisfied with many individual things, the whole still stood like an alien body before me. Nor did my heart drive me towards it. I had converted almost out of "duty over inclination," on purely intellectual grounds, and in the consciousness of bringing a sacrifice along with me. I wanted to "change my station within the whole of Christianity," to exchange that which seemed to me objectively less fruitful for another that seemed more productive to me. To a retrospective view, this attitude seems extremely presumptuous. Nonetheless, it contained a certain selflessness, and the latter was later rewarded beyond measure. I wanted to *give*, and I was *given to*. Among other things, I was given the insight that my giving was in a poor state, and that I was very much in need of receiving.

Even after I had gotten to know much that was positive about the Church, and even when in principle I no longer doubted that it was the chief Christian power in contemporary life, I lacked deep trust in it. I was far from thinking that it would also have the right view of just those questions with which I had occupied myself. Those things I had come to know which I have mentioned so far (whose clarity is partly owed to my describing them in the light of what I came fully to understand only later) would never have been enough to make me join the Church. Before doing that, I had to acquire a knowledge of individual questions and individual facts sufficient to satisfy me. My exertions stood under the sign of the words of the apostle Thomas: "Except I shall see in his hands the print of the nails, and put my finger into the print of the nails, and thrust my hand into his side, I will not believe." Later, at a Catholic youth day,

I heard our bishop, Johannes, approving of this attitude. "The Church demands of us nothing that we cannot observe," he said. I later found the truth of this idea confirmed. Knowledge does not stand in opposition to faith, but prepares the way for it.

Admittedly, I later saw that this attitude of mine ought not to be a general rule. Not everyone either could or ought to "see" for themselves and put their hand "into his side"—not, at least, as a condition of their faith, but rather as its consequence. The twelve apostles already bore their testimony to people who could not have the experiences they had had, and who nevertheless believed them. The Church would never have been built without faith. This too can be observed, and the consequences can be drawn from this observation. Even in the Church there can (and even must) be "knowers" (which does not mean "discoverers"), people who are capable of fully grounding their faith position not only as a whole, but also in detail.

Anthroposophy had prepared me for much in the Catholic church that is alien ("un-biblical"!) to Protestant Christians. On the governance of the Divine Hierarchies, for example, about which, with one exception, I had never heard a word from Protestants, Rudolf Steiner had communicated a great deal, and even in detail (publicly, he had done this in the foundational work *An Outline of Esoteric Science* in particular): that every person has a guardian angel, that the highest hierarchical beings are most strongly alive in sacrifice, that many archangels are rightly called by name—these and related matters had long been known to me intellectually. And on this subject Rudolf Steiner was not interpreting writings handed down by tradition, but giving expression to present experience. If there were a way to adopt them, all these insights could be received into the Church's thinking.

Rudolf Steiner also imparted many insights as to the fate of "the dead," so far as that fate is humanly expressible. According to his account, those who have died are by no means separated from the world of those alive on earth, any more than they are according to the teaching of the Catholic church. Because of this preparation, I was quickly and readily able to see that the Church as a whole—as *ecclesia triumphans* and *ecclesia patiens* (as the Church Triumphant and the Church Suffering)—also includes the faithful Christian departed. What the Catholic church teaches about "purgatory" is in substantial agreement with what Rudolf Steiner said about the purification of the soul after death, and can be understood even by one who does not himself "see." That a soul which indeed believes in Christ but is still suffering from the consequences of sin stands in need of cleansing in order to participate in the pure experience of God, and that this cleansing cannot be accomplished without suffering, can be understood even by someone unable to penetrate into the realm of the dead to experience it himself. Even on earth there are certain goods and experiences that can only be participated in after the necessary preparations are made; and inner maturity is never to be effected by external power. All deeper self-knowledge tells man that he stands in need of purification. Intimations of "purgatory" can already be observed amid life here on earth. Petitionary prayer, the living community of the faithful, and grace: these may, admittedly, be capable of removing the burden from an individual in an unfathomable way, without encroaching on his dignity. Who can fathom the transition from "purgatory" to "heaven"?

Above all, the truth of the Creed, the fundamental Christian truth, was deeply familiar to me. What Rudolf Steiner (after his own fashion, of course) says about the course of the world and becoming human not only agrees with the Creed, but can directly awaken a sense for the latter, if not at first for the verbal form in which it has been handed down. Here I had (in a general "spiritualistic" way) long since heard of the nature of the Church, and had understood and affirmed it. The life of the Trinity and God's governance, the *Et incarnatus est* ("He became flesh") and the *Et iterum venturus est cum gloria* ("He will come again in glory") had been variously and vividly expounded to me.

I have already mentioned that the idea of the priesthood, the idea that the sacraments were seven in number, and the idea of "transubstantiation" had long preoccupied me and persuaded me. At the time I am now speaking of I had to learn to recognize the law and the forms they are given in the Catholic church. Here, there were quite different and more favorable preconditions afforded to me than if I had had to make the step from the Protestant to the Catholic church.

It therefore seems to me appropriate to say something at this juncture about the principles governing the relationship between the
Church and Anthroposophy (and the Christian Community). Up
to this point some readers may have seen or supposed that Anthroposophy is something that is only harmful and risky, and their
opinion may only have been strengthened by my conversion,
despite everything that has so far been said in favor of Anthroposophy. The following, however, is in my judgment true. Anthroposophy was indeed intended by its founder to be a "science." It was
described by him as such, and according to his very words is supposed to be "neither a religion nor a substitute for religion" (as an
elderly anthroposophist once confirmed to me). In the hearts of
those who follow Anthroposophy, it has nevertheless for the most
part become either one or the other of these. This is evidenced,
purely externally, in the fact that there is hardly a single adherent of
the movement who actively participates in the life of the Church.
Hence it must be admitted that Anthroposophy *as a whole* is in conflict with the faith of the Church, and *as a whole* is to be rejected by
the Church. This said, further reflection is, however, called for.
True, many things in Anthroposophy cannot but be condemned in
the light of the doctrine of faith, for example, its theory of freedom
and its ideas about the Catholic church. Many things in it, however,
could be affirmed without qualification, and in my opinion ought
to be made use of accordingly.

I will try to explain what I mean by that, but let me first state the
following. Although For and Against, Yes and No, may become clear
from the whole of this work, it will perhaps be good to clarify matters right here. In chapters seven, eight, and nine I set out the reasons why I could not remain a member of the anthroposophical
movement in the long term, and yet much is said in favor of
Anthroposophy in this tenth chapter. How does this hang together?
Has the author himself arrived at complete clarity about the matter?
Isn't he contradicting himself? He is not. I have never doubted the
productiveness of the exercises given in the book *Knowledge of the
Higher Worlds*. I have never, for example, doubted the existence of

the "etheric" and "astral" worlds of which Anthroposophy speaks. Nor have I ever doubted that good and essential work is being done in the individual fields of anthroposophical study (pedagogy, medicine, agriculture, and so on). Consequently, I have in no way moved away from all that, nor are the misgivings presented in the previous chapters any part of that. Those misgivings concerned Anthroposophy *only* insofar as the salvation of the world is supposed to depend upon it. I myself also once shared that expectation and that claim. I could not be an anthroposophist just because Anthroposophy was good for me personally, or because individual anthroposophical undertakings were of essential value; I could only be an anthroposophist if and for so long as I held the view that the *most* important thing for the redemption of the world was happening there. This view disappeared from my life, and its disappearance was the condition for my conversion. But I never rejected everything anthroposophical on that account. Its values continue to exist, and I can acknowledge them even if today it is not Anthroposophy but the Church that seems to be *the* essential Christian power. The misgivings presented in the foregoing text and the acknowledgements presented in what follows stand on separate levels. They are not mutually exclusive; rather, they complement each other. The *logos spermatikos* can be understood, and always should be understood, in the light of the Catholic church.

It is true of what follows, as it was of what went before—but even more so—that this theme is inexhaustible. Everything living can and should be considered from a number of points of view. The relationship of the Catholic church to the anthroposophical movement and to the Christian Community resembles that between the Catholic church and Protestant Christianity. From the point of view of dogmatics, the latter is to be condemned only insofar as it represents a heresy and propounds doctrines that contradict those of the Catholic church (doctrines of original sin and justification, of the sacraments, of tradition, and so on). But everything in Protestant dogmatic teaching that is in accordance with Catholic doctrine (the Apostles' Creed, the doctrine of baptism, the doctrine of the significance of Holy Scripture, and so on) is to be acknowledged. But *people* are not to be condemned, as if they were dogmas. In the Una Sancta movement and elsewhere, one speaks always and everywhere of our "brothers and sisters."

It therefore becomes painfully clear here that it is impossible to speak about religious and ecclesiastical questions in such a way that all one's audience will be satisfied and have the impression that the truth has been sufficiently communicated. From the side of the anthroposophical movement (to which the Christian Community belongs) much that concerns the Church is unsatisfactorily expounded—often, indeed, with "incomprehensible" errors. I, for my part, have done what I can to portray these matters adequately. But no one on earth *can* actually speak "for everyone." I am writing here primarily for Catholic Christians, not for anthroposophists. I should like, however, to say once more that words taken out of context always distort the author's thought, rather than perfectly reproducing it.

First, on the Christian Community. It is by its nature a "church" with a claim to authority (for without such a claim there is no "church"), with a priesthood, with a sevenfold sacramental life, and so on; but unfortunately it is isolated within Christianity as a whole and does not sufficiently acknowledge the value of the other members of that body. Nevertheless, it champions the Christian life, and awakens that life in individual people, a life that is, can, and ought to be in accordance with that which is cherished within the universal Christian Church for individual people. There is much in the Christian Community that should be acknowledged by the Catholic church as valuable and true. Where these valuable and true elements lie can only be shown by a detailed account.

As a "movement for religious renewal" that was begun outside the Catholic church, and also brought to completion outside it, the Christian Community cannot, indeed, be condoned by the Church. Moreover, it harbors much within it that contradicts the Church's teaching. For example, flowing water is not used in its baptisms; its priests do not stand within the apostolic succession; it was founded

on its own authority "from out of the spirit"; the thought of reincarnation and of karma is fostered by it; it does not oblige its members to confess any particular articles of faith, even though it and its
priests typically (of course) believe the same things. This matter of
principle may suffice here, and the question can at once be asked
what it is that makes people find their religious life in the Christian
Community.

Inwardly or outwardly, many "modern" people have fallen away
from the Church. They are not reached by its message, are not
influenced by the its judgments, and have lost any relationship to
tradition. They can be won over again to Christianity in many ways
and in other forms, as I myself experienced in my own case. One
can lament that they for the most part regard as new in itself what
in fact is only "new" to *them* personally, and that they find themselves able to affirm traditional Christianity only with difficulty or
hardly at all. But that Christ—for it is indeed He, rather than some
phantom in his place—can still be alive in many souls, is not to be
lamented, but to be welcomed.

People are drawn to the Christian Community by something else
as well. Given its lack of any dogmatic presuppositions and its
upfront, unqualified affirmation of "modern consciousness," the
Christian Community is oriented towards individuals as thinking
and knowing beings. Now, just what is "modern consciousness"? It
is the consciousness of a person in whom the power of faith has
more or less disappeared, a person who possesses little or no experience of God's power, a person for whom "nature" (including the
human and earthly world) has become almost everything. It is the
consciousness of the person who wishes to acknowledge no ethical,
spiritual, or religious authority over him, who is or would like to be
his own master without becoming aware of his own essential nothingness. In the light of the Church's doctrine of faith, "modern consciousness" is a melancholy and dangerous late stage of the Fall into
sin. It is "You shall be as gods" put into practice. From such a consciousness one can proceed further only into nothingness (a step
that has only too often been taken both theoretically and practically) or into one's own being (and this is what is called for and nurtured in the Christian Community, although not of course in it

alone). From the latter point of view one can compare the work of the Christian Community with the service of the compassionate Samaritan who took care of the man waylaid by robbers. The message of the Christian Community is heard by many precisely because they do not feel that it demands of them something they cannot give, but are instead left "free" by it. The Christian Community does not aim, in any case, to subject people again to authority but to make them *so* "free" that they will lead a Christian and godly life from their own inner resources, without needing to be told what to do by authority. Now, what should be said about this from the Church's point of view?

The Church can never approve the idea of freedom fostered within the Christian Community. Man, who is under the spell of sin, will never be able to live a perfectly godly life unless he acknowledges God as an *authority*, thus subjecting himself to God's commandments, and unless he relinquishes the self-rule of a "modern consciousness." This is why the Church answers No as a matter of principle to the spirit of the Christian Community. But on the other hand, the message and the life of the Christian Community reaches people whose ears are closed to the language of the Church and to the meaning of life within the Church. Should that not arouse our interest? In the Church (thanks be to God) the old, eternal truth is championed without any compromise made to whatsoever particular trends of the age. And yet in many respects it still fails to reach what has, unfortunately, become of humanity in our time. In thinking about any heresy, then, the question to be asked is why and how that heresy came to be. In this respect, then, the Christian Community presents a task, not for dogmatics, but for method. While it is true that there is at present some support for "modern consciousness" even within the Church,[2] the Church as a whole—since it is today not a "young shoot" but an "ancient tree—is conservative and can only grow slowly, even though its divine nature can be presented to the consciousness of any given age in forms that are ever new. To this extent the Christian Community

2. The writings of Romano Guardini can be mentioned in this connection.

represents an admonition whose importance is not negated by the fact that as a whole it is to be "condemned."

And now, second, on the anthroposophical movement in general, whose child or component part the Christian Community seems to be. In the light of Catholic truth, the anthroposophical movement too can and should be spoken of in two ways. First, Anthroposophy offers matter for dogmatics and apologetics. Second, however, it is a spiritual phenomenon whose individual utterances do not for the most part fall into the area of dogmatics and apologetics at all, but only seem to do so. It is very difficult to achieve complete clarity on this point. For example, the author was once asked by a Catholic priest to tell him what Anthroposophy "was." He tried to give an account of its nature, but was soon interrupted by the observation that all that was "pantheist." But what does "pantheist" mean? St Paul said of human beings that we "live, and move, and have our being" in God. With this, he made a thoroughly "pantheist" statement. And it is in this sense (and no other) that Anthroposophy is in any way "pantheist." It sets out quite concretely the extent to which "in Him we live, and move, and have our being." Is "pantheism," then, to be approved of when put forward by St Paul, but be worthy of condemnation when put forward by Rudolf Steiner? In this comparison, let us think only of "pantheism." In other respects Pauline theology does indeed differ greatly from the teaching of Rudolf Steiner.

The main difficulty for any condemnation of Anthroposophy on the part of the Church lies, however, in the following. Anthroposophy is "neither a religion nor a substitute for religion" (see above!) but a science. Since the efforts of scientific researchers around the year 1900 were primarily directed towards what was material and sensible in the world, there was a risk that divine governance in the world and over human beings would be forgotten. It was in this setting that Rudolf Steiner showed, in his research and insights, that and how divine spirit governed the sensible and the material. Who moves the earth and the firmaments? How do plants come to grow? What distinguishes the animals from the plants? Who (quite specifically) brings about the change of seasons, human cultures, and the facts (at first so enigmatic) of the destiny of human beings? And so on. How does man acquire an organ for what is essentially at work beneath the orderly unfolding of phenomena? Rudolf Steiner did not "refute" materialism. Rather, after having demonstrated that, to those receptive only to material things, the world understandably only appears materially, he provided the method by which something *other* than the material—something "supersensible," essential, and divine—could be discerned. In the realm of knowledge he also cultivated the religious life and everything that lies at the basis of that life. Anthroposophy is all-embracing. It concerns the whole of the world, rather than (as in the case of the other sciences) only a certain part of it. This explains how easy it is for the Church to take Anthroposophy as something that is *only* to be condemned, according to dogmatics. But dogmatics can only engage meaningfully with the portion of Anthroposophy that touches on the truths of faith, *not* with what concerns life, being, the spiritual in itself. It is, however, difficult precisely to discern this point, since the spirit of heresy that Anthroposophy as a whole possesses affects the individual parts too. Anyone looking for a valid judgment of Anthroposophy, however, may not merely dodge this difficulty.

To grasp the nature of Anthroposophy it is not necessary to trace the career of its founder before the point where he publicly entered upon his "spiritual science"—just as, to see the importance of Augustine's theology, it is not necessary to trace *his* career before his entry into the Church. The truth of Augustine's theology is shown by that theology itself. Just so can Anthroposophy also be understood on its own terms. Moreover, anyone who wants to arrive at a sufficiently *demonstrable* judgment of Anthroposophy ought not merely to have read, but to have *worked through*, the following books from his "pre-anthroposophical" period: *Truth and Knowledge: Prelude to a Philosophy of Freedom*; *A Theory of Knowledge Implicit in Goethe's World Conception*; *Intuitive Thinking as a Spiritual Path: A Philosophy of Freedom*; and *Goethe's Theory of Knowledge: An Outline of the Epistemology of His Worldview*.[3] As regards Steiner's anthroposophical work itself, however, the essential testimonies are the books *Theosophy: An Introduction to the Spiritual*

Processes in Human Life and in the Cosmos; *How to Know Higher Worlds: A Modern Path of Initiation*; *An Outline of Esoteric Science*; and *The Spiritual Guidance of Mankind*. Exact knowledge of these books, and of at least part of the lecture series later published as books is a necessary precondition for arriving at an adequate judgment of Anthroposophy. Anyone who has not fulfilled this requirement ought not claim to speak on the matter with full knowledge of it. Critiques made of the work of Kant or Spinoza by those who have only read a few excerpts from their works rightly seem superficial and inadequate to us. We can all see without a second thought that valid judgments cannot result from fleeting and partial impressions, nor at second hand, but only from precise knowledge. What we take heed of in this case, however, applies to anything on which we wish to pass judgment, i.e., not only to Anthroposophy, but also to any intellectual work whatsoever. Anthroposophy is just especially difficult to penetrate. Platitudes and easily repeatable formulas will never get to the heart of the matter.

Now, Anthroposophy is not a sum-total of individual discoveries and individual statements that could somehow be understood or applied irrespective of the whole, or without grasping the nature of that whole. If anthroposophical natural science were set *alongside* the elements of Anthroposophy that deal with religion and theology, it would be easy in a dogmatic sense to grant the first its validity and consider the second separately. But in Anthroposophy, everything flows into everything else, not because of any lack of clarity, but owing to its unified vision and unified impulse. What Anthroposophy has to say about natural effects (in the broadest sense) cannot be separated from what it has to say regarding the "domain" of religion, Christianity, and worship. It is therefore unusually difficult to see what can be affirmed. Moreover, this task is only made more difficult by a second factor, one that in its turn is not an isolated individual idea within Anthroposophy but that both determines and is determined by Anthroposophy. What I mean is that, according to the worldview of Anthroposophy, human beings are on the path to

3. These books, and those listed immediately below, have been published in several translations and under several titles. Here the most current are given.

freedom. For Anthroposophy, history is essentially the history of consciousness. Moreover, consciousness is itself essentially a history, that is, something that comes into being and undergoes change. The goal of this coming-into-being is the free human being, who is above any law and who requires none. According to Anthroposophy's teaching, man arrives at this goal (which one could also interpret in a Christian way, according to the very words describing it) by overcoming every external authority (including, therefore, any ecclesiastical authority). And one surely cannot remove from the anthroposophical worldview or from Anthroposophy's stock of ideas the view that church-bound Christianity in any form is something that has to be overcome. Here the spirit of Anthroposophy is completely irreconcilable with that of the Church. Now, obedience belongs inseparably to the idea of freedom put forward and called for by the Church. Obedience is also inseparable from saying Yes to the Church founded by Christ upon earth, which includes saying Yes also to the forms through which the Church mediates salvation. The idea of freedom proclaimed by Anthroposophy does not stand in unconditional opposition to this obedience, but it does not *include* such obedience. Although Anthroposophy is by nature first of all a science, or spiritual science, the goal it works to achieve conflicts with the Church's idea of *its* goal. This conflict cannot be effaced by reinterpretations or apologetics, which makes it particularly difficult for the Church to acknowledge the value of Anthroposophy in any respect. But that value is real. And what is worthy and susceptible of acknowledgement ought to be acknowledged. To assist in this process of acknowledgement, then, let me say the following.

Rudolf Steiner created and championed Anthroposophy in order to give human beings (who in his view were in danger of sinking into an unspiritual state, and thereby, from a religious point of view, at risk) a new spiritual impetus, and thus a new religious impetus too. He almost wholly avoided employing the language of tradition. He spoke for people who understood Idealist philosophy and modern natural science, or who understood Goethe's spirit or theosophical ideas. He did not address ecclesiastical or denominational thinking. It is hard for anyone who thinks according to ecclesiastical usage, and who acknowledges its tradition, to discern what is Christian in the worldview resulting from the concerns of such people as Steiner spoke for. In many respects, what is Christian in Anthroposophy is found, not in the words used, but in the nature of Anthroposophy itself. One looks in vain in the anthroposophical stock of ideas for concepts such as faith, penitence, obedience, worship. Nevertheless, the worldview—its kernel, stem, and branches—in large part have the effect of shaping the organ for these concepts, even if this comes about while excluding any connection to the authority of the Church.

Now, Rudolf Steiner turned to the circle of people mentioned, people of (modern) intellect, and committed himself to them. Anthroposophy was for Steiner himself not something complete, but something in process. I suspect that he had the intention of championing in due course what was Christian (but not what was churchly!) more clearly and more compellingly than could be understood or accepted by people who had lived in the spirit of "Idealism," "natural science," "Goetheanism," or the "theosophical." There are at least the beginnings of a "proof" of this available: the methodological foundation of Anthroposophy, the book *Knowledge of Higher Worlds*, bears at its end the remark "end of Part One." But no Part Two was ever written. Such a Part Two would, as an experienced anthroposophist later said to me, have included what was openly and decidedly Christian. It was, however, never written, for the reason that those who had heard or read what Part One required of them had not yet made as much progress as Rudolf Steiner had expected they would. In a certain respect, Anthroposophy as a *whole* did not become what it wanted to become. What did come into being, however, has meanwhile (as one might put it) been "canonized" by its adherents, without developing the transformational power that had been expected to allow Anthroposophy to save the world. I should like to explain this with an example which is quite simple, but whose whole weight and illustrative power has to be seen if it is to be applied to the larger matter we are speaking of here.

It can happen to a priest that he finds himself in front of a group of people who are completely remote from the Church, and having to speak to them about the truth of the Church. What will he say in such circumstances? He will not blurt it out all at once. He will not immediately present these souls with the deepest truths, since they evidently (as a rule) will lack the capacity to grasp them as yet. Instead, he will accommodate himself to their own spirituality. He may speak of works of art, or of nature, or of something that allows these people to pay attention, but does not conflict with their ideas. If we assume that the priest has awoken some response in his audience, it will not be the last time he is among them. It is questionable whether he can speak of guilt and repentance, of the Eucharist, or of the Immaculate Conception as early as his second visit to them. Perhaps he will continue instead only to talk in a preparatory way, and hope for the time when he can bear witness openly and freely to what is most important in the Church. Perhaps this time will come; but perhaps it will not come, and the work must be interrupted before he is able to bear that witness for whose sake he had in the first place come among them. Has the priest, then, sinned by omission? Can one say afterwards that he has only spoken of nature and of works of art, and has left out what is essential? He has undertaken preparatory work, not because he himself has gotten distracted by it, but because his listeners held him to it. Many priests were in this situation during the war, when they were confronted in the field, not with a congregation of the faithful, but with a herd of the more or less "lost."

Now, this picture is certainly not exhaustive, and leaves open all that concerns dogmatics. But it may nevertheless help to explain how Rudolf Steiner's impulse can be Christian in its intention and nature, even though his thought as a whole does not seem to be Christian from the point of view of the Church, even including Protestant observers. We hear tell here of the *etheric body*, the *astral body*, the *I*, the *eyes of the soul*, the *ears of the spirit*, *karma*, *reincarnation*, *evolution*, *esoteric pupils*, and so on. And it is so that these words and the concepts that correspond to them are also part of a whole that if rightly understood can indeed awaken a Christian life, and *wish* to awaken such a life. But instead of calling for repentance, Rudolf Steiner speaks of the "guardian of the threshold"; instead of speaking of grace, he speaks of waiting until one is found worthy;

instead of speaking of faith (with whose nature Rudolf Steiner was of course familiar) he spoke of knowledge; instead of calling for obedience, he said that the "I" must work on the lower members of the being; instead of acknowledging the dogma of the Church (with the content of which his own statements are so often in agreement), he spoke of freedom in the search for truth, while adding that truth is unequivocal—and that, even in the case of two *esoteric pupils* who had come to maturity in their different ways, could only be grasped unequivocally. These are just pointers, and as such must suffice here. The author can testify that Christian being and striving dwells even within such unchurchly, untraditional, and "un-Christian" modes of expression. Rudolf Steiner, however (and here let us recall what was just said in the preceding paragraph of a priest coming among a non-churchgoing group of people), did not, taking a *very* wide view of the matter, get or progress beyond the first stage of his teaching. He remained with the pupils and with their mode of being; he did not bring this decidedly and openly Christian content further. Moreover, here as before, it must be remembered that Anthroposophy is science, not religion. There is no science of God as a science of *experience*. For its part, theology starts out from divine *revelation*, but it is not a science of experience in the same sense as natural science. Rudolf Steiner could speak about the "spiritual world" from experience, but not about the inner nature of the Most Holy Trinity, for only revelation can speak of this—and Rudolf Steiner was not a theologian, nor did he wish to be one. What is the result of this?

Catholic theology has until quite recently worked with an image of Luther that in our day is recognized as a distortion. Joseph Lortz's book *The Reformation in Germany*, which had already appeared during the war, overcame once and for all these caricatures and distorted images, acknowledging that Martin Luther's concern was justified, not only in religious but also in ecclesiastical terms, and raised Catholic discussion of his admittedly necessary denominational struggle to the only truly productive level. Similarly, Anthroposophy ("spiritual science") should in my view also be seen and discussed at an appropriately productive level as soon as possible, *not in several centuries' time*. This can only happen if Rudolf

Steiner's wish that Anthroposophy be regarded first of all as science, not as religion, is taken seriously, and if we can learn to separate its natural-scientific side (if I can call it that) from what stands to be judged by theological critique. Anthroposophical insights and their effects (the nature of man, the spiritual governance of nature, the relationship between spirit and matter, the doctrine of the hierarchies, and so on) have already shown themselves to be unusually productive, and they will continue to do so.

What can be said about Anthroposophy from a dogmatic point of view? In asking this question, I become painfully aware that for my anthroposophical friends the words "dogma" and "dogmatics" have a questionable, even an objectionable, ring to them. The word *dogma*, however, essentially describes a *statement of truth*, a teaching handed down. All the sentences of the Creed are, for example, dogmas. Now, no anthroposophist will doubt the truths of the propositions of the Creed. These propositions are in complete agreement with the doctrines of Anthroposophy, or rather, the latter are in agreement with them. These dogmas are, therefore, all believed by anthroposophists (no one will claim that he has acquired "knowledge" of these truths all by himself). What the anthroposophist queries, however, is the fact that the Church presents the dogmas as "to be believed"; to him, this seems to conflict with "freedom." The anthroposophical protest is not directed towards the *content* of the dogmas (nor would it be directed towards the content of any individual dogma, if only Rudolf Steiner had said something corresponding to it) but towards their *form*, towards the Church's claim to power. Anthroposophy *ought*, among other things, to reanimate Christianity. Part of this consists in believing and propounding truths that belong to the Christian worldview and to Christian reality—that is, in believing and propounding dogmas. The anthroposophical movement, however, lacks any understanding of the fact that a large spiritual community, like the Church, *can* only maintain itself if it is governed by *binding* statements of truth. On the one hand, there reigns in the anthroposophical movement doubt as to whether Jesus Christ really founded the Church, as Catholic doctrine supposes him to have done; on the other, there reigns belief that humanity is capable of a "free life of the spirit." The anthroposophical movement does not pose the question of truth in terms of content, but *methodologically*. Thus there comes about the paradox that people who reject dogma and everything "dogmatic" nevertheless are for the most part in complete agreement with the truth of that dogma, with the exception, of course, of everything concerning the Church, the Church hierarchy, and the dogma of the Church itself.

What is required is that dogmatics inquire into the agreement, or non-agreement, of anthroposophical teachings with those of the Church. However this or that element of Anthroposophy is to be explained, dogmatics must measure it against the teaching handed down by the Church. From this it follows that not only is Anthroposophy oriented toward people who have fallen away from the Church, but that it can also work—not so much with words as by means of the way in which it comes forward—to alienate people from the Church. The institution of the Church, its hierarchical ordering, its dogmatics, its method of instruction, are thought of and represented as obsolete. Emphasis is placed on a "freedom" that excludes the possibility of any subordination of one's own will. The capacity of the human being is appraised so highly that the valuation is obviously too idealistic—with the exception, perhaps, of one or two geniuses. *This* is where theological critique ought to begin. *With this* should be connected everything in Anthroposophy that appertains to the realm of theological critique, and as necessary ought to be denied by theological critique in accordance with the Church's teaching. The Church teaches that man can be deified by sanctifying grace and by the dwelling of God in the soul, which accompanies that grace. It also teaches that man should strive for this deification, but a theological critique can never see a sign of this in people's turning away from the Church, or thinking themselves to be above the life of the sacraments, becoming their "own father confessors" (the phrase is Rudolf Steiner's) and living, in principle, without any authority. Let it be left to a professional expert in dogmatics to specify all this in detail.

The Church, in any case, condemns heresies, and must do so. But it does not deny the possibility that those who are distant from the Church and who are separated from it by "invincible ignorance" may be saved. Such "invincible ignorance" is, generally speaking, present among anthroposophists. For them (as I know from my own experience and that of my friends in that period), the Church is hidden in darkness. More precisely, for them the Church is viewed in the light of what Rudolf Steiner said about it—which on the whole is nothing favorable. Nonetheless, anthroposophists who deserve that name live enthusiastically in a *bona voluntas* ("good will") that one can only wish were shared by the vast majority of Catholic Christians. This is why a critique of Anthroposophy is needed, and why one person's conversion does not imply any derisive judgment upon those who continue to live and work within the anthroposophical movement. I owe a deep debt of gratitude to many of them; many I can only now look upon with amazement; many I can learn from, now as then. It is not my purpose to deliver a judgment upon the fact that many of them consciously turned away from the Church.

But even with respect to the anthroposophical movement, this question is to be asked: What draws people to become anthroposophists, and what does this mean for the Church? Anthroposophy, as was said earlier in respect of the Christian Community, meets the need of "modern consciousness" for "freedom." It turns toward the drive for knowledge alone, and unleashes the creative forces that can spring from "spiritual knowledge." But it is not *only* about this. Furthermore, it is inaccurate to see *everything* anthroposophical (its pedagogy, its art, its biodynamic agriculture, and so on) only in the light of dogmatics. Even if the kernel of the anthroposophical spirit is to be condemned by the Church as unecclesiastical and as opposed to the Church, the task still remains of establishing a position as regards the fact that Anthroposophy does creatively and actively contest and defeat a materialism still prevailing among us. There is not only a materialism of thinking (this can be "refuted"). There is also a materialism of the way one leads one's life, of the instincts, of the organ for discerning that which is or is not spiritual. And this other materialism pursues its dark ends in many different ways, even in people who "reject materialism" and who "confess the Church." *This* is where the significance of Anthroposophy becomes manifest. However difficult it might be to work out precisely *how* to do it, this is where the necessary Yes to Anthroposophy must be spoken by the Church.

Clearly, were the Church to issue a prohibition, this would not impede anyone who does not recognize this command, has fallen away from a state of faith, or simply feels the need, from engaging with Anthroposophy as a practical aid in overcoming materialism in the way mentioned. By the same token, I have however often noticed in many Catholic Christians a need for what Anthroposophy calls the "path of knowledge," without their being able to find such a path. Without question, there are opportunities and means within the Church for spiritual schooling—but on the whole, they seem to me to be on the one hand more hidden (i.e., only accessible to people who actively seek them), and on the other, unable to provide that connection to "modern consciousness" and the relationship to nature that is peculiar to anthroposophical schooling. A phenomenon like anthroposophical schooling, however (think of the first exercise cited above from *Knowledge of Higher Worlds*) cannot meaningfully be either readily or simply "rejected." For anthroposophical schooling is not in principle opposed to the faith of the Church, but can instead prepare the way for it.

After my conversion, many people expected that I must now have completely "freed" myself from Anthroposophy, that I must now have completely "gotten over" it. These were people without any knowledge of Anthroposophy, and whose opinions regarding it were thus from somewhere else. The "freedom" and "getting over" that this sort of person wished for, however, will never come about. If in Anthroposophy it were a question of an unambiguous, single-layered matter that simply belongs in the realm of faith, it would *certainly* have no meaning for me any more. For it is in the very nature of the Church's divine truth that no one and nothing needs to be added to it, and that no one who has penetrated to this truth needs any other source of truth. However, I had turned away from Anthroposophy *only* insofar as it contradicted the teachings and directives of the Church, not in any other way; and that, indeed, is enough. It is not only a natural and lasting gratitude for what I received from Anthroposophy that still ties me to it, but the knowledge that a large part of Anthroposophy—a part very productive for life—in no way contradicts Church teaching or the life of the Church. It would be fruitless for anyone to hold out hope that, with regard to these aspects of Anthroposophy, some further personal development on my part might come that might open my eyes to the defects of the whole. It is my wish, rather, that the present study contribute to our being able to see and to judge separately, and in their own right, individual particulars that are admittedly hard to distinguish from one another. At first the Catholic church was at odds with the whole of Protestant Christianity, until at last a clear distinction was made and proper heed was paid to what should be rejected and what could be affirmed. Even if such a distinction and such close attention are easier in the case of Protestant Christianity than in that of Anthroposophy, the situation as it stands still calls for them; and in my judgment it would be a great misfortune if, when the Church condemns what it admittedly *must*, it were *also* to attack those elements of Anthroposophy that could very well be tolerated, affirmed, or—finally—made use of.

11

Conversion

ANYONE WHO IS EXPECTING THAT, AT THE END OF this book, the author's "rejection" or complete "condemnation" of Anthroposophy will be announced, will be disappointed. My hope, in fact, is that such readers may reconsider. I have indeed given up my membership in the anthroposophical movement, for one cannot serve two masters at once—and Anthroposophy was for a long time my "highest Lord." As a consequence of my conversion, however, I did come to see more clearly than before that, as a member of the Catholic church looking at Anthroposophy from the point of view of the Church's teaching, one is concerned with three different things. First, with what conflicts with the teaching of the Church; second, with what agrees with the teaching of the Church; and third, with what has nothing whatever to do with dogmatics. The teaching of the Church conflicts, for example, with what Anthroposophy has to say about the Church, about the sacraments, and about the nature of freedom. Anthroposophy is in agreement with the Church, for example, about the fact that Jesus Christ is our redeemer, and that by sacrificing Himself He has destroyed the power of sin and death over us. Moreover, nothing Anthroposophy teaches about—for example, the nature and development of man on earth. or the spiritual governance of nature and human beings' connection with that governance—has anything to do with dogmatics. I consider it unfortunate that a precise distinction between the three "domains" of Anthroposophy mentioned here is only possible for someone familiar with Anthroposophy, for which reason, of course, it is all too easy for the Church to lump them all together, with the result that what is valuable in Anthroposophy remains for the most part unknown to the Church, and is not made use of.

Anthroposophy is essentially science, not religion. That is why its language is "unreligious." Anthroposophy is also, however, essentially spiritual science, and not a church. This is why we must ask about its relation to the traditional faith, but must also acknowledge the Yes and No within it. These features can only be spoken about in a general way here. But let this at least be said in conclusion.

Anyone who consults an anthroposophical doctor can partake of many medicines and healing remedies that do not otherwise exist and that can come into being only out of the spirit of Anthroposophy. Anyone who enjoys produce from anthroposophically-inspired biodynamic farms benefits (for reasons that cannot be gone into here) from healthier nutrition than usually exists these days. Many considerations of this kind could be advanced. From personal experience, however, I can testify the following.

I owe it to the spirit of Anthroposophy that the nature of the Church was disclosed to me, and that I was able to penetrate by means of thinking much of what I later saw my later Catholic friends practicing. I cannot wish this fact away from my life. A Catholic Christian (in England) who had inwardly distanced himself from the Church once took part in a discussion of a lecture that had set out the nature of the Christian Community and its "religious renewal." Afterwards, he said that now he could participate once again in Holy Mass in a completely different way than before. I had a similar experience myself. Anthroposophy not only awakens a particular worldview in terms of content (a content that is in any case to be condemned by the Church) but also awakens an organ for the meaning and context of life that can be productive in any situation, in a completely universal way. On this topic, I must say that in my judgment it would be a good thing if Anthroposophy were studied by the Church in a *precise* way; and, moreover, if it were soon decided what the Church is and is not able to acknowledge to be of value (rather than some centuries down the road), so that no case like that of Galileo need again occur. Anthroposophy should not be taken as "religion," but as "science." Galileo's teaching of the earth's relationship to the sun has as little to do with dogma as does Anthroposophy's teaching (insofar as it is in the broadest sense true to nature). The relationship of the Catholic church to everything anthroposophical is essentially the same as the Church's relationship to everything Protestant. Just as the Protestant chorales *O Haupt voll Blut und Wunden* ("O Sacred Head, Now Wounded")[1] and *Vom Himmel hoch da komm ich her* ("From Heaven Above to Earth I Come")[2] have found entrance to the Catholic church even though Protestant Christianity is a heresy and even though many Protestant teachings are to be condemned, so anthroposophical knowledge of mankind, anthroposophical pedagogy, and much else in Anthroposophy could not and should not, in my view, be condemned by the Church as a whole and indiscriminately. If such condemnation could be avoided, not only would the many Christians who cannot be reached by mere dogmatic adjudications and behests be saved for the Church, but some things of value would be disclosed to the Church itself, things that are indeed more essential than many people today might think.

At this juncture, however, I shall give an account of my entry into the Church, which was so long obstructed by inner resistances that for some time remained strong.

The most essential difference between Catholic and non-Catholic Christianity seems to me (i.e., to me *today*, given that I first had to arrive at this insight!) to lie in the relationship to tradition, which differs within Catholicism from what is called tradition outside of it. All that differs in teaching, all that relates to the nature of the Church, the institution of the papacy, the church hierarchy, the sacraments, the Marian dogmas, and so on, arises from different stances towards tradition. One can say from a Catholic standpoint that Protestant Christianity has narrowed faith as a whole (we cannot enter into particular differences here) and depends essentially on "scripture." It is hardly possible in Protestant Christianity to treat something as divinely true and necessary to salvation if it can-

---

1. A Christian hymn of the Passion, based on a Latin text from the Middle Ages, of which a German version was written by the Lutheran hymnist Paul Gerhardt (1607–1676).
2. A hymn relating to the nativity of Jesus written by Martin Luther in 1534.

not be demonstrated from "scripture." On one hand, this faith in scripture holds Protestant Christianity together. On the other, it has led to its fragmentation, because scripture itself can be understood and interpreted in different ways. Anyone who only subscribes to belief in *scripture*, who doubts the correctness and truth of *tradition*, can never become a member of the Catholic church.

I was taught to have faith in scripture long before I could think for myself, and it remained at work within me as an anti-Catholic instinct in the depths of my soul. When I distanced myself from the Protestant church, however, I lost this faith in scripture; indeed, it may have been one of the reasons for my taking my distance in the first place, for this faith is not so living as it may at first appear. For we may, and we ought to, believe in the unfolding of revealed truth in the Church; we ought not to hold ourselves to something locked up in a book. In later years I also sought for an explanation of the fact that the Catholic church was able to create ever new feasts, while the Protestant church could not. The reason for this lies in the differences in their relationship to scripture and tradition. Only a faith in tradition, and in what is directly connected to it—i.e., faith in a presently living and authoritative Church that unfolds the truth, as well as in the reality underpinning this faith—can produce new feasts. Yet only in the most recent years did this knowledge dawn on me. In the course of my life I acquired from Anthroposophy an overcoming of a pure and exclusive faith in scripture. This overcoming was positive, rather than merely negative. I was also prepared by Anthroposophy for the Catholic doctrine of tradition, despite the fact that tradition has no place in the former. This does not mean, however, that such anti-Catholic impulses as had been present in me since my early years had disappeared. The latter could be removed only by sufficiently effective thinking. Hence what follows.

Martin Luther and the other reformers either already no longer believed in the divinity or holiness of the earthly Catholic church, or else they had lost their faith in the Church because of the sad state in which it seemed to them to have fallen during their lifetimes. Otherwise, it is not to be understood how individuals could have arrived not only at justified criticisms of Church abuses, but also at the audacity to trust more to their own inward inspiration (as one must call it) than to that which had given rise to the Church and from which the Church itself lived. In comparison with early medieval people generally, the reformers bore a different "consciousness" within themselves: they were so fashioned that they could seek for a reliable sign of what was divinely and ecclesiastically correct in "scripture" alone. Tragically, however, the first leaders of Protestant Christianity, without being able fully to see this themselves, proved to be standing, not on the ground of "scripture," but on that of their own personal understanding of it (which then thousands of believers and thinkers immediately discovered to be their understanding of it too).

Luther and Zwingli, both men of the greatest seriousness who had the most honorable of intentions, understood one essential (if not the most essential) passage of the New Testament quite differently from each other. According to Luther, the bread consumed in the Lord's Supper was to *be* the body of Christ; according to Zwingli, it only *signified* the body of Christ. Anyone who thinks about this calmly, without prejudice, and with an open mind, can see that only one of the two reformers can have been standing on "the" ground of scripture here. And yet both were firmly persuaded that they were propounding, not a personal judgment, but the objective truth. In conversation, I have occasionally drawn the attention of Protestant Christians to this point. They have conceded straightaway that I was right in my surmise, but nonetheless remained insistent that faith is based "on scripture." Deeply rooted habits do indeed exert great power in all of us. We can only find truth in our own thinking if we are able to question whatsoever we may have become accustomed to and been taught from our early years.

At Protestant services I have often heard, after the gospel has been read out, the words "Blessed are those who hear and who keep God's word!" These words can be taken as a fine appeal to receive sacred words according to their nature. But when Christ once spoke them, he was not directing his audience to a closed book. He meant by them something at work in a living way and beyond anything that is or can be written. The New Testament only came into being when the life of the Church was already strong. The New Testament emerged from the primitive Church. The canon of the New Testament was established by and in the Church. Why, then, should God be supposed to have inspired the New Testament, but not the Church from which the New Testament came forth? Moreover, if He inspired the Church that produced the New Testament, why should He not also have inspired the Church when it produced something else, namely the doctrine of the sacraments? Granted, "tradition" does not mean that new revelations were given to the Church, but the treasure of revelation certainly can be unfolded to us, and developed. And people can understand the word of God in an ever newer and deeper way, and so on, by means of epiphanies or inspirations The doctrine of tradition is to be *comprehended* after sufficient meditation. For someone coming from a denominationally determined perspective, the doctrine of tradition cannot, indeed, be more *persuasive* than the idea that scripture is the only essential source of Christian truth (so that if, for example, a sacrament cannot be given sufficient support from scripture, it should not count as valid).

No single person, not even the greatest genius, is in a position to understand the whole of Christian truth. Who would be able to discover the truth about the whole of world history, and the whole history of revelation? Protestant theology's research into the "life of Jesus" is a heart-rending example of how all too many people believe themselves to be in a better position than others to pronounce upon what is true, so that one "school" can always take the place of another. But what is truth? It must be somewhere, for otherwise it could neither be sought nor found. From this point of vantage one can arrive (as I can only say, rather than demonstrate here) at a recognition of the Church's teaching vocation. To illustrate this, we might say that whereas each "prodigal son" can take a different path back to his father's house, there is nonetheless only one such house. Personal truthfulness can call forth the most varied of thoughts, but there is One Thing that underlies these thoughts. Unity can never come about among us human beings if we only follow subjective truthfulness; it can only come about if we subordinate ourselves to the objective truth. If God wanted there to be one

Church on earth, He must also have communicated everything essential to it by means of the Holy Spirit.

Now, these are theological ideas rather than an account of my own experience; but even so, they also say something spiritually autobiographical. Every Catholic theologian will already have thought along the lines of such theological ideas. I had to find them out for myself, however. And even if it might hardly be possible to know and to set out how each such idea came to me, viewed from the perspective of my life as a whole they were like the blossoming of a flower—and who can describe such an unfolding in every detail? In my case, I bore within me a protest against any authority, a protest of at least an ordinary, and probably of a more than ordinary, strength. This protest of mine could be stilled only by sufficiently convincing ideas. Questions that *today* I would regard only as questions of objective truth were to me *then* questions of truthfulness, of method, of freedom, which I regarded the Church's dogma as restricting. There should not, I thought earlier, be any being on earth that simply "lays down" what one "ought" to believe. I did not wish to submit myself, nor could I have trust.

Furthermore, I regarded the commandments of the Church as sad relics of a genuinely lost age. When the Church first came into my field of vision, I said to an acquaintance of mine, about someone we both greatly respected, "he can't possibly go to confession!" My acquaintance rejoindered "why not?" and left me to my thoughts. At that time (1944) the idea that there could be such a thing as voluntary obedience was entirely foreign to me. I was filled through and through with the idea of independence. In the priests I saw people who wished illegitimately to rule over souls and consciences instead of seeing them as organs of the Church. It was only with difficulty and over time that I came to see that self-sufficiency can be developed into selflessness, and that such selflessness is unaffected by where and how one might fall into line or subordinate oneself. To frequent the sacrament of confession certainly can demand that one overcome oneself, which was just what I wanted, and had wanted then and previously, to avoid—and of course the conditions necessary for my avoiding it presented themselves easily enough. Christ certainly performed an act of self-conquest when he became human, an act greater than any human act and certainly greater than what the sacrament of penitence may demand of us.

As a student of anthroposophical epistemology, I also bore within me a deep aversion to the Catholic catechism, even though at the time I had never seen nor read it. To me it was self-evident that, since it was "dogmatic," it would impinge on my freedom. I was asking only "how do I find truth?" and not yet "what is truth, even if I do not yet comprehend it?" For many years, "ready-made formulas" seemed to me not to be invitations to come closer to truth, but deterrents from approaching it. At work here, it seems to me, was a trait common to many of our contemporaries, and here I include myself. It is not just that one "believes" certain propositions, even if they mean nothing to one, and thus lack any effect upon one's life. I was unable to see for a long time that the "ready-made formulas" of the catechism are only hieroglyphs—which of course one has to learn to decipher and animate. In reality, the formulas of truth in the catechism are like mathematical equations. To anyone who does not how to handle them, such equations appear to be dead objects. Anyone, then, who "believes" the formulas without their transparently becoming for him the living truth, is standing (if I can put it like this) on the lowest step of the ladder, and needs help to bring these truths alive.

This "help to bring these truths alive" (or, more precisely, a preparatory step towards this help) was what I had received in Anthroposophy. Through Anthroposophy I had learned to believe in the spiritual nature of the world, and in the effects of spirit and spirits on that world. Such things are discussed concretely and in a living way in Anthroposophy. And such a concrete and living introduction would certainly also be beneficial for many Catholic Christians. I do not know how I could have acquired the organ with which to approach the truths of the catechism without Anthroposophy. Or, to put it another way, I do not know what properly ecclesiastical voice could have succeeded in bringing me to acknowledge the truth. I cannot deny this fact. During those years, however, the time came when I *was* in a position to ask "what is the truth?" and when I *could* bring these "dead formulas" to life for myself. Let me try at least roughly to explain how I thought this through.

The laws, for example, according to which the sun, the moon, and the stars move, are objectively present and independent of human knowledge. True, Copernicus revealed a new picture of the world, but in doing so he merely made accessible to human thinking something that had long been objectively present and at work in the cosmos. Something similar must be the case with respect to Christian truth. The number of human beings who may know or acknowledge the truth of the Creed, for example, has in principle nothing to do with the content or with the objective validity of this truth. It would be true even if no human consciousness any longer received it as truth. What ought first to be asked about in relation to truth is its *being*, not simply the *method* of acquiring it. That I was now able to think in this way was, however, the consequence of the fact that I had had to undergo such a good education precisely in the "method of acquiring it."

In this sense, the catechism, whatever particular form it takes, contains truth. It is certainly not just a manual of instruction from which one can learn the method by which to pursue one's personal search for truth. Rather, it is a systematic work comparable to a popular study of astronomy in which one is given only the doctrines and results. It expresses what holds true. It does this clearly, soberly, and comprehensively so far as the principles are concerned, but it is based only on Holy Scripture and on the words of the Fathers, on the presupposition of their effectiveness upon the soul. "Modern" man certainly *does* believe in science and in scientific experience and the results of scientific research even if he does not himself possess the first inkling of how to demonstrate these things; but he *does not* believe in the least in the science of the divine, in the experiences that comparably gifted human beings have had, or in the results achieved by those who are gifted in the spiritual and religious field, in divine revelation, in the Church, or in dogma. For many years I was only able to believe what Rudolf Steiner had said, and this belief in turn was not only prompted by the *content* of Anthroposophy but also by its *method*. Rudolf Steiner had always offered proofs for what he said, and had shown how others could arrive at similar knowledge themselves. Could the individual propositions of the Church's truth be comparably supported, I asked myself? Was it possible here too to be justified—without being able to discover the whole—in trusting that an organism of truth, or even *the* organism of truth, was before us in the doctrine of the Church? Both Anthroposophy and the doctrine of the Church as a whole can be compared with a system of coordinates. Systems of coordinates, however, differ one from another, and all the particulars in them appear differently. The "coordinates" of anthroposophical thought might be approximated with the words "consciousness" and "development." The coordinates of the Church's thinking might be approximated with the words "sin" and "redemption." But "consciousness" and "development" have something to do with sin and redemption, just as "sin" and "redemption" have something to do with consciousness and development. The Catholic question of truth is first and foremost about the *what*. The anthroposophical question of truth is first and foremost about the *how*. Here there is much more in common between them, and much more that is mutually complementary, than might occur to someone who is an "outsider" to both "camps." As an anthroposophist, however, I was faced with the question: can all the truths propounded by the Catholic church be accepted and inwardly subscribed to upon trust, without being demonstrated?

Even though my trust in the Catholic church grew in the way I have indicated, and even though I began to see it with eyes increasingly more open than they had ever before been in my previous life, I would still never have been able to join the Church if to a certain degree I had not been able to understand and personally approve everything that was a personal question for me, everything that appeared questionable. By "understanding" and "approving" I do not mean an exhaustive fathoming, of which no single person would be capable. Indeed, I had heard the following words from the mouth of the most important anthroposophist I had ever met: "the truths of the Creed stand high above even the greatest initiate, like constellations." I mean, instead, an attitude that nevertheless stands opposed to the sort of "believing" that means merely to assent without oneself doing any intellectual work. This "understanding" and this "approval" are preparatory stages and impulses of a *living* faith, of a *pistis* in the New Testament sense. Such faith is what the simplest Catholic means when he prays to be "strengthened in his faith," for faith in the sense of assenting to the Church's doctrine is generally already present in him and so needs no "strengthening."

In the conversion lessons I attended for a long time (and which at one point I broke off for an extended period because of my resistance and doubt) I learned what the Church propounds as essential truth. All that was expected of me, really, was agreement with what was taught, and not what I called understanding. For a long time, my trust as a matter of principle in the catechism did not bring with it trust in all the individual statements of the catechism. For good or ill, I wanted to be able to see for myself that the Church and its scholars were right. But the Protestant-type bears a decided resistance within himself to much of what the Catholic church teaches. I had to try to discern everything foreign to me in the Church's "system of coordinates"; and only once I had really discerned it, could the question of conversion be seriously deliberated. What does it mean to "discern" something? Once all the struggles have been passed through and the beginnings (at least) of the power of faith have entered into one, then discerning and believing cannot be completely fenced off from each other. Life in and with the truth is not merely intellectual; it is deeper than that. With "discernment," however, one can describe finding something illuminating, one can demonstrate something, one can have no further doubts about something. The priest who gave me conversion lessons merely presented to me what was "to be believed"; my capacity to "see" what was to be believed (in the sense described) had in my case essentially been developed already by Anthroposophy.

The following facts about the teaching and life of the Church caused me particular difficulties. First, the veneration of holy Mary. As one who was born a Protestant, and who had always defended Protestantism, she was to me quite alien, and not only alien, but suspicious. My thoughts were roughly along the line that the veneration of Mary interposed something alien and disturbing between man and God. Instead of giving Christ his due honor, the Catholics were, I thought, worshiping "a mere human being." This prejudice on the part of non-Catholics is understandable, for from external appear-

ances (altars for Mary, images of Mary, prayers to Mary) this prejudice can only be removed in those who have an *exact* knowledge of
Catholic theology, Church liturgy, and Mariology. But of whom can
this be said? Moreover, I had never attentively concerned myself
with the figure of the Mother of God. I had always thoughtlessly
harbored the view that it was a sign of the "humanization" of the
Catholic church that it had put the Mother of God at the center of
its contemplations and religious practice. What does the non-Catholic Christian know of the difference between *latreia*, the "adoration" that only God, the Three-in-One, should be offered, *doulia*,
the "veneration" with which the saints are to be invoked, and the
hyperdoulia with which the Mother of God alone is to be invoked?
Non-Catholic Christians are almost necessarily faced here with a
fact incomprehensible to them; and even one such as I, who had
been freed from "faith in scripture," still approached the mysteries
of Mary in vain.

I had to find reasons for the veneration of the Mother of God. I
had to acquire an adequate understanding of it. And this was hard
work. On the one side this was because (as is the case in respect of
everything essential) it was not merely a question of intellectual
cognition, whereas on the other, we usually only open ourselves up
to insights to the extent that those insights correspond to our own
essential nature. In the Una Sancta movement, I had frequently
heard a Protestant theologian say "this is what we think!" Just such a
"we" (even though it was quite undenominational now in my case)
was also still at work within me. Only up to a certain point was I
able to let myself grasp the reasons for the veneration of Mary, to let
them have an effect on me, before this "we" proved victorious.

So I called to my aid what I had learned about the nature of the
Church as a whole and about tradition, and reasoned to myself
roughly as follows. It cannot be an accident that this one person
stood at such an important place for the whole of human history,
nor that she was connected to Jesus Christ in a closer way than anyone else. The Mother of God's destiny is a singular one. Why should
her nature not be singular also? I began to get an idea of what the
Fiat! ("Be it unto me!") holds within itself and of what it expresses.
The realization began to dawn on me that God and Man, creator

and creature, brought about the work of redemption together (if I may put it like that), even if the creature, of course, received all the strength, the grace, and the dignity needed for that work from the creator. I should like to express these ideas, which any Catholic believer can easily repeat and assent to, in the words of the suffragan bishop of Linz, quoted by Odo Staudinger in one of his books on Fatima:

> The holy Fathers themselves tell us over and over again how humanity fell into shame through a man and a woman, Adam and Eve, and how humanity, according to God's plan, is to be raised up again through a man and a woman, through the new Adam and the new Eve—Jesus and Mary. In the end, that is the deepest meaning of the very ancient Catholic panegyric: "Blessed art thou among women, and blessed is the fruit of thy womb, Jesus." And since the work of redemption continues until the end of time, Jesus and Mary are active until the end of time in this work of redemption—Jesus as the cause and source of all grace, Mary as the mediatrix of all grace. Jesus is the sole king of all the treasury of grace, and so his heart is the sign of salvation in which alone Church and world may find rescue and peace. Mary is the sole queen, as the most powerful intercessor, called to be mediator of Christ's grace, and for that reason her heart is the sign of salvation to which Church and world must turn in order to arrive at Jesus's heart.

Before my conversion I had merely thought such thoughts, without their having had any effect on my heart, and without my having drawn any personal religious consequences from them. Dogmas, however (perhaps I may say this to non-Catholics) are always in accord with reason, and yet they come about not only *from* human beings, but also *by means of* human beings. And since the human mind was not excluded from their coming about, one who thinks about them can understand the reasons for what is of course unfathomable by its very nature. One *can*, of course, extol on an earthly and human level those who closed themselves off from a dogma (after 1871, for example),[3] and see their resistance to the

---

3. The author is referring here to the First Ecumenical Council of the Vatican (1869–1870).

Church's authority as a sign of their spiritual freedom. But can one seriously still think today that the many others who assented to this dogma are, one and all, unfree and foolish? Just as Protestant Christianity stands towards Catholic doctrine, so do many non-Christian people stand towards Protestant doctrine in a comparable way today. These people, however, consider it a sign of unfreedom and folly that in Protestant Christianity certain ideas are propounded as firm and inalienable truths. Freedom is not shown by *what* a person confesses as truth, but in *how* he relates to that which he holds to be true.

Behind the figure of the Mother of God, however, lurk secrets that can scarcely be expressed in words. The reading for the Feast of the Immaculate Conception says:

> The Lord possessed me in the beginning of his way, before his works of old. I was set up from everlasting, from the beginning. . . . While as yet he had not made the earth, nor the fields, nor the highest part of the dust of the world. . . . Now therefore hearken unto me, O ye children: for blessed are they that keep my ways. . . . whoso findeth me findeth life, and shall obtain favor of the Lord.

These verses are about something other than the earthly virgin and mother; already in the most distant past there was talk of the being who once appeared to apocalyptic vision as the woman "clothed with the sun." It does not befit me to talk of this, but I can say that certain statements I learned from Rudolf Steiner prepared me to begin to fathom what these words are about—that there exists not only a "cosmic-masculine" but also a "cosmic-feminine," not only a "heavenly" Father but also an "earthly" Mother raised up to the heavens. This Mother is by no means a "goddess," as Goethe unfortunately called her at the end of *Faust*, and for which she certainly may be taken by many simple people, but a powerful being with far-reaching (creaturely, not creatorly) strength and love…

It is also imaginable, even demonstrable, that the mysteries of Mary *had* to remain more hidden than the mystery of Christ. It would not only have been impossible, but even unseemly, for more than a mere hint to have been said of the Mother of God in the scriptures. Does not the real life of a woman always unfold in a more hidden way than that of a man, which takes place in public?

And ought that to have been otherwise in the life of the God-man and his holy Mother? The gospel tells us of the deeds of Jesus Christ. The importance of his Mother was only expressed in later stories. However, just as we could never adequately imagine Jesus Christ, our Lord, the ruler of heaven, if we had only the picture of him given in the book of Revelation, but instead may and must think of him as a little child, as a twelve-year-old, as a man, and as man of sorrows, in order truly to participate in his nature, so we must also imagine "Mary" as a maiden, as a woman, as a mother, as a mother of sorrows, if we are to approach her unfathomable nature more closely. The image of the woman clothed with the sun is indeed the most sublime image, but on its own it would be both oppressive and inadequate. All this I was at first only able to think with (so to speak) a cold and unmoved heart. Yet one may perhaps say that a certain opening of the inner sense had come about in me, for otherwise this essential point would have resisted my thinking. At that time, the Lutheran translation of Greek *kecharitomene*[4] as *holdselig* (meek, sweet, fair, lovely)—seemed to me inadequate, and *voll der Gnade* (full of grace) seemed to me to get closer to the matter.

And then again, the Catholic veneration of the saints presented me with a riddle I found hard to solve. The veneration of the saints is foreign to non-Catholic Christianity, and is rejected as "unbiblical." But many people love the images of the saints when they are of artistic value, and it seems to me that, in this love, what holds sway is not only an encounter with art but also a remnant of, or an opening to, a relationship to the saints themselves. In the Protestant view, however, the dead have disappeared from any community with the living. They are not prayed for, nor are they asked to intercede for us. If one is used to this and has known nothing other than this since childhood, one must either be attracted to the Catholic church as to a magnet of truth, or else one must fight against admitting Catholic life and thought into oneself. The latter was the case with me. The idea that the living and the dead belong together was familiar to me from Anthroposophy, but not in a way that would permit a living veneration or a request for intercession to arise from it.

4. The salutation of the Archangel Gabriel to Mary at the Annunciation.

Here, the idea that the whole of Christendom, indeed the whole of humanity, was a single spiritual family was helpful to me. That one person might be able to have beneficial effects on another seemed to me not only possible, but consistent. But first of all I had to get rid of the idea that the dead were now "with God" in a quite different way from the living, an idea that contains a certain dualism.

If we believe the intercession of a living person can be significant, why should we not believe the same of the intercession of a dead person? Moreover, if we hold the intercession of an average person to be essential, why not that of a great and especially blessed spirit? First I had to learn that the canonized saints are not the only people who deserve the description "holy," that the word "holy" means two different things, and can be used both in the universal Christian sense and in a particular sense as a description of those who "enjoy the honor of altars." Furthermore, I learned that at the deepest level "holiness" is a gift from God, and is in any case not simply the work of man or a human act of service, as Protestant apologetics once assumed (but perhaps less often assumes in our day). What I had to learn did not consist of simply adopting the opinion that "the Catholic church will certainly have the correct doctrine," but in meditating on the reasons, facts, and experiences that had led to the doctrine, and were at first so alien to me. Wondrous and more than wondrous is the idea—or rather, the reality—of the community of saints, and the fostering of it in the Catholic church. In any case, there also exist others ways of venerating the saints that do not conform to the dignity of Catholic teaching, and are therefore more likely to attract the attention of precisely those people who are not Catholics, since "people see what is before their eyes." And how great an obstacle this can be to truly seeing the "heart" of this teaching—in this case the "heart" of a doctrine and of a way of life! Yet all these things were, before my conversion, essentially only ideas, rather than perceptible blessings.

Third, the "problem of the chalice" for a long time caused me severe difficulty. Perhaps the Catholic Christian may not be in a position to sympathize with this feeling, since he may never have seen a "problem" here at all. Yet I must tell the truth. It is well known that since the high Middle Ages, lay people (apart from only a few exceptions) have been served only the sacred host, not the chalice with the divine blood. The chalice is, as they say in non-Catholic Christendom, "reserved" from the lay faithful. From my youth onwards I had always thought (as I had been taught to think) that this clearly and incontestably demonstrated the will to power of the Catholic clergy. Even the "pre-Reformation reformers" had fought for the "lay cup," and the reformers introduced it. It was (and still is) regarded as a sign of Protestant freedom that in Protestant Christianity the lay faithful were given the chalice as well as the host.

I had also already found out that some doctrines accepted in early youth can take possession of one almost ineradicably, making it almost impossible to think unimpeded by presuppositions. If I wanted to progress, if I wanted to freely overcome my present position, I had to approach the question as if I were not full of anti-Catholic instincts, and as if I had not for years, or ever at all, inhaled such instincts from the atmosphere. That was not easy. True, the actual source of Protestant thought, the belief in "scripture," had never had any sway over my waking thought. I was concerned with the "substance" itself, rather than the words. But it was just the "substance" here that was causing difficulties. Even Christ's words, "*drink* ye all of this," are not only words, but also a matter of "substance"; and as a result of Rudolf Steiner's directions, the Christian Community, in which I had for so long lived, administers communion by distributing in both kinds, like Protestant Christianity, and the words spoken allow one to imagine a secret distinction between the "bread" and the "wine." Was there not, I wondered, something essential contained in the wine that the bread did not supply? Is not something being "reserved" when bread alone is distributed? The question lay heavy on my heart, and I would never have been able to convert if I had not been able to solve it. Conversion could founder on one such point alone, for I was not ready to make any sacrifices when it came to my own thinking.

At first I attempted to think from immediate experience, together with my own observations. I asked myself: Did the Protestant Christian, who for hundreds of years had communicated by means of the chalice as well as the host, thereby participate in a charisma that the Catholic Christian in some way lacked? I looked at the question from all possible angles, and thought I could answer in the negative. Then I asked another question. Had the Catholic clergy had access to a charisma by means of communion through the chalice that had been denied to lay Catholics by the removal of the cup? I believed I had to answer this question in the negative also. To believe that Christ's efficacy was essentially bound up with the substances themselves would be to place the purely spiritual basis of that efficacy in question, and to imagine that the substances themselves possessed some sort of magical power. "The spirit blows where it listeth," and the Church admonishes: "Whoever does not communicate at the altar, may he at least communicate in the spirit!"

From there, I arrived (and perhaps the experienced and well-informed reader may smile here, since the results of my "cogitations" are already familiar and self-evident to people of faith) at the thought that the nature of Christ and of His efficacy must, after all, be indivisible and always entire. It did not then seem to me either possible or meaningful—nor to correspond with the nature of Christ—that He should be communicated otherwise in the wine than in the bread. He is, then, *one* spirit after all, and yet spirit is something incommunicable.

Here I had hit upon the Catholic doctrine of the sacraments, which emphasizes and propounds just these thoughts, which I had also long since read somewhere else, but which I could not, precisely, accept from outside. According to the teaching of the Church, "the whole of Christ" is present in both of the holy substances after they have been transformed, as a result of "transubstantiation" into the body and blood of the Lord. The wine in the chalice does not signify anything essential that is not also in the bread, nor does the bread signify anything not also in the wine. "Under the form of bread we receive the living Christ, and thus his holy blood."

Then I could see that the "reservation of the cup" (which expression for the non-Catholic Christian lacking precise knowledge of the subject is either just a formula without any particular content or else can appear as an untruthful stipulation), or chalice procession, has no dogmatic, but only pragmatic reasons. As I write this, I become painfully conscious of the fact that in the non-Catholic world there is in many ways a widespread ignorance of the nature

Catholic dogma, as of so much else, that can permit the most unfortunate suspicions to arise. On one hand, the dogmatic rigor of the Catholic church is objected to, especially the "rigidity" with which it holds to its doctrines; on the other (just as happens here), that dogma is not taken seriously by its opponents. I must admit, however, that it is very difficult for non-Catholics to take the Church's doctrine on its own terms and in accordance with truth. Catholic dogmatics is like the great cathedrals of the Middle Ages. Anyone who wants to get to know it needs to do more than just walk around inside it. The gargoyles sit high up on the cathedral. And who can grasp how the cathedral has been built apart from an architect who has mastered the laws of gravity, of structural engineering, of vaulting? Anyone who understands the nature of dogma also knows that if the chalice had been reserved to the priesthood on dogmatic grounds, then this would have been stated in dogmatics, just as there are completely unequivocal teachings about the priesthood, the religious orders, and the hierarchy. Thus, it can be a great deal of work to question spiritual customs and to acquire new knowledge. But only when the "problem of the chalice" had been solved was the way into the Catholic church to this extent open for me.

Fourth, I had to bind myself at my conversion to interpreting Holy Scripture only "in accordance with the agreed interpretation of the Fathers." Now for me, as someone who had once fallen completely away from the Church and from Christianity, a new way of accessing Christianity had essentially been opened up by the expositions of Rudolf Steiner. The latter, however, were very different indeed from any usual exegesis, or at least any I had hitherto encountered. I cannot go into this matter in detail here, but I will say this, which will perhaps be enough: I did not find it easy, yet found it acceptable, that the formula of conversion warned against "erroneous doctrines" that had never occurred to me, and that could never have occurred to me. The formula does not demand that one should not think anything that has never been thought before, but that what one goes on to think of should be in inward agreement with the Church's doctrinal heritage. I could stop worrying about this part of the conversion formula, which had long troubled me, with a good conscience.

Fifth, I also found it not a little difficult that I was to obey the Holy Father and all papal decrees unconditionally, or at least to accept, affirm, and comply with all the dogmas of the Catholic church without contradicting them. However much my spirit and heart had opened up to the Catholic church, or come closer to it on the whole, or in the depths of my being, I still harbored a deep mistrust towards the Catholic hierarchy. I sensed, or, so to speak, everywhere imagined in it a desire to exert its power to restrict freedom. So I am all too familiar with doubts about the truthfulness of the Catholic clergy and its statements. If I was to convert at all, however, I could only do so with complete sincerity, and would be unable to swear obedience to the Holy Father if I was not ready to abide my vow!

On this point I thought a great deal might be demanded of me that would go against my convictions and my conscience. If I may put it like this, I was reckoning with the possibility that the Holy Father might wish to test the obedience of his believers in a very arbitrary way. I did not see in Christ's representative a champion of freedom, but of imperiousness, a figure of the will to power rather than of lawful compliance. And this as late as 1945! I greatly lament this fact today, but so it was. I had to reflect further on this aspect or foundation of the Catholic church. Thinking was the ice-pick with which I took purchase on the next steps in terrain I sometimes supposed to be icy and impassable without the help of this implement; and yet thinking, as a God-given divining rod, was held in the hands of my guardian angel just as much as it was held in mine.

The question of spiritual obedience was solved when, in considering it, I looked at the *whole* of the Church and its history. Christ had said that "if a kingdom be divided against itself, that kingdom cannot stand." This might also apply to the organism of the Church. The dogmas, as I was only then beginning to be aware (not all at once but gradually), had developed consistently. Never had any of them been revoked or altered. The popes, unlike any earthly rulers, are not bound to themselves and to their immediate circumstances, but to the whole of the past and the whole of the future; and their decisions arise from their awareness of this fact. The non-Catholic Christian,

Conversion

who is unacquainted with any such existing and future spiritual
kingdom, hardly suspects the obligation resulting from this, which,
furthermore, is always fulfilled not morally, but spiritually.

In one volume of the journal *Die Christengemeinschaft* (January
1948) it was possible to read that Christ's descent into hell had been
concealed from the faithful at an early stage, which was why it finds
no mention in the Niceno-Constantinopolitan Creed or in the
Creed of the Holy Mass. The writer of the essay concerned was
unaware either that every Catholic child learns the Apostles' Creed,
and that that Creed, including the words "he descended into hell," is
uttered in every telling of the rosary; or that a dogma, once it has
been proclaimed, is never retracted, but is disseminated wherever
possible. I too had to come to understand these facts and connections. Church and papacy are guardians and heralds of the objective,
divine truth, within a world that has on the whole made itself over
to the spirit of worldliness—and in which, admittedly, the truth is
often sought with the greatest subjective sincerity. In order to
understand what this means, as was said before, one must consider
the whole of Christianity and its whole history. A Protestant who
thought everything through from first principles once admitted to
me that without the influence of the Catholic church, non-Catholic
Christianity would either no longer exist, or would be in a much
worse situation. I also take to heart what he added to this: that it
would be good and needful for the Catholic church to see that in
Protestant "poverty" (this was meant as a term of praise!) the highest values might be served, and that "not all wine was kept in Catholic cellars."

Apart from this, I had to commit myself to all the stipulations of
the Council of Trent and the First Vatican Council. I was to "believe
everything" that had been promulgated as truth at these two coun-
cils. I well know, even now, that I was full of doubts about what sort
of questionable propositions I should thereby be compelled to
affirm! Spot checks then showed me that these decrees were not, as I
had imagined, subjugations of the soul, but instead expressed
truths. Only later did I notice that the Council of Trent had saved
the Catholic church. My doubts were those of a "Protestant" who
had never engaged with the whole of the "matter" but had only had

269

an opinion about it, admittedly a very deep-rooted opinion. Naturally, the dogma of the pope's infallibility was exceptionally questionable to me, in fact not just questionable but to be "rejected." My objections soon disappeared, however, when I understood in what way and to what extent "infallibility" was spoken of. If only all those who understand by this word something quite erroneous could be enlightened about its sole and true meaning!

Popes can indeed fall into error, as they did in the Middle Ages and in the Renaissance, but not into such terrible errors as, for example, we find Adolf Hitler making. If only the foundations and contexts of Catholic teaching were better understood outside the Catholic church, no person guided by a spirit of truth would any longer raise his voice to object against it. One example: I once had to explain to a Protestant Christian why, and in what spirit, the Catholic church has converts "conditionally rebaptized" when it is not certain whether or not they have been legitimately baptized. I sought to remove the strength of his objection that the Catholic church recognized no baptism performed outside it. But he stuck to his opinion that all this was only a pretext. It was impossible to make him attend to the relevant dogma of the Catholic church. And how ancient and how completely unequivocal is the Catholic church's teaching that baptism cannot be repeated, and that every act of baptism is valid!

Once the questions just mentioned, along with some others that can be omitted here, had been answered to my satisfaction, my conversion could take place. It was by no means the case that all resistance to the Catholic church had been removed from or stripped of their power within my mind. I just saw conversion as what was right and what was mapped out for me. I no longer had to question whether it should take place; and what was going to happen ought to happen quickly. It happened on May 18, 1946, in the chapel of the Maria-Rosenkranz-Church in Kassel—the one part of the building left standing after the war. I knelt at the communion rail, together with my wife, who had traveled the same spiritual path as I, and held a burning candle in my hand. I spoke the words of the formula of conversion, about which I no longer had any complaints, and received the priestly blessing. When we came into the chapel, it was empty of people. When we left it, a congregation that seemed full of joy had gathered. The act of being received into the Church was festive and joyful; it was not merely objective, but also subjective. For me, as someone quite unused to it, my first confession was no pleasure. The day after that, I legitimately took communion for the first time, and it filled me, despite all the resistance of my heart, with a first gentle breath of peace.

12

In the Church

THE STEP OF CONVERTING TO CATHOLICISM COULD BE compared to moving into a new house. Now you "have" it, but you have to settle into it. That can happen quickly; but it can also happen slowly. For me it happened slowly. At first it was satisfying to know that a deed which had been difficult for me, and almost seemed to go against my nature, now lay behind me. It would have suited my character better to have remained "free" in the sense I had always given that word. Now I had bound myself. It had, alas, been a sacrifice, and I felt grateful to have made it.

Almost all people belong to the church or the denomination into which they were born and in which they were brought up. Not everyone can bring themselves to question this. In my case, no Christian or church connection of any kind followed me in later life from my Protestant childhood. I lost any sense of identity, and for a while (in retrospect, this is hardly credible) I thought of Sigmund Freud's psychoanalysis as a significant and sufficient "worldview" (which in any case its creator could never have intended). Later on, I became a student and follower of Anthroposophy, which even today seems to me the most important worldview outside that of the Catholic church. And now I was a Catholic Christian. In my new "post," nothing was any longer reminiscent of the outset of my life. With two large, if not easy, steps, I had distanced myself from that. I had "freely" become a member of the Catholic church, which filled me with gratitude. But initially this was t gratitude for the fact that the way was now behind me, rather than gratitude for the place where I now found myself. As far as conscious comprehension was concerned, I still had no interest in the mystery of the Church. I was still a stranger within the Church.

I could not encounter real disappointments in the Church, of the kind that well-meaning friends had predicted for me. I had already considered the possibility of these beforehand. I knew only little of the history of the Church as a whole, but the main corruptions that had taken place in it were familiar to me. No one could surprise me by telling me anything about the popes of the Renaissance or the deviations of the Inquisition, or the many deficiencies of those in the religious orders or among the priesthood who were not completely up to their difficult office. And it is hardly astounding that the present-day Church on earth is not perfect. The friends who had given me well-intentioned and insistent warnings thought that I had fallen prey to a need for personal satisfaction in the simplest sense, and that I was going to wake up from my delusory expectations. I had no such expectations, however. When I decided on converting, I was ready to bear all the consequences, even if they were painful ones. Karl Adam, in the last chapter of his book *The Nature of Catholicism*, on the "Church" whom we can call our "mother," says that a perfect mother would be a burden. A poor, suffering, dusty, even stooping, mother is closer to our hearts. —That is how one who loves speaks, and if the word love does not signify a sort of feeling but rather a willed decision, then I can say that even at the beginning of my time as a Catholic, I loved the Church.

What man or woman upon earth would be loved, if only the perfect could be loved? Why should only a completely perfect earthly Church be loved? Why do many Catholics, who are dissatisfied with this or that in the life of the Church, or those who are still outsiders, believe that the Church's imperfections must spoil our love for it? We do not belong to a perfect Church, yet it is nevertheless the holy Church, and the word holy points to its inmost divine nature. It hides this nature behind earthly defects, as the individual Christian (according to St Paul) hides the "new man" he bears within himself beneath his everyday appearance. Insofar as the Church—even though it is a divine being before and beyond all time—can only flourish on earth with the help of human beings, we have indeed to serve the Church and not merely to receive things from it. If there were no longer any human beings, who have their own deficiencies and are willing to remedy them, the Church could no longer exist on earth. Just as one continues a marriage not so as to be "satisfied" with it, but because it is the right thing to do, so one can keep faith with the Church, howsoever its earthly countenance may be shown.

I still had a great deal to learn however. Before my conversion I had been of the opinion that I could not possibly (on health grounds!) attend Holy Mass every Sunday. Behind this was doubtless hidden a disinclination to obey the "commands of the Church," as well as my own convenience and a lack of experience. I had, first of all, to discover that the Holy Mass is a source of strength that cannot be sought out often enough, and so I still considered other sources to be more important. Initially, I nevertheless attended Holy Mass every Sunday, and later did so even more often when possible. Thus, I have never broken the Church's commandment. I was able to settle in, gradually, and ever more strongly, to the essence of the mystery. It became increasingly familiar to me, at first from the content of the words, but then as a liturgical event. Soon I was completely in sympathy with it at every point; and the less I had to summon the power of my intellect, I the more the strength of my heart was freed. My love grew, and it did not take long before I understood that the "commandment of the Church" that prescribes attending Mass every Sunday merely carries in objective form, as an admonition to congregants, what ought in a very real sense to be a demand they make of themselves. If all Catholics were living members of the Church, we would not need a commandment of the Church to call us to regular attendance at Mass—everyone would go gladly and voluntarily. Thomas à Kempis says "If this most holy sacrament were celebrated only in one place, and only by one priest, with what urgency would not men make their way to this place and to this priest, in order to participate in this divine mystery!" That is indeed true, but it is also true that this truth often lies far distant from "modern" people. The Liturgical Movement has been a decisive help to many Catholic Christians in this respect. Anthroposophy, too, was of essential assistance to me here. I cannot deny that through Anthroposophy a sense for the "supersensible" was opened up within me—and the mystery of the Mass certainly is something "supersensible."

I went with increasing gladness to Holy Mass, and it also increasingly saddened me that I could only to such a small extent keep up with or come close to its spirit. How quickly the holy event flies by! In what sublime thoughts and facts does one not share, or not share in enough! How insufficient is the greatest possible gathering and devotion at the altar! Just now the paten was elevated for the sacrifice; but had I fully comprehended this? Can I attend to the elevation of the chalice with a whole and waking heart? Does the *Kyrie eleison* really resound within my inmost being, and do I have the strength to utter the unfathomable *Sanctus!...* with the others only at a distance? The one who strives will indeed be accompanied by such pangs until the end of his life, but apart from them, it must also be said that growth, life, grace, was present despite all the failure. But then: who as an ordinary person, one who has not had any sort of special experience, can speak of these things?

Before my conversion, a Catholic friend once said to me that he had only "actually communicated" three times in his whole life, perhaps only once, perhaps never. I now had to experience for myself what he had meant by that. Nevertheless, however sincerely meant this thought was, it starts out too much from personal experience, and not enough from objective reality. Even great saints—indeed, precisely they—were familiar with "aridity." Higher experiences are gifts of grace, not anything that lower ones could make questionable; and in every communion, we meet the Lord, whatever our state of mind.

One thing however can be said as a consequence and a benediction of participation in the life of the Church, because it touches only on my attitude, rather than on the nature of the thing itself: I was able to comprehend that everything that is beautiful and significant in the "world" was of less significance than the divine mystery. I could not say that any of the "church events" from my Protestant and anthroposophical periods had been more important to me than the great events in the cultural sphere in which I was now able to take part. Nor was there a specific day on which this changed. Today, however, the meaning of this is clear to me: that the greatest literary compositions, the most sublime works of visual art, and the most powerful musical masterpieces only point towards the divine mystery, but are never equal to it—any more than, in their effect upon the soul, they can replace it. Here, too, belongs the experience expressed in the simple song, "Fairest Lord Jesus":

> Fair are the meadows, fair are the woodlands,
> Robed in the blooming garb of spring:
> Jesus is fairer, Jesus is purer—
> Who makes the woeful heart to sing.

Previously I had thought these verses too emotional and world-denying, and it is true that what they say could be more powerfully expressed; but they speak the truth. The *lumen de lumine* (light of light) is brighter, stronger, more essential than anything it produces, anything it reveals, even if what it produces and reveals may also be in turn seminaries of light.

> I wandered long in willing blindness,
> I sought Thee, but I found Thee not,
> For still I shunn'd Thy beams of kindness,
> The creature light fill'd all my thought;
> And if at last I see you now,
> 'Twas Thou to me didst bow!
> (Angelus Silesius)

When I entered the Church I was like someone about to take my high-school diploma. He has completed his schooling, and thus stands to that extent on a summit. But at the same time he is, in the old joke, a pack-animal (*mulus*), facing once again a climb he must commence at the lowest rung.

Foreign to me for a long time was the use of holy water, as well as much else in the life of the Church that is unfamiliar to the outsider—and for that reason can seem unappealing. The salvation of our souls (so I thought), and our strength of belief, did not in any essentials depend upon external forms. Here my sense for the *sacramental* (as distinct from or as supplementing the *sacramentum*) had to awaken, as well as a sense for the beautiful and the symbolic—which is nevertheless more than merely beautiful and symbolic. One should not overvalue what happens in a single place, perhaps inconspicuously, but one should also not mistake its living connection to the whole. The KMB (the initial letters of the names of the three holy "kings," Kaspar, Melchior, and Balthasar), for example, which I had so often seen written over Bavarian peasant doors by the hands of priests, can certainly become a mere form, a pure externality; yet if treated reflectively, they are nevertheless a sign from which blessing can flow.

The priestly blessing distributed with the help of the monstrance is a similar case. One certainly does not take "more" home with one, in some magical way, because the blessing has been dispensed by the priest with the consecrated host rather than with the sign of the cross alone. Yet the solemn form of blessing with the monstrance is indeed more than, and something different in principle from, an aesthetic symbol. Moreover, it is always up to the particular individual what he receives from something objectively offered to him. At first, blessing with the consecrated host seemed to me to be a questionable, "magical" act. Later, I accepted it more calmly and more readily. Who may seriously censure anything that allows our devotion to grow? I knew and loved a beautiful poem by Christian Morgenstern in which he expresses the wish that his soul should come to resemble a "spirit-illuminated monstrance." What is a "spirit-illuminated monstrance"? Only a person who had learned to venerate a monstrance can discover this—a person who seeks to encounter Christ in the sight of it, a person for whom it is a reality, not merely an image.

As a former non-Catholic and "Protestant," the wealth of forms of the Catholic liturgy also gave me some difficulties, since the Protestant service, even in its richest form (with which I only later became acquainted), is poor and sober in comparison with the liturgy of the Catholic church. Here too I could make progress only as a result of thinking, not from experience; and this thought helped me: not even Protestant Christianity has destroyed and negated the meaning of forms; it has only diminished it. Why do not Protestant Christians regard the two candles that are usually used in Protestant services, or the ecclesiastical vestments, the black cassock of the vicar, or the folding of hands in prayer, as "merely external"? It would be consistent either to get rid of all such forms, or to admit that forms *can* be ever more richly developed without having to become "merely external." As time went on, I discovered that the forms of the liturgy are themselves a form of proclamation, and are more essential than any works of art created by human beings, marked as they always are by the peculiar characteristics of their creator. One cannot listen to the Matthew Passion of J. S. Bach without being reminded of Bach, or to that of Heinrich Schutz without being reminded of Schutz; but the kissing of the altar, the paschal candle, and the gestures of the servers do not remind us of any particular people. They speak a language that is objective and divine. I looked upon it with growing delight.

Much of what a lavish ecclesiastical life brings with it was hard for me to put up with at first, as was the fact that not all believers are able to follow the holy events with sufficient devotion. I had to learn that the Church as a whole offers more than the assembled collectivity, more indeed than any individual, is able wholly to grasp. Catholic liturgical life is (paying due attention to the point of comparison) like the performance of a majestic symphony. Who among those in attendance can fathom, can grasp, can follow everything about it? Who, however, could wish to exclude those who are unable to follow it? Who could be in a position to decide that it befits this person but not that person to participate? I could more and more readily apply the truth of this comparison. Was it about other people, was it about my judgment about other people?—Indeed, it was about how I *myself* was adapting to the life of the Church. Whoever wishes to participate in the liturgy in a collective group does not have the right, as an outsider might think, to object to the comportment of those who are not devout. He must do what he can to ensure that they find less to complain about.

About so, a year and a half after I had been received into the Church, I was a little nervous in advance of my confirmation, for this was supposedly to take place together with a huge number of other confirmands in a relatively small church. This meant that people would be pressed up against each other, pushed this way and that, and that the individual confirmations would be completed very quickly (there were about five hundred confirmands, as well as their sponsors and their families). It was precisely in this hurly-burly that I saw more clearly than ever before that how well people can compose themselves, and to what purpose, is entirely dependent on the individual people themselves. I saw mere girls who (I don't know for how long, for I wasn't there as a spectator) without attending to the disturbance around them, knelt in prayer, evidently quite composed in their demeanor—a composure of which not everyone is capable. Later, I thought that even for outsiders it would have been better to exercise composure than to remark upon a lack of composure among those not capable of it—and for whom a great deal of what made up Catholic life seemed to resemble a public holiday. "Seemed," I say, for no one knows what is passing through another person's heart, and those capable of greater reflectiveness should not look down on others, but stand by them. Let anyone who thinks he may reproach the plenitude of forms of the Catholic liturgy on account of its "externalizations" examine whether it is not his pride that is speaking! This I may say, perhaps, for non-Catholic readers. We Catholic Christians, however, ought always to reflect on how things that seem quite familiar, self-evident, and not worth thinking about to us, can affect outsiders.

When I entered the Church, I was indeed filled with a will "to make common cause with simple and ordinary people," but in fact I was full of reserve and pride towards "ordinary" people. Was I not a person of "advanced consciousness"? Could I be required to take part in mere congregational prayers? I still well recall the horror that struck me when, about a year and a half before my conversion, I for the first time unexpectedly heard another member of the congregation saying the rosary, which was then wholly unfamiliar to me. The rapid, expressionless speech seemed spiritless and irreligious to me, a sign of what Christ had called "using vain repetitions, as the heathen do." Now, the rosary really does have to be discovered and learned by non-Catholics—not merely in their heads and according to the text (which is easy) but in its essence and by practicing it (which is difficult). For the non-Catholic Christian is not used to praying in repeated brief formulas, but only through thoughts, which bear on consciousness in a different way than the rosary does, and is supposed to do. I had to come to understand the meaning of this way of praying in contrast to what I had been used to. And nobody can well understand it who has not given themselves up to its flow (the image is just right: it is a question of a flow of time that bears you up). No one who has never swum can know what it is like in the water; no one who has never grown accustomed to praying the rosary can know what grace and what mysteries it holds. I had been prepared for the rosary, incidentally, by some of Rudolf Steiner's statements, not about the prayer life of the Catholic church, but about the meaning of the repetitions in the discourses of Gautama Buddha.

My experience of the rosary was like my experience of everything else about the teaching and life of the Catholic church: I had to win my way through by thinking. I first meditated upon the rosary, then tried to pray along with it, and finally set myself the goal of learning to pray it. I once heard a Protestant pastor say that he himself could only say the Lord's Prayer once at any given time, and only wanted to say it once. If I had also remained with what I was used to in this way, I would never have taken a step towards the Catholic church, let alone have been able to join it. No one says, "I can only speak German and don't wish to speak any other languages: English, French, and Latin don't exist for me!" But that is just how most people behave in the field of ecclesiastical and religious life. Every church and every "movement" has nevertheless gone through powerful disturbances and changes, and they were never started by people who stuck to what they were "used to." In one way or another, the divine admonition should apply to all Christians: "Get thee out of thy country, and from thy kindred, and from thy father's house, unto a land that I will show thee." There are various levels of the soul at which this injunction demands to be applied. One of them is the level at which a religious practice to which one is accustomed can be changed; and this need not lead to conversions until a long while later.

It would be very tempting here to say a good deal about many individual features of Catholic life, about the use of Latin in the liturgy, for example, or about the justification and significance of the sacrament of confession, about priestly celibacy, the meaning of monasticism, the teachings about the Mother of God, or the early first communion of Catholic children. I had meditated on all this. I had to allow it to disclose itself to me (which is all I mean by "meditating") and could thus also, indeed, set out how such a disclosure becomes possible… To a faithful Catholic Christian, perhaps it may seem needless that I wanted to "understand" everything before I would give myself over to it. But so it was. And this shows that there is a path of *thinking* that leads into the Church too. If in the end one looks at everything from a sufficiently broad perspective, one will nevertheless say once again that *how* any given convert came, each in his own way, to join the Church pales in significance before the fact *that* he did so. With me, too, the heart followed along later. My conversion was the second great spiritual blessing in my life—but I can only mention this, not depict it.

I see two sorts of traits or needs running through my whole life from my early years onward, traits or needs about which there still remains something to be said at the end of this "spiritual life story," and in the light of my conversion: the drive towards an objective and liturgical Christianity, and the drive towards the universality of a spiritual life with real effects.

Objective and Liturgical Christianity. So far as I can see, Protestant Christianity had lost me through its lack of liturgical power, and was unable by any means to win me back, however much I understood and acknowledged Protestantism's great significance. I was later able to find a strong liturgical life in the Christian Community, and this liturgical life deeply challenged, educated, and formed me. Why did I not remain rooted there my whole life long? I think this is connected with what it most values, which is at the same time its limitation: its "up-to-dateness" or "newness" and its emphasis on "awareness." For what is "up-to-date," "new," and "aware" today can be swept away tomorrow by something more "up-to-date," "new," and "aware." From a certain standpoint, the liturgy of the Catholic church can certainly be seen as out-of-date, old, and insufficiently aware. But, as does the "dead" language Latin today, it transcends time and is thus always new and always accessible to any awareness that can find a way into it. In the Church's liturgy I had a much stronger feeling than I did in the worship of the Christian Community that I was participating in something that transcended time.

282

Forms that come from history endure much better than anything a later period can produce. Anyone who seriously seeks Christ can find Him anywhere. But anyone who loves His Church (in a "realist," not in a "spiritualistic" sense) will seek Him in the Church. To this extent, my conversion is the result of a long working out of my destiny, guided by a higher power whose goal this conversion apparently was.

Universality of a Spiritual Life with Real Effects. And then, from my childhood onwards—even in my schooldays and then at university—I had always struggled against the fragmentation and secularization of the life of the spirit in general. Here Anthroposophy, which seemed to offer the possibility of overcoming fragmentation and secularization, helped me in a decisive and life-saving way. I hoped that Anthroposophy would alter the world's outlook, that it would put a stop to disasters and lead humankind to come together as one. And yet the world's outlook has remained rigid, disasters have continued to occur, and the oneness of humankind is further off than ever. This means that the forces or realities which have really shaped history have shown themselves hardly to have been influenced by Anthroposophy at all. Thus the hope has disappeared that "fragmentation" and "secularization" could be defeated for the whole of humanity. On this account, a will grew in me to join the strongest positive "spiritual power" present in history, which will defend spirit, humanity, and Christianity until the very last, even if the counter-forces grow ever stronger. Small movements, as we have seen, are easily destroyed and prohibited. The Church is the last, the strongest, the unconquerable bulwark—at its root—of the spirit of Christ on earth. I increasingly sensed something of the truth of the promise that the gates of hell would not overpower it. I gave up the relatively recent beliefs that the world as a whole can be healed—and I gained another faith, given me by "the cross." Linking to something said above, I can put it like this: I moved from a system of coordinates whose axes were "consciousness" and "development" to another system of coordinates whose axes were "sin" and "redemption." These, of course, are only inadequate markers, and there would be a good deal more to say about this. Just as the

Church's liturgy seemed more strongly to contain eternal spirit, rather than a temporal one, so also did a "system of coordinates" with the axes "sin" and "redemption" seem more strongly to contain eternal spirit. After my conversion I thus had the impression, certainty, and joy of finding myself in the "right place."

In various quarters it was expected that my conversion would bring me a satisfaction I myself neither expected nor wished for. I had, they said, "come home," and now I had to be happy about it. One female reader of my essays even wrote, appreciatively, that I would comport myself as a "rightful heir" within the Church. Now, I certainly am grateful to have found my way to the Church, or, what is at bottom the same thing, to have been guided towards it. But I never intended, nor do I now intend, to feel "at home" on earth, not even in the Church. The notion of being a "rightful heir" seems highly questionable to me. When confronted with this notion, two of Christ's sayings come to my mind, sayings that are at once a promise and a warning: "The first shall be last, and the last shall be first" (Matthew 20:16) and "For here have we no continuing city, but we seek one to come" (Hebrews 13:14).

True, it is possible to experience the Church, the "Mother," as being like a home, but in my view one should never connect this with a feeling of security and entitlement, but should instead chiefly be aware of having a task to perform. We should, in the Pauline expression, "work out our own" blessedness. But wherein lies "blessedness"? Eternal bliss is certainly promised us, if we "endure unto the end"; but to strive for it, to engage in a life-and-death struggle for its sake, seems to me still to be too self-seeking. If God has destined me to eternal bliss, I wish to accept it, when it is time to do so (or in eternity). The "blessedness" that we are to lay eyes on here on earth, however, seems to me essentially to be a community of life with Christ, and this is a community of suffering—even if this expression is inadequate, and even if one *could* say the opposite. Do we not set eyes on the continuing sacrifice of the God-man in every Holy Mass, and do we not have a share in His being every time we sacrifice together with Him?

St Paul left behind him a confession that he made good what was lacking "of the afflictions of Christ in my flesh for His body's sake, which is the Church" (Colossians 1:24). There is, then, something "lacking," and this lack has to be "made good." The same Paul also once announced his readiness to be damned to hell if he could thereby save his brothers, the Jewish people. This seems to me to show the correct and the only exemplary attitude towards life; here is the "salvation" or the "blessedness" that has left all self-seeking behind. I am "blessed" if I do not ask about my own blessedness, but about the blessedness of others. I participate in an essential way in "salvation" if I no longer wish for salvation for my own sake. Who can manage that? But the great saints were great precisely because they bore this attitude within themselves, and anyone who sees what is essential in this cannot set for himself any lesser ideal.

The second prayer of the Eucharistic Mass points to this mystery, or to this goal. It asks that we might be *consortes* of Christ. *Sors* is, in German, *Schicksal* (fate). We are thus at bottom praying to share the fate of the God-man, not only to participate in his divine nature. What, however, was, and thus what is, Christ's fate? It begins, so far as we can see it, with the *descendit de coelis* ("he came down from heaven") and leads through the cruel passion, endured in pure self-lessness, the descent into hell, the resurrection, and finally the heavenly ascension to lasting works of love in and with humankind. The prayer for community with the saints at the end of the Canon of the Mass (*nobis quoque peccatoris*—"with us sinners too") contains the thought of a common fate. We are asking, that is, to be permitted to continue to exist *intra consortium* with the saints. This cannot only mean that, because of the service the saints have done, we would like to find an undeserved happiness for ourselves. Essentially, however, it means that we wish to comprehend the sacrificial will of these great figures, and wish that God might bestow upon us the perfection this sacrificial will requires.

Life in this world, as well as in the next, shows that one is only in community with another person or spirit to the extent that one can *comprehend* that person or spirit. Whether it is with Goethe, with Bruckner, or with anyone else, no one has more community than his own capacity permits. Why should it be any different with the great saints? Because their legends can be told? Because we "love and honor" them? Because we "invoke" them? And why should it be different with the God-man? I am so far connected to, or one with, Christ as I succeed in receiving, or it is given to me to receive, His divine will into my own. All this stands under the sign of sacrifice. One of the blessings of my membership of the Church is that fact that I am permitted to find out how to do this and what belongs to it. We should certainly invoke the saints "in all things," but there are also "things" in connection with which it would be better not to do so, and at heart every Christian prayer must proclaim: "Not my will, but Thine be done!"

In my Protestant youth I never heard this idea of sacrifice wholly and purely championed. Perhaps things are different in the Protestant church now. But perhaps Protestant theology stands in the way of this. For Protestant theology is unable directly to expound a theory of ascesis. If one starts out from the idea that man is "justified" *sola fide*, by faith alone, then the idea of sacrifice can only ever be justified as a consequence of faith, not immediately deduced from the relationship of human beings to Christ. No one need suffer with Christ *sola fide*, nor become like him in form.

Even in my anthroposophical period, although it led me into the world of the essentially real, I had still not grasped the idea of sacrifice in its purity. I never regarded myself as an advocate of "myself-through-Christ," as Christian Morgenstern puts it somewhere, for my gaze was much too strongly directed both by Anthroposophy (as well as by everything I absorbed from the Christian Community) towards the "resurrected Christ." I was too determined by the idea of a "Christianity of resurrection" to be able to give equal attention to the Passion (as a voluntary *achievement*) in the fate of the individual. Moreover, where authentic Catholic religious practice is considered to have actually survived (what Protestantism pejoratively calls "Good Friday" Christianity) the gaze of those who are striving is far too focused on the *objective* forms of "Christianity" for the "cross" to find the central respect that is necessary in the context of *subjective* life.

No one who does not regard following Him through the horror of the Passion as his highest task can, however, share in the life of the *resurrected* Christ. To them belongs Gethsemane, to them "My God, my God, why hast thou forsaken me?" It also seems difficult to me to follow Christ without reservation if one is thinking (no matter in what way) of one's own *karma*, which could be, or should be, "improved upon." So long as I am thinking of my own *karma* (and I did then think about it) I am thinking of myself. Anyone who seriously tries to imitate Christ, however, will in the long run be as little concerned with his own *karma* as a person, while running fast, will be thinking about his body.

Only in the Church did I learn, in my thinking and in my intentions (certainly not in what I could achieve) to be serious about imitating Christ; and I believe I have now understood the meaning of the Passion. The consequence, however, is that one must become ever more deeply aware of one's own weakness, of continual renunciation, of the indestructible continuous workings of the fall into sin. Christian self-consciousness, as Rudolf Steiner once described with perfect clarity in one of his lectures, has two sides: one's own human insignificance, and that which pulls us out of such insignificance and fills us with a new, divine, nature. The essential effects of my conversion were what meant that, in the Catholic church, I was able to come noticeably closer to an unqualified understanding of sin and to an understanding of divine grace.

To belong to the Catholic church is certainly a gift of grace, but it is a gift one must show oneself worthy to receive. Christ said: "From everyone to whom much has been given, much will be required." (Luke 12:48) What will one day be required of a Catholic Christian? In the words of the centurion, *Domine, non sum dignus, ut intres sub tectum meum, sed tantum dic verbo, et sanabitur anima mea.* "Lord, I am not worthy to have you come under my roof; but only speak the word, and my servant will be healed." (Matthew 8:8)

APPENDIX

Book Reviews

BERNHARD MARTIN'S AUTOBIOGRAPHY AWAKENED A
great echo in the "relevant" circles, so that a second edition was
already called for only a year later. The book, printed with the
imprimatur of the Episcopal Ordinariate by Pilger-Verlag Speyer,
received considerable attention, both from Catholic and from
Anthroposophical circles, especially from the Catholic side, as the
following review excerpts show.

> People are reading Bernhard Martin's very painstaking, conscien-
> tious, and careful book. And they are coming to see (in many cases,
> perhaps, as if struck by a lightning-bolt) that one must first have
> studied Rudolf Steiner and Anthroposophy adequately before per-
> mitting oneself to stand in judgment over either.... For the first
> time, the book offers from a Catholic (yet nevertheless objective)
> standpoint deep insights into the nature of Steiner's Anthroposo-
> phy and into the religious life of the Christian Community. [...] I
> recommend Martin's book most warmly to all seekers after truth.
> It is not only interesting as the story of a conversion, but is valuable
> also for us priests in understanding the soul of these two currents
> which want to renew the world spiritually and religiously.[1]

There were also reviews in the anthroposophical press, whose criticism was, however, in part destructive, although among these the
review by Herman Jülich in the *Blätter für Anthroposophie* [Anthro-
posophical papers] stands out for its objectivity.[2] When the second
edition appeared, Jülich also reviewed it, this time in the periodical

---

1. Quotation printed on the dustjacket of the second edition, excerpted from
Natur und Kultur and *Ambrosius*.
2. Hermann Jülich, "Droht uns eine katholisierte Anthroposophie?" [Does a
catholicized Anthroposophy threaten us?] *Blätter für Anthroposophie* 7 (1951), 246 ff.

Die Kommenden [Forthcoming events], where, in issue twelve (June 25, 1951), he writes: "There are books whose testimonial power exceeds what their author seems to have intended." Martin himself observed that Jülich came very close to the concern of his book in trying to do justice *both* to the anthroposophical and to the Catholic Bernhard Martin (who nevertheless remained a member of the Anthroposophical Society his whole life long). In this reviewer, Martin encountered an attitude that could not always be taken for granted among anthroposophists, for which reason he wrote the following reply to Jülich.

> There is a growing tendency among modern people to set up ready-made camps; and so it happens all too often that one person "is" a Catholic, another "is" a Protestant, another "is" an anthroposophist—and all that remains is to classify and label everything around them in accordance with what each of them happens to "be." Now, that the Protestant church and the Catholic church champion particular forms and formulas of truth belongs to their essence, and can be conceived of in no other way. In the anthroposophical movement, however, if judgments approved by "us" or by "one" should come to be regarded as sufficient, sooner or later this will be the death of it. […]
>
> The book not only intends to bear witness to what we might call the positive aspects of Anthroposophy for Catholicism, but to give voice also to what is positive for Anthroposophy in the Church. Only in the earthly world (on the "physical level") are Anthroposophy and the Church tragically irreconcilable with each other. In higher spheres, there are paradoxical harmonies; and in the end, Anthroposophy and the Church stem from the same highest cosmic sphere. The purpose of the book is essentially to point to these higher realms, from which stem all earthly forms, and from which alone originates the power of understanding all earthly forms. […] Truth lives both in the anthroposophical movement and in the Church. If only the proponents of both would ask whether they had understood each other, rather than seeking only to understand themselves, many sources of salvation would be unblocked. […]
>
> Just as the Church cannot live from the precisions of its theological formulas, but requires that they be brought to life in individual people, so also is Anthroposophy not complete when its

objective meaning is expounded, but requires to be demonstrated in the individual's thinking, feeling, and willing. [...] What Rudolf Steiner wished for, gave us, and inaugurated, may be as "timely," etc., as you like. But whether it is going to "save the world" is not an impersonal question. It is, rather, a question of the practice of the individual; and to this practice belongs alert, open, unprejudiced observation of what exists in our environment, including the Church.

In the same issue of *Die Kommenden*, Jülich answered Martin in considerable detail. Here is the core of his response:

If I have understood him rightly, Martin finds himself situated between two "camps." Catholicism has given him an experience he could not find in Anthroposophy; but it is Anthroposophy that makes it possible for him to understand this experience. On the one hand, Martin would like the Church not to overlook the possibility of this understanding; one the other, he wishes anthroposophists would consider his experience—if not have it themselves. It is from this position that Martin views the two "camps." [...] The goal Martin has set himself is a truly adventurous and brave undertaking. From the standpoint of developments up till this point, one can describe this goal as fantastical or even dangerous. But there ought to be people, even on the anthroposophical side, willing to take up this goal as seriously as can be. One should not let oneself be overly affected by the impression Martin's book must inevitably make on many anthroposophists, or by its possible lack of success. For the mortal danger in which Christianity stands today surely justifies *any* attempt at honest mutual understanding between the Church and Anthroposophy. Rudolf Steiner would never have stood in the way of Martin's experience of receiving a blessing from the current of grace in the Christian sacraments, a blessing Martin can understand by means of Anthroposophy—in other words, that he can also intellectually grasp the nature of the current of grace within which he is standing. Steiner always left it to his students to take up a position in relation to the religious life in accordance with their needs. Over and over again he said that Anthroposophy did not wish to cut anyone off from their existing contexts; but that Anthroposophy ought instead to help people grasp more fully the context in which they stood.

For the sake of clarity it must be reiterated that Anthroposophy is in no way a substitute for *religion*. It is a spiritual *science*. The fact that, as spiritual science, it wishes to stimulate artistic and religious feeling and endeavor, in no way alters its scientific character. This is why, as I see it, Martin is fundamentally mistaken when he laments that Anthroposophy is taken too much in a scientific, rather than in a religious and Christian, sense. Anyone who takes Anthroposophy in too religious and Christian a sense (as Martin has manifestly done) must remain dissatisfied with it. That which participation in authentic Christian worship can do for a person (and I am not thinking only of Catholic worship, but equally of the Christian Community, the Church of England, or others) cannot be supplied by Anthroposophy. But then, to supply it is not at all the intention of Anthroposophy!

Nevertheless, Anthroposophy *does* offer an important contribution to the ecclesiastical and religious life of our age. It supplies a new and overarching understanding of the historical religions, of Holy Scripture, and of the sacraments. It makes it possible for Christians to know that Christ is not a god among the gods of other peoples, but the redeemer who became man in order to enable humankind as a whole to re-ascend to the spiritual world, and thereby to free itself from bondage […] to the body. By this means, Anthroposophy can also help to deepen ecclesiastical and religious life. By means of Anthroposophy, one can intellectually grasp (i.e., without direct spiritual vision or clairvoyance) Christ's sacrifice at Golgotha as the central mystery of human evolution. And one can learn (again, without clairvoyance) to find a new path to Christ in a mode of thinking that makes it possible to grasp such thoughts—a new path that, of course, by no means excludes us from Christ's effects on us through the sacraments. With regard to the fact that thinking has so far mostly had a destructive impact on the strength of faith—and that, indeed, the intellect's powers of doubt have entailed a dangerous decline in religious life—people will learn in the future to regard the intellectual path to Christ, which Anthroposophy presents, as the greatest possible help to an endangered Christianity.

"Humanity today," Rudolf Steiner said, "needs to move towards spiritual knowledge. Spiritual knowledge, however, mostly resists the dogmatic ecclesiastical confessions that have gradually taken form in the West. The Church as such cannot really be hostile to spiritual-scientific knowledge—that is quite impossible. For the Church as such ought really only to have to do with people's feelings, with ceremonies, with worship, but not with the intellectual life."[3]

3. *Die geistigen Hintergründe der sozialen Frage* [The spiritual background of the social question], volume three in the edition by the administrators of Steiner's estate, distributed in Germany by the Novalis publishing house.

Letters from
Valentin Tomberg

EARLY IN 1952, BERNHARD MARTIN RECEIVED FROM Tomberg a letter evidently in reply to a letter from Bernhard evincing some emotional disturbance which Jülich's second review[1] had raised up in him:

Dear Friend,

Today, on the last day of the year and in the middle of the thirteen Holy Nights of Christmas, I should like, with reference to your latest letter, to say a few things that are on my mind.

When I look back at the years of my life (already quite few) I find a long series of hopeless situations, and one lesson taught by them all: that there is no such thing as a hopeless situation. True, no one (apart from Maria)[2] knows how many there have been, how wide their extent, or their particular nature. But it is perhaps enough to say that we are talking of hundreds of situations in which there did not seem to be any humanly foreseeable possibility of finding the money to pay for food (I mean this literally and in the most basic sense). This is the earthly and material side, which is not the most important. But how did it stand with things that were more important?

Five times, death just barely passed us by, touching us with its breath and its wings. I do not mean sickness and the hospital, but death, i.e., a "hopeless" situation, and agony. Faith and hope, those two rays of love in human life, always helped. And how did it stand with the purely spiritual side? The "most important" side, as spiritually-yearning people are accustomed to call it? There is no favor-

---

1. See final book review in preceding section.
2. Tomberg's wife.

itism in the spiritual world. Its revelations are consolation. One who receives many revelations is much consoled. Much consoled also is the one among men who needs consolation in order to *endure* the suffering that life brings with it. *Consolation* and *suffering* are in direct proportion to each other. Why should one need a doctor if an ordinary household remedy will do? Why should an angel or an archangel reveal itself and intervene where human remedies and materials suffice? Only a suffering for which there is no human remedy—a spiritual emergency, a question, a difficult task—creates the prerequisites for the concrete personal revelation of spiritual beings.

I could tell in this connection of many years of hourly and daily exertion, work, and longing—with no ray, no gleam of concrete, tangible spiritual reality to be seen... And what came later was not at all what one had striven for: as if someone who had for decades longed for a library received as a consolation a piano instead!

Could it be said, then, that no one has it easy and no one is in a better state than anyone else? Yes, certainly—and why, moreover, should it go better *privately* for one person than for another? But goodness, happiness, is offered to all people universally. And consciousness of this universal happiness is precisely a spring of gladness in human life, a spring of a *pure* joy—a joy that has nothing to do with some advantage over one's fellowmen.

No matter in what way one's private destiny may be shaped (and here it is true that *as a whole* no one has it easier than others), it is important and salutary to remind oneself from time to time of the *actual* rank of the precious things one *does* possess:

The first and most precious thing is *being*, that one *is*—a wondrous gift in comparison with which all other gifts pale.

Then, the wondrous capacities of the light of thinking, of the warm music of feeling, of the ardently desiring will!

Then, all the wondrous organs that rescue us from being solitary and let us be surrounded by a magnificent world—our senses, of every kind, and in particular our ability to speak, which makes it possible for us to *interact* with our brothers and sisters!

Then, our brothers and sisters themselves, those wondrous creations—with their countenances, gazes, and voices, full of mysteries of the soul!

And the dearest and nearest among these, the saints and angels, the Virgin Mary, Christ himself, his sacrifice and miracles, his Church with its gifts and sacraments.

Then, everything good, beautiful, and true in human culture as such.

Then, nature: the firm reliable earth, water, the wondrous air we breathe, all warmth, the fruits of the earth, all plants and animals, *light*, the sun, moon, and stars... and much, much more.

This calling to mind of the precious things given to all human beings, I call "taking an inventory" of human life. This is what I recommend to you, dear friend, from the heart. It creates a distance from what is purely private, and in so doing brings us close to the great treasure of *being* by showing us the true hierarchical ranking of values—which in its turn awakens the gratitude and gladness necessary to overcome private difficulties.

All *strength* is of a joyful, courageous kind, whereas regret, discontent, and dejection are good for nothing—they are the *weaknesses* of the so-called "weakling" (which none of us are, in and of ourselves). *Each* of us, however, *can* become the weakest weakling, if, forgetting the great goods of *being* (thus becoming ungrateful), we give ourself over to private dejection and discontent.

I did not write all this in order to say anything new, but to make the breath of love detectable in some way, between you and me as well. If I have failed, put the letter in the fire and forget it. We wish you happiness for the New Year.

Your Valentin

On April 16, 1956, Tomberg replied to a letter from Bernhard Martin, occasioned by Martin having learned from their mutual friend Gertrud von Hippel why Tomberg had not wanted to meet him [which had troubled Martin] during his stay with the von Hippels in Eichstätt in 1953. Tomberg had later replied to an enquiry on this topic from von Hippel, that it had been "too early" for such a meeting, after which the correspondence had understandably come to a standstill. This letter, and the one following, are included here particularly for the light they cast on the paramount themes of Catholicism and Anthroposophy in the present book. Tomberg wrote in explanation to Martin as follows:

I should like to make clear here, in the first place, just what "too early for a meeting," as Gertrud put it, meant. Our correspondence had been interrupted since your letter in which you wrote that Catholicism alone was not enough, and that you had the intention of bringing (or had a need to bring) Catholic and anthroposophical elements together, and to work with other people towards this end. (I am summarizing the content of your letter in much too "simplified" a form here, I know; but I just want to indicate which letter I am talking about.) When I learned of this intention from your letter, I said to myself: "You cannot say anything, and you *may* not say anything—you cannot say yes, because you are against it from your own experience; and you cannot say no, because you cannot and may not in all honesty be certain that Bernhard might not have a different and better experience if he tries it. Until he has tried it and has the results of his experience in front of him, it is too early for me, with my perspective and my views, to appear before him. I must draw back for a while—until the results of his experience either strengthen or refute my perspective. In either case, only then would it be opportune to resume the conversation (about this very important matter), for if the experience has been a favorable one, I can learn something important and adjust my point of view, which would be a great joy to me. If, on the other hand, the experience turns out to be a negative one, we would be agreed, and also then have a conversation." This is what was meant by the expression "too early."

Now I would like to ask you whether you have had any definite experience of Catholic-anthroposophic work in the meantime. If so, I would be very grateful if you would tell me the results.[3]

As a letter of Tomberg's of April 29 (i.e., some two weeks later) shows, Bernhard wrote back very quickly, though we do not have his reply to the particular question Tomberg had put regarding the connection of Catholicism with Anthroposophy. Martin's response seems, rather, to have posed many specific questions associated with this topic, which Tomberg was glad to answer. But he wanted to do this thoroughly, and that was not the right moment because "first he had to cope with the move on May 7 to Green Trees in Peppard." Although not responding immediately to Martin's specific questions, Tomberg did write the following about himself:

---

3. Valentin Tomberg to Bernhard Martin, letter of April 16, 1956 (RKT-Archiv).

Through Anthroposophy to the Universal Church

I am now particularly concerned with arriving at a retrospect over the past, a view of the spiritual present, and a prospect over the future of humankind. Much that is new has surfaced in my field of vision—especially when looking at the present situation of spirit and its tendencies. As you know, the present day is extremely pre-occupied with psychology, and especially with depth psychology—almost to the same extent that the eighteenth century was preoccupied with metaphysics, and the nineteenth with natural science.

I have now made myself more thoroughly familiar with this field—that is, with Freud's psychoanalysis, Adler's psychology of the individual, and Jung's analytical psychology. The latter (the Jungian school) has made a deep impression on me. Although it grew out of the same soil as Freudianism and Adlerism, it has developed in a manner markedly distinct from both. It has arrived at the empirical discovery that a person's essential core consists neither of the sexual drive (Freud), nor of the "will to power" (Adler), but of religion. Jung "came upon" the fact (his expression) that beyond the threshold of ordinary day-time consciousness, subconscious and superconscious forces are active, working out of religion, through religion, and for religion ("religion" understood here in the sense of communication with the "higher worlds").

The juxtaposition with Anthroposophy is, to my mind, favorable to Jungian research. For in Anthroposophy, "mystical facts" are converted into concepts from ordinary everyday consciousness, whereas in the Jungian school concepts of ordinary everyday consciousness are converted into "mystical facts" (symbols). Here, the "scientist" becomes a "mystic," whereas in Anthroposophy the "mystic" becomes a "scientist"—or aspires to. The result is that out of the Jungian tendency come people who are reverential, open to any new revelation of spirit, and value every ancient revelation of spirit, whereas anthroposophists obscure everything, are not open to anything new, and scorn or undervalue everything traditional. P. W. Martin's book *Experiment in Depth: A Study of the Work of Jung, Eliot, and Toynbee* (showing that the psychotherapist C. G. Jung, the poet T. S. Eliot, and the philosopher of history Arnold Toynbee all arrived at the same conclusion),[4] as well as Dr. Brown's book *Psychotherapy,*[5] provide (along with the works of Jung him-

---

4. NY: Routledge, 1955.
5. Presumably Dennis Brown's *Psychological Methods of Healing: An Introduction to Psychotherapy* (London: University of London Press, 1938).

self) valuable material in this line. Frieda Fordham's *An Introduction to Jung's Psychology* also gives many precious "keys" to his spiritual direction (Jung himself recommends the book in a foreword).... In short: I see in the Jungian spiritual direction a new ally for religion, for the Catholic church, and also a breath of fresh, revivifying spiritual life in the sense of spiritual experience as such.

As it happens, at almost the same time Tomberg wrote this letter, Martin was also occupied with C.G. Jung—perhaps because they had alerted each other to this "soul-spirit" researcher.[6] It should be noted that Jung repeatedly stressed that his field was that of the soul, and not primarily the spirit.

In the meantime, Valentin Tomberg had thought more about his answer to Martin, until at last, on July 24, 1956, he was able to respond. It was to be an extraordinarily long letter—perhaps the longest Tomberg ever wrote—which took him almost a week to write. Because of its significance, it is given here in full.

Dear Bernhard,

I will try to respond as truthfully and responsibly as possible to your letter of April 13, a letter that, as I have already said, is of the highest merit. I have read the letter over again. It is fresh in my memory and right in front of me on the table. So, even if I may *seem* to be writing about "other things" not mentioned in the letter, this is not because I have forgotten or overlooked what is in it, but is only what seems to me a necessary expansion of the subject.

As a starting point, I would like to emphasize that it is true that the Church (i.e., the *clergy*) is conservative. The forward-moving impulse in the Church comes mainly, if not entirely, either from lay people or from the general world situation. Over time, the clergy does come to recognize everything that has shown itself to be true and necessary in this way—but that occurs after some delay. This is why, as far as the clergy is concerned, the "strip of

6. It is conceivable that Bernhard Martin had continued to send Tomberg his periodical *Neue Schau*, on whose editorial board he worked. In January 1956 Martin published in it a review of C.G. Jung's recently published book *Answer to Job*.

land" (so to speak) of what cultured lay people have recognized to be true remains for a time a *terra incognita*, but then comes to be recognized by the Church (as an example, we may take the long since discarded belief by the clergy that the history of the earth is to be counted only in thousands of years). This is just how it is.

Having said this, let us now ask ourselves how matters would stand if the Church did *not* function in this way—i.e., if it were not "conservative," but "progressive"? Then two things would happen. First, the whole strength, focus, and activity of the clergy would be devoted, not to the truths of salvation, but to "cutting-edge developments" in the fields of life bordering upon those truths. There would be a danger that the truths of salvation—which are of eternal value—would be pushed into the background, or even be overshadowed by "progress." Second, scope for ongoing development in other fields would *ipso facto* be made impossible for lay people, since any and everything "just discovered" would immediately be grafted onto the Church's body of doctrine, and thus irreversibly rigidified. In other words, as lay people, we have scope to carry out our own research, express our opinions on points of doctrine, and then (perhaps years later), if need be, change or even retract them. But the Church cannot afford to operate this way. It cannot "take sides" again as it once did in the well-known "Copernican-Ptolemaic" controversy.

Progress, then, is the *task of the lay person*. You write (correctly, in my view) that it is even the *duty* of the lay person. Yes, it *is* our duty: and thousands upon thousands of us *do* take part daily in the further development of the sciences, the arts, and social relationships.

As you write, there is, however, still one area that stands in need of "progress": the *supersensible* domain... The supersensible, as experienced in depth psychology of a Jungian bent, in parapsychology (hypnosis, suggestion, telepathy, clairvoyance), and as taught by metaphysical philosophers (Pythagoras, Plato, Leibniz, Fechner, and others), by mystical doctrines (Yoga, Vedanta, Kabbalah, Gnosis, Christian nature-mysticism), and by esoteric doctrines (Alchemy, Astrology, Magic, Hermeticism, Theosophy, and, lastly, Anthroposophy), is *not* identical in its meaning with the "supernatural" of theology or with the "supernatural" of natural science. It is obvious, however, that to a certain extent they do all cross a given border experienced as real. This much is explicitly admitted by these thinkers and traditions themselves. Not only is this border (the "super" of the "supersensible") acknowledged, but warnings are frequently issued regarding it in various respects. Thus, we find in tractate Chagiga 14b of the Talmud (the collection of post-biblical Jewish ethical, religious, and mystical literature extending from the second century BC to the fifth century AD), the following story: Four scholars (rabbis from the beginning of the second century AD) attempt to find entry into the heavenly paradise—that is, to penetrate into the secrets of divine creation. One of them, Ben Asai, loses his life in the attempt; the second, Ben Zouma, loses his reason; even worse, the third, Elisa Ben Abuja, loses his faith; only the fourth, Rabbi Ben Akiba, succeeds in getting in and returning safely.

This story, written eighteen centuries ago, comprises two very different themes: on the one hand, *encouragement* to penetrate into the supersensible (since Rabbi Ben Akiba succeeded in getting in and returning safely); on the other, a *warning* that the supersensible is "super" sensible for the good reason that crossing its border brings with it danger to life, intellectual health, and moral health—for, as the story tells us, the three failed scholars lost, respectively, life, reason, and faith.

Admittedly, this is an extreme case, given that, for the four rabbis, it was a matter of the "heavenly paradise" and the "secrets of divine creation"—and not everyone either wants or needs (as they say in Cologne) "to go whole hog." But even so, history records in varying degrees the same universally valid teaching: crossing the border to the supersensible brings with it danger to health, reason, and faith; and the further one wishes to trespass, the greater the danger. (Rudolf Steiner, too, spoke of attendant dangers for thinking, feeling, and willing—i.e., coldness, over-sensitivity, and a violent nature—in *Knowledge of Higher Worlds*, and elsewhere.)

The border to the supersensible *is* a reality, and to cross it carries risk. For this reason, one cannot, by means of lectures and writings, *encourage* or *call upon* people to cross this border; nor can one *promise* them spiritual goods if they do. The *Church* does not do this—instead, it guides people to the truths of salvation and to universal earthly duties and tasks. *Science* does not do this—instead, it protects itself and people at large with its method, which is limited to a universally testable and verifiable protocol that proceeds step-by-step on the basis of experiments. So then, who *does* aspire to cross the border of the supersensible, and for what reason?

This is the important question to answer if one wishes to act and to know in a responsible manner. Let us therefore take a moment to explore it with a view to understanding clearly when the border must be respected, and when it may be crossed—and, perhaps, even when it *ought* to be crossed.

I am personally aware of only *two* circumstances in which the border between the sense-perceptible and the supersensible may and ought to be crossed (I do not means speculatively, but in one's own experience).

The *first* occurs when—neither sought for, nor owing to any known cause—the supersensible simply *appears*; when it so to speak *breaks in upon* one's life. In such a case, one must engage with it.

The *second* circumstance I am thinking of is when a person simply cannot do otherwise (not in a manic way, but out of true "hunger and thirst") than seek the supersensible. In the latter case, a person *may* strive for the supersensible. Thus, for example, when a person loves another person or other being who is "beyond" (whether "gone" or "not come"), this love, if it is real and true, justifies his entering the supersensible. Orpheus's journey to the underworld in search of Eurydice is justified because (as it seems to me) love carries within itself a justification for everything in the world.

Apart from these circumstances, I really cannot offer any others of a *justified* attempt to cross the border to the supersensible. Summoning the supersensible solely out of a desire to "know" seems to me insufficient grounds to justify making the attempt. It is not "serious" enough. It is playing a game—indeed, playing with fire, as we learned above from the Talmudic story of the four rabbis.

Now let us come back to the question of *who* ought to cross the border to the supersensible, and *why* (in the sense of *supplementing* science and religion by investigating the supersensible). In the first instance, those who *ought* to do it are practitioners duty-bound by their vocation to help others (though not themselves) whose lives have been *broken in upon* by the supersensible, and whose health is for this reason at risk. This holds, at any rate, for therapists and pastors. As he has often said explicitly, C.G. Jung was forced by the experiences *of* his patients, and by his experiences *with* his patients, to engage experientially with the domain of the supersensible. As far as the second circumstance is concerned (that of a love stronger than forgetting, sleep, and death), however, it can only be a matter of individual and purely *private* exertions, methods, and results, even if the love in question concerns God Himself—this being the domain of private mystical experience. It seems to me, then, that a study of the supersensible that goes beyond the borders of what is *private* is justified only for *therapeutic* purposes. Now, the objection can be made that anything, or almost anything, *could* have therapeutic significance, and that therefore even Anthroposophy could be evaluated from this angle. Thus, your doctrine of the *Ahrimanic* element in the world, for which the Church (as you write) fails to account, *could* conceivably be considered from a therapeutic point of view.

The above proviso is justified, and so, in the interest of the problem with which we are both concerned, I would like to explore the question of the therapeutic value of Anthroposophy as a possible, even if only a partial, supplementation of the doctrine and practice of the Church. In treating the problem of the Ahrimanic, I would like to begin from the *particular* (in order to move on then to the *general*) therapeutic value of Anthroposophy in comparison to other existing and possible paths to the supersensible.

   That there exists a whole series of beings in the hierarchy of evil (Lucifer, or the devil; Satan, or Ahriman; Mephistopheles, Samael, Azazel, and others) is familiar enough to us. Nor is it contested by the Church, although the Church prefers to deal with one being as the "monarchical" leader of the hierarchy of evil, in the same way (with respect to the hierarchy of the good, with its saints and hierarchical beings) it insists that it is God who matters first and last. For the Church, the leader of the hierarchy of evil is not on a level with God, but fulfills a function *permitted* by God. The Book of Job contains a sufficient treatment of the question of the relations between God, the devil, and man. Here, the devil (Satan, *not* Lucifer) appears, not as an enemy of God, but as a champion of the thesis that "only what has been tested, and proven in the test, is genuine and of value." This thesis is recognized as being justified by

God; and under certain specific conditions (which must be strictly adhered to), the devil obtained *permission* from God to test Job's relationship to God on the matter of Job's selflessness.

From the story of Job, which as part of Holy Scripture is absolutely binding for the Church, it follows that the effect of the devil in relation to human beings rests on a *covenant*. In other words, it is *permitted* by God. This covenant is aimed at the testing or temptation of human beings (otherwise, what could be the meaning of the sixth petition in the Lord's prayer: that God "lead us not into temptation"?). It thus relates to complying or failing to comply with the Ten Commandments. In Job's case, the first commandment ("You shall have no other gods before Me") was being tested. Now, *killing* people, subverting their consciousness, causing them to fall asleep through hypnotic means, mechanical devices, or other forms of *coercion*—none of these are *temptations*, and so are not *tests*, for they lie outside the domain of the God-devil-man relationship, and thus beyond both the relationship of good and evil and the covenant whereby human freedom is preserved and protected.

If, for example, a Moscow secret agent offers me a large sum of money to betray professional secrets to him, he is *tempting* me. But if he throws me into prison and paralyzes the operation of my will with chemical injections (as happened in the case of Cardinal Mindszenty, for example), so that I capitulate to his demands, this is not *temptation*, but *coercion*—which means *evil* has gained nothing by all this, and *good* has lost nothing thereby. For according to the covenant, and according to reason, the "struggle" between good and evil consists in garnering the *free decision* of a person involved: the struggle is a purely *moral* one, not a matter of *power*. An coerced evil deed is as worthless to the devil as a coerced good deed is to God. It is the *law of freedom* (the moral realm as a reality) that holds sway over and within the struggle between good and evil. Without this law of freedom, any temptation loses its meaning—i.e., ceases to be "evil," but instead works mechanically, just as does any good deed.

Since the whole affair we are speaking of is a purely moral one, it is in fact a question here only of good and evil, not of strong or weak, healthy or sick—let alone of living or dead. If, however, there is in the world an absolute force that can *coerce* people to do anything whatsoever (a force such as that applied by Hitler and Stalin, for example), then whatever may come of this is neither God's will nor the devil's will, but the will of a *person* able to cross the line of the *law* (the "good-evil" covenant) in either of two directions: that of the good (for example, voluntarily *seeking* martyrdom) or that of evil (for example, *martyring* others by the misuse of *force*).

To put it crudely: if, with the help of the state's means of coercion and of modern science, a tyrant achieves absolute mastery over a nation, then, throughout the period of the tyrant's rule of coercion on *earth*, this nation is lost both to God and to the devil. Why? Because this nation stands outside the domain where good and evil (in the moral sense) apply. It has *fallen out* of the realm of merit and sin. But this is *not* a result attributable to the spiritual world in the sense of the hierarchy of evil; it is, rather, a result of arbitrary human will, i.e., the misuse of human freedom. A *great deal* more could be said about this, but for the sake of the main problem we are concerned with here, I must forego exploring any further ramifications of this subject, in order to move on to the question of the relationship between the Church and the Ahrimanic, considered now from a therapeutic point of view.

From what has been said so far, it follows that the *mechanical* does not belong to the realm of the *moral* (that of good and evil). The mechanical "in itself" has as little to do with the concept, idea, and being of evil (i.e., of the devil) as it does with the good. This is why singling out the intellectual mechanism of a sort of "world-hypnotizer" hypostasized as Ahriman in contrast to a "tempter misleading us into sin" hypostasized as Lucifer (as promulgated with such glaring schematic convenience in Anthroposophy), *blurs* the moral question by seeming to place responsibility for the creation of arbitrary human will and fantasy on an hypostasized Ahriman— thereby absolving human beings of these commissions, and distorting the whole God-devil-man relationship by transposing it from the purely moral to the mechanical.

If, on the other hand, the anthroposophical formula "Ahriman is the karma of Lucifer" (meaning that Lucifer's "evil" becomes mechanical in Ahriman) is brought forward here as an objection to the account just given, one must consider that "karma" never means the "becoming-mechanical" of anything, but means, rather, the intervention of a correcting and restraining *law*: karma is law, not mechanism. If, in the present context, one means to apply the anthroposophical formula that "Ahriman is the karma of Lucifer," it would quite unexpectedly mean that Ahriman enters into Lucifer's sphere of action and brings the latter's arbitrary will within the bounds of the *law* and *covenant*, in order that no chaos should arise there.

I write all this with the particular intention of showing that the Church (whether consciously or unconsciously, being irrelevant to our present purpose) has very important and biblically-founded grounds for disregarding the Ahrimanic, and focusing instead in this regard on the "devil" who negotiates with God over Job.

Let us now resume our consideration of the problem of the Ahrimanic from a therapeutic point of view. In what does the need for a therapeutic effect consist? It consists in the fact that we find ourselves confronted by a monstrous abstraction pieced together from elements drawn from politics, technology, institutions, and intellectualization. We are faced with an impersonal force of iron necessity, a sort of world-clockwork that wants to engulf us. *Fear* arises in face of this mechanism of force, which seems all the more daunting given that planets and stars move as a sort of clock-work also. But fear is the strongest contagion there is. *Fear* is the poison of the life of the soul. A terrible fear-mysticism—the *shudder*-mysticism of a bleak, frigidly-intelligent world-spider spinning its web around all things—arises if one really takes the doctrine of the "Ahrimanic in the world" seriously; if one not only thinks it but feels it.

Moreover, this feeling will sooner or later be accompanied by an ever-growing sense of *impotence*. How can this monstrous thing ever be overcome? Yes, "Christ has overcome it," but it has become three times more powerful in the human realm since Christ's sacrificial deed! When taken seriously, the doctrine of the Ahrimanic can give rise (on a global level) to a metaphysically-grounded, worldwide *neurotic anxiety*; and (in the case of individuals) to an equally metaphysically-grounded personal "inferiority complex" or sense of impotence, to which individual human beings *as such* can fall victim.

Or we can seize upon an *antidote* to this sense of omnipotence. We can say to ourselves: "what I need to meet this danger is a *strengthened ego*," and (in Jung's terminology) resort to the "infla-tion" or puffing-up of the ego—that is, to "supermanhood." We will want to be installed as an "initiate" in the "circle of initiates"—as a "superman," as the "future man" of *manas, buddhi,* and *atma.*

Now, as anyone with even a modicum of experience of psycho-therapy knows, the sense of impotence at play in an inferiority complex *can* easily switch over into delusions of grandeur. More-over, delusions of grandeur ("ego-inflation") appear in graduated stages, both pre-clinical and clinical. The prevalent, animating conviction of the anthroposophical community that they belong to a chosen "community of the Archangel Michael"—a commu-nity standing in no need of the sacraments of the Church (peni-tence *in particular!*), called to replace all faith with "knowledge," pioneer new pathways in science and art, organize the state in a threefold manner, and so on—is symptomatic of just such delu-sions of grandeur, if perhaps still at the pre-clinical stage.

To the Church by contrast, the devil is (like Faust's Mephistoph-eles, the "joker who is the least of the Lord's burdens")[7] an incen-tive to *remain awake and responsible* in one's endeavors and decisions. The devil occasions no reason for fear, even fear of one's own sin. Yes, temptation is a serious thing, but who among us (if he has a truly good will, is aided by his guardian angel, and is sup-ported by the sacraments, Holy Scripture, and the saints) is not in a position to resist it? No matter that one may have fallen victim to temptation: there are still a hundred opportunities to turn back, to make amends, to begin anew… What is there to fear here? The devil is only as *strong* as I am *weak*: not weak in terms of ordinary health, but weak morally (that is, insofar as I am *undecided*). The power of the devil is my indecision. If I am decided, his power is null.

At this point, intimately, friend to friend, I would like to whisper something in your ear. What do you think is happening when the devil, as a *tempter*, becomes null? He becomes a *friend* to man, a *devoted* friend. The gospel says of Christ Jesus that after he resisted the temptations in the wilderness, the angels tended him. What does this mean? Recalling that the *angels* had been devotedly tend-

7. *Faust II*, lines 338–339.

ing him right along, that they had never forsaken him, it means that the "angels" mentioned in the verse as devotedly tending him *after* the temptations had been overcome were the *transformed temptations* themselves!

Not only do we human beings have no cause to fear the devil— or better, to fear *any* and *all* devils (Mephisto, Beelzebub, Samael, etc.)—but, quite to the contrary, shining before us is the great hope that sometime... on some occasion... after all is said and done... we may liberate the devil himself from temptation and redeem him from his devilry. Indeed, we can do no greater service to the devil than successfully resist temptation. To whom do you think Job owed his later happiness, after having withstood his trials? To God? Well, of course, for all good things come from God. But by *whose hands* was all the suffering and loss of Job's time of trial made good once more? This I have whispered in your ear.

Now I will resume speaking directly person to person. I see no reason, then, to *supplement* the Church's doctrine or practice with the Ahrimanic. There are however all sorts of reasons (therapeutic, moral, and biblical) to *support* the Church in its idea of the *devil* and of *devils*, and even to *deepen* this idea. The deeper idea I have in mind may only be whispered in one's ear; but even so, the "ordinary" ecclesiastical idea of the devil already comprises everything one could ask for through such deepening. And so, having laid these things before you, let us now turn to consider Anthroposophy as a whole from a therapeutic point of view.

As you well know, Anthroposophy is a *spiritual science,*[8] by which I mean that it is neither a religion nor any branch of science resting upon *experience* of the sense-perceptible world. It is "science" only in that it interprets experiences of the supersensible "scientifically." Spiritual science translates supersensible experience into the language of *unambiguous concepts,* just as ordinary science does with sense experience. *Spiritual science is the supersensible intellectualized.* What makes of supersensible experience a spiritual "science" is its intellectualization. On the one hand, this spiritual science is

---

8. *Geisteswissenschaft.* The usual translation of this common term in anthroposophical writings is "spiritual science," although in more literary or academic contexts it would usually be translated as "cultural science" or "humanities."

distinguished from *religion* by the fact that although it also treats of the supersensible truths of salvation (it, too, speaks of the Father, Son, and Holy Spirit; of the mystery of Golgotha, of original sin, of the resurrection, of Pentecost, of the Ascension), it presupposes no *faith* in them—considering them instead as *objects of knowledge*. On the other hand, this spiritual science is distinguished from science in the ordinary sense by the fact that it treats as known, or as knowable, things that are beyond the reach of ordinary science (which explains why ordinary science generally relegates such things to the realm of belief or superstition).

Now, all this is familiar enough. Our present concern, however, is to *test* these familiar things for their therapeutic significance. Let us make a start with the first thesis given above: that, since "spiritual science" is science or knowledge, "no faith is presupposed." How does this thesis play out, though, if we *really* take seriously the thesis that *even* the truths of salvation (which are indeed a knowledge representing results of research) do not require faith? The *immediate* effect will be that the search for knowledge finds itself greatly encouraged and elevated, whereas the life of faith finds itself discouraged and depreciated. In other words, the life of faith will thereby have become superfluous because (according to this first thesis regarding spiritual science, that "no faith is presupposed") everything *can* indeed be known—making of faith no more than a childish and incomplete *substitute* for knowledge. This in turn means that man brings about a reversal in his scale of values: *faith and knowledge switch places.* What actually happens is that man directs his capacity for faith and trust towards knowledge and towards "someone who knows." Faith becomes the handmaiden of knowledge—*fides ancilla scientiae.*

Moreover, this means that as long as *we ourselves* have not come to know everything essential, we place all our faith (the very faith we would otherwise have bestowed upon the body of Church doctrine or upon the academy) in "someone who knows"—in other words, in a *master.* Both physically and psychologically, this helps explain how, in the eyes of his followers, a "spiritual researcher" or "initiate" may so readily take on the role of an "anti-pope," that is, someone whose "infallible *ex cathedra*" knowledge represents a competing community and doctrine alongside the Church and

311

religion in general. The "He Himself has said" of the Pythagore-ans, and the "The Doctor has said" of Anthroposophy are two cases in point.

What is *really* happening, then, with regard to the "no faith is presupposed" theme, is not an *emancipation* from authority, but a *changeover* of authority! What has one gained by this? Many new concepts perhaps, and some possible enrichment of the concep-tual life. What has one lost? The honesty and sunlight of faith, now relegated to half-silent, dusky back alleys. The "therapeutic" effect of this changeover is obvious. On the one hand, when the sunlike nature of *faith* is relegated to nocturnal paths, it becomes moon-like, which sets in motion fear of losing one's way—giving rise in turn to intolerance and desperate exclusivity. On the other hand, when the moonlike (coolly reflective) nature of intellectual *knowl-edge* assumes the position of the sun, it waxes exuberantly specula-tive: although retaining the moonlike quality of cool reflectivity, it becomes instead *active* (corresponding to the solar position it has now acquired), expressing itself as an intellectual impertinence or cavalierness in consequence of which the affected person believes himself qualified to cast judgments upon, and have something to say about, everything in the world—for example (in the particular case of anthroposophists), that since the West is Ahrimanic, the East is Luciferic, and the Center is Christian, it must be that Bol-shevism is Luciferic, Americanism is Ahrimanic, and Germanity is Christian (along with many another such rampantly uninhibited, sweeping judgment).

A moment's reflection on what has just been said makes clear that, from a therapeutic point of view, it is *disadvantageous* to put the knowledge-function in the place of the faith-function in the life of the human soul.

The other point to be made about Anthroposophy concerns the above-mentioned intellectualizing of the supersensible. This pro-cess converts the supersensible into concepts, for example that of the "Ahrimanic," just discussed. These concepts are then coordi-nated into a system, which is to say, into a *spiritual science* or worldview. But then one is caught in a web of concepts and can no longer think without presuppositions! Put another way, immedi-ate experience ("naive" experience, in Goethe's sense) is no longer possible, since the web of concepts arising from *spiritual science* intercedes between oneself and the immediate problems or facts of experience—that is, of course, unless one has found the strength to break through this web, and by means of *actual* practical exercises and exertions gain immediate access to the things themselves.

Here we may ask whether such intellectualized concepts of the supersensible can help us gain immediate access to things themselves, by immersing ourselves in their content, for instance. The answer is that as long as these concepts remain just that—*concepts*—they do *not* lead to the reality to which they refer. On the contrary, they become *obstacles* on the path that leads to reality, regardless whether the reality in question be sense-perceptible or supersensible.

It is *not* true, then, that man is *free* in the domain of the concept, and that symbols shackle him. Just the opposite is true! A Hegelian, a Marxist (yes, even an Anthroposophist), has generally fallen so far under the sway of his conceptual system that he can no longer think in any other way, or along any other lines, than those of that system. Much nonsense has been bandied about on the topic of "occult imprisonment," but the truth of the matter is that this occurs *whenever* anyone is caught in a conceptual system.

One *is* free, however, if one works, not with *unambiguous* concepts, but with *symbols* (which have *multiple* meanings); or, alternately, when one at least considers and uses concepts themselves *as* symbols.[9] Symbols such as those of the *Tabula Smaragdina* of Hermes Trismegistus, the Book of Revelation, the Kabbalah, and the Arcana of the Tarot, are *incitements* to know the supersensible in the way, and to the degree, corresponding to each person individ-

---

9. The same year (1956) he wrote this letter to Bernhard Martin, Tomberg began work on a text concerned with symbolism in this same sense. The first sketch of this text was entitled "On the Nature of Symbolism," but the work was left unfinished. A German edition of the unfinished text was finally published in 2012, of which an English translation was published by Angelico Press in 2023 under the title *Personal Certainty: The Way, the Truth, and the Life.* After abandoning this work, however, Tomberg commenced writing what many consider his greatest work, *Meditations on the Tarot: A Journey into Christian Hermeticism,* which picks up the theme of the *analogia entis*—of symbols, the method of analogy, and moral logic—and develops it to new heights.

ually. They are guiding *stimuli* that function like well-formulated *questions* in a conversation. Multiple sharp, unambiguous concepts can be formed on the basis of symbols, but it will never be possible to exhaust symbols by means of such concept-formation. This is because symbols are pathways *to* the real, not relics of *turning away* from the real (as is the case with abstraction). Symbols do not compel. They "ask" and "say" exactly as much as the person concerned *can* and *wishes* to ask and say. They leave people *actually* free. The most salient reason people who speak of the supersensible from their own experience make us of symbols to do so is that, although they want to tell others something, they want to tell them in such a way that they not only remain free, but become *even more free* (more creative). St John, the writer of the Book of Revelation, spoke in this way. This book has endured for over two thousand years; but who has ever in any way been coerced by it? No inquisition has ever arisen on account of symbolism, whereas every conceptual system by its very nature seeks to exert sole mastery over people.

A significant scientific (i.e., both *critical* and *empirical*) twentieth-century discovery with regard to symbols was made by C.G. Jung, who repeatedly came up against the experience that the "unconscious" (that is, in his terminology, everything found in human beings *outside* ordinary everyday consciousness, including "superconsciousness") speaks in symbols, and that these symbols are *healing*—that is, they possess a significant therapeutic value.

Jung found, for example, that the mandala symbol appeared in the most diverse variants in the dreams, visions, and fantasies of both his patients and his healthy colleagues. Moreover, he had to acknowledge that alchemical, gnostic, and ancient mystery-symbolism also emerges from the depths of the souls of modern salespeople and bank-clerks with no notion whatsoever, intellectually and culturally, about these symbols. Nor is this emergence of symbols a "mere curiosity"; it is, rather, a significant therapeutic and developmental symptom. Even more than that, their emergence from the soul's depths is often an *efficacious* means of cure. In this way, Jung showed that the mandala symbol not only illustrates the process of "individuation" (the finding of the self and the striving to achieve integration of one's total being) but also helps to *accomplish* this process.

On the basis of this discovery, a practice of veritable *interaction* with the supersensible has been developed that in its significance and influence has grown far beyond the level of individual therapy, and keeps being developed further by others in the field, [...] all of whom, especially Jung and Schultz, are alike in having embarked upon their work with no presuppositions in tow. Moved, as *therapists,* by their concern for others, they arrived at the beginnings of the *rebirth of mystery.* They commenced with small things, and arrived at great things. They proceeded from experience. They drew all their concepts from experience, and in so doing came in the end to a world of symbols. Moreover, since this world could not be "explained away" (that is, converted into concepts), they humbly opened themselves to its instruction, never calling their process into question.

Now, this is quite the opposite of what most anthroposophists do. They set out armed with a panoply of ready-made concepts, and only *then* seek to arrive at direct experience. But this burden of ready-made concepts keeps them confined in their world. Because *they* are doing the speaking about the spiritual world, the *spiritual world* remains mute. They don't let it get a word in! It is otherwise with the people I am speaking of. They are silent. They let the spiritual world speak. And the spiritual world speaks in *symbols.* It speaks in the language of mystery, today as in earlier times.

Now at last we are coming to an answer to the question put at the outset of this letter: What can and must a lay person do to help the Church move forward in the direction of what is spiritually living? The answer I suggest is that lay people do *not* help the Church forward in this way by importing into it anthroposophical methods that represent and treat the supersensible in terms of unambiguous concepts of the scientific kind. Moreover, they do *not* help the Church forward in this way by importing into it a "spiritual science" that is neither *real* science (because it is not presuppositionless) nor *real* religion (because it wants to replace the life of faith). Rather, lay people help the Church move forward to what is spiritually living through *immersing* themselves in Christian liturgical and biblical symbolism—an immersion that can be *complemented* further with symbolisms that have likewise arisen through "interaction with the supersensible" in *other* epochs and cultures. Yes, *intellectual crystallizations* that may from this immersive "work"

inevitably become "formulas"[10] of a sort; but, since the world of *symbols* stands behind them, they are of no use in the public world of ordinary science or religious doctrine. They are, rather, formulas of *personal certainty* for individuals. They are formulas (or mantra) for the *private* use of those who possess personal certainty in relation to the supersensible, and who, on the basis of this certainty, can make their way with all the individual questions and individual tasks both of the Church and of science.

It is a matter, therefore, of a calm, unpretentious *Mysterium* that wishes neither to rule nor to lecture, but that in an intimate (i.e., *mysterious*) way exercises an animating, spiritualizing, and healing influence *indirectly*. The *Mysterium* is called to *serve*, not to rule. Just as a symbol does not instruct, but *stimulates*, so is the modern *Mysterium* meant to work in the world like a symbol: not to lecture, but only to *stimulate*. It seems to me that the modern Catholic lay person is called to become such a stimulus in the Church, as also in science—and in fact, everywhere.

10. *Formeln*, with the sense also of patterns, rubrics, canons, theorems, etc. ED

316

Christ in
Rudolf Steiner's
Knowledge of the Higher
Worlds and Its Attainment

RUDOLF STEINER'S LOFTY SPIRITUAL WORK STANDS
there, alone in history, misunderstood and attacked by the outside
world, but accepted by those who seek to live according to the
impulse of that work, which they take as an inexhaustible and
unfathomable spiritual act on the part of the great initiate. It would
seem that Steiner's lifework is intelligible only on its own terms,
that there is nothing against which to measure it, that we can only
come close to understanding it by following it, not by comparing it
with anything else. Yet Rudolf Steiner had a master above him, to
whom he dedicated his whole life, all his research, all his work. This
master is Jesus Christ. Rudolf Steiner's greatness can be specified
from many different points of view, but they all culminate in this:
he was a servant, despite and along with his greatness; he was the
herald preparing the way for another, greater figure; he did nothing
in his own name, but everything for humankind—that is, for its
divine "representative," Jesus Christ. The greatness of this Christian
figure is shown by the way in which, and by the extent to which, he
served the greatest and the highest.

For this reason, it is not only possible, but right and proper, to
view Rudolf Steiner's lifework in the light of the acts of the one who

---

* This unpublished essay, written between 1954 and 1956, presupposes familiarity with the foundational books of anthroposophical spiritual science.

317

was *truly* the greatest: Jesus Christ. The service Rudolf Steiner performed becomes clearer and more comprehensible in this way, whereas without viewing it in this light it must remain incomparable, immeasurable, ungraspable. Our purpose in what follows, then, is to consider anthroposophical teaching in the light of the acts of Jesus Christ.

It goes without saying that only a sketch can be given here. Both the impulse of Anthroposophy and (especially) the activities of Jesus Christ are inexhaustible. We can only point toward both, for many books would have to be written to even remotely characterize their nature. In what follows we can offer only a few indications of the fullness of the impulse of Jesus Christ and that of this great pupil of his. These indications will follow the text of one of the foundational books of the anthroposophical method, *Knowledge of the Higher Worlds and Its Attainment*.[1] This text has been chosen both because in the whole of Anthroposophy there is nothing essential that cannot be derived from it, and because it is more difficult to bring out the Christian elements from the text of the other foundational book of Anthroposophy, *The Philosophy of Freedom*. No other anthroposophical book presents the method of Anthroposophy in the same way as *Knowledge of Higher Worlds*. Just as we can come to know the essence of Jesus Christ from his Sermon on the Mount, the Last Supper, and the Passion (and can likewise come to understand the rest of his activity from this standpoint), so the whole of Rudolf Steiner's work can be understood on the basis of *Knowledge of Higher Worlds*.

The author would not have ventured to record the thoughts that follow, but for the fact that the influence of Christ in Rudolf Steiner's lifework is often misunderstood. For this reason, it is to be hoped that a modest and imperfect contribution such as this present one might contribute to the correct interpretation, the correct use, and the correct pursuit of that lifework.

Rudolf Steiner did not speak about "higher worlds" merely to furnish his readers and listeners with new ideas. He did so as a means of giving impetus to the *how* of life, of guiding them on a

---

1. Hereafter abbreviated *Knowledge of Higher Worlds*.

way: the way of Christian initiation; the way of the soul-becoming-Christian. The only wish of this great follower of Jesus Christ was to stimulate his own pupils to become followers of the Highest also. This is clear from his definition of the nature of Anthroposophy as "a way of knowledge that wishes to lead the spiritual element in the human being towards the spiritual element in the universe," as well as from his statement that, as to its core, Anthroposophy is meant to prepare humanity for a meeting with Jesus Christ at his second coming, when he appears again in what Steiner called the living or "etheric" world.[2]

The expression "way of knowledge" must be understood in its full depth. Knowledge is not merely a matter of the head and of cognition, but is at bottom a matter of the will. Thus, at the beginning of Genesis we read "Adam knew his wife"; and Jesus Christ says "and this is eternal life, that they may know you, the only true God, and Jesus Christ whom you have sent." (John 17:3) Now, a way of knowledge is certainly not possible without an increase in knowledge, without developing one's ideas; but, since knowledge is itself always a matter of the will, it is bound up with the *maturity* of the being of the knower, with that being's *moral and spiritual progress*. This is how the impulse of *Knowledge of Higher Worlds* must be understood and put into practice. Moreover, if Anthroposophy as a whole is meant to prepare humanity for the second coming or etheric return of Jesus Christ, then this impulse must surely not be lacking in its foundational book.

There are two difficulties that stand in the way of coming to this insight. The first is that Anthroposophy as a whole comes forward more as a system, more as an intelligible, comprehensible edifice of doctrine (together with its practical applications) than as a course of instruction. The second is that there are no direct references in *Knowledge of Higher Worlds* to the workings of Jesus Christ. Taken

2. The several allusions in this article to Christ's second coming or "etheric return" refer to spiritual research on the part of Rudolf Steiner that cannot be adequately described in the present context, except to say that several biblical mentions of "clouds" and of Christ's return "in the clouds" bear reference to this. See, for instance, Revelations 1:17, Matthew 24:30, and I Thessalonians 4:17. ED

together, these two difficulties have had the effect that the influence of Christ in Rudolf Steiner's own work is most often overlooked, or else not fully seen, even by his pupils—and consequently that this influence of Christ has not been fully appreciated.

The first difficulty to consider is that Anthroposophy came forward as a *worldview* in the sense that its statements about the world, the earth, and man can be illuminating and helpful even to those who do not at the same time take up the core method of Anthroposophy. Such anthroposophical insights as man being of a ninefold or sevenfold nature, the laws of reincarnation and karma, the doctrine of the spiritual hierarchies, the relation between spirit and matter, the rhythms of the evolution of the world as a whole, and so on, can be "seen" well enough even by those who do not themselves possess spiritual vision. Moreover, when such insights are imparted, they can often be experienced as liberating and redeeming by comparison with other conceptions of life and the world current outside Anthroposophy in our day.

Furthermore, Rudolf Steiner said that the *prerequisite* for attaining such insights through *personal* spiritual knowledge was to study, think through, and assimilate the teachings comprising the anthroposophical worldview (and those who have put such study into practice can attest to the truth of this). But since these teachings are so extensive that very few could possibly ever reach the end of them, it is understandable that, for many, the default approach is to study ever on, laying claim to an ever broader swathe of the teachings. As a result, the "systematic" side of Anthroposophy is more cultivated than the "methodological" side by virtue of which the teachings were place *discovered* through spiritual research in the first.

Now, every act of assimilating the teachings *is* indeed a feeding of the soul; it *is* already (as Steiner describes in *Knowledge of Higher Worlds*) part of the "way." But even if this assimilation forms *part* of the aspirant's apprenticeship, it does not *exhaust* that apprenticeship! No, the *method* of knowledge to be striven for and brought to realization "under one's own steam" demands something different. Complicating matters further, the individual fields of practical work that have arisen out of Anthroposophy can likewise be fruitfully cultivated by anthroposophists *even if* they have not embarked assiduously upon the "way" of a centered, conscious apprenticeship in Christianity.

It seems that we human beings have an innate tendency not to take seriously even what is most serious, but prefer to dawdle at the fringes of life. For this reason, we do not like to acknowledge to ourselves with full transparency that a course of instruction cannot lead to anything essential if rigorous testing, renunciation, overcoming, sacrifice, and self-surrender are lacking. Those active in one or another field of anthroposophical work can of course experience their work as a blessing, even if as yet they lack "complete seriousness" in the sense described. But they can and do often say to themselves perhaps rather too assuagingly that since they have not come to the end of the vast body of "delivered" teachings, they may as well get on in the meantime with assimilating even more of them… There are so many excuses for letting ourselves off the hook in face of the demands of becoming really serious about the *way*!

The fact of the matter is, however, that ultimately the assimilable and practicable contents of anthroposophical spiritual science are only there to further our progress on the *way*; and that too much mental assimilation of Anthroposophy as the "subject matter" of a worldview is a deviation from the *way*. The deviation can be "Luciferic" or "Ahrimanic"—i.e., it can originate in a personal desire for enjoyment and comfort, or it can originate in an overestimation of thinking or head-knowledge (in *Knowledge of Higher Worlds* Steiner provides the means to cure both of these dangers)—but in either case, what is needed is that each individual apply these means *through their own initiative*.

The second of the difficulties mentioned lies in the fact that *Knowledge of Higher Worlds* contains no *direct* reference to the impulse given by Jesus Christ, but proceeds in an exclusively "humanistic" mode of expression. That is, it makes no appeal to authority, not even to that of Jesus Christ. There are two reasons for this. On the one hand, Steiner developed the *method* of Anthroposophy out of modern natural science specifically for the mentality of modern people, who for the most part lack any ties to dogma (and of course modern natural science contains no connection to the works of Jesus Christ). Such a connection, however, *can* be provided by consideration of the actual *results* following from anthroposophical thought and research. But at the same time, Rudolf Steiner had such respect for human freedom that he avoided anything that might impose any tinge of necessity on others. His purpose was to contribute in whatever way he could to opening up a way for the impulse of Jesus Christ to spring up *independently* in individual human beings. For this reason, there is no "You ought to" or "I believe" in Anthroposophy as Steiner presented it. It is only because Steiner made a point of avoiding terminology steeped in the usage of two millennia of Christian life and tradition, that Anthroposophy is presented in the form of more universal formulations of the truth. Nonetheless, for anyone who knows how to "read" *Knowledge of Higher Worlds*, the substantive, essential, and spiritual connection with Christian tradition is more than evident—for example, in the following sentence found early in the text:

> At the very beginning of his course, the student is directed to the path of veneration and the development of the inner life. Spiritual science now also gives him practical rules by observing which he may tread that path and develop that inner life. These practical rules have no arbitrary origin. They rest upon ancient experience and ancient wisdom, and are given out in the same manner, wheresoever the ways to higher knowledge are indicated. All true teachers of the spiritual life are in agreement as to the substance of these rules, even though they do not always clothe them in the same words. This difference, which is of a minor character and is more apparent than real, is due to circumstances that need not be dwelt upon here.

Rudolf Steiner, then, considers the difference between anthroposophical instruction and, say, medieval Christian instruction, to be "of a minor character," meaning that they signify the same thing, even if drawing upon different words and concepts.

Naturally, the purest consequence of Rudolf Steiner's own discipleship to Jesus Christ (that is, *in relation to human freedom*, in which quality he exceeded all other proclaimers of Christianity) is too much to ask of most people. The impetus Rudolf Steiner gave in service to Jesus Christ must not only *rise up* independently in each individual, but must also be *found* independently by each individual. The publication of the esoteric materials Steiner bestowed upon the world was enormously bold and trusting; but it was also risky. Only hints are found in his work about how the anthroposophical stimulus for training (which always appeals to human activity) harmonizes with earlier Christian training in thinking and awareness of human *destiny*, so that, however much talk there may be in anthroposophical training of the *activity* of human striving, it also includes suffering, endurance, purification of the innermost, and implacable *passivity*.

The fact of the matter is that anyone who very attentively thinks through, or even begins to experience, what it actually means to transform the astral body into "manas," the etheric body into "buddhi," and the physical body into "atma," comes to the conclusion that the *same* impulse described in these terms was in earlier times thought, willed, and "walked" in direct connection with the gospel and the Passion of Christ Jesus. It is significant that when Steiner speaks of the nature of grace in his lectures (for example, in those published as *From Jesus to Christ*), he proceeds sparingly, since it is better to *acknowledge* and *turn toward* grace than to speak overmuch about it. For this reason, these passages too often escape notice, while most readers come away overshadowed by notions like a "higher I" that they imagine could somehow be brought into life by human power alone, whereas in fact our human capacity extends only as far as establishing the *conditions* on the basis of which the "higher I" can be formed in us. If we do not pay sufficiently close attention, we can all too easily remain caught at the "exoteric" level, even when we *think* we are cultivating the "esoteric." But in accordance with a universal law that Rudolf Seiner often mentions when describing initiation (as he does in *Knowledge of Higher Worlds*), everything esoteric is reached only through devoted susceptibility.[3]

3. *Passionen.*

Rudolf Steiner left it to his pupils to take his individual statements to heart and draw the relevant consequences from them. He always makes demands on the *individual's* power to *act*. This will become clear from the following examples.

Steiner speaks relatively seldom in *Knowledge of Higher Worlds* about the "content" that makes up the knowledge of higher worlds. At one point, while summing up, he says:

> There is in reality only *one* possible view about higher truths. This *one* view can be arrived at if, through devotion and labor, one has raised oneself to a sufficient height from which to see it.

Not only are historical, human, and natural-scientific truths being spoken of here, but above all the "core" of the world, its basic structure—i.e., the things Christianity had previously spoken of in the Credo. And yet nothing is said here in detail about this connection because Rudolf Steiner did not wish to re-found the faith as it had been practiced *up to that point*. His purpose was to call his readers to set out upon the *way*. This way, however, is not meant to lead to whatever goals may "happen to be" agreeable to us as natural human beings, but to the goal of evolution in its entirety—which goal is only to be reached by the *way* of the Passion. Accordingly, in *Knowledge of Higher Worlds*, all "cosmic" Christian truths are veiled These Christian truths are not veiled, however, so that they will go unnoticed, but in order that people may *find them for themselves*. In this veiled form, they are to be found everywhere in the book. Indeed, the book's method is crafted in just such a way that modern human beings, integrated in the non-dogmatic and natural-scientific spirit of today (a spirit that conforms with human development), may of themselves be able to discover a new discipleship[4] of Jesus in relation to Christ. How could Anthroposophy be preparing humanity for the second coming or etheric return of Jesus Christ if it did not call upon us to be his "successors"? And how could humanity meet the returning Christ of the second coming if we

---

4. *Nachfolge* can also mean "succession" in the sense of apostolic succession.

were not appropriately purified by *following* him? Knowledge of Christ is also a matter of will and action. Basking comfortably in the way of thinking and looking at things set in stone by an all-too-familiar worldview is just not sufficient.

If we carefully consider *Knowledge of Higher Worlds* in light of how its inspiration relates to that given by Jesus Christ, we become aware of how, from beginning to end, the demands the book calls for parallel those Jesus Christ made of his disciples (although the book naturally expresses those demands in contemporary language, concepts, methods, and orientation). The freedom that Jesus Christ brought in place of the "Luciferic freedom" already long since at work in humanity is in actual fact a "lawfulness" binding us on all sides. Only the law makes us free: the law we give ourselves, and that we can then follow.

The kingdom of heaven cannot be attained in an approximate or partial way; nor can it be attained by mere trust. As St Paul says, man must "make" his blessedness; but even so, no single jot of the law will be done away with, as Jesus Christ himself told us. Today, many people believe that being "bound by law" makes us unfree. But *only to the unfree does the law seem unfree*. The free man not only can, but must, live with the law. The law received from without can nevertheless be freely obeyed. According to Rudolf Steiner's way of putting it: law can result from the "moral imagination," but this does not do away with its compulsory character. In both cases (Christ's original teaching and Steiner's contemporary manner of expression in *Knowledge of Higher Worlds*), it is at bottom a question of the law of *discipleship*, of "carrying the cross" in its various stages. The redemption Christ seeks, and the "knowledge of higher worlds" the spiritual pupil strives to attain ("And this is eternal life, that they may know you, the only true God, and Jesus Christ whom you have sent." John 17:3), are in essence one and the same, and stand at the end of an arduous path. For the "Christ-I" is born as the "higher-I" in man *only* when the lower-I is trodden down through pain and sacrifice, self-denial, and self-surrender. This is something that can be attained in many ways, but ought also to be attained through spiritual instruction. What is important is not what words are used to describe this, but that one passes through these stages—or at least, that one makes an effort to pass through them so far as one is able.

Rudolf Steiner contrasts the intention behind *Knowledge of Higher Worlds* with two errors (the "Luciferic" and the "Ahrimanic") met with in those aspiring for such knowledge:

> Some effects produced upon the soul of the student will here be indicated. For only those who know such things as they are here communicated can undertake in full consciousness the exercises that lead to knowledge of the higher worlds. Without the latter, no genuine esoteric training is possible, for it must be understood that all groping in the dark is discouraged, and that failure to pursue this training with open eyes may lead to mediumship, but not to exact clairvoyance in the sense of spiritual science.

Here, Steiner is referring to the Luciferic temptation. In short, anyone who rests content to simply absorb the content lecture after lecture without ever undertaking the necessary exercises demanding renunciation, falls victim to a Luciferic temptation.

Elsewhere, Steiner says that there are other paths of instruction which lead to the goal more quickly, but are dangerous. Here, an Ahrimanic (or Satanic) temptation is being referred to. It could be added that the view according to which everything hinges on a vast fund of knowledge, and that absorbing volume upon volume of lectures offers sufficient nourishment (an opinion that many anthroposophists do not wittingly adhere to, but nonetheless unwittingly embody), represents a compromise with an Ahrimanic temptation. Rudolf Steiner only ever described the absorption of the truths of spiritual science as a *condition* of, and an *aid* to, instruction—never as a *substitute* for those truths. Just as in the gospel we see Jesus Christ between the two thieves, and in Steiner's well-known sculpture of the same name we see the "Representative of Man" between Lucifer and Ahriman, so in *Knowledge of Higher Worlds* we see the path of spiritual instruction, of discipleship, as a middle way—with all the stringent and indispensable "lawfulness" that appertains to this path. Man can only progress towards knowledge of Christ in Anthroposophy by undergoing instruction and *applying* it. A course

of instruction always demands the whole person, never only a particular "cognitive" part of the person. So it is today, so it was yesterday, so will it be tomorrow.

The message Jesus Christ brought into the world can be described
in one word as that of *love.* Jesus Christ explained, and also (far
more importantly) *lived out* the way whereby one attains to love: the
natural man must be transformed; egotism must be brought to selflessness; a higher element must seize the earthly, purify it, and elevate it. Our human exemplar of this is the man Jesus of Nazareth
making his way to the baptism in the Jordan. Our hope is that we
might be filled with the being of Christ, even as Christ entered into
Jesus of Nazareth at his baptism in the Jordan. The natural world in
all its forms will finally pass away, but the divine powers that once
created the natural world can work anew in us, bringing us to participation in an everlasting life. This is what people of earlier times
believed; and their belief gave them the power of discipleship. The
power of belief has now for the most part disappeared; but even
those who lack this power can attain insight into the law of the
coming-into-being of man and of the world—and upon this insight
they can found a course of instruction that will sooner or later grasp
(but now at another level) the same truth that centuries ago could
be reached by faith.

Grasping truth is a matter of the *core* of our being, of the element
in us that survives the moment of death, the element in us that
passes from earthly life to earthly life. It is a matter of the purification and strengthening of *this* element, which is why spiritual
instruction is meant to lead us towards the experience of our own
death—or through and beyond it. Seen from this point of view, it
becomes clear that Anthroposophy is a contemporary proclamation
of the mystery of Christ (although it is of course not the only way of
experiencing the mystery of Christ). Moreover, it also becomes clear
not only that the mystery of Christ can to be seen in the light of
Anthroposophy, but that Anthroposophy can be seen in the light of
the mystery of Christ.

Anyone whom Anthroposophy has actually led to an *experience* of the mystery of Christ is no longer bogged down amid "more teachings still to be assimilated," for such a one is now a *participant* in the mystery, and can see from this point of vantage how Anthroposophy is related to this mystery. In truth, Anthroposophy prepares the way for that mystery, as will now be illustrated with some passages drawn from *Knowledge of Higher Worlds*.

The very first sentence of the book ("There slumber in every human being faculties by means of which he can acquire for himself a knowledge of higher worlds") expresses the Christian principle that salvation, the kingdom of heaven, awaits *every* person; that everyone can become a participant in it: the only difference being that, as formulated in Steiner's early twentieth-century text, this truly universal proclamation is directed to contemporary humanity in a non-dogmatic fashion making no direct appeal to the tradition of faith. The "higher worlds" of which Steiner's book tells, however, are no other than those in which the Father, the Son, and the Holy Spirit prevail, in which the angels and archangels serve, in which all the spiritual hierarchies go about their work, and in which the human being is by origin at home. Moreover, everything that supersensibly underpins individual earthly creatures, and dwells within them, belongs to these worlds also. But *knowledge* of all these core truths of the world is only a preparation for *grasping* them. For so long as the divine beings from whom the moral powers of the world flow are hidden from us, it is of no *decisive* importance whether or not we are aware (for example) of elemental spirits, folk souls, the etheric body of an oak tree, or the astral nature of an animal.

True researchers of the spirit instruct us that in our feeling life and in our thinking we ought to concern ourselves with the knowledge of higher worlds *solely* a means to render ourselves more capable and more useful *for the earth*. Rudolf Steiner does not speak specifically of the dimension of morality in the opening sentence of *Knowledge of Higher Worlds* quoted above; but what, other than morality, could he have had in mind when the meaning of the knowledge of higher worlds is defined so unequivocally? The "materialism" we are meant to overcome is only overcome if we have attained *personal contact* with the beings of the higher world; it is certainly *not* over-come by acquiring an assortment of notions regarding spiritual sci-ence that, with a certain self-satisfaction, we believe somehow make us less materialistic than those who lack them. Just as the Christian message is at the same time a rigorous demand made upon us, so is it also with anthroposophical spiritual science.

To continue: as early as the preface to the third edition of *Knowl-edge of Higher Worlds*, we read that there is a category of spiritual-scientific disclosure that

> will be found to elude purely mental judgment more or less; but the right relation to these also will be achieved without great diffi-culty by one who understands that not the mind alone but healthy feeling as well is qualified to determine what is true.

Rudolf Steiner goes on to explain, regarding "healthy feeling," that

> when this feeling does not permit itself to be warped by a sympa-thy or antipathy for some opinion or other, but really allows higher knowledge to act without prejudice, a corresponding sen-tient judgment results.

This proposition, like every anthroposophical proposition, must be absorbed literally and soberly. What is being discussed here is that *particular* feeling which does not permit itself to be driven by sym-pathy or antipathy, but that has become selfless: a pure and free instrument. In other words, it is that *particular* feeling which, as a consequence of the Christ-impulse, can be supra-personally devel-oped within the human being; for without the Christ-impulse, there would *be* no feelings that could rise beyond the horizon of sympathy and antipathy. Moreover, anyone who speaks of such feel-ings is by implication appealing to Christ, even where Christ is not named. We might say further that in this context even sympathy with spiritual science *itself* can, under certain circumstances, be described as dangerous: "Some take pleasure in asceticism just as others do in drinking wine!" Even sympathy for a spiritual world-view can stem from the spirit of Lucifer, and will in that case most assuredly not lead straight to the path of Christian discipleship.

The instruction offered in *Knowledge of Higher Worlds* serves the strengthening and transformation of our thinking, feeling, and willing. All the exercises begin with thinking. But as has been said more than once, they also need to take hold of feeling, and can only be executed by a strong will. According to the terms Steiner makes use of in the book, the astral body is to be transformed into *manas*, the etheric body into *buddhi*, and the physical body into *atma*.[5] This demand is served by the exercises in *reverence* at the outset of the book, which include: the prescription that although the student of the esoteric must make use of pleasure, he may not remain stuck in it; the demand that the student learn to distinguish the essential from the inessential, together with looking at himself as a stranger, and living out the "purely human"; and as well, further demands made by the whole series of meditations that follow. All these exercises in fact stand in perfect concord with those Jesus Christ made of his pupils, even if they most often have a different point of departure than active discipleship and service in the life of faith. Regarding this, Rudolf Steiner wrote the following:

> For every human being bears a higher man within himself, besides what we may call the work-a-day man. This higher man remains hidden until he is awakened. And each human being can *himself alone* awaken this higher being within himself.

The higher human being within man is just what, in Christianity, is called Christ-in-us. There would be no *manas, buddhi,* or *atma* without Christ. But are we really to understand by these words that we alone can awaken this higher human being within us? This makes it sound as though this awakening lies entirely within our own power. But we can only create the *conditions* under which the higher human being can come to life within us; we cannot ourselves compel this higher being to do so. On the other hand, it is indeed the case that *if* we create the conditions for this to happen, *then* the higher human being will of necessity rise up within us. Now, since the spiritual world most surely does not close itself against anyone

5. These Sanskrit terms were in common use in the esoteric spiritual circles at the time Steiner wrote *Knowledge of Higher Worlds*. Over the years, Steiner replaced these with German terms, generally translated into English as "spirit-self" (*manas*), "life-spirit" (*buddhi*), and "spirit-man" (*atma*)—which latter, as the "spiritualized" physical body, may be thought of as related to the "resurrection body."

who seeks it worthily and in all seriousness, to *this* extent it *does* lie in our power to enable such a development. Indeed, the spiritual world responds to our appeals and our efforts more reliably than any human being ever responded to another. We may depend upon it. Hence the "awakening" of the higher man we are speaking of arises from the interplay between above and below, between man and God, between effort and grace. Although presented without reference to traditional Christian concepts, Rudolf Steiner said all this very clearly. For example, in *Knowledge of Higher Worlds* he had this to say:

> When, by means of meditation, someone raises himself to that which connects the human being with the spirit, he begins to bring to life that which is eternal in himself, that which is not limited by birth and death.

Note carefully that according to this account we ourselves neither can nor ought to try to raise ourselves up to the spirit, but only up to *that which connects the human being with the spirit.* Here we have, in a veiled yet unequivocal form, the statement of the true spiritual researcher that we do not attain to the spiritual *itself* by the power of our own will: all we can do is raise ourselves up to that which *connects* us with the spirit. Yes, if we do this, we will surely be connected with the spirit, but we ourselves do not *make* this connection; rather, we *are* connected. The concept of "grace" is chiming here, if not the word itself. Accordingly, in the exposition of the unfolding of the organs of spiritual perception (the so-called lotus-flowers or *chakras*), it is said that we need only unfold *half* of this spiritual organ, and then "the other half appears by itself." That which *we* develop is indeed the *precondition* of the appearance of the rest—but without this answering response, the accomplishment of those preconditions would have had no decisive importance. In other words, the answering developments are bestowed both as a *necessity* and as a *gift*, since what is divine never withdraws itself, nor can it ever be compelled. In this regard, we read elsewhere: "Do not expect immediately to see and hear in the world of soul and spirit, for all you are doing is but contributing to the development of your higher senses." In other words, one must learn in the innermost core of one's soul to wait—that is, to reckon on "grace."

331

⊕

The exercises in *Knowledge of Higher Worlds*, which in terms of content are mostly connected with nature, all have a strong, unequivocal, essential, moral feature. Selflessness, dedicating oneself to the needs of others, silencing in oneself everything to do with one's own "I," with all egocentrism—it is around such moral qualities as these that the exercises again and again revolve. The spiritual pupil is to arrive at a position in which he lives for others, not for himself. Only for the world and for the sake of others is he to develop himself towards what is lofty and good. The spiritual pupil is to become a servant, as the initiate is a servant, and as Jesus Christ was the greatest and most selfless of all servants—the one who taught the "washing of feet," which all of us must learn. Rudolf Steiner says that in correcting slander against one's own person we should remain objective and calm, as though correcting slander against another on their behalf. Here we have a nod toward the conduct of Jesus Christ, who answered with calm resignation and no personal affect when dragged by his enemies before the judgment seat. Such traits can be discerned throughout *Knowledge of Higher Worlds*.

But what "knowledge" is Steiner speaking of when he refers to "knowledge of higher worlds"? What are the traits of this "knowing"? These traits must not only be understood, but must also be put into action. The exercises in *Knowledge of Higher Worlds* will fully awaken us, and thus most fully "open our eyes," when we both *know* and *will* that our dedication to them is not a matter of studying nature, or of cultural work, but is a matter of Christian discipleship in contemporary dress. The student of the esoteric must learn

> to sacrifice his deeds, and indeed his whole being, to the world, however these sacrifices of his might be received. Anyone who wishes to become a student of the esoteric must declare himself ready for such sacrificial service.

This is *discipleship* in the service of Jesus Christ, or if you like, preparation for his second coming or "etheric return." For this is just what Jesus Christ lived out on the grandest scale and in the loftiest manner. Those who attempted this service on earth *before* him lived already in his *light*; those who attempted this service *after* him lived in his *strength*.

Why are ideas just as important as outward actions? Why is hatred just as wicked as striking blows? Not only because, as is said in *Knowledge of Higher Worlds*, ideas are "facts," but also because the kingdom of God is not of this world. "Behold, the kingdom of God is within you!" Here, in this proposition as well as in its guiding thought, it is easy to see the book's connection to the ethos of the Sermon on the Mount. Jewish law contained no rules with respect to thoughts. In the gospel, however, we read: "But I say unto you that if you are angry with a brother or a sister, you will be liable to judgment." (Matt. 5:22); and: "But I say to you that everyone who looks at a woman with lust has already committed adultery with her in his heart." (Matt. 5:28)

But we need not keep listing one example after another. Those just given start by addressing the thinking intellect alone. As was said above, it is always a matter of knowledge in a *real* sense also, that of the will, of one's actions. Anyone who brings his will to life in the sense intended by *Knowledge of Higher Worlds* discovers further examples. What he discovers (not by comparing and contrasting thoughts, but by experience) is that the commandments of Jesus Christ have the same effect upon us as do the suggestions given in *Knowledge of Higher Worlds*—or, rather, that the suggestions in this book lead us towards the same purifications and sacrifices as does Jesus Christ himself. There are many kinds of Christian life and striving in the world, but there is no Christian instruction that exceeds in clarity and urgency what is offered in anthroposophical spiritual science. And yet, it is not by virtue of an attraction to spiritual science, or of a desire to profess it, that we participate truly in spiritual science, but only by traveling the path ourselves. "Not everyone who says to me, 'Lord, Lord,' will enter into the kingdom of heaven, but only the one who does the will of my Father in heaven." (Matt. 7:21–32) The thought prepares; only the deed sets free.

Jesus Christ said, "If any want to become my followers, let them deny themselves and take up their cross and follow me." (Matt. 16:24) Accordingly, in *Knowledge of Higher Worlds* we read that a man must learn to see himself as a stranger and must be open on

every side to the lives and needs of others; that he must feel responsible for everything that happens; that he must overcome all prejudices of rank, race, and so on; that he must strive towards pure
humanity, must learn to sacrifice himself, must strive towards universal love. Hence, also, the golden rule of true spiritual science
given in the book: "For every one step that you take in the pursuit of
higher knowledge, take three steps in the perfection of your own
character." Moral progress is the *prerequisite* for spiritual progress.
Put in Christian terms, the *prerequisite* for attaining grace is the law
and its fulfillment.

This is why Rudolf Steiner himself pointed out over and over
again that what is at stake in spiritual progress is not so much
knowledge of a certain content, but rather a transformation of one's
being. The *habits* of our earlier earthly, material, creaturely life are
what we ought to overcome: we ought to do away with anxiety and
fear, and fill ourselves with faith; we ought to carry out tasks that
others are incapable of mastering; we ought gradually to distinguish
ourselves by means of our *actions* and by means of our *being*, not by
means of what we think about, or by our pastimes.

But at the same time, in all our work arising out of anthroposophical spiritual science, we have always to do with the Luciferic
and Ahrimanic temptations as well: it is not an easy matter to walk
the middle way. In the description of the third of the trials, the "air
trial," we read that

> in this test, no goal becomes perceptible. Everything is put into the
> pupil's hands, who must find his way all by himself. Things or per-
> sons that move him to something are not present. Nothing, and
> no one, apart from himself, can now give him the strength that he
> needs. Everything needed consists in rapidly coming to terms with
> himself. For here one must find one's "higher self" in the truest
> sense of the words.

At this point on the way, we stand within nothingness, without any
external support, without any source of strength in our own, lower
I. This means that we must find the Christ-in-ourself in a situation
like that on Golgotha when the words "My God, my God, why hast
thou forsaken me?" were spoken. This is a test of faith. Rudolf
Steiner calls it a test of the "presence of spirit"—not of the presence

of spirit one has already had as an ordinary person, but rather the presence of the World-Spirit, who can enter into those learning to sacrifice, learning to believe, learning to be of courage. In *Knowledge of Higher Worlds*, however, all is described solely in "humanistic" words formed out of ordinary, direct experience. The truth is that Rudolf Steiner expressed himself on every subject as neutrally or accommodatingly as he could because, although throughout his lifework he *himself* approached the teachings of spiritual science by way of his personal experience of Christ—his primary purpose was always to help *others* make a start at finding their own way towards this experience.

In the discussion of initiatic experiences in *Knowledge of Higher Worlds*, a "Guardian of the Threshold" is mentioned. This "truly terrible spectral being" that one confronts at the threshold to personal spiritual knowledge is nothing other than an accurate depiction of one's own being. We are left in no doubt about the fact that the pupil perceives something dreadful here, and that this dreadful thing is his own self! Now, how might this experience be described in Christian language? It is the experience of *sin* to a degree we ordinarily never suspect, an experience of horror so overwhelming that, as a matter of grace, it is generally concealed from us (even from the pious among us) behind the familiar securities of our everyday consciousness. It is understandable that such an unflinching, terrifyingly accurate portrait of ourselves can be withstood only by those in whom a higher strength has previously arisen—by those who, in Christian terms, have already entered into a truly efficacious relationship with Jesus Christ. In this context, *Knowledge of Higher Worlds* explains with most fitting words *that*, and *how*, sins can be overcome; and, moreover, that there is no fruitful redemption from sin without an ultimate, deadly-serious commitment on the part of the spiritual pupil himself.

This meeting with the "Guardian of the Threshold" is followed by another such meeting, this time with a "noble form of light" Steiner describes as the "Greater Guardian of the Threshold." This noble form of light is Jesus Christ himself (even if he goes unnamed in

Knowledge of Higher Worlds). This Greater Guardian says: "You will some day be able to unite with me, but I cannot be exalted so long as others remain unredeemed." Thus are we addressed at this point on our way. Universal love and sacrificial power must now become perfect reality. Those who wish to serve the true progress of worlds must become pupils and followers of Jesus Christ. We can summarize the pupil's experience of the Greater Guardian of the Threshold with one of the final sentences of *Knowledge of Higher Worlds*: "No one therefore should expect esotericists of the true path to offer instruction for the development of their own egotistical self."

After all this, it will readily be understood why, to those unable to surround themselves during their course of instruction with "the inner dignity and loveliness of nature," Rudolf Steiner suggested that they read four works of world literature: the "sublime doctrines" of the *Bhagavad-Gita*, the Gospel of John, the *Imitation of Christ* of Thomas à Kempis, and expositions of the results of spiritual science. The *Bhagavad-Gita*, the most sublime of the pre-Christian, non-biblical revealed writings, is mentioned first as a sort of preliminary stage because it serves as a better preparation for the Christ-impulse than the discourses of Gautama Buddha. The second-mentioned, the Gospel of John, is the deepest of the four gospels and the foundational book of esoteric Christianity. The third-mentioned, the *Imitation of Christ*, replete with the faith, and rich with the experience, of Christian discipleship, is the crowning work of Late-Medieval Christian counsel. The fourth-mentioned, finally, is the contemporary literature of spiritual science, whose meaning can only be fulfilled through the emulation of Christian discipleship. These brief mentions constitute the sole overt reference to the world of Christianity in the whole of *Knowledge of Higher Worlds*. It is sufficiently weighty and unequivocal, however, given that it belongs to very nature and character of the instruction given in this book, that this one central reference illuminates the whole as by a stroke of lightning from above. The more mindfully and close to our heart we hold these links between *Knowledge of Higher Worlds* and the truths of Christianity, the better we will fare in our quest.

It is only in the matter of its *method* that *Knowledge of Higher Worlds* comes forward shorn of any historical or religious affiliation. This is because its method adheres to that of modern natural science. In terms of *content* and *meaning*, however, its method does continue the tradition of the Christian life. As Rudolf Steiner put it, what is yet to come will develop out of the past. In other words, it is not those who think that everything must be thought-out anew (and if possible created anew) from our present point of vantage who will press on into the future in the richest and most promising manner, but those who carry within them the past and its values. Anthroposophical instruction does not stand in opposition to the Christian life of the past; it wants, rather, to *open* Christian life to a whole new stage of its development. The impulse of Jesus Christ is at work throughout the *whole* of history; it is only that its manifestation differs in successive stages. Still, we *cannot* ascend to a higher stage by misunderstanding, denying, belittling, or depreciating a lower one. Those who adopt such a view are far indeed from the universal love, patience, and mildness that Rudolf Steiner expected of the student of the esoteric—and that he himself exemplified. This is of special importance, in Steiner's view, for only by living in a loving, patient, and mild discipleship of Jesus Christ are we preparing rightly, in full awareness, for Christ's anticipated second return "in the etheric."

One of the challenging tasks of the anthroposophist is to unite *voluntary attentiveness* to this anticipated Christian impulse of such grave relevance in our day with *loving respect* for all the forms of Christian life that have previously arisen in the course of history, forms that for the most part still surround us today. Whoever knows something of the loftiness and power of the meditative life of earlier times can only look to those times with a sense of shame in comparison to our own state in this regard today. Let this be a reminder that, in the anthroposophical path of schooling, we have been given a means (of karmic provenance) to further our salvation, but that this means is of value *only* if we follow it of our free will and actively progress along this path.

We are all open to the temptation (Luciferic on one hand, Ahrimanic on the other) to regard our participation in the anthroposophical movement as a good in itself. But this is not the case. Viewed from the vast perspective of evolution as a whole (as Steiner presents it), Anthroposophy *per se* possesses no absolute value. It wishes only to serve the *furtherance* of this same evolution. At best, one might put it this way: Christ "calls for" what the anthroposophical impulse intends in service to the further unfolding of the Christ-impulse, but the anthroposophical impulse is *not* the Christ-impulse itself; it is there to *serve* the Christ-impulse *for the sake of* evolution as a whole.

To render this service, a certain wisdom is necessary, including "knowledge" we can acquire outwardly and convey to others—that is, knowledge we can grasp with our understanding even if we are as yet unable to experience it directly. But all this is only ever a means to an end. In both Christian discipleship and Christian esoteric instruction there is no special entitlement, no support in the outer world, no value in itself. Rudolf Steiner never tired of drawing attention to the fact that, insofar as the anthroposophical worldview (with all its resultant spiritual research) is itself a "system," it also can be pursued in the same materialistic, intellectualistic way as any other purely exoteric science. This danger can be circumvented only by spiritual instruction itself, which (as has also been said repeatedly, and as anyone who puts it into practice finds confirmed) to be worthy of its name must bring about a transformation of the pupils's *being* and *habits*. Through spiritual instruction, stages of development are anticipated that in the regular (i.e., fated or karmic) course of events would only have been reached later. But the intention of this development "beforehand" is solely to serve others, not for our own delight! Moreover, these anticipatory stages are not attained without pain, without great effort, without transformation, without renunciation, without experiences of death. They are attained only through sacrifice and suffering, through the positive acquisition of qualities and powers that otherwise only fate brings us.

It cannot be said often enough that insight is not a matter of the mind or head-knowledge, but of the *whole* person. But just because we assent to the *idea* that insight is a matter of the whole person doesn't mean that without further ado we ourselves immediately become whole persons enjoying insight! From the simple, observable fact that many do indeed assent to this idea but nonetheless quite evidently lack this insight, we see that it is entirely possible to assent to something without putting it into practice. Only when we take the path of spiritual instruction in *bloody* earnest do we approach *discipleship* in the service of Jesus Christ in a form appropriate to our time.

For this reason, Rudolf Steiner repeatedly demanded of the student of the esoteric a relentless, truthful self-knowledge—an open, unconditional admission of weaknesses together with the readiness and fortitude to look at one's true state with no attempt to gloss over it. Anthroposophists are all too fond of comparing themselves with others—"outsiders"(!)—and inclining to the view that their "insider" status (which for practical purposes usually means nothing more than access to the research results of spiritual science) is valuable in itself. We can free ourselves from this view by realizing that Rudolf Steiner's aim was to cultivate stages of spiritual instruction (not to propagate particular ideas or even cultural initiatives), and that these stages, or the journey through them, can only be seriously spoken of if they are understood as entailing blows of fate and tests of the *weightiest* kind. For this reason, Rudolf Steiner says:

> A person initiated today without further ado would lack the experience that he will gain during his future incarnations before he can attain to higher knowledge in the normal course of his development. At the portal of initiation, therefore, this experience must be supplied in some other way.

If we have come this far, we can easily assess the level of experience at which we stand. At the same time, it is good to remind ourselves that, beyond doubt, others who may never have heard of Anthroposophy or of its spiritual schooling have undergone experiences through their life and fate that constitute tests going beyond our own. It is just in this way that we begin to develop that humility which the spirit-researcher names as one of the prerequisites for students of the esoteric—as well as the will to do what is necessary and possible to proceed further on this path. Sectarian attitudes, in whatever guise they come forward (those holding them being the least aware of them!), are contrary to the spirit of spiritual instruction and to the spirit of Anthroposophy. It is not the world's task to become "anthroposophical." It is the task of Anthroposophy and of anthroposophists to serve the world. Moreover, by "world" we do not mean only that portion or conception of it that may happen to conform to our personal sympathies. We mean *the world as such*. And what is the task and the meaning of the world as such? It is to be filled ever more with the spirit of Jesus Christ. Or, to use Rudolf Steiner's expression, to become a "cosmos of love" instead of a "cosmos of wisdom." Everything comes down to sacrificial love as an infinitely high goal, standing far above us all. Everything comes down to real service in the spiritual school of universal love. What is demanded from the outset in all esoteric exercises is the practice of reverence and love—right through to the highest possible love, a love we cannot exact out of ourselves, a love we can only prepare for, a love we can only await as a gift.

As students of the esoteric, we must place ourselves within the stream that fills the world (the "cosmos of wisdom") with the power of Jesus Christ's love. We must do this with our thinking, feeling, and willing. We must do this with our willing, feeling, and thinking. The course of instruction must make us humbler, more open-hearted, more fearless, more reflective than we were before embarking upon it. Moreover, we ought never to forget (as Rudolf Steiner so often emphasized) that, apart from this course of instruction, there also exists an "unconscious initiation through life itself" that is accessible to everyone—whatever their fate and whatever their presiding worldview may be. We must be ever mindful that we can "know" a great deal about higher worlds and about initiation, yet live all unknowingly alongside others who, although they perhaps "know" nothing consciously about higher worlds and initiation, may have "unconsciously" experienced more of the way of initiation, and accomplished more along it, than have we ourselves.

It is no depreciation of the anthroposophical impulse then, but is on the contrary the right way to praise it, to view it in the light and in the service of Christ. Belonging to the anthroposophical movement should never be a crutch for our self-confidence; it should, rather, be a mission we accept and undertake to become ever more aware of the inner agreement of the path of spiritual instruction with the general course of humankind's development under the guidance of Christ Jesus. Rudolf Steiner said that as students of the esoteric, we ought to know what the spiritual exercises are *for*, and that we ought also to know that we only find Jesus Christ when we *go towards him*. Jesus Christ, too, is known only through *deeds*, only by those who follow him in the washing of feet, in the scourging, in the crowning with thorns, in the carrying of the cross, in the crucifixion, and in the burying in the tomb. These experiences must be *undergone*. They must even be undergone repeatedly in the *core* of our being. The spiritual development of our "I" for the sake of the world *consists* in undergoing these experiences.

> Anyone, therefore, really following the instructions of the good esotericists will, upon crossing the threshold, understand the demands of the Greater Guardian; anyone, however, not following their instructions can never hope to reach the threshold. Their instructions, if followed, produce good results or no results; for it is no part of their task to lead to egotistical felicity and a mere existence in the supersensible worlds. In fact, it becomes their duty to keep the student away from the supersensible world until he can enter it with the will for selfless *collaboration*.

These are principles that hold not only for putting into practice the spiritual instruction offered in *Knowledge of Higher Worlds*, but also for all true anthroposophical life and effort. They are, like all the instructions in this book (and like Anthroposophy itself), taken from the impulse of Jesus Christ, and are there solely for his service. As Rudolf Steiner and true Anthroposophy understand it, there is no student of the esoteric who is not also a student of Jesus Christ, or who is not obligated by the impulse of Christ.

Made in United States
Troutdale, OR
08/21/2024

22219105R00224